ISLAND BRITAIN

THE OBSERVER

ISLAND BRITAIN

EDITED BY PETER CROOKSTON

BLACK CAT

CONTENTS

INTRODUCTION

In the early 1960s, when I made the transition from newspapers into magazine journalism and was casting about for clues to what made people read magazine articles, I stumbled on a nugget of information. One of London's biggest advertising agencies had commissioned a survey of readers' reactions to headlines and their research had shown that one word brought a bigger 'reading and noting' response from the people of Great Britain than any other: it was the word island. Put 'island' into a headline and the chances are that everyone will plunge like gannets on to the copy below it. We are, it seems, in thrall to the call of islands, which is strange when you come to think about it. We live on an offshore island of Europe, or on islands that are satellites of that larger island. Why should we be so fascinated by what we already know? It would surely be more explicable if we were locked into a massive land mass, hedged about by frontiers. But the fact that there are always dozens of prospective buyers when an island is put up for sale, and that Mr Roy Plomley's 'Desert Island Discs' is one of the most popular and longest running programmes in the annals of radio broadcasting, give further and better testimony to the fascination of small areas of land isolated by the surrounding sea.

When we began publishing 'Island Britain' in its original form as a series in *The Observer Magazine* in the summer of 1980 there was an immediate and

heartening response from our readers. Many of them took the trouble to write to me personally to enthuse about the series, and to suggest that it would make a good book. And the demand for back numbers of the magazine from readers who had missed issues while on holiday was astonishing. All of this strengthened our resolve to expand the series into a book. There are several new sections and illustrations which were not in the original series. We have commissioned leading authorities on their subjects to write about the birds, boats, lighthouses, plants, animals, beach life and geology of our islands, and there are new drawings to illustrate each of these chapters. We have also expanded the information sections on sightseeing, activities and 'how to get there'.

The original idea for 'Island Britain' came from my colleague Richard Findlater, to whom I am deeply indebted for his wise counsel throughout the preparation of the series and the book. I would also like to give special thanks to Pamela Brown and Sarah Howell for their meticulous and inspired organisation of the research. All of us on *The Observer Magazine* would like to think that this book will stand as a definitive guide to the islands of Britain and the joys that can be found in them, and that it will bring as much pleasure to you in reading it as it has given us in producing it.

PETER CROOKSTON
London 1981

SHETLAND

BY JAN MORRIS

The Shetland Islands are inset islands. They lie so far north of the Scottish mainland that on nearly all United Kingdom maps they are shown only in a box in the corner. This has subtly affected our conception of them. They are much, much further away than most people suppose. They are much more foreign places, much harder, older and more distinct. They are closer to the Arctic Circle than they are to London, as near to Bergen as to Aberdeen, as far north as Anchorage in Alaska, or Leningrad. There are more than a hundred Shetland islands, 17 of them inhabited, and they are strung out in a long and skinny archipelago, like a distinctly un-coral reef dividing the northern oceans – at a spot half-way down, so the geographers say, you can throw a stone from the North Sea to the Atlantic.

This remote and arcane nature is the compelling interest of the Shetland Islands, which are different in kind from Orkney, the Hebrides and the other British islands of the north: but it is compounded by another immense abstraction – the impact of the international oil industry, which has fallen upon these innocent outposts with all its fateful implications of change and disillusion. Like an invasion from another planet, this gigantic force has affected every aspect of life in the islands, and has made of them a disturbing allegory of our times, where profound dilemmas of human aspiration are enacted, floodlit upon a windy stage.

The quandaries of Shetland suggest themselves the moment you fly into Sumburgh airport, at the southern tip of the main islands group. It looks exactly like a map down there. Below the wing of your old Viscount rises Sumburgh Head, fringed in surf and crowned with a lighthouse just like an Ordnance Survey symbol: and there are sheep and Shetland ponies grazing the contour lines, and scattered crofts, and small boats beached in coves; and jagged at the water's edge, as though in the

'. . . a very northern town, Scandinavian, Baltic, Hanseatic perhaps'.

ornamental script they reserve for Non-Roman Antiquities, is the ruined 17th-century house of Jarlshof, which was named by Walter Scott himself, and which stands on a site riddled with the tunnels and chambers of the haziest island ancients.

But when you come in to land at the little airport beneath the hill you find some less conventional signs. A hundred helicopters seem to be twirling their blades upon the tarmac, oil-rig departure boards announce destinations like Treasure Finder, Uncle John or Chevron Two, jet-props come and go from Aberdeen or Bergen or Scatsta, and outside the terminal a long line of taxis waits to whisk executives up the island to sales conference or avocado vinaigrette.

Almost treeless (the odd thicket vociferous with starlings), rolling rather than hilly, the Shetland Islands are more like rocks than islands, and their people indeed call them generically 'The Old Rock'.

Wherever you look across the black peat-turfed moors, there shows the sea, in a silent loch twisted among the headlands, in a foam-lashed reef surging at the feet of some tremendous precipice, or in the genial sheltered sound that is Lerwick harbour. Seals, whales and myriad sea-birds haunt these coasts, and their human inhabitants have always been amphibious. The crofter-fisherman is the Shetlander par excellence: in the Shetland farmyard the boat is much more common than the tractor, and broken oars, net-buoys or rusted anchors (not to speak of old cars apparently washed up by the tide) give to almost every croft an unmistakable tang of the foreshore.

Magnificently lonely though the settings are, these are not exactly romantic islands. Mendelssohn never got this far, and there is no dream in the air. The terrain is too harsh, the wind too violent – 177mph has been recorded – and Shetland's horses, neat dogs and little brown sheep are

Fishing boats in Lerwick harbour, 'a genial sheltered sound'.

all proportioned to it. The islands' cultural traditions are essentially practical, and the history of the place is stern. Norsemen settled in the eighth century, and the Shetlanders still feel half-Scandinavian: the islands became Scottish only in 1469, and the rapacious dynasties of lairds who took them over have long since vanished anyway, leaving scarcely a kilt, a sporran or a snob behind. The original language of the islanders was Norn, the ancestor of Norwegian, and though this was infiltrated and largely supplanted by Lowland Scots, much of it lives on still in the tough and angular dialect that is spoken to this day.

'Dip dee,' says your Shetlander kindly, showing you into her parlour, 'and hae a crack!' – 'Sit down and let's have a chat!' She says it with no mellifluence, though. The Shetlanders, though infinitely courteous to strangers, lack the easy charm of the Celtic peoples, the blarney or the flatter. The fiddle is their instrument, not the resonant harp or the braggadocio bagpipe, and the great festival of their year is certainly not an eisteddfod, but the winter celebration called Up Helly Aa, when the island worthies dress up in horned helmets, sing the Up Helly Aa song –

From grand old Viking centuries Up Helly Aa has come.
Then light the torch and form the march and sound the rolling drum –

burn a Viking galley and spend all night in booze and high jinks.

The only real town in the islands is Lerwick, and here the oddly brittle character of Shetland is concentrated. A jumbled old town of granite houses around the harbour, it is crowned by the square Victorian tower of its town hall, and falls in narrow stepped lanes down to the quays, where the lifeboat lies, the Bressay ferry comes and goes, peculiar oil-ships stand about and fishing boats from Norway, Russia or the Faroes often put in for shelter or supplies.

Lerwick's main street winds a sinuous way in parallel with the waterfront, paved throughout its length and lined with a sturdy variety of shops – butchers selling Shetland sausages and salted legs of mutton, licensed grocers doubling as ship-chandlers, a homely café or two, lots of Shetland knitwear shops ('Urgently Required from Home Knitters, Shawls, Cockleshell Scarves, Fair Isle Yokes . . .'). The pubs can be boisterous with seamen of many nations, not infrequently moved on to make their appearances in the Sheriff Court: when I was there recently one defendant admitted hauling the barman of the Queen's Hotel over the bar by his hair, but said it was just a joke.

It is a very northern town, Scandinavian, Baltic,

Hanseatic perhaps. The bookshops sell Icelandic dictionaries. There is a Norwegian seamen's centre, and for some months of every year a Norwegian lifeboat is based on the port. Lerwick began life as a settlement of trading booths established by German merchants in the 15th century, and it has never quite lost its burgherly character. I called one day upon the editor of the *Shetland Times*, a splendidly idiosyncratic journal, and sitting with him in his panelled room above Commercial Street, surrounded by galley proofs and pictures of old ships, while the pale sun streamed through the windows and the sounds of the little town echoed in the street outside (clatter of boots down steep stone lanes, hoot of a ship's siren from the harbour) – sitting thus on a Lerwick morning, I felt myself to be inhabiting a page of pure Ibsen.

There is a sort of stealthy excitement to Shetland. I was standing one morning on the ramparts of Fort Charlotte, above the Lerwick waterfront, when there sailed into harbour a British sub-

marine, black and predatory, pennant streaming from the radio mast, bearded officers muffled in the conning-tower. I thought she looked perfectly suited to the scene, stealing in like that out of those northern seas.

This is Buchan country, just made for derring-do. The Shetlanders are terrific seamen, who used to fish their open boats hundreds of miles out in the North Atlantic, and who made disproportionately heroic naval sacrifices in both world wars. It was from these islands that the Norwegian adventurers of the 'Shetland Bus' smuggled their spies, saboteurs and refugees into and out of Nazi-occupied Norway, and even now Shetland brings out the conspiratorial in one. Up a thousand lonely inlets lie the long-stemmed island boats, directly descended from the Viking galleys, and in the long summer nights, the Simmer Dim when it never gets dark, they seem to beckon one down

to the shore for skulldug voyage or forbidden ferryings.

If there is a magic to these hard-headed islands, it is this sly magic of the sea, in the gull-speckled cliffs that hang above the tides, in those waiting boats on deserted beaches, even in the kipper-smell which, emerging from the processing plant on Scalloway harbour, fragrantly pervades the village quays, and impregnates the stonework of the wicked Earl Patrick Stewart's long-ruined castle. The Shetland dialect has an inner vocabulary used only at sea, to evade an immemorial series of verbal taboos. Priests, pigs and sunshine all have their particular words in this mystic glossary, which reaches back to the days of the vengeful water-gods, and nothing emphasises more queerly the old sea-separateness of the islanders. Who else would call a cat 'da skaavin', 'the shaver', one who seems to shave his nose when washing, lest a more explicit

'Like some implanted cell or strain, Sullom Voe is mutating the very character of Shetland.'

mention of that land-lubber mammal might arouse the ocean furies?

Upon this singular community the North Sea oil industry has fallen in monstrous visitation. If you drive on a wet and windy night down the west coast of Mainland, the principal island of the group, you will be told eerily of its presence by a diffused glow in the night sky, like the shine of some immense grounded UFO, over the sea-inlet called Sullom Voe. Here, in one of the remotest and most peaceful corners of all Europe, there arose during the 1970s one of the world's great oil terminals, the head of two pipelines from the North Sea fields to the east: and when you cross the ridge from Northlee, and run down towards the sea, all around an alien civilisation seems to close in upon you. There are lights in the haze everywhere – lights on ships, lights on beacons, a searchlight probing the cloud base, winking lights, steady lights, airstrip landing lights, urgently flashing lights ordering you to stop. A deep hum sounds from somewhere, like the murmur of some tremendous turbine, unresolved shapes loom on the hillside in the mist, and as you wait tensely before your warning signal, with a sudden whine the evening flight from Aberdeen swoops low over the car to land in the drizzle.

Sullom Voe is the most formidable thing to have hit the Shetland Islands since the first Viking force disembarked at Harold's Wick 12 centuries ago. In the daylight, actually, it does not look so dramatic: a cluster of big oil tanks over the hills, a supertanker at a jetty, a row of modernistic tugs, hundreds of parked cars and a few unobtrusive buildings. The airfield looks a drab little affair in the daylight, and the most spectacular things in sight are two passenger ships which are moored off-shore as workers' dormitories.

But like some implanted cell or strain, Sullom Voe is mutating the very character of Shetland. Its effects are inescapable, physically in new roads and buildings all over the islands, economically in jobs, high wages and new expectations, ethnically in its armies of imported labour, aesthetically in its quickening of the island pace, morally, or spiritually perhaps, in the mighty jolt it has given to island habits and convictions.

'Oil-related' is the most common dialect word in Shetland now. Far up at Baltasound, on the northernmost island of Unst, almost as far north as you can get in Britain, English voices easily outnumber Shetland in the pub: oil-related incomers, as Shetlanders call immigrants, now outnumber the indigenes. Across Yell Sound at Toft a vast labour camp sprawls over the moorland, horribly suggestive of Gulag were it not for the scurry of

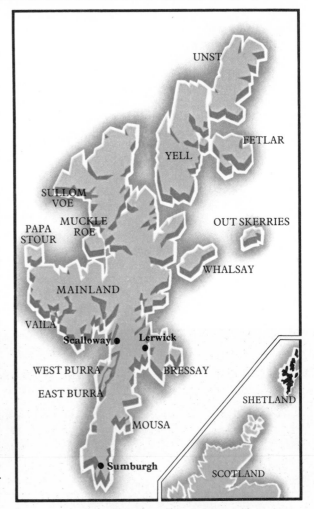

cars going in and out, the village bank and hair-dresser and the proliferation of beer barrels. There is always something, even far from Sullom Voe, to hint of the giant extraneous energy which has seized upon these islands: the unnaturally efficient telephone system, perhaps – a scurry of cars along a road that seems to go nowhere – the clatter of a helicopter in the silent sky – an oil-subsidised golf club or an unctuous public relations reminder that Oil-Related Contractors have generously repaired the church bells at Brae: 'It's gratifying to know that a large organisation is finding the time and the inclination to look after the small things. . . .'

For inevitably the oil companies, treading care-fully down their own pipelines, have adopted in Shetland those attitudes of calculated paternalism they perfected during colonial times in Mosul and Abadan. Softly, softly! Like the Iraqis and the Iranians, the Shetlanders are not deceived: sundry folk-movements stand up for tradition, the Shet-land Islands Council fights bravely to preserve the island character, the Shetland Movement demands Home Rule. But still a cloud hangs over the archipelago, vague and threatening, drifting outwards from Sullom Voe south to Dunrossness, north to Muckle Flugga, and even to the far outrider islands like Out Skerries or Fair Isle. Shrewd and resolute the Shetlanders may be, one feels, and loyal to their heritage, but even the bold helmsmen of Up Helly Aa are no match for the multi-nationals.

Somehow, though, this portentous intrusion makes the Shetlands feel more isolated still. They feel all on their own, like survivors from some frightful catastrophe. The very names on the Shetland map sound like futurism or SF – The Nev, the Haa of Stova, Grind of the Navir or Flubersgerdie. It is hard to remember that the island of Foula, say, humped far out there in the western gales, is really part of contemporary Britain: the familiar red telephone boxes, the royal cipher on the post office, seem like tokens of some previous or perhaps impending age.

And in turn this encapsulated or disoriented suggestion reinforces the allegory of it all. It is as though the Shetlanders, subjects of some dark experiment, have been deliberately insulated among their terrible seas, exposed to new irradiations for a trial of values. Which is the stronger, earth or oil? Which will survive in the end, the old or the new, and which is more truly modern anyway? Is it doomwatch up on the Old Rock, or hope eternal after all?

Not many islands raise such questions in the mind, or illustrate them with such haunting images.

JAN MORRIS

BASICS

Watery maze of islands 200 miles north of Aberdeen, 600 north of London, stretching 70 miles from head to toe (not including Fair Isle) and 35 east to west. Even on largest, Mainland, coastline is so intricately patterned with voes (inlets) and peninsulas that you are never more than 3 miles from sea. You could come to Shetland just to watch the waves.

It is cold (hat especially advisable) but birds, wild flowers – a reminder of how meadows used to look – archaeology, fishing and magnificent and desolate scenery are well worth it. When whipping wind dies down, glassy blue sea seems all the more miraculous. Hotels and farmhouses are usually well heated, electric blankets commonplace. There also tends to be a lot of light misty rain in summer, but days then are exceptionally long with only two hours semi-darkness mid-June. It's a geologist's paradise. 2,000 million-year-old gneiss rocks at extreme northern tip of Mainland are some of oldest in world.

Shetland Tourist Organisation, Lerwick, is a mine of information on boat trips, fishing tackle and permits, events etc and generally getting around. Good idea to visit it on arrival. Market Cross, tel Lerwick 3434.

WHERE TO GO
Mainland Towns

LERWICK
Shetland's capital. Sheltered by island of Bressay opposite, Scottish baronial turrets and solid stone houses slope steeply down to busy waterfront. Almost divided into three tiers – from administrative section at the top with Town Hall, Anderson Educational Institute (endowed by archetypal local boy made good Arthur Anderson, co-founder of P & O), library etc, you descend via narrow steps and alleyways to paved Commercial St, the shopping centre, and then again to harbour full of trawlers, screeching gulls and sou' westered fishermen talking in foreign accents. For a closer inspection, The Dimriv, an authentic replica of a Viking longship makes occasional trips around the bay. Check details with Shetland Tourist Organisation. There are fine views of harbour and Bressay Sound (in 17th c so thick was the Dutch herring fleet you could walk to Bressay stepping from ship to ship) from Scottish baronial-style Town Hall, 1882, open Mon-Fri 10-12 and 2-3, and Fort Charlotte, built by Cromwell to protect the Sound, open daily. Both in Hillhead.

West Lunna Voe: 'this sly magic of the sea'.

Shetland Museum, above library in Hillhead, which also has excellent Shetland Reading Room. Fascinating collection including two splendid ship's figureheads, sea-chests with painted lids and intricate rope handles made by ship's carpenters, iron Age and Celtic finds, folk-life gallery with special display of everyday objects, delicate 19th c 'fine knitting' and bridal veils. Open Mon, Wed, Fri 10-1, 2.30-5, 6-8; Tues, Sat 10-1, 2.30-5; Thurs 10-1. Tel: Lerwick 3868.

Up Helly Aa Exhibition, Galley Shed, Sunniva St: photographs and full-size replica of Norse galley sent to Valhalla in flames in January festival. June-Sept, two evenings a week. Details from Tourist Organisation.

Isleburgh House Exhibition, King Harald St: demonstrations of carding, spinning, knitting and craft displays. June-end Aug, two evenings a week. Details from Tourist Organisation.

SWRI Exhibition, Town Hall, Hillhead: knitwear and crafts exhibition with demonstrations of carding etc plus morning coffee and afternoon tea. June-end Aug, one day a week. Details from Tourist Organisation.

Shopping: not much diversification in spite of oil boom. Plethora of traditional knitwear shops selling variations on same theme, but individually made. The Shetland Times Shop is a wide-ranging bookstore with excellent local selection and Stove & Smith is a splendid old-fashioned ironmonger-cum-toyshop where paraffin is measured out by the copper jug. Food shops are in short supply with little variety in fresh fruit and veg, but Malcomson's fresh warm bannocks, Scotch pancakes, baps, help a picnic along. Smith & Co's haggis and mealy pudding are home-made and J. & M. Fraser have wonderful displays of foot-high crisscross piles of fresh fish. Apart from Frasers, on Esplanade, all are on Commercial St. Most shops in Lerwick close all day Wed, food shops from midday.

Eating and Drinking is done in hotels rather than pubs and restaurants. Not a lot of choice – Queen's Hotel, Commercial St, has newly decorated lounge bar; public bar with darts, pool, dominoes; lunches, teas, dinners served in dining room. Tel Lerwick 2826. The modern

Kvelsdro House nr Water Lane, like plush 1970s equivalent of a gold-rush saloon, has comfortable bar thronging with people. Also has restaurant, on the expensive side. Best to book, tel Lerwick 2195. With effects of North Sea oil (staff wages have to compete with those paid at Sullom Voe) eating out in Shetland can be pricey. Fresh fish and chips are good value – three shops in Lerwick – and the Noost, Commercial St, serves cheap cafeteria-type lunch. The Golden Coach, Hillhead, Britain's most northerly Chinese restaurant, makes an inspired and welcome change with home-grown beansprouts, tasty chicken with ginger and spring onion, sweet and sour pork etc. Long and tempting menu, reasonably priced, also take-away. Very popular – book early. Tel Lerwick 2452. Scottish beef, game and locally caught fish and seafood are served at Chapel House, Mounthooly St, tel Lerwick 3804. Semi-self-service lunches are good value.

SCALLOWAY

Oddly shabby and bizarre. Old fishing port and former capital of Shetland lies in sheltered bay, with almost cottagey gardens sloping down to water's edge and harbour full of noisy seagulls and clanging boat repairers. Pleasantest approach is along road by Tingwall Loch. Overshadowed by Scalloway Castle, built c 1600 by tyrannous Earl Patrick Stewart, nephew of Mary Queen of Scots, who ruled both Shetland and Orkney at end of 16th c. Castle now looks straight out on to fish processing factory. Gaunt, 4-storey ruins open weekdays April-Sept 9.30-7, Oct-March 9.30-4, Sun from 2. Key from cottage opposite. Visitors are welcome at Williamson's Fish Processing Factory at Westshore, Mon-Thurs 9-3 – good for a rainy day.

Not a busy commercial centre but there's a sprinkling of shops along main street by harbour – Nicholson's is a nice old-fashioned general store, bank, a couple of hotels where you

Dry-stone wall on Lunna hillside.

can eat or get a drink, and right by the harbour, The Fisherman's Arms, a large pub with pool, darts, and serving snacks. Early closing day Thurs.

SIGHTSEEING

Sumburgh Lighthouse: one of many Scottish lighthouses designed by Robert Louis Stevenson's grandfather. Looking much as it did when built in 1821, plenty of immaculately polished brass, and still using 1914 pendulum mechanism rather like a clock. Three-ton lens floats on mercury bath – rare in Scotland. Rotating beam installed 1914 but changeover from paraffin to electricity not effected until 1975; light now, unbelievably, from 250-watt bulb. Fog-horn, installed 1906 and very much in use, involves elaborate procedure explained by lighthouse keepers as part of colourful and informative tour. From 2pm to one hour before dusk. Always telephone first, Sumburgh 60375. End A970, southern tip of Mainland. (Other lighthouses – see *Bressay*.)

Jarlshof: remarkable archaeological site sandwiched between busy Sumburgh airport and the seashore. Windy spot has attracted dwellers over thousands of years, first probably arrived around 2,000BC. In between waves of Stone Age, Bronze Age, Iron Age, Viking and medieval settlers, sand blew in covering the traces of their houses or else new arrivals built on to what was already there. The jumbled remains include circular stone huts with underground earth-houses c 5-600BC; broch from around 100AD with wheel-houses added some time during next two centuries; Viking and medieval farmsteads; and finally early 17th c Laird's house, partly built by infamous Earl Patrick, and christened Jarlshof by Sir Walter Scott. D of E. Small admission charge. Open daily April-Sept 9.30-7, Oct-March 9.30-4, Sun from 2. Southernmost tip Mainland.

Clickhimin Broch: on promontory in some marshy ground incongruously close to modern housing estate on outskirts of Lerwick. Fairly substantial and easily understood remains of Iron Age broch – a tapering circular tower that combined defence and shelter from winds in communal living quarters for a whole clan. Walls, up to 20ft thick, are honeycombed with stairways and galleries leading to top. Open daily April-Sept 9.30-7, Oct-March 9.30-4, Sun from 2. A970 out of Lerwick towards Gulberwick. (See also *Mousa*)

Stanydale 'Temple': strange horseshoe-shaped remains dating from 1,600BC, linking early Shetlanders with Mediterranean. Called a temple because of its similarity to temple sites in Malta and Gozo. May have been a public meeting hall. Two holes in floor would have supported roof poles and low chunky walls have small bays. A pleasant ½-mile walk across marshy moorland with sheep and ponies (wellies advisable). Well-signposted – take Gruting turning off A971, west Mainland.

Croft Museum: caretaker William Manson, born and brought up in similar croft nearby, gives lively account of daily life, including a tune on the fiddle, in typically furnished 19th c croft-house and steading with box beds, butter churns, household utensils, corn kiln etc. Has one of Shet-

land's few remaining thatched roofs. Open May-Sept, Tues-Sun 10-1 and 2-5. To check opening times tel: Lerwick 3868. Small admission charge. At South Voe, Bunrossness, off A970, south Mainland.

Tingwall Agricultural Museum: fascinating collection of Shetland bygones including crofting and fishing implements, breadmaking equipment used over open peat fire, 'rivlins', primitive cowhide shoes, 'haps' and 'mutches' – shawls and bonnets. Open May-Sept Tues, Thurs, Sat 10-5, and also 6-8 Thurs or by appointment, tel: Gott 344. Admission charge. At 2 Veensgarth (¾ mile north of Tingwall Loch), off A971 just before B9074 turning to Scalloway.

Tingwall Loch: traditionally annual meeting place of Norse Althing or parliament on holm (islet) at north end of loch, once reached by stepping stones, now a peninsula. Ancient law lords are supposed to have dealt out justice ceremoniously seated on circle of stones, although Eric Linklater thinks they would hardly have chosen such an uncomfortable spot and suggests it was used for holmgang – a legal ritualistic duel or trial by ordeal. Good for trout fishing. By B9074, north of Scalloway.

St Ninian's Isle: juts out on long curving stretch of white sand dividing the ocean. A geological rarity, this tombolo (sand-bar joining island to land or other island) is said to be one of finest in world. In late 1950s, schoolboy helping with dig on site of old church found amazing hoard of 8th c ecclesiastical silver hidden in wooden box, perhaps by fleeing monks. Includes seven shallow bowls, intricately worked cones that might have been caps for ceremonial staves, and ornate, rather worldly-looking brooches and buckles that would have delighted Viking marauders. Splendid replicas on show in Lerwick Museum, originals having been whisked off to Edinburgh. Signposted – take turning off B9122 at Bigton, track leads from farm entrance at corner. South-west Mainland.

Lunna: long spindly finger of land pointing towards Fetlar. At narrowest part overlooking bay stands Lunna House, a grey, brooding mansion (now hotel – nice home-baked high teas) dating back to 1660 that would make admirable setting for World War II spy drama. It has an appropriate history. In 1940, with barns and outhouses used as arsenal, it became headquarters of Norwegian resistance. Using a couple of sturdy fishing vessels, they ran the Shetland Bus (later run from Scalloway) carrying ammunition and saboteurs into Norway and returning with refugees.

Nearby, delightful Lunna Kirk, a plane tree smothering one side, is one of Shetland's oldest churches still in use. Built 1753, it has two monuments from an earlier family mausoleum incorporated into porch; inside, honey-painted pews and blue canopied pulpit lack the usual dourness. Outside staircase leads up to gallery. Misty graveyard, dotted with ethereal-looking monuments of glass-domed white flowers, looks out over the sea. B9071. East Mainland.

Sullom Voe: by 1982, Sullom Voe will be capable of handling 1.4 million barrels of oil a day – two-thirds of Britain's total consumption. Because of excellent planning and forethought by Shetland Islands Council and BP, vast terminal lies well hidden in sheltered deepwater inlet, marring landscape far less than some of the new roads and building. Oil is brought ashore from the platforms through two pipelines, the gas is separated and processed, and then both oil and gas are dispatched by tanker to refineries and petrochemical plants elsewhere. No facilities for visitors to look around terminal but it's certainly worth driving up B9076 for science fiction-scape of giant storage drums and twinkly lights looming through mist. North-east Mainland.

Weisdale: at top of Weisdale Voe, B9075 turns off A971 and runs through some of Shetland's prettiest country – a gently wooded valley with green pastures and farmhouse hidden behind walled orchard, quite unlike the rest of the island's treeless landscape. The burn also has reputation as one of the best places for sea trout fishing. In 1786, Weisdale was birthplace of John Clunies Ross, one of Shetland's more spirited emigrants. After marrying the daughter of house he had hidden in to evade press-gang, he left Scotland and became uncrowned king of the Cocos Islands. Queen Victoria granted these islands in perpetuity to his descend-

ants who ran them as a paternalistic welfare state until the last, 'King Ross V', lost the fight with the Australian Government over future of his Indian Ocean realm.

Hillswick: sheltered fishing hamlet with a few fine old grey stone houses prettily clustered around bay in Ura Firth. Away from church, tiny graveyard amid clumps of yellow iris looks westward to stark mauve-grey cliffs. Up from harbour, past well-stocked village store-cum-PO-cum-petrol station and eccentric shell-covered outhouse. St Magnus Bay Hotel, splendidly timbered with a John Buchan flavour, overlooks bay. Excellent centre for mineralogists, walkers, fishermen, ornithologists and painters. Hotel, with its lovely pine-clad interior, is one of nicest places for a drink in Shetland. Also good restaurant (tel Hillswick 209 for booking).Further up the road, Shetland Knitwear and Crafts has pleasing range of locally made trinkets, mugs, knitwear – especially good for gloves. Local salt Tipsy the cat accompanies visitors around the village. A970, north-west Mainland.

Esha Ness: wild north-west corner with some of most magnificent cliff scenery in Britain. On southern side guarded by the Drongs, fearsome stone fangs jutting out of the sea, and great rocky arch, Dore Holm. Road then forks either to Stenness, with remains of old haaf station on edge of shore where fishermen lived during season, drying and salting fish on pebbled beach around, or past square-walled ruins of medieval church to lighthouse and ragged coastline where sea crashes against precipitous cliffs, competing in noise with puffins and fulmars that nest there. Excellent walking ground. B9078 from Hillswick.

ISLANDS

BRESSAY

Very close to Lerwick, but locals are determined it shouldn't become capital's island suburb. Car ferry (departing from Alexandra Wharf, booking not necessary) crosses ¾-mile wide Sound frequently, on some days in summer until 10pm. Population of around 300 is spread mainly over western side. Good walking around deserted north, the flatter end with

voes and lochs, the eastern side overlooking spectacular bird reserve of Noss (see *Flora and Fauna*) and southern end, perhaps the best, with marvellous views over mainland from cliffs, even better from 743ft conical Ward of Bressay behind. It takes about three hours to walk to Bard Head from Ord Lighthouse – another built by the Stevenson family, 1858. Visitors welcome summer afternoons 2-6, Sun excepted, winter phone first Bressay 282. (Also see *Mainland – Sumburgh Lighthouse.*)

Maryfield House, quite close to pier, is the island inn and guesthouse, serving bar lunches in summer, also evening meals, but book first, tel Bressay 207. Weather permitting, Robin Hunter does boat trips around the island and if sea is calm enough might include a visit to the echoing Cave of the Bard, with its marble-like walls. Book either direct (tel Bressay 285) or through Tourist Organisation.

There's a nice little sandy beach in north at Beosetter, and look out for rusting 40ft World War I guns at Aith Voe and the Ord, hauled into place by mules; and two ruined churches – at Gunnista, with roofless family vault of the Hendersons, early Bressay lairds, and St Mary's at Cullingsburgh (burgh pronounced broch) where there is a 17th c tomb of Dutch sea captain Claes Janssen Bruyn.

If you visit Noss (as you should) there's a fascinating tale about the Holm of Noss, rocky islet just off south-east corner. 17th c fowler from Foula was charged with task of scaling 160ft-high vertical cliffs in order to fix a rope railway with oblong box large enough to carry a man and a sheep. In wager for a cow, he was challenged to climb down again rather than use the device but fell and was killed in the descent. Every summer for the next 100 years, 12 sheep were put to graze on the holm. Dismantled 19th c. The 'Tystie' which sails around Noss, leaves from the small boat harbour, Lerwick. Details from the Tourist Organisation with whom bookings should be made.

EAST AND WEST BURRA AND TRONDRA

Three long, narrow, green islands, pleasant for walking with unexpected and contrasting views. Linked to each other and to Mainland by bridges

Weisdale Voe, a great inlet running deep into Mainland.

south-west of Scalloway. Hamnavoe, at northern end of West Burra, is a delightful natural fishing harbour with mirror-calm sea; yet a few hundred yards away on other side of headland, mesmeric waves crash against rocks sending white spray flying feet into air. Papil, in south, was an early centre of Christianity. Two Celtic crosses found here – the Monk's Stone, a prized piece in Shetland Museum at Lerwick, and much more fantastically inscribed Papil Stone depicting creatures part-man part-bird, now at Edinburgh Museum of Antiquities. Some accommodation on Burra.

FETLAR

North-eastern island, roughly 5 miles by 3, green and fertile. Was only nesting site in Britain of the snowy owl, on southern limit of its breeding range. Royal Society for the Protec-

tion of Birds' 1,700-acre reserve at Stakkaberg was established when pair of snowy owls began to breed here in 1967, but old and grumpy male drove out the male offspring and since he died in 1975 the four or five females have been without a mate. Stronghold of the delicate red-necked phalarope and whimbrel, Fetlar has highest density in Britain of breeding waders besides being one of top sites for arctic terns with about 4,500 pairs. Visitors should contact RSPB warden at Bealance, tel Fetlar 246, who will tell them where they might see the rarer birds and which areas to avoid because they may disturb nesting sites. There are seals all around the island – grey seals breed on several beaches Oct-Nov – and there's a good chance of seeing otters under the turf banks if sea is calm. Brough Lodge and Urie are favourite haunts.

Of great interest to the geologist –

gneiss in the west gives way to serpentine in the east where there are some fascinating cliff strata.

Fetlar in Norn means 'fat land'. It has good grazing for cattle and ponies and a prettiness about the landscape in the south especially around Papil Water and Tresta, which has island's best beach. Centre of population (about 100) is at Houbie with shop, and two guest-houses nearby in the old manses. Also some self-catering accommodation. For taxi service call Thomason's, tel Fetlar 225. Car ferry runs three or four times a day from Gutcher, Yell, to Oddsta on north coast (book vehicles, tel Burravoe 259 or 268). Loganair service Mon-Fri, for details and reservations tel Gott 246.

FOULA

Rocky fortress rises up out of sea 27 miles west of Scalloway. Extremely remote and isolated island with population now only 40 – one-third old-age pensioners. No natural harbour, main settlement Ham Voe only has storm-lashed jetty, and problems in getting there are formidable. Mailboat, kept on Foula, sails once a week to Walls, Mainland, but with mighty seas is often cancelled in summer, and in winter for up to six weeks at a time. Special Loganair service, in conjunction with Shetland Islands Council, operates mid-June to end Aug. For details tel Gott 246. Until arrival of trawling fleets, abundant fish supported population of 300 – Foula men renowned as tireless oarsmen, fearless rock-climbers after birds' eggs, and energetic dancers of the Foula Reel. Norn spoken here until 1800.

Towering rocks form five pinnacles, grim Sneug the highest at 1,370ft, while the Kame is second-highest sheer cliff face in Britain. Breeding place for thousand upon thousand of sea-birds (Foula means 'bird island'). Boss of the roost is piratical great skua or 'bonxie'. Once

nearly extinct – 18th c conservation act fined anyone killing it or stealing its eggs 16s 8d, but rule fell into disuse and with Victorian passion for egg-collecting and stuffed birds, by turn of the century it was down to a couple of pairs on Foula and a couple at Hermaness, Unst (guarded there by a paid watcher – the farmers liked to have them around because they kept sea eagles from attacking lambs).

Remarkable population explosion followed and the great skua is now widespread in Shetland, 3,000 pairs nesting on Foula. A rather vicious bird, it attacks smaller birds forcing them to vomit up the fish they've just caught. In nesting season, well-known for its dive-bombing technique on intruders, humans included. Usually bluff but it can give you a good thump!

MOUSA

Attractive little island just off south-east coast, used for grazing sheep and ponies. Has best preserved Iron Age broch in Britain. One of about 500, almost all confined to north Scotland

with 95 in Shetland. 40ft-high cooling tower-shaped structure shows how they all must once have looked. All based on same prototype suggesting that their builders were part of a well-defined political unit. Built of island stone, which also provided Lerwick's paving stones, intricate arrangement of galleries and staircases within thick walls not only led to top but provided ingenious masons with form of internal scaffolding. Setting for two early runaway romances. Victorian traveller John Tudor gleefully recounts how in 1152 Margaret of Atholl, an ageing beauty of easy virtue, and Shetland chieftain lover Erlend Ungi spooned in the broch while her ineffectual son Earl Harald lay siege outside. 200 years earlier, an Icelandic saga tells how young Norwegian Bjorn eloped with 9th c heiress Thora Jewel-Hand and honeymooned there for a year.

Certainly worth a visit and picnic. Flower-spangled meadows, storm petrels and rock doves nest in broch walls and it's one place you can be just about certain of seeing seals

Hercules Irvine outside his croft. He is one of the few still making these baskets, 'kishies'.

basking around shore – tidal pool on eastern side a favourite haunt. During summer, day trips from Sandwick – for details ring boatman Tom Jamieson, Sandwick 367. Mr Jamieson also sells HMSO guide to the broch.

MUCKLE ROE

Means 'big red island'. Small, almost circular island of red granite, perhaps solidified roots of ancient volcano. Linked to Mainland by a bridge, road runs only around south-eastern side – a fertile stretch of land with farming community of about 100. After shower of rain, countryside becomes a misty kaleidoscope of reds and greens, bright fields and stooks of corn sloping towards shore and watery maze of islands and peninsulas opposite. South Ward rises darkly behind.

On north-west coast are high red cliffs, particularly spectacular at The Hams. Take first left turning out of Brae passing Busta House hotel – charmingly converted 18th c laird's house with wooded gardens leading down to sheltered bay. Just right for special evening out – restaurant serves five-course dinners, nice home-cooking and fresh fruit and veg including such exotics as green peppers and courgettes. Not Sun – book first, tel Brae 209.

OUT SKERRIES

Remote group of small rocky islands covering about 600 acres, 5 miles north-east of Whalsay. Two inhabited – Housay and Bruray – linked by bridge. Very little grazing or arable land but rocky coves and inlets make good harbours and fishing grounds. Small community of about 90 (risen since early 19th c) has staunchly maintained that the children should not be sent away to be educated. When present headmaster, who doubles as minister, came to the school, his own children, 7 and 11, neatly complemented the nine existing pupils so that there was one child for every year.

Few high cliffs so no large sea-bird colonies but it's almost as good as Fair Isle for rare and exotic migrants in spring and autumn. By boat from Lerwick, twice weekly in summer, or from Symbister on Whalsay, but rough seas sometimes cause cancellations. Loganair runs special service mid-June to end Aug, tel Gott 246. Some accommodation available.

PAPA STOUR

Looks like misshapen starfish with stacks and skerries – rock-pillars and reefs – liberally scattered around edge. Early home of Celtic missionaries or hermits; name means 'big island of priests'. Looks deceptively easy to get to, but mile-wide channel is treacherous with strong currents running over submerged rocks and in heavy seas you can be stranded for a few days. But when calm, it's possible to see some of Britain's most spectacular caves – weird cathedral-like caverns glistening and tinted many colours, some sinister, some romantic, tunnelled out of volcanic lava and ashes.

At entrance to Housa Voe, on top of isolated Frau Stack, are remains of stone hut where c 1300 Lord Thorvald Thoresson is said to have imprisoned his daughter to keep her from the company of men. In vain, she was pregnant when brought out. Nearby Brei Holm was leper colony till 18th c. A later prisoner, the Hon Edwin Lindsay, was dispatched to Papa Stour at beginning of 19th c for refusing to fight a duel, thus bringing disgrace to his family. Declared insane, he was kept there for 26 years until Catherine Watson, a Quaker preacher, helped him escape and claim his inheritance. Spring at southern end of island where he used to bathe is known as Lindsay's Well.

Green, fertile land, aromatic with wild flowers and pleasant for walking, but lack of peat used to be a problem.

By 1973 numbers had dwindled to under 20, until some young newcomers wanting self-sufficiency instead of city life settled there and helped turn the tide. Stable community now of about 40.

Boat sails from Melby, west Mainland, three times a week; contact boatman John Jamieson, tel Papa Stour 225 (also for cave trips). There is a combined post office/general store, and some accommodation available including self-catering.

UNST

Northernmost of British isles. Remote and beautiful, inhabited in Shetland folklore by giants and trows (trolls).

Fishing boats drawn well up for the winter on Muckle Roe.

Near ferry landing at Belmont is Muness Castle. Built 1598 according to inscription above doorway, by Laurence Bruce, a relation of Earl Patrick Stewart and almost as nasty. Burnt down by avenging neighbour or French privateers, it fell into disuse within 100 years. Three-storey ruins open weekdays April-Sept 9.30-7, Oct-March 9.30-4, Sun from 2. If not in door, key from cottage opposite. Back on main road, turning to Westing is well worth detour. Passing a few scattered standing stones, road leads to sadly dilapidated 18th c house with most stunning view over Lunda Wick. Walk takes you around bay to ruins of medieval church. Further on at Underhoull near Westing is excavation site of 9th c Viking long-house.

There are two hotels at Baltasound, the Baltasound Hotel and Hagdale

Lodge hotel, both with restaurant and bar. There is also some b & b and self-catering accommodation plus private youth hostel at Uyeasound (bookings essential, ring A. Fraser, Uyeasound 237).

Postcards sent from Haroldswick Post Office (Britain's most northerly PO) bear special frank. Rolls of barbed wire round RAF base here put up only after unfortunate NATO exercise when site was all too easily captured. RAF is useful local employer providing islanders with cinema and dentist.

From Norwick, steep bumpy road leads to smashing little beach at Skaw. Saxa Vord looms blackly behind, once home of Saxi the giant but now topped by enormous early-warning radar scanner. In 1962, gust of 177mph measured here – Britain's wind-speed record. Worth driving up winding road, which has plenty of stopping places, for breathtaking view over Burra Firth.

North-westwards from Haroldswick road runs down into valley and strange bar of bright marshy turf with delightful sandy shore that separates Burra Firth from Loch of Cliff, before reaching entrance to Hermaness bird reserve (see *Flora and Fauna*) and shore station for Muckle Flugga lighthouse.

Second largest of the Shetland Isles, it's a good place to stay with excellent walking, sea and trout fishing (tackle not easily obtained, wise to bring it with you), sea angling, especially during long summer nights, wild flowers, ponies and birdlife. Apart from huge sea-bird colonies, look out for shy red-throated diver; whimbrel, in valley at Watlee; along shores redshanks and other waders too numerous to mention (identification book and binoculars a good idea).

If you don't stay there, do make a day trip, but if you want to see Hermaness properly, overnight stop might be necessary. Easily reached by car ferry from Gutcher (allow about ¾ hour to drive across Yell); almost hourly, early morning to early evening. Book first, Burravoe 259 or 268. Loganair service Mon-Fri – details, tel Gott 246. Several petrol pumps, licensed grocers (for basic picnic), and mobile Bank of Scotland calls alternate Thursdays. Useful guide available from Tourist Office.

John Buchan set his gripping tale 'Sule Skerry', a story in 'The Runagates Club', here.

VAILA

Tiny west coast island sheltering Walls harbour. Dominated by battlemented Vaila Hall, the laird's home which was started in 1696 but greatly added to in 1894. 800 acres, mainly moorland, are ideal for studying birds and otters and over 100 species of wild flowers are to be found here. Details of day boat trips from the Tourist Organization, Lerwick.

WHALSAY

Three miles from north-east coast of Mainland, lively and genial fishing community has steadily risen over this century to 1,000. Dialect a bit harder to understand here. Shellfish and lobsters are caught around rocky coastline with its endless reefs and holms, while Whalsay's large fleet of modern trawlers provides prosperous livelihood for islanders who prefer unpredictable seas to farming grassy pastures.

Close by pier at Symbister, the 'Bremen Böd' is fine example of a Hanseatic Booth, windlass still intact. Built 17th c by German merchants for storage of brandy, tobacco, linen, muslin, salt, fruit and other delicacies, which they bartered with Shetlanders for salted dried ling, cod and herring.

Much older, heel-shaped stones at Yoxie, like Stanydale, are thought to be remains of temple dating from c 2,000BC, with Benie Hoose, a roofless ruin about 100 yards away, perhaps the living quarters of its pagan priesthood. Close to shore between Yoxie and Whelsie Geo, leave road at Challister. Most eye-catching piece of architecture is Victorian extravaganza, Symbister House, built by wealthy Shetlander who preferred to spend £30,000 on a second home rather than leave any money to his heirs.

Like neighbouring Out Skerries, good place for spotting rare and exotic migrants, including in recent years hoopoe, red-rumped swallow, Pallas's warbler etc. Accommodation difficult, but day trips easy via car ferry from Laxo (sometimes Vidlin in bad weather). In summer frequent service, book first Symbister 376. Loganair service – for details, phone Gott 246.

YELL

'You need to pull the car blinds down, driving through Yell' is an unkind local joke. Though interior is dull, dark and monotonous – raw peat deposits recently estimated at 200 million tons – the coastline, eaten into by voes on east and with splendid views towards Mainland on west, is attractive and good for walking. Best parts, inaccessible by road, are along wild cliffs from beach at West Sandwick north to Neeps of Graveland and from Vollister on other side of Whale Firth northwards again to Vigon and Gloup. A good otter-watching place (see *Flora and Fauna*).

Some accommodation available including small guest-house at Mid-Yell, the main town. Keith's Kitchen, West Sandwick, does take-away curries, pasta, fish and chips. Car ferry (holding about 10 cars) operates almost half-hourly approx 7.30am to 7pm summer, dawn to dusk winter, between Toft (Mainland) and Ulsta. Booking advisable, tel Burravoe 259 or 268.

SPECIALITIES

Shetland Ponies or Shelties: short stumpy Thelwellian figures with bright eyes, bulging sides and knotted manes. Not as many as you'd expect, but Fetlar and Unst are good places to see them. Average height 38in. None is wild – all have owners. Once of great economic value to the crofter for transport (few tracks had surface good enough to take a wheel), and tail hair was used for making fishing lines, cords etc. In 16th and 17th c to cut the hair from the tail of another man's horse was a serious offence. During 19th c many were shipped to north-east England to replace children in coalmines, hauling tubs along low seams. Numbers dwindled between wars but export market picked up again in 1950s when they became popular as pets. Annual sales held in Unst (end Oct) and Lerwick (beg. Nov).

Plantie-Crubs: shallow round stone-walled enclosures often dotted over a hillside, in which cabbage seedlings were (and in many places still are) raised, sheltered from the wind.

Peat-Cutting: hillsides are seared by peat-cuttings like long black gashes. From May onwards, surface turf is removed, peat cut into slabs and stacked, allowing air to circulate. When dry, taken home and stacked outside the house for winter. Peat rights are usually traditional and go with the croft.

Knitting: distinctive patterns, perhaps of Moorish origin, once said to have been introduced by Spanish sailors wrecked in Armada – a theory now disputed. Now done while watching TV, but once women knitted as they walked to and from the croft, peats, potatoes and cabbages loaded on their backs. A few older women still card and spin their own wool but famous lacy shawls, delicately worked using wool plucked from sheep's neck, are rare and prized possessions now. Several workshops where knitwear is assembled and finished – visitors generally welcome. At T.M. Adie, Voe, delightful old wooden buildings also house Shetland tweed looms – advance booking for guided tour essential, ring Voe 332 – and Thuleknit, Brae, often have excellent seconds on sale. Demonstrations of carding, spinning etc – see *Lerwick*.

Shetland Fiddlers: traditional reels, jigs and marches played with gusto and enjoyment at practice sessions Wed evenings 7-9, Isleburgh House Centre, Lerwick. Not to be missed. (Donations welcome.) Also look in local paper for any dances at which they are playing.

Food: reestit – lamb salted and dried in peat fumes – and young cod-like fish called piltock salted and dried in same way, are eaten in most Shetland homes, especially in winter. Rarely found on uninspired restaurant menus, they can be bought in shops and taken home.

ACTIVITIES

Angling: brown and sea trout fishing: over 200 lochs with good and varied fishing, some also stocked with rainbow trout. Permits needed for Mainland but not generally on islands – available from Shetland Tourist Organisation, who will also advise on hotels offering special fishing facilities. Sea trout season runs from end Feb-end Oct, best fish caught at beginning and end; brown trout mid March-early Oct. All lochs on Mainland but Gonfirth, near Voe, have

Spinning, knitting and carding wool 'Urgently Required . . .'.

brown trout – some of the best are Tingwall; Spiggie; Benston, near Nesting; Sand Water, near Weisdale; Pundswater, near Aith; Houlland, near Bixter, which has especially big fish. Good sea trout waters include Laxo Voe, which also has grilse of about 5-11lb; Stromfirth, Whiteness Strand, Lax Firth. Girlsta Loch, south of Nesting, has char – a rare silvery trout-like fish only found in extremely deep waters – and ferox trout – large cannibalistic brown trout weighing 6-7lb.

Sea angling: haddock, whiting, ling, skate, saithe and pollack in abundance. 100lb of fish can be caught in 6-8 hours. Shetland has held records for giant skates and porbeagle sharks. Suitable for beginners too. Tourist Organisation will give details of fishing holiday hotels, tackle and boat hire. If you make an exceptional catch, let Tourist Organisation know in case it's a record.

Sailing: only for those with a good boat, good equipment and expert knowledge. Clyde Cruising Club, S.V. Carrick, Glasgow G1 4LN (tel

Glasgow 552 2183), publishes manual 'Sailing Directions and Anchorages Around Shetland', from bookshops/chandlers or direct from them. Lerwick and Scalloway Boating Clubs welcome visiting yachtsmen and provide clubhouse facilities.

Sub-Aqua Diving: again for the experienced only. Very cold but exceptionally clear waters with close-up views of seals and plenty of unexplored shipwrecks. There were important 16th-17th c sea lanes here and area rivals the Caribbean for finding cannons, pieces of eight, doubloons etc. Keep an eye open for dramatic and sudden changes in weather. Shetland Diving Club offers reciprocal facilities to members of branches of Scottish Sub-Aqua Club, and will sell air to competent divers and advise on best spots etc. Enquiries to Andy Carter, 83 Nederdale, Lerwick, or ask at Lerwick Swimming Pool, Hillhead.

Walking: marvellous all round coastline and, with few enclosed fields, inland also. On Mainland, best in northern part past Mavis Grind, the 100yd-wide isthmus dividing Atlantic and North Sea. Beyond Ronas Hill, the highest point in Shetland at 1,486ft, lochs are connected by burns with spectacular rapids and waterfalls – at Lang Clodie Wick 240ft high – and long shingle beaches run under towering cliffs. Magnificent but lonely area with no road or track, where you're unlikely to encounter another human being. Compass useful. Other hills, like Fitful Head in south, make splendid vantage points; and inland following a stream to its source makes a pleasant diversion. Ordnance Survey map (nos 1, 2, 3 and 4), wind- and waterproof clothing, stout shoes essential.

Swimming and Beachcombing: swimming restricted to the very hardy (or Lerwick's indoor pool) but clean stretches of firm white sand are superb for walking, beachcombing, shell-collecting etc. Some of the best are: sheltered Maywick and Spiggie, south-west Mainland; Levenwick and Gulberwick, south-east Mainland; west Sandwick, Yell and Skaw, Unst (reached by bumpy almost vertical track from Norwick).

Golf: 18-hole course at Dale, 3 miles north of Lerwick. Visitors are welcome and clubs can be hired at course.

FLORA AND FAUNA

BIRDS

Spectacular sea-bird breeding colonies, numerous rare migrants and northern species on the very edge of their breeding perimeter, make Shetland an extraordinary bird-watching spot for both layman and ornithologist. The best time to see the breeding colonies is from mid-May to mid-July; for migrants end April/May/early June and Sept/Oct. Carried on easterly winds, the eastern isles – Out Skerries, Whalsay and east Unst – and of course Fair Isle, are the best places to see them.

Reserves include: **Hermaness** (Nature Conservancy Council), north Unst – bird city – grassy, rocky 600ft cliffs packed with layers of nesting puffins in the grassy slopes, guillemots on the lower ledges, razorbills and shags in the boulders at the bottom, and every nook and crevice filled with nesting kittiwakes and fulmars. The last has multiplied enormously since it came to Shetland in 1878 and now causes some annoyance to farmers because the musky smell of its spit contaminates sheep's wool. It also lingers on clothes for months. But most spectacular is the gannet colony, increased from a few pairs in 1917 to 5-6,000 pairs today, and sitting in their midst on the point of Saito, eyeing them hopefully, a lone but ever-optimistic black-browed albatross. (Sturdy waterproof boots necessary.) **Fetlar** (Royal Society for the Protection of Birds) – see *Islands*. Good place to see red-throated divers, Arctic skuas and rare northern waders like whimbrel and red-necked phalarope.

Noss (NCC), East Bressay – 700-acre rocky island, every square foot of cliff face taken up by segregated layers of guillemots, shags, kittiwakes, puffins and 5-6,000 pairs of gannets sitting on large untidy nests decorated with multicoloured scraps of old fishingnet, all supervised by the great skuas or bonxies (see *Islands – Foula*). Elsewhere eiderduck, lapwing, ringed plover, oyster-catchers, snipe, rock doves, wrens and wheatears. Walk round island takes approx three hours, avoiding central part where some of the rarer birds nest (when birds are scared from their nests, eggs or chicks may quickly be snatched by skuas). Visitors are ferried across regularly in small inflatable dinghy if they wait on opposite shore at Bressay and wave vigorously to catch boatman's eye. Check weather conditions and tides before leaving Lerwick with Tourist Organisation (who sell useful inexpensive guide) or NCC Office, tel Lerwick 3345. Boat trip round Bressay and Noss (good also for seeing caves), $2\frac{1}{2}$ hour trips most days from Victoria Pier, Lerwick. Book at Tourist Office. **Lochs of Spiggie and Brow** (recently created RSPB reserve) south-east Mainland, have lots of wintering duck and whooper swan. **Ramna Stacks** (RSPB), north tip of Mainland – huge sea-bird colonies but seldom accessible.

Non-ornithologists will find it frustrating not to have good identification book with them. Binoculars always useful. Excellent small guide by Bobby Tulloch and Fred Hunter is published by Shetland Times Ltd. Some of the rare species come under Schedule 1 of Protection of Birds Act and permission is needed to photograph them at the nest – details from Nature Conservancy Council headquarters at 20 Belgrave Sq, London SW1X 8PY or 12 Hope Terrace, Edinburgh EH9 2AS. For RSPB enquiries, Shetland officer is at Lüsetter, Mid Yell.

OTTERS

Together with Orkney and Western Isles, one of last domains of the otter. Good chance of seeing one especially if you're prepared to get up at dawn and wait patiently by a muddy creek or shore. Uninhabited offshore islands, north-west tip and south-east side of Yell, Fetlar and Unst are good spots.

SEALS

Common and grey seals all around coast. You will almost certainly see them at Hermaness in Unst and Mousa. Common seals pup all around the offshore islets midsummer but you can often watch them from the land; grey seals come ashore to pup Oct/Nov particularly around the coast of Fetlar where you can see their cream-coloured young.

WILD FLOWERS

Traditional agricultural methods mean that in spring and summer countryside is carpeted with flowers now rarely seen in England – ragged robin, hayrattle, different types of orchid, buttercups, monkey flowers and many others. On the cliffs, pinks, sea campion, mayweed, scurvy grass and roseroot (in Shetland called lady's footstool) – so named because the base of the stem has a delicious rose scent. Ronas Hill has been designated a site of special scientific interest because of sub-arctic flowers that bloom there. Again, worth having a book with you to help you identify them all.

EVENTS

Up Helly Aa: not a tourist attraction but pagan midwinter fire festival celebrated with much merrymaking by people of Lerwick. Last Tuesday in January, 10ft high Proclamation containing year's local humour and gossip is exhibited at the Market Cross while 30ft Galley is escorted through the streets by Guizer Jarl and his Viking squad. Galley is then displayed on sea front for the day before being carried by torchlight to brass band accompaniment up to George V Playing Field, where, to proud rendering of 'The Norseman's Home', it's set ablaze. Feasting, drinking, dancing continues all night in 12 Halls (to which you have to be invited) with guizers and their squads, in humorous or satirical costume, visiting each in turn and performing their secret but carefully rehearsed act to loud cheers.

Agricultural Shows: held at Walls first Sat in August, and Cunningsburgh, following Sat.

Sheepdog Trials: three or four during summer – dates and venues announced local Press and radio.

Regattas: almost one a week during summer in numerous voes and harbours – local Press for details.

Angling Competitions: lots throughout Shetland with all-night competition mid-June. Details local Press.

Tourist Organisation publishes a comprehensive list in its 'Shetland Holiday Planner' (see *Useful Information*), and look out for barn dances, fetes, etc in local Press.

Briefing by Pamela Brown

FAIR ISLE

BY DEREK COOPER

Fair Isle is a pinpoint in the sea halfway between Orkney and Shetland. Since the evacuation of St Kilda in 1930 it has been the remotest inhabited island in British waters. It is a 50 mile round trip in the island's only boat to the nearest landfall in Shetland.

And were it not for the imagination and determination of one man it might well have followed in the desolate wake of St Kilda. George Waterston who died in an Edinburgh hospital in September 1980 after a courageous fight against kidney disease bought Fair Isle in 1947 from its owner Robert Bruce of Sumburgh for £5000. He wanted the island not for his own private pleasure but as a permanent bird observatory. George first visited

Sunrise lighting the natural buttresses of Fair Isle's coast.

Fair Isle in 1935 and like the pioneering birdman Dr William Eagle Clark of the Royal Scottish Museum he realised its great potential for the study of bird migration. He saw too that the only natural resources on the island were the ingenuity and determination of the islanders themselves. Without some kind of life support and encouragement it was unlikely that they could survive for much longer.

And then the war came. George Waterston was captured in Crete and made a prisoner-of-war. But a chain of coincidences began to connect, a chain that secured the future of the island. In 1974 I was lucky enough to fly from Aberdeen to Fair Isle with George Waterston and he told me the story.

'In the camp with me was another ornithologist, Ian Pitman and we used to talk over what we were going to do after the war. I had this mad idea of setting up a Bird Observatory on Fair Isle and Ian seemed to be taken with the idea too and he said "well let's get together on this"'.

The strangest coincidence of all came towards the end of a long voyage back to Britain, to which he was returning because of his ill-health. The Red

Cross ship on its journey from Sweden passed Fair Isle and that was the first piece of his native land George sighted.

It was the final omen. With the island bought, George began to raise money to set up the Fair Isle Bird Observatory Trust, a centre which would be permanently manned by a trained ornithologist and which would provide accommodation for visiting enthusiasts and naturalists from all over the world.

Of all the British offshore islands Fair Isle is ornithologically the most important, as George Waterston told me on the second stage of our journey, a short flip in a Loganair Islander from Sumburgh airport: 'You see it acts as a kind of stepping stone for birds moving between Orkney and Shetland and you get concentrations of birds here which you don't get anywhere else on the mainland. You can, as it were, keep your finger on the pulse of migration from day to day'.

It's not just sea birds, the puffins, the fulmars, the gulls, the guillemots that command attention. There are small land birds to be recorded, birds blown off course and caught in traps placed cunningly about the treeless windblown plateaux of the island.

The bird observatory, a £50,000 hostel and research centre, was built in 1969, and between three and four hundred visitors stay for varying periods each year. The Shetland Islands Council, the Highlands and Islands Development Board and the National Trust between them have provided the islanders with an air strip, electricity, modernised housing, an improved pier. Some bird enthusiasts have stayed on to try their hand at crofting and whenever a croft is advertised there's a fistful of hopefuls vying with each other to secure a foothold on this bleak and remote landfall.

But this is no place for escapists or eccentrics. The residents of Fair Isle know only too well the tensions that isolation brings so they vet carefully any incomer who wants to join them. It is a fragile community where you have to work your way to acceptance. When I was there there were sixty souls living on six square miles of rock and treeless turf. All the boat work is more or less communal; the sheep are worked communally too, and there is a strong tradition of work-sharing.

The new life on Fair Isle, the spin-off from the Observatory, has given the island a *raison d'être* which other less fortunate islands lack. However dark and long the winter, when spring and the first migratory birds arrive, the naturalists return in ever increasing numbers. Fair Isle is no longer cut off. It is, thanks to George Waterston, the most viable of all Britain's small offshore islands.

DEREK COOPER

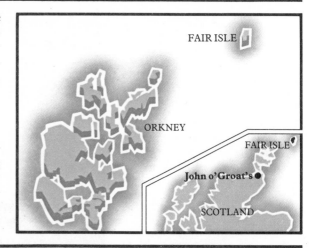

The remotest inhabited island in British waters.

NOTES

Visitors (not just ornithologists) can stay at the Observatory and help, if they have sufficient knowledge, with counting and catching birds for ringing. Best to book well ahead especially for spring and autumn migration periods. Details from The Warden, Fair Isle Bird Observatory, Fair Isle, Shetland, tel Fair Isle 258. There are also huge sea-bird nesting colonies in the spectacular 4-500ft-high sandstone cliffs – some of the best in Shetland – all along the western side, particularly around Malcolm's Head, and in the east by the Observatory at Sheep Rock and Buness.

Crofting is confined to the southern part of the island with general store at Stackhoull, and hall where lively dances are held most summer weekends. Two or three crofts have old beehive-shaped corn-drying kilns still intact and horizontal water mills. Just down from the Hall at Kirkigeo, little graveyard overlooks beach where fishermen used to winter their yoals (open boats) in hollowed-out noosts. Demand exceeds supply for Fair Isle knitwear so regular sales have been abandoned, but you may be able to buy direct from a knitter. Hardy bathers might be tempted by the rock pool at Gunglesund, south-west corner, and North Haven has a sandy if cold stretch of beach. In moorland-covered north, where skuas nest, look out for juniper, growing as ground cover, and milky white flowers of chickweek wintergreen, normally a woodland plant but prehistoric survivor here from time when island was covered with scrub.

'The Good Shepherd' crosses the 20 choppy miles from Grutness, near Sumburgh, twice a week in summer, once in winter. $2\frac{1}{2}$ to 3-hour journey, to book tel Fair Isle 222. Longanair flights from Tingwall Airport nr Lerwick make a day trip possible (details tel Gott 246), but to see the island properly you need a good 3 or 4 days.

Briefing by Pamela Brown

ISLE OF WIGHT

BY HUGH CASSON

'That over there,' said my governess, pointing a gloved finger across the misty Solent, 'is the Isle of Wight. It's about 20 miles long and 13 miles across and it can accommodate all the people in the world put together.' '*All* the people?' I piped incredulously. '*All* the people,' she said, firmly screwing down the Thermos, 'provided they stand shoulder to shoulder of course . . . and I see you have got tar on your left shoe, we'll have to get rid of *that* before we get on the bus . . .'

The image was breathtaking . . . that softly moulded landscape on the horizon goosepimpled solid with millions of black, white and brown heads. And true or false I've never forgotten it. The island doesn't help you to forget it either. From the north as you

Windsurfing off Ventnor. Isle of Wight has good beaches, strong winds and tricky tides.

approach it – it's moored about four miles off the Hampshire shore to which it was once joined – the coastline has hardly changed in the last hundred years. Low clay-coloured cliffs topped with dark woods yield to multicoloured farmland and the gentle swell of the chalk downland beyond. Even the landmarks ('conspic' on the charts) are the same. To the east the high Victorian spire of All Saints Ryde – one of Sir Gilbert Scott's best – and the Metropolitan-Water-Boardish campanile of Osborne House (Prince Albert and Thomas Cubitt in partnership), the French Baronial Royal Yacht Squadron at Cowes holding the centre, and far to the west beyond the bird-haunted salt-pans and oyster beds of Newtown, Yarmouth castle and the Needles.

Like all islands, 'The Island', as the residents always call it, is touched with magic. Not the magic of remoteness – you are unlikely to be marooned or weatherbound there and from Ryde you can imagine you see the time on the clock tower of Portsmouth Town Hall. Not the magic either of frowning cliffs and scurrying clouds – the Island is about as ferocious as a teapot – but the magic of the miniature, a Victorian miniature.

Everything about it – its buildings and gardens, its seaside villas and pier-ettes, its Gothic vicarages and forgotten signal-boxes, its tiny terraces and toy-town halls – is miraculously preserved as though beneath a domed Victorian glass. True, there have been some sad losses: East Cowes Castle has gone. It was built by John Nash to retire to, visited by Turner on a sketching tour in 1827 – and described as a 'tawdry specimen' by *Black's Guide* in 1865. John Nash died there in disgrace and in debt, and was buried nearby under the wall of the little church he had designed himself, his coffin secretly hurried across the fields by night because his creditors had planned to arrest his corpse. Gone too are the old Red Funnel paddle-steamers with their stovepipe funnels, grained panelling, and fine Victorian names – Lord Elgin, Balmoral, Duchess of Cornwall – painted on their paddle boxes. On a fine summer evening you could hear them coming from miles away, their paddles thumping the water like a spaniel's tail.

But by geography, luck and the energy and foresight of those who care about such things, the Island is still largely unspoilt. It is still possible (just) to share a deserted village street with a sunstruck cat, to walk the top of the downs with only the larks for company, to anchor for the night alone in a quiet creek . . . and all this under a hundred miles from London.

The coastline is amazingly varied. Bird-haunted mudflats, luxuriant semi-tropical undercliffs, dramatically carved dazzlingly white chalk cliffs guarding a soft centre of tiny meandering little streams, meadow sweet valleys and gently contoured farmland.

The river Medina almost splits the Island in two from north to south. It's big enough to allow coasters up to the Island's capital Newport, an

Ryde Pier, opened 1814, one of the oldest in Britain.

underrated and self-possessed little town full of charm and dignity, with some handsome warehouses and Victorian terraces. John Nash designed the Guildhall and the County Club and in the north aisle of St Thomas's Church is a touching little memorial (given by Queen Victoria) to the 15-year-old daughter of Charles I, who died in her father's prison, Carisbrooke Castle nearby. (The flagpole on the keep, incidentally, is the spinnaker boom from King George V's old J-class yacht 'Britannia'.)

There are no really grand houses on the Island. The grandest are Appuldurcombe, a D of E-preserved Palladian shell that stands magnificently roofless, its smaller sister Gatcombe, and Osborne House, bought for £26,000 by Prince Albert and reconstructed as a family house for Queen Victoria. Here they spent much of their married life. Here the Queen retired to as a widow. It was here, behind the still-shuttered windows of her bedroom, left almost undisturbed ever since, that she died. It is a place not to be missed. The state apartments with their cargo of oddities – tusks from Nepal, China pugs, antler-legged chairs, a crocodile skull, and 23 paintings of her favourite dogs, Noble, Minnie, Fern, Scamp, Sally and the rest . . . and across the embroidered lawns and down by the sea the children's tiny Swiss-style playhouse, fully furnished to miniature scale, the toy fort and the Queen's green high-wheeled bathing machine. (The dottily pinnacled Royal church of Whippingham nearby [1849] is another of Prince Albert's architectural efforts and contains his monument and some very pretty candleholders.)

Apart from this there are a score or so of good-sized manor houses, a handful of picture postcard villages, plenty of good Victorian churches, and plenty too of delightful unpretentious seaside buildings, wharves and jetties, prettily balconied lodging houses, lots of gaily painted and lettered stucco – and everywhere flagpoles and masts and the noise of sea-gulls and slapping halyards. The oldest borough in the Island, Newtown, is best visited by boat – silent (except at weekends), plaintive sea-birds, the impatient suck of the tide against the marshy grass. The great trees are gone but the grass-grown streets of this once busy little town remain, and its tiny little 18th-century Town Hall – sensitively restored and guarded by the National Trust – still presides over the few cottages above the salt-pans.

But all is not loneliness and sea-birds. Cowes is a thriving semi-industrial town whose tiny narrow streets and alleys seem always to end in the glint of water or the flick of a flag. Ryde is a day-visitors' place, popular and crowded but still keeping much

Night falls on the pier at Shanklin, a traditional sea-side resort.

of its Victorian charm. Bembridge is still rather posh in a Frintonesque sort of way but the unusual Ruskin Museum and the Oglander tomb in Brading Church are worth a visit. Sandown's setting is better than its architecture – much of which is seaside ticky-tack – bingo halls, funfairs and caffs. Shanklin keeps its old village centre and scores of charming Victorian houses – though not so many as Ventnor, a beautiful little once-fashionable Victorian watering place, luxuriantly shrubberied and rockeried and steeply stepped. Freshwater is famous for Tennyson and Julia

Cameron, its gentle little river valley joining it to Yarmouth – a ferry port, jaunty, crowded, guarded by a castle and packed to the brim with boats all the year round. (It must have the busiest harbour master on the south coast.)

History? Not much. No Wars of the Roses. No Civil War – the Island was Parliamentarian. It was occupied by the Romans in 43AD (they called it Vectis) and was the last bit of the United Kingdom to receive Christianity. It had its share of invading Saxons, Danes, Normans, though William the Conqueror excluded it from his realm, and French, who burnt Yarmouth, Newport and Newtown in 1377. This was really the last great disturbance and for the next 400 years the Island drowsed away happily farming, smuggling, fishing and ship-building, until the Victorian seaside holiday boom and the arrival of the first paddle-steamers (1826) and Queen Victoria (1845).

Celebrities? The Royals of course, plus Nash and Turner. Dr Arnold was born in Cowes. The Countess of Albemarle, who sold the Isle of Wight to Edward I in 1293 for a jumble-sale price, lived at Carisbrooke. David Garrick and Lewis Carroll loved Sandown. Samuel Wilberforce was Vicar of Brighstone. Garibaldi planted a tree at Farringford. Tsar Alexander's visit to Chale is commemor-ated by a monument. Sophie Dawes, the fisher-man's daughter who became mistress to the Duc de Bourbon in the early 19th century, lived at Brading. Dickens and Thackeray stayed at Bon-church. Tennyson wrote 'Maud' at Calbourne, 'The Idylls of the King' in his attic study at Farringford (now a hotel) and 'Crossing the Bar' en route to Yarmouth from Lymington. Tenny-son's old coachman William Knight died at Fresh-water aged 80 after a lifetime diet of hardboiled eggs and dried goat's flesh.

This part of the Island is for my money the high-spot of the Isle of Wight: the long low fancy-Gothic house of Farringford sheltered by trees, the green shoulder of the downs behind, then on its summit (by the Tennyson Monument) not a house in sight, nothing but gorse tugging in the wind and sea-gulls wheeling below. You can walk over the turf with Tennyson's wrinkled sea crawl-ing hundreds of feet below on each side of you until the hill narrows to a point, and then to the Needles, each with its name – Old Pepper, Wedge, Roe Hall, Frenchman's Cellar – with the yellow-funnelled pilot boat rolling gently in the swell and finally the striped lighthouse, as gaily painted as a croquet mark, to signal the end of your journey.

HUGH CASSON

Towns and Villages

NEWPORT

Pleasant little working town which became the 'new port' in 1180 when Lord of the Island Richard de Red-vers ruled from nearby Carisbrooke. Busy commercial and administrative centre, streets lined with solid 18th and 19th c houses. Tuesday cattle and general market, which is now in South St, used to be held in St James Square with its half art nouveau, half Gothic monument to Queen Victoria and colonnaded Guildhall by Nash. St Thomas's Church, 1854-5, has par-ticularly fine Jacobean pulpit saved from earlier church, and pretty white Carrara marble monument to Prin-cess Elizabeth, 15-year-old daughter of Charles I. 2nd-3rd c Roman Villa in Avondale Rd marks Newport's earlier history. Smaller than Brading (see *Sightseeing*). Open April-Sept Sun-Fri 10.30-5.30. Admission charge.

County Press in High St, sedate mahogany-filled newspaper office, publishes nice range of booklets and postcards using old engravings and photographs. National Trust has an

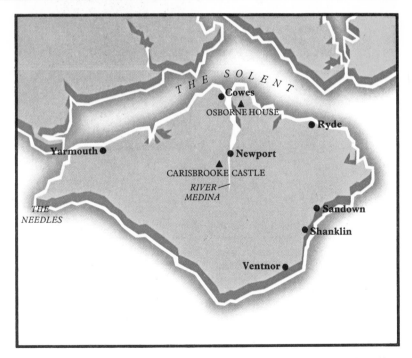

information centre at 35 Upper St James St. Early closing Thursday. For real beer try Calverts, Quay St, a small town hotel, and the Rose and Crown, a friendly local. Excellent range of information sheets and bro-chures from Tourist Board main office, 21 High St, tel Newport 524343.

BONCHURCH

Steep wooded hills with winding paths slope down to a bay criss-crossed with stone breakwaters. Half-hidden among the tall trees and shady gardens are picturesque cottages and some fine big early 19th c houses. The focal point is a pond with willow trees and ducks. It's all dankly romantic like the background of some Pre-Raphaelite painting. In spite of a sprinkling of modern houses, the atmosphere has changed little since Keats came here in 1819. 'Bonchurch a very delightful place – cottages all covered with creepers and honey-suckle, fit abodes for the people I guess live in them – romantic old maids fond of novels.' It has many literary associations. Swinburne was born here, and despite all the scandals is buried with the rest of his family in the graveyard of the Victorian parish church. Thackeray and Macaulay spent holidays here. Dickens stayed at a house called Winterbourne and wrote six chapters of 'David Copper-field'. At St Boniface Old Church, tiny Norman building set in flowery churchyard, Charles I attended the funeral of a cavalier killed in his service. Bay House Café specialises in crab and lobster caught by the proprietor. Bonchurch is the best place on the island for a special meal. As well as the very civilised Copper-field Room at the Winterbourne Hotel (tel Ventnor 852535), there is the Peacock Vane Hotel Restaurant (tel Ventnor 852019) – sedate country-house feeling, log fires, nice wine list and 'Good Food Guide' tureen award.

COWES

The River Medina divides the town into two distinct parts linked by a ferry bridge. East Cowes is industrial and unattractive, and out of season, Cowes itself has a surprisingly sleepy, slightly run-down air for a place with such an international reputation. But from the last week in April when the yacht racing begins it becomes more animated, and by the beginning of August and Cowes Week it's packed with excited crowds and rowdy yachtsmen. Every other year, when the Admiral's Cup Race makes it the focus of world sailing it regains all the hearty glamour of its Edwardian prime.

Boat building began here in the

12th c – there are still lots of boat yards – yacht racing in the 18th c. The Prince Regent made Cowes the height of fashion. There are now nine yacht clubs – the Royal Yacht Squadron is still the grandest and most exclusive. Twenty-one brass cannon stand near-by on Victoria Parade to start the races and fire royal salutes.

Pleasant walk from there along the edge of the sea as far as the stone lion that marks Egypt Point at the northernmost tip of the island. Good place to watch yacht races and, especially at night, big ships which come close in shore here as they turn into Southampton.

Alum Bay : choose various coloured sands and make your own souvenir.

The twisting shopping streets are full of ship-chandlers supplying everything a yachtsman could need – at the Marine Gallery, High St, you can even commission a portrait of your boat and the Book Cabin specialises in nautical publications. Pubs, mostly small and cosy, get packed to overflowing in the summer. Nice ones include the Vectis Tavern – ancient with low ceiling, local Burt's beer – and the Britannia, another small local serving Whit-bread real ale. Ruth's in High St is very good for superior picnic food, also self-service café. Early closing Wed.

You can arrange boat trips round the harbour or further afield with F. Cole, tel Cowes 293990 or M. Ray-ment, tel Ryde 64602. The National Sailing Centre, tel Cowes 294941/2, or the Medina Yacht Co, tel Cowes 292179, can arrange individual sailing tuition. See also *Activities, Sailing*.

At Dottens Farm, Baring Rd, Curds and Whey make special island-shaped Isle of Wight cheeses. Talks and demonstrations Easter-Sept weekdays 11.30 and 2.30 while cheese is being made. Admission charge. Shop open all year (closed 1-2 and Sun).

GODSHILL

Goes right over the top – not long ago it was just a pretty village, but now it's a feast for lovers of kitsch, with at least six purpose-built wishing-wells, dozens of tea gardens and ye olde gifte shoppes, gnomes galore and quantities of coach parties. There is a nicely jumbled natural history museum in a Gothic cottage with palm trees outside. Open April-Sept daily. Admission charge.

There is a model village in the Old Vicarage Gardens, part of it a minia-ture copy of Godshill itself, complete with thatch and flowery gardens – a model village in a model village in a model village. Open April-Spring Bank Holiday and Sept 10-5.30, Spring Bank Holiday-Aug 10-dusk. Admission charge. Only the 15th c church is still unselfconscious, with lovely views from the churchyard over hilly countryside and fine monu-ments inside to the Worsley family who lived at nearby Appuldurcombe House. Big, very handsome old pub, The Griffin, serves Whitbread real ale.

Other pretty, less commercialised inland villages are Calbourne, famous for Winkle St, row of cottages beside a stream, and Brighstone with its thatched Post Office.

NEWTOWN

In the Middle Ages a thriving port famous for its oysters, but as the creek silted up it went into a dramatic decline. All that remains are four or five cottages and a little Georgian town hall, silhouetted against the fields and sky. Inside are old regalia, maps and furniture. Open some days Easter-Sept, check times with Nat.

Trust Information Centre, Newport, tel Newport 526445. Admission charge.

Some of the layout of the original town is still visible, the small fields were once gardens and the grassy walks where cows graze were once roads. The whole place has a lovely remote feeling. The creeks and abandoned salt-pans of the estuary are haunted by wildfowl and waders. The National Trust owns the river, quays and four miles of Solent foreshore with anchorages for yachts, and much of the land has been turned into the Newtown Nature Reserve (see *Flora and Fauna*).

Oysters are still bred in Newtown at the Newtown Oyster Fisheries Ltd in Waters Copse, tel Calbourne 452. They also specialise in clams. You can buy direct from them or sample their produce at the New Inn, a delightful little pub in Shalfleet, a nearby village. Many islanders' favourite pub, the oysters have to be ordered in advance, tel Calbourne 314. They also specialise in other shellfish and game.

RYDE

Looks charming as you approach from the sea. Regency and Victorian houses framed in trees rise steeply up from the esplanade. The pier is half a mile long, one of the longest and oldest in Britain, opened in 1814. London Transport tube trains, retired from the Piccadilly Line, trundle down it to greet waves of new arrivals from the ferry. There is a jolly esplanade with bandstand, an esplanade pavilion with blue and gold chinoiserie turrets, and seats for a grandstand view of all the big ships in Spithead.

The town behind the seafront bustles with shoppers, traffic and trippers. Keep a look out in the hilly streets for pleasing architectural details around almost every corner, eg classical portico at 15 Union St, The Royal Squadron Hotel, where Queen Victoria stayed as a girl, and the grandly balconied facade opposite, Royal Victoria Arcade. All Saints' Church, Queen's Rd, big and ornate, is one of Sir Gilbert Scott's most successful buildings and St James's Church has a pretty Regency Gothic interior.

It's the best place for shopping in the island. Several decent bookshops; Heritage Books in Cross St, a very pleasant second-hand bookshop and print seller, specialises in books about the island. Lots of bric-à-brac shops and stalls in the Royal Victoria Arcade and good hunting ground for bargains at the Snuff Box and the Sedan Chair next door to each other in the High St. Early closing Thursday. Nice pubs include the Castle – local clientèle, Gales' beer – and Yelf's Hotel, bar very popular with non-residents, variety of hand-pumped real ales.

Blue Funnel Cruises, tel Ryde 63478, and Sealink, tel Ryde 62560, provide boat trips and N. Whellan, tel Ryde 64389, and M. Rayment, tel Ryde 64602, will take you on fishing trips, as well. Tourist Information, Western Gardens (summer), tel Ryde 62905.

SHANKLIN

A traditional seaside resort with a good sandy beach, pier and amusements. It's lifted rather out of the ordinary by its chine, cliffs and old village – straight off an embroidered tea-cosy. Immaculately thatched cottages, gables outlined with frilly white-painted barge-boards, sit snugly in gardens full of hollyhocks and honeysuckle. There is a pretty and popular pub, the Crab Inn – too popular, perhaps, service can be off-hand – lots of places to eat, craft and antique shops. At the Rock Shop opposite the Crab, there are weekly rock-making demonstrations, usually Mon.

The chine, a steep ravine that leads down to the shore, entrance off Old Village High St, is well worth a visit. It's still genuinely picturesque and romantic (*see Specialities*). At the bottom, right on the beach, is the thatched and pleasantly pokey Fisherman's Cottage Club – temporary membership only a few pence per week. A good place to sit drinking – they have a wide range of liqueurs – and eating crab sandwiches while keeping an eye on children paddling or building sandcastles. Open till 12.30 at night.

The main part of the town is at the top of the cliff reached by steep steps or a lift. Lots of handsome Victorian houses, now mostly boarding houses and hotels, and a jolly Edwardian theatre for summer shows. Newnhams, 26 High St, is a splendid old-fashioned grocer's. In the arcade just below, the Odd Shop holds promise of a bargain among an assortment of junk. Tourist Information, 67 High St, Esplanade (summer), tel Shanklin 2942. Early closing Wed.

VENTNOR

The oldest seaside resort on the island, apart from Ryde – and the most attractive. It's a sun-trap, facing south and protected from winds by St Boniface Down. Its climate, pronounced specially beneficial for pulmonary disorders in the 1820s, was the making of the town. From the

The Square in Yarmouth, once the island's most important town.

Esplanade, bow-windowed villas and white-painted hotels with glassed-in verandahs zigzag up to the cliff top. Plenty of shaggy palm trees and bright gardens to evoke wistful comparisons with the Riviera. Stream runs underground through the town and cascades from the clifftop to a boating lake with a little island in the middle shaped like a miniature Isle of Wight. Eccentrically seaside details: the scaly onion dome of the Gaiety Bingo Hall on the Esplanade, the seafront villa with a wrought-iron fence shaped like a musical stave. The notes spell out themes from 'Die Meistersinger von Nürnberg' and 'Die Fledermaus'.

Most of the shops are at the top of the cliffs. In Pier St there are a couple of nice antique shops, I. W. Mercury at No 83 and A. & S. Keen at No 19, which also sells second-hand books. Pubs include the Mill Bay down on the front, the Blenheim, which serves nice pies and puddings for lunch, and the Hole in the Wall, much patronised by longshoremen, which serves Burt's beer, brewed in the town since the 1840s. A fine Botanic Garden, on outskirts of town. All sorts of exotic trees and shrubs flourish in the open here which only grow in glasshouses at Kew. Restaurant and adventure playground. Admission free, but parking charge. Museum of Smuggling History also in grounds, open daily Good Friday to Sept 10-5.30, June, July, Aug, also evenings 7.30-9. Admission charge. Tourist Information: 34, High St (summer), tel Ventnor 853625. Early closing Wed.

YARMOUTH

An engaging, self-assured little place. There is little more to it still than a quay, a castle, a square and a long high street, but in the Middle Ages it was the most important town in the island and, till the 18th c, the headquarters of its governor.

The castle stands guard over the animated harbour. Built by Henry VIII as one of his chain of defences against the French, it consists of a gun-emplacement with living quarters behind. Open April-Sept weekdays 9.30-1, 2-6.30, Sun 2-6.30, closed Fri. D of E. Admission charge. Nearby in the square is the Georgian town hall and handsome George Hotel, once the Governor's house. It

was here that the 18th c artist George Morland was arrested for spying – the incriminating document, his unfinished sketch of a spaniel, mistaken for a map of the island.

Inside the modest church, mostly 17th c, is a striking monument to Sir Robert Holmes, governor of the island and privateer. He looted the statue from a French ship and substituted his own head for that of Louis XIV – it doesn't fit too well but has a suitably defiant glare.

The High St runs parallel with the shore – lots of private jetties and Georgian houses, one disguised as a fort with dramatic castellations. At the end of it is a sloping green lawn with seats overlooking the sea.

Shops include a pleasant bookshop, Holdings, off the square and Marlborough House Antiques in the High St for good furniture and china. Pubs: four, all pleasant, including the Bugle, old oak-panelled inn.

Hire yachts, dinghies and life-rafts from West Solent Yacht Brokers and Charterers, tel Yarmouth 760202. You can learn to sail as well as hire a boat from J. Sleight, tel Yarmouth 760752, who specialises in teaching children. Fishing trips arranged by T. Haward, tel Freshwater 752399, and for parties R. Johnston, tel Freshwater 752380, D. Thomas, tel Newport 523848. See also *Activities, Sailing*.

Tourist Information Office on the quay (summer), tel Yarmouth 760015. Early closing Wed.

SIGHTSEEING

Osborne House: Queen Victoria's overpowering personality still pervades Osborne. It was her favourite house, designed in the 1840s by Albert himself and Thomas Cubitt as a seaside retreat in the Italian manner. Here, where she revelled in domesticity, spent much of her widowhood and died, time seems to have stood still – especially in the private apartments which were shut up undisturbed for 50 years after her death on the instructions of Edward VII. They are touchingly ungrand. The sittingroom is quite small with modest chintz curtains, plain walls covered in family portraits, a curving balcony where Victoria and Albert used to stand admiring the view over

the Solent and listening to the nightingales. The tables where they worked elbow to elbow on their state papers still stand side by side. Their children, often in fancy dress, pout and smile in white marble, in photographs, and innumerable paintings – some very competent oils by the queen herself – and their pudgy, disembodied marble limbs, carved when they were babies, lie about on cushions.

The state rooms downstairs are far more exotic and formal. In the queen's presence no courtier was ever allowed to sit down on the uncomfortable-looking chairs in the state drawingroom. As well as some elabo-

Queen Victoria's room at Norris Castle, scene of a childhood holiday.

rately hideous furniture and a glaring colour scheme – Lord Rosebery said he had never seen such an ugly room till he went to Balmoral – there are charming details like the painted marbled columns and Albert's fancy slate billiard table. The Durbar Room decorated in the Indian style with extremely elaborate white plasterwork is astonishing.

The grounds where Albert supervised the planting of rare trees are impressive. Don't miss the delicious Swiss Cottage, about half a mile from the house (minibus takes you there), where the royal princesses learnt to cook in a blue and white tiled kitchen with miniature range and copper pots. Open Mon-Sat, early April-June and

The eighteenth-century windmill at Bembridge, the last on the island. Much of its original machinery is still intact.

Norris Castle: Norris stands dark and melodramatic against the sea. Designed at the end of the 18th c by James Wyatt, a master of the mock-medieval, its stone walls look thick enough to withstand a siege. Inside are beautifully proportioned rooms and elegant stone staircase, a feat of engineering. A pleasing jumble of curios includes a bath specially designed by the Kaiser. He used to stay here when visiting his grandmother Queen Victoria at Osborne, and she herself first acquired a taste for the Isle of Wight during a childhood holiday at Norris.

The guidebook – a publication of inconsequential charm dashingly illustrated by Mrs Lacon, the present owner – lists the contents of the rooms. 'The withdrawing room – gilt sociable owned by Queen Caroline, Lady Randolph Churchill's parasols, ghosts of former occupants. The courtyard – stuffed warthog's head, fan of old polo sticks. Dyak hats from Sarawak, a Victorian WC from Parkhurst Prison.' There are also kestrels nesting on window ledges, signed photographs of Cecil Rhodes, crowds of dolls. Unless you like stately homes to be highly polished museums, it's a great treat. Fitting somehow that the castle and 400 of Mrs Lacon's protegées from the Pony Club starred in 'The Wildcats of St Trinian's', described by *The Guardian* as "without doubt one of the worst films ever".

The grounds slope down to the sea and make a splendid grandstand from which to watch yacht racing in Cowes Week. Open Good Fri-Easter Mon and mid-May-mid-Sept Sat, Sun, Mon and every day in Cowes Week, 11-5. Admission charge. East Cowes.
Appuldurcombe House: stands roofless and melancholy in a beautiful wooded park planted by Capability Brown. Its interior was completely destroyed by a landmine, but its Palladian stone shell is still almost intact. Built by an unknown architect for Sir Robert Worsley in 1710, it was by far the grandest and most sophisticated house on the island and makes a most impressive ruin. Open mid-March-mid-Oct weekdays 9.30-6.30, Sun 2-6.30, mid-Oct-mid-March weekdays 9.30-4, Sun 2-4. D of E. Admission charge. Wroxall.
The Ruskin Galleries, Bembridge School: at the turn of the century, the

Sept-early Oct 11-5, July, Aug 10-5. Admission charge. D of E.

The Osborne estate church, St Mildred's, Whippingham, is a weird, spiky building, worth a look. Prince Albert was in charge of the design.
Carisbrooke Castle: very dramatic and well-preserved. Begun by Normans, has tall 12th c walls and imposing keep, but most of buildings and ramparts are Tudor, defences against the Armada. Famous for its association with Charles I and his family. He stayed here as an unwelcome guest and later as a prisoner from June 1647 to September 1648.

The castle's museum contains several touching relics including a lace nightcap he wore the night before his execution. Also has interesting well laid-out sections on the social history of the Isle of Wight and a particularly charming series of watercolours of the island at the end of the 18th c by John Nixon. Don't miss the contented donkeys that draw water up from the deep well by treadmill, and it's worth climbing the 71 steps up to the keep for dramatic views over the tilt yard converted to a bowling green for Charles I and out to the Solent. Open mid-Oct-mid-March 9.30-4, Sun 2-4, mid-March-mid-Oct 9.30-6.30 including Sun. Admission charge, half-price in winter. D of E. Carisbrooke Church – Norman, with 15th c tower, interesting effigies – also well worth seeing.

founder of Bembridge School, John Howard Whitehouse, amassed the most complete collection in the world of manuscripts and books by and about Ruskin plus hundreds of his paintings and drawings. These range from astonishingly precise architectural drawings he made as a child prodigy of seven to his last sketchbook of 1889 and include beautiful studies of trees and rocks and famous watercolours of Venice. Also works by Millais, Burne-Jones and other contemporaries. Visits by appointment only. The curator, Mr Dearden, prefers people to write telling him when they want to come, but appointments can be made by telephone, tel Bembridge 2101.

Maritime Museum: excellent small museum opened two years ago by four enthusiasts – two pilots, a deep-sea diver and a yachtsman – partly to display their own collections. Exhibits include old diving equipment, treasures rescued from wrecks, a section on Ethel Langton – gallant lighthouse keeper's daughter and the island's own Grace Darling – splendid ship models and old photographs of life on board. There are worksheets for children, changing displays and a shop selling really interesting seafaring souvenirs, not the usual downmarket tat. Open Easter-Oct 10.30-5.30; Aug 10.30-8.30. Admission charge. Providence House, Bembridge.

Bembridge Windmill: 18th c windmill with much of its original machinery still intact – a landmark for yachtsmen and the last remaining windmill on the island. Check opening hours with Nat. Trust Information Centre, Newport, tel Newport 526445. Admission charge.

Lilliput Museum of Dolls: fascinating collection of every conceivable type of doll started 20 years ago when owner's daughter wrote to Nikita Khrushchev and was sent a wooden nesting doll. Now includes elegant 1920s sofa dolls, dumpy homemade ATS and WRAC wartime dolls, 1790 wax doll in remnant of Queen Caroline's wedding gown, film star dolls and so on. Open mid-March to mid-Jan, Spring Bank Hol-end Aug daily 10-10, otherwise 10-5. Admission charge, under-fives free. High Street, Brading.

Osborn-Smith's Wax Museum: theatrically ingenious push-button light-up tableaux. Queen Victoria disconcertingly taps her toe. Duc de Bourbon lurks behind rippling curtains in Sophie Dawes's bedchamber. All accompanied by colourful and racy captions reassuring torture-chamber enthusiasts that executioner's axe etc 'have actually been used'. Open daily all year, May-Sept 10-10, otherwise 10-5. Admission charge. High Street, Brading.

Brading Roman Villa: well-preserved mosaic floors in remains of home of wealthy Roman Briton. Panel of chicken-headed Gnostic god Apraxes in Room 2 is unique. Open April-end Sept weekdays 10-5.30, Sun 10.30-5.30. Admission charge.

Quarr Abbey: new Benedictine Abbey built 1908–14 near ruins of old Cistercian monastery by monks exiled from Solesmes in France. Architect Dom Paul Bellot, one of the community, was pioneer of 20th c expressionism – 'a virtuoso in brick' says Pevsner. Essentially a place of worship but church is open daily to visitors. Signposted off A3054 between Binstead and Fishbourne.

Geological Museum: wise to examine collection here before exploring the island's beaches, a rich hunting ground for dinosaur bones, fossils etc – one of early attractions for Victorian seasiders. Exhibits include dinosaur footprints, giant ammonites and minuscule insects perfectly preserved in rocks for millions of years. Once you know what to look for, Compton Bay and Atherfield Point are good spots for finding dinosaur bones – usually black with porous texture; fossils are found all over southern half of island and around Culver, the huge ammonites coming from Whale Chine. Open all year

The Needles, at the westernmost tip of the island.

except Bank Hols, Mon-Fri 10-5, Sat 10-4.30. First floor, Sandown Library, High St.

St Catherine's Lighthouse: very handsome, white-painted lighthouse. Open daily mid-March-mid-Sept at the discretion of the Keeper in Charge 1pm-sunset, closed Sun and in fog. Tel Niton 730284 Niton.

Arreton Manor: gabled manor house of local honey-coloured stone, rebuilt 1595-1612 around fragment of earlier 14th c building. Fine Jacobean furniture and carved panelling. Houses several exhibitions including doll collection, models of stately homes in England, and assortment of vintage wireless receivers. Teas served in Jacobean kitchen, in fine weather on the lawn. Open daily one week before Easter-first week Nov, Mon-Sat 10-6, Sun 2-6. Winter Sat only 10.30-5. Admission charge. Arreton. There is a charming pub in the village, the White Lion, which serves good food and beer from the

barrel. On other side of village is Haseley Manor, recently restored.

Barton Manor: newest of island's three vineyards with wine-tasting room and display of wine-making equipment. Gardens originally laid out by Prince Albert and Queen Victoria, whose collies are buried there; the royal skating rink transformed into water garden with black swans and waterfowl. Open early May-late Sept daily, Easter Mon and Suns in April 12-6. Admission charge. On A3021 between Whippingham and Osborne.

Calbourne Water Mill: still in working order, has lovely setting with peacocks and water birds wandering about. Rural museum with display of farm implements. Refreshments and picnic area. Open daily Easter-Oct 10-6. Admission charge. On B3401 just outside Calbourne towards Freshwater.

Yafford Mill: 18th c watermill, restored and in working order. Plenty

for children with grey seals living in pool below mill-race, several rare breeds of cattle, sheep and pigs in meadows around, and collection of waterfowl. Playground, refreshments and picnic area. Open Easter-Oct weekdays 10-6, Sun 2-6. Admission charge. Off B3399 between Shorwell and Brighstone.

Steam Railway: from Havenstreet Station, nr Ryde, 1½-mile ride along part of once flourishing network. Display of island railway and rolling stock, up to 100 years old, and small museum. Check trips with Isle of Wight Railway Co, tel Wootton Bridge 882204. Summer Steam Show Aug Bank Hol Sat/Sun/Mon.

Robin Hill Country Park: popular place for tourists and children covering 80 acres of down, woodland and meadow. Birds, animals and insects range from budgies to eagles, tortoises to tarantulas. Also commando-style assault course, donkey and pony rides, etc. Picnic gardens have pretty view, open-air barbecue stays open until midnight Tues-Sat July-Aug, otherwise open daily 10-6 March-Oct. Admission charge. Between Arreton and Downend off A3056.

The Needles: the Isle of Wight's most famous landmark, three jagged islets looking more like teeth than needles jutting from the sea at the western tip of the island. They mark the end of the ridge of chalk that stretches right across it like a backbone. If you get the chance, see them from the sea – there are occasional boat trips from Alum Bay – but they also look splendid from the path through the National Trust's land that leads over West High Down and along the top of the White Cliffs.

Farringford, Tennyson Down and Mrs Cameron's Portraits: Farringford, on the road to Alum Bay just outside Freshwater, is the house where Tennyson lived for 30 years. It's a pretty Georgian Gothic building surrounded by trees and paddocks, now a hotel. Non-residents can have a drink, lunch or dinner there and take a look at the poet's study – turned into a television room – with some of his original furniture; guests can wallow in the poet's bath. It's still a most impressive walk from Farringford along Highdown towards the Needles with chalk cliffs dropping sheer 500ft to the sea – Tennyson did it every morning. On top of the down is a stone monument to commemorate him, which can be seen all over the island.

Tennyson used to dread being buttonholed as he walked by his neighbour, the pioneer photographer Julia Margaret Cameron, who was always trying to get him to pose for her – an uncomfortable and lengthy business, but it produced some marvellous images including the famous portrait of him described by its subject as the 'dirty monk'. Some of Mrs Cameron's portraits hang in the council chamber of the municipal offices in Freshwater; most mornings, when the room is not in use, the Clerk to the Council will show them to members of the public. But in an island so full of little museums she surely deserves one to herself.

SPECIALITIES

Chines: these steep, narrow ravines are striking features of the island's coastline. They do occur on the south coast of England, but never as dramatically or as frequently as here – there are a dozen between Shanklin and Freshwater. They are caused by coastal erosion combined with streams cutting through relatively soft rock. The steep sides of chines form an enclosed environment and vegetation within them is often lush and quite different from that in surrounding areas. The cliffs along this part of the coastline are still crumbling and the chines are changing all the time – Barnes Chine has been almost completely eroded, Ladder Chine, which could once easily be climbed down, now has a 150ft drop to the sea, and Whale Chine – perhaps the most spectacular, is still eroding several feet each year.

Shanklin Chine, admired by Keats, Darwin and George Eliot, retains the picturesque charm that enchanted the Victorians. Near the entrance there is a dramatic 40ft waterfall, ivy, moss and ferns cover the sheer sides of the ravine. Open Easter-late May 9.50-5.30, late May-Sept 9.30-10.30 floodlit at night, Oct 10.30-3.30. Admission charge.

Blackgang Chine: a cleft in the ominous dark cliffs makes an unlikely setting for a home-grown Disneyland with plaster dinosaurs, a working sawmill, Buffalo Creek reconstructed

from Pinewood Studios and a whale with an aquarium in his tummy. All great fun for children. Open daily April-late Oct, floodlit every evening late May-late Sept. Open 10-5, 10-10 during floodlighting. Admission charge.

Alum Bay Sand: the sandstone cliffs at Alum Bay are famous for their extraordinary stripes of colour – 21 distinct shades ranging from white to brick red to brown. Their freakish appearance is apparently due to the varying amounts of iron salts and clay in the sand. They look especially spectacular after rain. Ever since visitors first came to the island, souvenirs have been made of Alum Bay sand. The Victorians composed pictures out of it and put layers arranged in rainbow patterns into all sorts of glass containers. There are examples of 19th c Alum Bay sand work at the Maritime Museum in Bembridge and the museum in Carisbrooke Castle (see *Sightseeing*). Today at the shop at the bottom of the cliffs you can choose samples of the coloured sands and make your own souvenirs by putting them in stripes into a choice of different glass shapes.

You can get down to the shore by a daunting-looking ski-lift. On top of the cliffs is a memorial to Marconi who made his first experiments with wireless transmission here.

ACTIVITIES

Sailing: Uffa Fox who lived in Cowes said the waters of the Solent were like a really exciting golf course, full of hazards and rewards. It's experience of the tricky, fast-running double tides in the western Solent and the treacherous winds that gives local yachtsmen a distinct edge over competitors. They get used to all the hazards – especially dodging approaching craft in the crowded water.

The island buzzes with regattas almost every weekend from the last week in April to the end of Sept. There's a full list of these and other events in 'Treasure Island', Tourist Board's guide. The most democratic and exhilarating is the Round the Island Race every June. In Cowes Week, the first week in August, the crowds make it impossible to find a

berth anywhere on the north side of the island unless you are a competitor or have reserved one nearly a year in advance. Best to moor off the mainland and sail out to watch the races. At other times it's quite informal and the harbour master will usually be able to find you a berth. Worth telephoning ahead in summer to make sure, tel Cowes 293952.

Most of the social life in Cowes and other sailing centres revolves round yacht clubs some of which welcome visitors from other clubs outside the Solent, eg The Island Sailing Club – very well-equipped and friendly with good food, busy bar – and the Cowes Corinthians. Don't try strolling boldly into the Royal Yacht Squadron – it has reciprocal membership only with the New York Yacht Club.

Yarmouth harbour often gets very full at weekends – if you're not there by midday on Saturday, forget it. Moorings on first come, first served basis. Bembridge harbour can only be entered 2 hours before and 1 hour after high water, dries out at low water except for marina. In spite of this fashionable with yachtsmen – has its own class of racing boat, the Bembridge Redwing.

The Tourist Board produces a useful information sheet on sailing with lists of yacht clubs, chandlers, sailing schools, boat hire etc. It also publishes a brochure on Activity Holidays with details of several sailing holidays as well as riding, fossil-collecting (for fossils, see also *Geological Museum*) etc. Southampton Weather Centre, tel Southampton 28844, provides local weather forecasts. See also *Where to Go, Cowes* and *Yarmouth*.

Bathing: a huge choice of places to swim, beachcomb, make sandcastles or explore rock-pools. Sandown and Shanklin are perhaps the best traditional beaches with all the trappings, beach huts, deckchairs, boats for hire etc – both huge expanses of sand and safe bathing. There are lots of big but comparatively uncommercialised beaches: Totland Bay – trees and grassy slopes come down almost to the water's edge; Colwell Bay – safe curving beach, good for children; Compton Bay – good sand backed by high cliffs; Woodside Bay – trees to the edge of the sea; Whitecliff Bay –

Shanklin Chine was admired by Keats, Darwin, and George Eliot.

low cliffs, shallow, curving shore. Some of the most attractive places for rock-pools and seclusion are at the bottom of steep cliff-paths like Luccombe Bay and Steephill Cove. By boat you can reach little coves on west coast, inaccessible from land and deserted even in high summer. Public open-air swimming-pools at Newport, tel Newport 524826, and Ryde, tel Ryde 64921; an indoor one at Freshwater, tel Freshwater 752168 and Newport, tel Newport 527767.

Golf: 18-hole courses at Freshwater Bay and Sandown, 9-hole at Newport, Osborne, Ryde, Cowes and Ventnor – all open to visitors at most times.

Walking: by far the best way to see the rolling countryside in the centre of the island and the beautiful downs and cliffs of west Wight is on foot. There is an outstandingly well-signposted and organised system of trails and footpaths for walkers – altogether 148 miles of footpath including a 60-mile path going right round the coastline. The County Council has produced a series of excellent leaflets on the seven main inland trails and four sections that make up the complete coastal path. These include precise directions, details of places of interest en route, flowers, animals and birds to look out for and bus services that run near paths for those who only want to walk sections of a trail. County Council also

publish eight 2½in to 1 mile maps, 'Long Distance Trails and Other Rights of Way'. They, and the leaflets, can be purchased from the County Surveyor, County Hall, Newport, or Tourist Board.

There are three very pleasant walks through Forestry Commission land. Parkhurst Forest near Newport has a great diversity of species of trees, Brighstone forest walk leads out on to downland with splendid views, Firestone Forest between Ryde and Newport offers a short but charming walk down to the waterside at Forest Creek, lots of wild flowers.

Windsurfing: with good beaches, strong winds and tides, interesting spot to try it. Couple of places give tuition: International Windsurfing Schools have two centres at Toll Rd, Seaview and Littlestairs Slipway, Sandown Bay, tel Seaview 3649. Book in advance. They hire boards and wetsuits to competent windsurfers. Mustang Yachts make and sell sailboards and give tuition: tel Cowes 292179 or Wootton Bridge 8821570.

Surfing: best at Compton Bay, spring and autumn – not so many big waves in summer. Small surfboards or 'bellyboards' can be bought from the National Trust kiosk at the top of the cliff.

Fishing: freshwater fishing mostly in the eastern River Yar, good for roach, bream, perch etc – trout only in private waters, no salmon on island. Permits available from Hon Sec, Isle

of Wight Freshwater Angling Association, 12 Manor Rd, Lake, Sandown, tel Sandown 403994. Also rod licence required from Southern Water Authority, 58 St John's Rd, Newport. Tourist Board has useful information sheet with details.

Good light sea fishing for plaice, flounder, mullet etc at Wootton Creek, Bembridge Harbour, Whippingham etc. Fishing trips (see *Ryde* and *Yarmouth*) also with Sea Tac, tel Sandown 403654. Open sea angling competitions between May and Sept, details Hon Sec, NFSA, 28 West Hill Rd, Ryde. 'Angling in the Isle of Wight', useful booklet available from tackle shops etc.

FLORA AND FAUNA

The great variety of habitat in the Isle of Wight produces a comparable variety in species of plants and animals. There are few parts of Britain where chalk cliffs, salt-marsh, downland and woodland are so close together. A very good place for people with a general interest in natural history.

Birds: kittiwakes, guillemots, razorbills and the occasional puffin nest near the Needles on the chalk cliffs at the western end of the island – an official bird sanctuary. Newtown Nature Reserve (see *Where to Go*), an unspoilt estuary, is a good place for ducks, geese and waders in the winter. The black-tailed godwit can be seen all year round and there are small colonies of Britain's rarest nesting sea-bird, the little tern.

Flowers and Plants: botanically the island is like southern England in miniature, with over 1,000 species of wild flowers, including one, the wood calamint, that grows nowhere else in Britain. 22 species of orchid can be found, mainly on the downland – but never pick them. Newtown Nature Reserve includes good examples of salt-marsh plants like golden samphire and the original English cord grass, now rare. Hedgerows and woods are at their best April-May, chalk downs and marshland June-Aug, salt-marshes July-Oct. Serious botanists should get 'Flora of the Isle of Wight' published by The Isle of Wight Natural History and Archaeological Society.

Briefing by Sarah Howell and Pamela Brown

The sun sets behind Ryde Pier, the second longest in Britain.

LIFE ON THE BEACHES

BY TONY SOPER

Most of us tend to visit beaches in fine weather, but the seaweeds and seashells which make a living there are adapted by time and experience to withstand an astonishing range of conditions, from icy cold to sweltering sun; lashing rain to pounding sea. They manage in different ways, some riding with the current, some retreating into impenetrable castles, hiding under rocks or migrating deep underground when the going is rough, but always taking advantage of the plankton-rich sea when the going is easy.

Tides are the most powerful influence on a beach community. Twice a day the shore is swept and inundated by life-giving seawater; twice a day it is exposed to the damp of night

and the drying effects of the sun. The position on the beach at which an organism lives is crucial in determining the amount of drying, heating or cooling it has to withstand, and it also governs the length of time during which it may feed. The top of the shore, near high water mark, provides the most extreme physical conditions. Here the creatures must endure long periods between feeding, but on the lower shore the beach is denied the life-giving sea for only short periods in each tidal cycle. The most cursory examination of seaweeds on a rocky shore will reveal the effect of this gradation in conditions. At the top of the tide they will be weedy, thin and straggly. At the bottom they will be large and luxuriant. Very often this gradation is dramatically shown on a sheltered harbour wall. From the sparsely colonized area of lichens just above the highest point reached by the sea, the different species of weed, each in its place as ordained by the amount of daily exposure to the air, are displayed in horizontal bands. Green lettuce-like weed at the top gives way to the brown channelled wrack, then the middle-zone wracks, then long-fronded *Laminaria* with its anchoring stalk (known as the holdfast) rarely knowing the air.

Down below, in the depths, browns give way to reds as the weeds grow ever more luxuriantly, bathed in perpetual sea, till somewhere around the ten-fathom line the lack of penetrating light begins to inhibit growth, even in clear water.

But the zoning which is most clearly seen on a vertical wall is equally apparent on the open rocky ledges which offer such enjoyable hunting for the naturalist. Trace the life-forms downhill from the thinly populated high water mark to the richly populated low water mark and you move through an ever denser jungle. The toughest live at the top, but most live at the bottom!

The monster weed of the lower shore is commonly, though loosely, called kelp, a word more correctly ascribed to the ash produced by burning various brown seaweeds. In the old days, collecting *Laminaria*, *Saccorhiza*, and *Fucus* for the manufacture of kelp was a major industry in remote islands from Scilly to the far north. In Orkney, for instance, 20,000 men were employed for the whole of the summer. The weed was collected, dried in the sun and then burnt in shallow pits. While the mass was still hot it was sprinkled with water to break it up. From about 20 tons of the wet weed the residue was about one ton of hard, dark grey ash. Sodium carbonate and potash were subsequently extracted. The soda was used in the glass and soap industries, while the potash was sold as fertilizer.

The British kelp industry went into a decline after the Napoleonic wars, when the ash was more cheaply imported from France, but it revived after the discovery of iodine in 1811. For a long time kelp was the only source, although the preparation was fraught with difficulties. If the untreated weed was washed by rain, for instance, nearly 90 per cent of the iodine was lost.

If you collect seaweed for the garden, the best time is after a summer storm, when great quantities

LIFE ON THE BEACHES

1 *Laminaria digitata.* **2** Eggs of common dog whelk. **3** Eggs of netted dog whelk. **4** *Fucus vesiculosus*, bladder wrack. **5** *Littorina littoralis*, flat periwinkle. **6** *Laminaria saccharina*, sugar kelp. **7** *Patina pellucida*, blue-rayed limpet. **8** Egg cases of common whelk. **9** *Electa pilosa*, sea mat. **10** *Chondrus crispus*, Irish moss. **11** *Semibalanus balanoides*, acorn barnacle. **12** *Echinocardium cordatum*, sea potato. **13** Discarded tubes of sand worms. **14** Pod razor shell. **15** *Entada gigas*, West Indian bean. **16** *Cerastoderma edule*, common cockle. **17** Worm casts. **18** Dogfish egg case. **19** *Chrysaora hysoscella*, compass jellyfish. **20** *Physalia physalis*, Portuguese Man o' War. **21** *Mytilis edulis*, common mussel. **22** *Asterias Rubens*, common starfish. **23** *Monodonta lineata*, toothed winkle. **24** *Crepidula fornicata*, slipper limpet. **25** *Actinia equina*, beadlet anemone. **26** *Buccinum undatum*, common whelk. **27** *Patella vulgata*, common limpet. **28** *Fucus ceranoides*, wrack. **29** *Littorina littorea*, edible periwinkle. **30** *Nucella lapillus*, dog whelk.

of rich kelp will have been torn from its anchorage and piled upon the shore. Transport and spread it before rain reduces its mineral value. On St Martins, in the Isles of Scilly, we used to go down to the sandflats after a storm to fork great bundles of the sweet-smelling sea-hay into a cart, the horse dragging it back to the bulb-fields loaded high above the gunwales. Hebridean crofters are said to have reckoned that one cartload of farm manure was equivalent to two and a half loads of seaweed. But one of the advantages of storm-tossed weed is that it is free from harmful crop-weeds and fungi. Fields treated with seaweed manure demonstrate a clearly superior yield.

Some of the bladdery wracks from the middle shore are an important source of alginates, organic substances used for thickening soups, emulsifying ice-cream and soft drinks, gelling confectionary and jellies. They can also be persuaded to form the thin films used for the best quality sausage skins. Irish moss, or carragheen, *Chondrus crispus* was thought to have important medical properties, and was used to treat bronchitis, for example. Washed and boiled, it was infused as a beverage, or concentrated to make table jellies, after the addition of sugar and fruit juice. Dulse, *Rhodymenia palmata*, has been eaten in quantity in Ireland and Scotland, where the cry of 'dulse and tangle' used to be heard in the streets. One of the most common of seaweeds, it grows from disc-shaped holdfasts fixed to large brown seaweeds. It may be chewed fresh or dried, or boiled in milk. It has even been used as a substitute for chewing-tobacco.

Laver, *Porphyra umbilicalis*, is still eaten with relish by remote communities. Washed, boiled with a little vinegar and then fashioned into sea-weed cakes which you roll in oatmeal and fry, it is much enjoyed with bacon and eggs. The fact is that all seaweeds are edible, though some more so than others, and none are particularly likely to feature in gastronomic guides. They are hard going, but good for you.

One of the kelps, *Laminaria saccharina*, is sweet to taste, as its scientific name suggests, because of the coating of mannite, a sugar alcohol, on its fronds. This is the seaweed that has a single frond crumpled like a giant ribbon, sometimes five feet long, and is beloved of weather forecasters. Hung up in the front porch, it acts as a humidity indicator, usually telling you what you can see outside the window – that rain is falling. It becomes soft and limp when damp is in the air.

The fronds and holdfasts of weed provide food and shelter for many animals. Just take a close look at any of the brown seaweed fronds and there may be the characteristic rasp marks showing where limpets have grazed. The delicately patterned blue-rayed limpet may still be nestling in the depression it has formed by feeding. Tiny mussels may be attached by the *byssus* threads to the crevices of the holdfasts. There will probably be periwinkles feeding – some of them shaped and coloured to resemble the float bladders of the wrack. There may be the almost fluorescent mossy mats made of communities of *Bryozoa* – sea mats – each minute compartment occupied by an animal which extends feeding tentacles to the plankton when the tide is in. Polychaete worms live in limy tubes which spiral and snake about on the surface of the weed.

Examine the weed for the variety of eggs which may be attached: the small egg capsules of sea slugs and snails, the purses of netted whelk, ribbons of sea lemon, strings of sea hare and collars of necklace shell. At extreme low water mark of the biggest spring tides, you may find the elegant creamy purses of the dogfish egg, lashed to the kelp by twisty threads. They are easy enough to find if you wade amongst the weed in a foot or so of water. Most fish spawn uncountable numbers of eggs into the open sea, but it is typical of the cartilaginous sharks, dogfish, skates and rays, that they produce a small number of eggs which are more carefully attached to a seaweed nursery. The dogfish embryo incubates for about six months inside the purse, growing on a diet of yolk before it finally emerges as a little fish when the case splits open. Other 'mermaid's purses' may be found lashed to low-water seaweeds; for instance the darker eggs of skates and rays, each containing a young fish with its supply of yolk.

On, in, around and under the rocky ledges there are hosts of animals exploiting both the seaweed community and the food brought in by the tides. One of the largest groups lives out in the open for all to see: these are marine snails – gastropods. With few exceptions they have a single spiral shell which comes in a number of variations, some plain and dull, some very fancy and highly coloured.

The most easily seen are the limpets, with their flattened conical shells. Very often they live side by side with acorn barnacles (which are in fact crustaceans, cemented to the rock, and which, when covered by water, wave their legs about to collect the plankton). The limpets start life as free-swimming members of the plankton, but then settle on a patch of rock which they proceed to farm. They move about in a given area, a couple of square yards, grazing the seaweed. Usually they feed at night, some species returning to the same 'home'.

If the rock is soft then over a period of time, through erosion, the limpet will find himself returning to a well-marked depression. The low-profile shape of the shell offers least resistance to the force of the sea, and as you will know if you have given advance warning when trying to lift them, they have a foot muscle with a very strong grip.

Brown algae exposed by the receding tide in Loch Eynort, South Uist.

Both periwinkles and dog whelks are also common sea snails, to be found in profusion on rocky shores. They do not grip the rock surface with anything like the tenacity of the limpets, but find their safety from the force of the sea by retreating into crevices and crannies, or by hanging on to seaweed which bends to the ebb and flow. The periwinkles feed on seaweed and on lichens, and are very diverse in colour. Some are a beautiful yellow, others are green, brown, red or black. Different species span the life-zones from extreme low to extreme high water, one surviving by virtue of an occasional sea splash, and one screwing up courage to make the leap ashore to become a land snail as part of the evolutionary advance.

The dog whelk is a carnivore and a predator, especially equipped for boring through the shells of other snails. When you consider that his relatives have developed techniques which defy the shattering force of the sea, clearly the dog whelk must have powerful weapons to defeat them. He finds a suitable victim and bores a hole through its shell, using band-saw teeth which are extended at the end of a proboscis. Having bored an entrance, the teeth cut out the meat from the prey, and convey it back to the throat of the whelk. When it has been

feeding on mussels, the whelk shell itself changes colour to a browny-black or mauve-pink. In fact the whelk secretes a purple dye – purpurin – which was used by monks to illuminate their manuscripts and by Roman emperors to dye their togas. A toxic sustance, it is yellow when first exuded, then green and finally purple, the changes taking place through the action of the sun.

Sandy shores are, at first glance, deserts devoid of life, unless perhaps a few gulls or oystercatchers are standing at the edge of the water. But the birds are there because there is food, quite apart from the peace and quiet. While it is true that sandy shores are inhospitable to plants, since there is nothing for the seaweeds to hold fast to, there is a profusion of life just out of sight, waiting to emerge as soon as the tidal deluge arrives.

Provided there is little or no grinding action, the salt-wet sand conceals a lot of activity. Burrowing underneath the surface, a worm or a shellfish can retreat downwards if life gets uncomfortable on the surface – if it is too hot from the sun, too fresh from the rain or too turbulent from pounding surf. When conditions are suitable, the worm can show his face and feed from the passing show of constantly renewed waterborne nutrients. There may be many millions of shellfish living within a single acre of tidal sand, feeding on the current-borne plants which flourish in the top layers of the sea. The phytoplankton blooms in the spring, as the days grow longer and there is increased light and radiation to stimulate them. Then in early summer they are at their most plentiful. A second harvest comes along in autumn, triggered by the availability of deep-water nutrients which have come to the surface. When the days get shorter there is a winter decline in sea-plant activity. So, although the sea and shore may appear unchanging to the casual observer, there is in fact a procession of seasons as we know it on land.

Although many of the sandy-shore animals are hidden out of sight, it is easy enough to trace them. Sand masons, for instance, live in a tube which they make from grains of sand and shell particles and a mucus secretion. The worm migrates up and down the tube according to tidal conditions. The top end reaches out above the surface of the beach so that the worm has access to the sea when the tide is in. Then its tentacles emerge and fan out to sweep the adjacent surface for food. The construction of the house is a very precise affair, the sand grains fitting to each other like a tubular jig-saw puzzle. Indeed the casing may well last longer than the worm. After a storm large numbers of the empty tubes may be thrown up on the strand-line, but for live specimens look near low-water

Traig Uis and Scurrival Point, Barra. The fronds and holdfasts of weed provide shelter for many animals.

mark, round places which make a break in the beach – a groyne, a weedy outcrop or depression.

The lugworm is the commonest sand worm. The familiar conical mound of castings is defaecated by the worm which lives in a U-shaped burrow. Above its head is a tell-tale depression in the sand. This is caused by the caving-in of the sand as the worm eats away underneath. Unlike the sand-mason, the lugworm does not construct a permanent burrow, although he strengthens his tunnel by lining it with mucus. He may live in one place for some weeks, feeding by ingesting quantities of sand and then extracting the small portion which is edible. Periodically he backs up the burrow and adds to the mound of castings. Lugworms are large, juicy beasts, very attractive to fish, and that is why you often see fishermen with fork and bucket digging away on the sand or mud, collecting them for bait.

You may also see fishermen armed with buckets and short rakes. They are not searching for bait, but directly engaged in fishing for marine molluscs. For lying just underneath the surface of the sand there will be a whole regiment of shellfish. Cockles, for example, live just below the surface, where they find some safety from predators. They are surprisingly mobile, with a strong foot which they use to dig themselves in or jump about on the surface. A whole population of cockles may migrate if conditions change and better feeding is found elsewhere. They feed by siphoning in water from just above the sand-surface, sieving it through gills, and then ejecting it through a second siphon.

Cockles are an easy catch, but other burrowing bivalves are by no means easily collected. Some may burrow faster than you can dig. Razorshells, for example, have a very powerful foot which pulls the smoothly designed shell vertically downwards. And at low-water, when a hot sun is drying the surface of the beach, they will need to get down into the damper, more sympathetic regions to avoid the danger of dessication.

The burrowing starfish, too, is quickly under the surface, digging with the many feet under the five arms. Safely out of sight, it will attack the molluscs and almost anything else encountered on its journey. Embracing perhaps a cockle, the suction of its feet forces the shell to open. Then the starfish extends its stomach through its mouth and presents it to the prey, devouring it at source. They are not loved by inshore fishermen, who say that if you have a starfish in the pot then there will not be any lobster. Before they realised the folly of it, fishermen used to deal with starfish by breaking them on the boat's gunwale, tossing the pieces back to the sea. Since the arms are capable of separate regeneration the result was to increase the population of starfish.

Sea potatoes, low-water creatures, burrow into sand and extend a lined tunnel up to the surface from which they siphon food. Sometimes their empty 'shells' (more correctly their skeletons, known as tests) are strewn along the tideline in fair numbers. Hold them gently, and against the light you will see the rows of foot-holes in a five-rayed symmetry which reveals their relationship to the starfish.

A diligent search of the strand-line – the trail of old seaweed, odds and ends of this and that lying in an endless ribbon where the retreating tide deposited it at high water – is the highlight of the beachcomber's day. The proper name for this activity is wrecking, not to be confused with the apocryphal nonsense of false lights luring innocent seamen to their doom. Wrecking is the practice of combing beaches and especially strandlines for treasures of all sorts, from crab-pot floats, pit-props riddled with shipworm and encrusted with goose barnacles, cuttlefish 'bones' and, once in a lifetime if you're the sort who wins football pools, amber or even ambergris.

Cuttle shells, empty egg-masses of common whelks, mermaid's purses, whelk-nibbled seaweed, sea potato tests – all these are indicators of the sort of creatures which live near the beach you're standing on. But there may also be the remains of ocean travellers, from turtles to jellyfish. Sometimes deep sea jellyfish are stranded on our beaches in large numbers. This happens, mainly on western coasts, after a long period in which south-west winds have persistently blown them towards us. Both the species stranded in this way are wind-borne sailing creatures, unable to govern their own movements in the way used by the common jellyfish, which swims by opening and closing its discs, thereby producing a sort of slow motion jet propulsion.

The first is called the 'by-the-wind-sailor' and is somewhat like our own well-known jellyfish but more oval and with a hard ridge 'sail' which extends right across its diameter. Deep blue round the edge, it is four inches or so across. The second is the Portuguese Man o'War, which is a most wonderfully constructed creature. The bladder, which is the part you are most likely to find on the beach, is up to six inches long, and looks very much like some kind of child's balloon. Indeed it can be difficult to persuade someone that it is animal and not man-made. The float is pale blue, and there is a crenellated crest of a pinkish colour. From the float hangs a complicated cluster of stinging cells in long tentacles. If the jellyfish is alive, do not touch it, as it can deliver a powerful sting. This is its method of capturing small fish in the ocean. Often the Man o'War is somewhat battered by the time it reaches our shores, and the bladder is the only part left. When they do appear, it may well be in very large numbers over a long stretch of coastline.

Home-grown jellyfish are frequently stranded. *Aurelia* is the commonest, usually about six to eight inches across, with its four purple rings. A larger, and stinging, animal is *Chrysaora*, milky-white with a central brown spot and radial brown streaks. Then there is *Rhizostoma*, the biggest, up to two feet across and quite harmless; it is pale green or blue, with a darker purple fringe.

Two species of tropical bean quite often arrive on western coasts, driven here by winds and currents after a long ocean journey which starts in the Caribbean. Both are about the size of a large broad bean; one of them, *Entada gigas*, is the same shape. It is a seed which comes from the West Indies, has a uniform brown colour and a hard shiny skin. The other, *Mucuna urens*, shaped more like a disc, has a black creamy bordered rim on a dark purple-brown background. It probably comes from Central America.

The great joy of a strand-line is that you never know what you might find next. Anything from a fish box to a dead whale. Take the fish box home, clean it up and use it for furniture. Tell the Coastguard about the whale. It comes under Her Majesty's protection and must be treated with respect.

TONY SOPER

ORKNEY

BY GEORGE MACKAY BROWN

Orkney is no extension of the Highlands, mountain and glen, deer and torrent. It is an archipelago of gently-contoured hills, 'like sleeping whales'. And the hills, from shore-line to heather, are fertile and well-cultivated, with cows among lush grass 'in coats of silk'. Only one island – Hoy – looks as if it might be a piece of Sutherland or Perthshire. Hoy means, in Norse, 'the high island', and its tumult of blue shoulders contrasts starkly with the patchwork fields of the islands all around it. Hoy contains, as well as the famous rockstack The Old Man of Hoy, and the heroic lifeboatmen of Brims, a beautiful valley in the west called Rackwick. With the beauty is mingled melancholy, for the slopes of the valley are littered with ruined crofts, and only one farmer is left. But some of the crofts have been restored – one of them, Bunertoon, is now the home of the composer Peter Maxwell Davies, who has transmuted much of the natural sound of the island valley into his unique art.

A typically colourful shop in Kirkwall.

The largest of the Orkneys, called Hrossey ('horse island') by the Vikings, is now marked insipidly Mainland on the maps. It has two towns, Kirkwall and Stromness, and a cluster of villages here and there. The farmhouses look immemorial as if they and the earth belonged to each other – 'sunk in time', in Edwin Muir's phrase. Kirkwall is an old town. It lies right in the centre of Orkney, where journeys by sea or land intersect, and so it was natural that merchants and earls and sailors would at last do their settled business there. There too began to be built in 1137 the Cathedral of St Magnus, one of the most beautiful minsters in Britain. In Kirkwall are played twice in midwinter the famous Ba' games, fierce anarchical tussles between the two divisions of the town, 'uppies' and 'doonies'. There is the St Magnus Festival of the Arts in June (mainly held in Kirkwall) and a St Magnus Fair in August.

Stromness, the town in the west, began to grow in the late 17th century, when larger ships were trading between Europe and America. It had its heyday during the long wars of the 18th century, when it was safer for ships to go by the north of Scotland than through the English Channel. In the fine natural harbour here, they found shelter, good water and bounteous provisioning. The little seaport and market town has survived almost unspoilt into the late 20th century – a single surging twisting street, with closes stepping down to the piers of fishermen and gulls, and closes and gardens swarming up the granite hill that shelters it from the west.

What kind of people live in Orkney now? They are a mingled weave of many races. The first settlers are anonymous, dark shadows on the dark moor; yet some of their houses and burial places survive. There followed an ingenious folk, from the south, possibly from the Mediterranean – driven outwards by who knows what economic or population pressures. They were mighty hewers of stone; they built the stone circle at Brodgar between the two lochs and, more impressively still, the burial chamber of Maes Howe. What dead priest-kings lay in the Maes Howe chambers? No names, no fragments of language, survive. There is only the marvellous symbolism, in midwinter, of the last sunbeam striking, through the long corridor, one of the walls of the dead; it is like a promise of resurrection. All the rest of the bright year the interior of Maes Howe is a bourne of shadows and darkness.

A brave, ingenious Celtic people came and they farmed and fished beside the sea and on the loch margins. The tribes of Europe were still migrating west and north. Was it to deter their land-hungry cousins that they built so many brochs – little round primitive stone keeps that were almost impregnable to the torches and stones and arrows of a

---

Marwick, on Mainland: fertile and well cultivated.

besieger? Enough fragments of brochs remain to assure us that they were marvellous defensive structures against the weaponry of the times. There a little community could sit at peace round their well of sweet water and their fish and meat and corn until the enemy, dispirited, sailed on towards Shetland and the Faroes.

The Picts who followed the broch-builders were no match for a new race breeding among the fjords of Norway, superlative shipwrights and seamen. It was soon time for them to test their skills 'west-over-sea'. The bright-bearded men from the dragon-ships entered Orkney – so to speak – by the back door. The Picts were expunged and razed. The Norsemen do not even refer to them in 'Orkney-inga Saga', the history of the Norsemen in Orkney. That is something of a mystery; one might have expected a resounding piece of prose about their victory in the islands of the west, full of vaunt and boasting. Perhaps Picts survived and mingled with the Vikings. Perhaps, out of deference to wives and kinsfolk, a silence was observed.

For a brilliant piece of prose narrative, all the more impressive for its understatement, 'Orkney-inga Saga' has a unique place in our island history and literature. With a few swift strokes the character of this earl and that Viking is laid bare. A few paragraphs build up an episode towards its inevitable climax. No time is wasted on such irrelevance as description, conjecture, comment. The saga is full of marvellous real characters: Thorfinn the Mighty, King Magnus Barelegs of Norway, Hakon and Magnus, Sweyn Asleifson 'the last of the Vikings', Earl Rognvald the crusader and poet and cathedral-builder.

Who was the St Magnus that is so honoured in hewn stone, and in festival and fair? In the early 12th century two Norse earls ruled in Orkney – Hakon Paulson and Magnus Erlendson. They were first cousins, and their joint rule prospered to begin with. But Earl Hakon was a statesman of ability and Earl Magnus was a mystic. Quarrels broke out, the peace of the earldom was endangered. At last, friends of both earls arranged a peace conference in the island of Egilsay on Easter Monday, 117. The earls were to come to the island with two ships each and an agreed number of conciliators. Earl Magnus arrived first, true to the terms. Earl Hakon landed in another part of Egilsay with eight armed ships, and a swarm of ruffians.

What follows is a moving and beautiful story. Magnus sheltered all night in the church in Egilsay and had a Mass said for him. In the morning he walked out, 'as cheerful as though he had been bidden to a feast', among the swords and the axes.

There was some parley. Earl Hakon was anxious to spare his cousin's life, but that day he was overruled by his counsellors. In the end Hakon ordered his standard-bearer, a man called Ofeig, to strike the axe into Magnus's head. Ofeig refused very indignantly. At last the cook Lifolf was forced to be the executioner. Magnus comforted him, and promised him his clothes. And Lifolf, weeping, brought the axe down: a flash and a splintering under the ploughman's sun. . . .

After a time Magnus's body was brought for burial inside the little church in Birsay. Then began the miracles of cure that at last convinced even the sceptical bishop that he had a saint buried in his church. Not long afterwards the body was taken to the new-begun cathedral in Kirkwall; and there it rests, in a martyr-red pillar, to this day, cloven skull and all. Earl Hakon went on to become one of the wisest and most loved governors that Orkney ever had.

The period covered by the saga is Orkney's golden age. Orkney was the centre of an earldom that reached far down into Scotland and the Western Isles, included Shetland, and even influenced affairs in Ireland. But as Scotland increasingly realised itself as a nation, and as the power of Norway lessened, Orkney was inevitably drawn into the Scottish orbit. That mingling of races was

not successful, to begin with, for the native-born Orcadians. Gradually their laws, their language, their possessions were trimmed to suit the convenience of the incoming Scots, who assumed ever-increasing control. One of the mightiest medieval earldoms shrank over the centuries to the status of a minor Scottish county. It was the end of an old heroic song.

Yet history was to impinge more than once on the islands. Scapa Flow was a naval base in the wars of 1914–18 and 1939–43, a safe harbour for the great ships of the Royal Navy. But early in the Second World War a German submarine penetrated the defences of Scapa Flow and sank the Royal Oak. To lock that door forever barriers were thrown across the eastern end of Scapa Flow, and five islands were connected by a road buttressed with massive blocks of concrete.

The island of Flotta, inside Scapa Flow, is a terminal for the North Sea oil that lies east of Orkney. The Flotta gas flare illumines the winter nights. Uranium, in some quantity, lies under the tilth and pasture of many parts of Orkney. Orcadians, who are folk not given to show or outward flourish, have demonstrated with great firmness that that is where they want it to remain.

Harbour at St Margaret's Hope, South Ronaldsay.

What is probably the most striking thing about Orkney and living in Orkney is the stark drama of light and darkness. In summer it is never dark. On clear nights the glow of the sun never leaves the north; the sun is just under the horizon; the fires of sunset and dawn intermingle. In winter the lamps are lit at three o'clock. But the midwinter skies are beautiful with moon and stars reflected in the many waters of burn, loch, quarry, rock-pool, ocean. Five or six times a winter the aurora borealis is abroad.

> *The Arctic girl is out tonight*
> *(Come to the doors.)*
> *She dances*
> *In a coat of yellow and green patches.*
> *She bends*
> *Over the gate of stars.*
>
> *What is she, a tinker lass?*
> *Does she carry flashing cans*
> *From the quarry fire?*
>
> *I think*
> *She's a princess in a silk gown.*
> *She turns*
> *A jar of cut green crystal.*
>
> *Come to the doors!*
> *She's walking about in the north,*
> *   the winter witch.*

On those long winter nights, there was once a great treasury of lore and legend for the country folk to draw upon; trows (trolls), sea-monsters, seal-men and seal-maidens; and stories of smugglers and pirates and witches. The coming of newspapers, compulsory education, radio, television, the cinema diluted that native culture. But modern Orkney can still show achievements in art and music and literature. A symbol of that perhaps is the new Pier Arts Centre in Stromness, a small beautiful complex of rooms and galleries played on by the shifting harbour gleams. Here, among a permanent collection of works of the St Ives school, are changing exhibitions of artistic work from Orkney and elsewhere, poetry readings, lectures and film shows.

The population, which had been in steady decline since the mid-19th century, has now levelled out. To an already rich and complex racial mix a new strain has recently been added: scores of families, mostly from England, have settled in the islands in the last two or three decades. Surfeited with industrialism and the ratrace, most of them have soon settled down to be good Orcadians.

Orkney has always kept its doors wide and welcoming.

GEORGE MACKAY BROWN

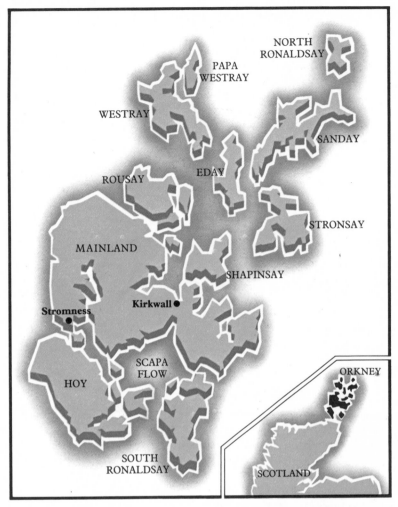

getting round islands etc. Produces many useful leaflets including five about different areas of the islands. Go there as soon as you arrive.

WHERE TO GO
Mainland Towns

KIRKWALL

Capital of Orkney, busy port and attractive old town with winding streets and grey stone houses. Many buildings have steep gables with stepped edges, called crow steps. Main shopping streets paved and look to English eyes as if they are pedestrian precincts – don't be misled, cars come belting down them. General greyness relieved by Orcadians' strange colour sense – they seem especially fond of lemon-yellow houses with maroon trimmings – and by red sandstone of cathedral and two ruined palaces that dominate the town.

Cathedral of St Magnus is most impressive building anywhere in Scottish islands. Begun in 1137 by Norse Earl Rognvald in memory of his uncle murdered on island of Egilsay 20 years earlier. At beginning of this century Magnus's remains were found buried in cathedral by workmen – an axe wound in his skull just as described in 'Orkneyinga Saga'. Exterior massive but dour, inside has tall arches, sandstone soft golden pink. Primitively carved 18th c monuments along both aisles – look out for Mary Young's with comic praying maiden. Good medieval heads above choir. Open Mon-Sat 9-1, 2-5.

The Earl's Palace: home of 'Black Pate' – wicked Earl Patrick, nephew of Mary Queen of Scots and one of the Stewart Earls who tyrannised Orkney at end 16th c. Built by local slave labour, but bears no trace of grim origins. Even in roofless, ruined state very elegant with distinctly French flavour. Great hall where Patrick held court has magnificent fireplace and curved oriel windows. Open April-Sept weekdays 9.30-7, Sun 2-7; Oct-March 9.30-4, Sun 2-4. D of E. Admission charge includes admission to Bishop's Palace.

The Bishop's Palace: 12th c, much altered by Earl Patrick; now a rather ominous shell. Climb Bishop Reid's tower for view of cathedral, town and

BASICS

About 7 miles of choppy sea lie between the northernmost tip of the mainland of Scotland and the most southerly of 67 islands that make up Orkney (not, locals insist, 'the Orkneys'). Largest island, called Mainland, has greater acreage than all others combined. Most of Orkney green and fertile – majority of islanders still make living from land, chiefly cattle farming. Old saying: 'The Orcadian is a farmer with a boat, the Shetlander a fisherman with a croft.'

For 500 years Orkney was ruled from Norway and Denmark, until in 1468 given to Scotland as part of dowry. People here used to speak Norn, form of Old Norse, not Gaelic, and language lives on in many place-names and clear, slightly sing-song accent of the people. Orcadians still treasure Norse links – thriving Orkney-Norway friendship societies, exchange visits etc. Before Norsemen, Picts, Celts and neolithic people all had settlements here.

Main tourist attractions as well as beauty of scenery – less dramatically wild than Shetland, but very varied and tranquil – are fascinating variety of archaeological sites and ancient buildings (see *Where to Go, Mainland* and *Islands*), excellent fishing, both fresh and sea water (see *Activities*), and birdwatching (see *Flora and Fauna*). People most relaxing company, with wry humour, genuinely friendly and welcoming.

Weather often cool and rainy, sometimes biting winds. Never exactly hot, but can be brilliantly sunny.

Orkney Tourist Information Office, Broad St, Kirkwall, tel Kirkwall 2856, invaluable for finding places to stay, information about

out to sea. Same hours as Earl's Palace.

Tankerness House Museum opposite cathedral in handsome old house with beautiful sheltered garden. Touring exhibitions plus toys, farm implements, Norse brooches, whaling weapons etc. Open all year daily except Sun 10.30-12.30 and 1.30-5.

Public Library, Laing St, founded 1683, is oldest in Scotland. Has outstanding reference library of over 5,000 books on Orkney. It's a good place to retreat to in bad weather. There is also one cinema in the town.

Shopping: some splendidly old-fashioned shops, eg James Flett & Sons, Bridge St, ironmonger and general store with frontier post atmosphere. Foubister's, Albert St, with trade cards, posters and biscuit tins unchanged for at least 30 years. At Scott's Fish Shop in Bridge St you can buy the most delicious smoked salmon we have ever tasted and Kirkwall kippers, 'Famous in Orkney and the adjacent island of Great Britain'. They send both by post all over the world. The Longship in Broad St sells work by many potters who have studios in Orkney, also silver jewellery made on premises by Ola Gorie – watch her at work. Early closing day Wed.

Eating and Drinking: pubs as such hardly exist in Orkney. You drink in hotel bars, mostly cosy but without much individuality. Lots of juke boxes and young people. Best are near harbour. Try comfortable bar of Ayre Hotel – disco Sat – or the St Ola nearby with unlikely mural of Chicago gangsters. For meals go to Ayre Hotel for good plain food, or Pirate Gow Restaurant at the Torvhaug Inn, Bridge St – stick to excellent steaks – or the Old Ship Inn, Bridge St for coffee and light lunches.

STROMNESS

Beautiful setting – hills rise steeply behind town which faces bay overlooking green island of Graemsay with mysterious shape of Hoy looming in distance. Main street snakes along edge of sea. It's narrow and paved, with houses on both sides, so you get sudden enticing glimpses between them of stone jetties, boats and the water. Sheltered harbour still alive with ships. Stromness became important in 18th c as last port of call

Ancient Monument signs in Earl's Palace, Mainland, for the winter.

for whalers and ships making for Arctic. Inscription in main street on site of Logan's Well: 'There watered here the Hudson Bay Co ships 1670-1891, Capt Cook's vessels "Resolution" and "Discovery" 1780, Sir John Franklin's ships "Erebus" and "Terror" on Arctic exploration 1845.' Its unexpected delights include a huge pair of antlers which decorates a garden shed in main street.

The Pier Arts Centre is another surprise. Opened in 1979 in converted 18th c stone warehouse backing on to bay and facing Victoria St, it has internationally famous collection of works by Ben Nicolson, Barbara Hepworth etc. Also gallery for local artists, it has friendly, unpatronising atmosphere as well as austere good taste. Open Tues-Sat 10.30-12.30, 1.30-5; Sun 2-5 in summer.

Stromness Museum has a pleasing mixture of curios – sea-chests, stuffed

birds, splendid old photographs, model boats – enough to while away several wet afternoons. Open Mon-Sat 11-12.30, 1.30-5; Thurs 11-1 (July and Aug from 10.30). Admission charge.

Some excellent shops – in main street Christine Clarke's antique shop, the only one in Orkney, full of bargains with an especially nice line in teapots. Manson's, Victoria St, is a grocer's that would do Soho proud, piled high with exotic foreign food as well as local produce. Stromness Books and Prints, serious and friendly bookshop with particularly good selection of books about Orkney and Shetland and works of Stromness's own literary lion George Mackay Brown. Early closing day Thurs.

To quench your thirst there are several hotel bars. For home cooking and a pretty room go to Richan's Restaurant, tel Stromness 850139.

Golf course and indoor swimming pool, also lobster pool you can look round. Branch of Tourist Information Office in Ferry Terminal Building open mid-June–mid-Sept, tel Stromness 850716.

SIGHTSEEING

Skara Brae: marvellously well-preserved village built 4,500 years ago. Cluster of interconnecting circular houses stands right on edge of beautiful Skaill Bay on the west coast. Walls of many houses still stand up to eaves, alley ways still roofed over by original slabs. Life of village ended by great storm that left it choked with sand – much original furniture still where it was buried. Here term 'Stone Age' becomes a reality – there are stone food boxes once lined with clay to act as fridges, stone grinders, stone-sided beds,

even stone dressers. Open April-Sept 9.30-7, Sun 2-7; Oct-March 9.30-4, Sun 2-4. D of E. Admission charge. Off B9056 about 6 miles north of Stromness.

Maes Howe: call at farm across the road for someone to show you round, cross field, bend double and grope down a narrow entrance tunnel that emerges into dramatic megalithic burial chamber. Finesse of masonry and grand scale most impressive. Three cells off main chamber where chieftains must have been buried perhaps with great treasure, for carved on walls are series of runic inscriptions lamenting its loss cut by visiting Norsemen in 12th c. Open same hours as Skara Brae (above) but closed weekends June, July, Aug. D of E. Admission charge. On A965 about 8 miles west of Kirkwall. Several similar but less grand chambered tombs on Mainland eg on

Cuween Hill nr Finstown, Wideford Hill nr Kirkwall and Unstan nr Stromness.

Ring of Brodgar and Stones of Stenness: two mysterious stone circles that stand not far from each other in wild country between lochs of Stenness and Harray. Stones of Stenness probably slightly earlier, dating from 3rd millennium BC. Ring of Brodgar even more impressive, surrounded by deep ditch. Only 36 stones stand of original 60, but mathematical precision of their placing still very evident. Both off B9055.

Birsay and Brough of Birsay: straggling little village with one of the ruined 16th c palaces built by the Stewart Earls of Orkney, now a sombre shell. The Brough of Birsay is a beautiful little grass and sea-pink covered island off the nearby Point of Buckquoy. At low tide can be reached on foot along concrete causeway.

Birsay Bay on Mainland. Orkney's shores are a beachcomber's delight.

Shore itself beachcomber's delight – rock-pools, sea anemones, sea-weeds, shells. On island remains of Viking and early Christian settlements including churchyard with gravestones. Also remains of Norse buildings including bath-house. Open same hours as Skara Brae (above). D of E. Admission charge. Check tide times with locals; being marooned here could be bleak. Off A965 and 986, north-west point of Mainland.

Click Mill: in middle of very muddy field, small, primitive water-mill still in working order. Earliest type with wheel set horizontally instead of vertically – this one probably 19th c though similar introduced by Norsemen. Charming little building, worth the mud. Key on site. On B9057, $1\frac{1}{2}$ miles north-east of Dounby.

Gurness Broch: on Aikerness overlooking Eynhallow Sound, ruined fortified tower encircled by ditches probably built 1st c BC but surrounded by remains of much later houses and fortifications that show it was still being used as a refuge 10 centuries later. Open same hours as Skara Brae (above). D of E. Admission charge. Off A966.

Yesnaby: dramatic, sinister cliffs, track off B9056 leads straight to top. Splendidly wild place on a rough day, in good weather stunning views of island of Hoy with coast of Scotland in distance.

Marwick: lovely little rocky bay surrounded by flowery pastures. Above it on Marwick Head stands tower monument to Lord Kitchener, who went down in HMS Hampshire which sank near here in 1916. Marwick Head is a Royal Society for the Protection of Birds reserve – cliffs from May to July covered with breeding guillemots and kittiwakes, also puffins and aggressive great skuas. A spectacular walk northwards to Birsay from Marwick Bay, but be wary – cliffs can be dangerous.

Corrigall Farm Museum: old farmhouse and outbuildings give good idea of traditional crofters' life. Box beds, fish drying above fireplace, cheese-making implements, old hand-looms, corn-drying kiln, ploughs etc. Open April-Sept weekdays 10.30-1, 2-5, Sun 2-7. Signposted on turning to Harray off A965.

ISLANDS

COPINSAY

Sea-bird island south-east of Mainland off Deerness. Purchased as memorial to James Fisher, naturalist and broadcaster who worked for seabird conservation. Now administered by RSPB. On 200ft cliffs at south-east of island kittiwakes and guillemots nest in thousands May-July, also razorbills and puffins. On Corn Holm, little offshore island that can be reached on foot at low tide, there are arctic terns. Telephone boatmen in Deerness, David Foubister, tel Deerness 245 or S. Foubister, tel Deerness 252, to arrange trip from lighthouse pier at Newark Bay. Visitors are asked to go to information room in farmhouse on the island for advice about what can be seen there and where to go.

EDAY

A hilly, narrow island, about 8 miles long. Declining population, now only about 100. Has some standing stones and chambered tombs, but its archaeological remains are less striking than those of most of the main islands and the landscape, apart from the bright sandstone cliffs at the Red Head of Eday, lacks drama. A mile or two south of its southern tip are the Green Holms where colonies of shag nest and seals breed (see *Flora and Fauna*) and to the north, across the often furious waters of Calf Sound, is the Calf of Eday. Here in 1725 the ship of an ineffectual pirate named Gow, son of a prosperous Stromness merchant, ran aground and at Carrick House, the local laird's house overlooking the sound, there is a stain on the floor said to have been made by his blood. Gow is a notorious character in Orkney with restaurants and shops named after him. Perhaps his gruesome end made him such a part of local folklore – he had to be hanged twice. The first time the rope broke.

The island of Hoy : its tumult of blue shoulders contrasts starkly with the surroundings.

HOY

The gaunt cliffs and hills of Hoy make a dramatic backdrop to the benign landscape of Mainland. It is the second largest of the islands and by far the most desolate, very beautiful, but wild and depopulated. Since the naval base for the fleet at Scapa Flow closed in the 1950s, there has been little employment and much of the land is too inhospitable to farm. Only one proper road, running down its east coast past the ugly ruins left by the navy at Lyness, impressive Martello towers that guard the deepwater inlet at Longhope – built as a defence, not against the French, but against American ships in 1812 – then across the narrow isthmus that joins green, prosaic South Walls, where most of the islanders live, to the rest of Hoy. At Osmondwall cemetery in Longhope there is a memorial to the brave men of the Longhope lifeboat which was lost with all hands in 1969. You can see the new lifeboat at Brims.

The interior is a hilly, heather-covered wilderness haunted by legends of trolls and giants. There are many little lochs and burns, rare alpine plants (see *Flora and Fauna*) and Ward Hill at 1,565ft is the highest point in Orkney. The strange Dwarfie Stone, a hollowed-out neolithic tomb, once thought to be the home of a malevolent dwarf, stands overlooking the valley that leads to the lovely, almost deserted village of Rackwick. It is just beginning to come back to life, three or four crofts are lived in again and local people are working to make others habitable. Jack Rendall, who owns some of them, also runs a taxi service from Mo Ness where the ferry from Stromness lands, to Rackwick, tel Hoy 262.

The cliffs along Hoy's north-west coast are much the most spectacular in Orkney, more than 1,100ft high at St John's Head. You get a splendid view of them from the Scrabster to Stromness ferry. The island's most famous landmark, the Old Man of Hoy, a sheer tower of rock 450ft high surrounded by roaring waves, was first scaled in 1966 and remains a supreme test of ability for rock-climbers.

Few places to stay except two hostels (see *Accommodation*). Only one shop in North Hoy where the ferry lands – run by Jack Rendall in Rackwick – so if you are going on a day trip take a picnic and wear wellingtons, the hills are very boggy. There are daily boats from Stromness to Hoy, sometimes cancelled in bad weather. Check with Captain Sutherland, 126 Victoria St, Stromness, tel Stromness 850678/850276. Also Orkney Island Shipping Co Services (see *Getting Around*).

NORTH RONALDSAY

High stone dyke keeps the native breed of sheep out of the fertile interior, reserved for comparatively pampered cows. Sheep happily share beaches with seals and sea-birds, living entirely on seaweed, which gives their meat a unique pungent flavour – an acquired taste. Island only 4 miles long – several archaeological remains including Iron Age Broch of Burrian. Fine striped lighthouse, highest built on land in Britain, was first lit in 1789, and still beams out over North Sea – this is the northernmost island in Orkney. Loganair and Orkney Island Shipping Co services (see *Getting Around*).

PAPA WESTRAY

Fertile little island famous for birds, archaeology and the shortest scheduled flight in the world – 2 minutes from Westray to Papa Westray by Loganair. Faced by a falling population, something that has led to the desertion of many Scottish islands of similar size, the 100 or so islanders set up community co-operative 3 years ago – first of its kind in Orkney, though there are several in the Western Isles. They have built new shop and are now trying to encourage tourism. Last year they started enterprising scheme, 10-day holidays, 5 in comfortable, modern Foveran Hotel on mainland, 5 staying on Papa Westray in home of islander with guided tours of ancient monuments, nature reserves etc. Details from Manager, Papa Community Co-operative, Beltane House, Papa Westray.

North Hill nature reserve has biggest colony of arctic terns in Britain, 100 pairs of arctic skuas and a few great skuas. Foul Craig is where last great auk in world was shot in 1813. All visitors to reserve between May and July must contact RSPB reserve warden beforehand. He stays at house near reserve entrance, but would prefer letter in advance – RSPB Warden, Gowrie, Papa Westray.

Oldest known settlement in Orkney and probably oldest standing houses in Europe are at the Knap of Hower on west coast of island – considerable remains of two houses more than 5,000 years old. On little island to east, the Holm of Papa Westray, is fine chambered tomb, its stones decorated not by later intruders as at Maes Howe, but by original users themselves. Loganair and Orkney Island Shipping Co services go there (see *Getting Around*).

ROUSAY, EYNHALLOW, EGILSAY

Rousay is an idyllic island – beautifully varied scenery, hillier than any of the others except Hoy. Has trout-filled lochs, wild heath, rolling farmland – yellow with primroses in late spring – rocky sea-bird-haunted cliffs.

Exceptionally rich too in archaeological remains. 'The Egypt of the North' say locals, exaggerating but not outrageously – many ancient buildings on island date from same period as Pyramids.

Boat scheduled twice daily from Tingwall Pier, tel Rousay 203. Also Orkney Island Shipping Co service (see *Getting Around*). Island only 5 miles long and 3 wide – would be lovely place to explore gently by bike. Hire them near pier from Tommy Gibson. Even better, hire a pony and trap – the driver will tell you about the sights and will also provide a picnic, cost about £10 for a day's outing, tel Rousay 330. Chris Soames, tel Rousay 234, runs a taxi service and will also show you round the island.

Only two shops, one delightfully old-fashioned general store at Hullion where your bill is made out in fine copperplate handwriting. Orkney Pottery near Hullion welcomes visitors to watch potters at work and sells their pleasing, practical ware. Friendly bar at Taversoe Hotel. Accommodation limited – hotel has only two rooms – but some islanders take guests, including young English couple, the Gowings, who have old farmhouse and serve delicious ice cream and cheese made from milk of their own Jersey cow. Tel Rousay 244.

North-west side of island more affected than most of Orkney by early 19th c clearances – many ruined crofts there and little cultivation. Ancient remains concentrated on west coast; lots of impressive things including neolithic chambered tombs at Midhowe and Yarso. Midhowe's central burial chamber 80ft long, divided into 24 burial compartments. Several ruined brochs also stand along shore of Eynhallow Sound – Midhowe Broch especially well-preserved. This shore was also much frequented in later centuries. There is Norse cemetery, and recently Viking burial ship was unearthed. All monuments open all the time. Booklet 'A Rousay Heritage Walk' available from Tourist Office, full of useful information.

Eynhallow, west of Rousay, is deserted except for birds and seals. Was monastic site in 12th c and ruins of church of period survive.

Egilsay to the east, where St Magnus was murdered, has far better

preserved church of same date with fine round tower. Boats 3 times a week from Tingwall pier. Check with Rousay boatman, tel Rousay 203 – he might also be persuaded to take you to Eynhallow.

SANDAY

Good place to take children for holiday. Green, low-lying, bat-shaped island with miles of curving sandy beaches linking the spindly peninsulas – stretches of foreshore attract huge flocks of wading birds. Hardly showing above the waterline in a fog, it has caused many a shipwreck – once welcomed by islanders, because with no peat here, ship's timber provided winter fuel.

Kettletoft village and harbour has hotel with pleasant if basic bar, but best place to stay is with postmistress Mrs Foubister, who also runs the island's restaurant (Belsair, Kettletoft, tel Sanday 206). There are also some b & bs and self-catering cottages to let. The Sanday Knitters, successful local women's co-operative, have sales of seconds every other Wednesday evening in the Wool Hall. Mainly machine-knitted Shetland wool with Fair Isle decoration or chunky hand-knitted Nordic wools – nice mittens, hats and slipper-socks. Details on local shop's notice board along with news of dances, drama club productions etc. Two more perhaps surprising ventures for this remote corner are thriving electronics business Sykes Robertson, whose Morse code and communications equipment is exported all over the world, while Stuart Christie publishes the anarchist fortnightly *Black Flag* from here.

South-western corner, The Wart, is highest part looking out over Red Head of Eday; a walk leads down from here to Stove Bay, secluded little beach of bright white sand. Other long sweeping bays like Backaskaill are superb for walking and beach-combing, while bird-watching is best around northern peninsula at the Holms of Ire and Roos Wick. Seals can be found all around the coast. On eastern side of Elsness peninsula, Quoyness chambered cairn is spectacular example of neolithic masonry dating from 2,900BC, similar to Maes Howe but with elongated central chamber and more cells. Open

April-Sept 9.30-7, Sun 2-7, Oct-March closes at 4.

There are two taxi and car hire firms, Moodie's (tel Sanday 325) and Wilson's (tel Sanday 321). Wilson's also hire bikes. Regular Loganair and Orkney Island Shipping Co services (see *Getting Around*).

SOUTH RONALDSAY, LAMB HOLM

Linked with the mainland by The Churchill Causeway. These islands form the eastern arm of the great naval anchorage of Scapa Flow. It was here that the German fleet scuttled itself in a final heroic gesture in 1919. At the beginning of Second World War after HMS Royal Oak was sunk by a German sub, Churchill ordered the closing of the narrow but deep channels between the islands. Thousands of huge concrete blocks were sunk to make barriers. Now it's a strange, surreal landscape with ramshackle-looking piled-up blocks topped by a narrow road, rusty half-sunken wrecks line route between islands.

Italian prisoners of war built the barriers, and on the little island of Lamb Holm is charming relic of their presence – the Italian Chapel, a Nissen hut they painted and embellished so intricately that when, years after the war, it began to decay, the Orcadians had become so fond of it that they broadcast and advertised in Italy to find the original prisoners, who returned to restore it.

St Margaret's Hope in South Ronaldsay has a seaweed-filled harbour, lots of boats tied up, grey stone houses. Several artists and craftsmen have made their homes here. The Workshop is a good craft centre. The Creel Restaurant, near harbour, is perhaps best in Orkney – unpretentious cooking, good local scallops, crab, fish and lobster if you order in advance. Popular and small, so book. Tel St Margaret's Hope 311.

At Burwick at south end of South Ronaldsay is a nice example of the many plain but well-proportioned little 18th and 19th c churches, some now decaying, scattered all over the islands. Graveyard on edge of sea – everyone seems to have lived to very ripe old age – with views of north coast of Scotland and several winking lighthouses on islands between.

STRONSAY

Green and fertile little island consisting of three peninsulas with sandy bays in between. There are some fair-sized farms – population about 400, but was 2,000 at turn of the century. 17th to early 20th c was one of the capitals of the herring industry with five fish-curing stations on the little island of Papa Stronsay alone and 15 more at Whitehall, Stronsay's harbour and main village.

Visitors can look around the Lobster Pond here – long low stone building at end of harbour – if manager isn't there, ask at PO. At Old Handweave, Tom Shearer demonstrates traditional weaving techniques and sells handwoven cloth.

Pleasant walks around craggy headlands like Burgh Head and Lamb Head, where there's a curious geological formation called Dane's Pier, formed by two currents meeting but once thought to have been constructed by the Vikings. Good spot to see seals and sea-birds. In early summer the bays are fringed with clumps of yellow iris and sea-pinks. Along sandy beaches look out for low stone platforms where the 'tangles', tree-trunklike seaweed, is stacked and dried. Hard and laborious work often done by women – it takes four tons to get one ton of dried seaweed.

Hotel in Whitehall and some excellent guest-house accommodation. Whitehall's general store is the place to look for news of local events. Taxis and self-drive car hire from Mr Swanney (Stronsay 244). Bikes can be hired, but sometimes you can't even go downhill against the wind. Gusts of over 100mph not unknown and great wind of 1952 that blew all the hen-houses away still talked about. Regular Loganair and Orkney Island Shipping Co services (see *Getting Around*).

WESTRAY

One of Scotland's rare boom islands with increasing population of more than 750, thriving fleet of fishing boats and modern lobster and crab processing plant with a successful export record in spite of the island's only recently having acquired mains electricity. Landscape varied and pleasing with white sand beaches, flat farmland in the east and considerable hills and high cliffs in the west.

Among them on Noup Head, an RSPB bird reserve with the largest colony of guillemots, razorbills and kittiwakes, and a splendid viewpoint, is 'the gentlemens' cave'. Here after the Battle of Culloden a group of lairds who supported the Young Pretender went into hiding for a whole year.

The island's most dramatic and sinister monument is Noltland Castle, a dark ruin standing on a hill above the main village of Pierowall. It has two towers and 7ft-thick walls pierced by 61 gun-loops. Its builder, Gilbert Balfour, was implicated in the conspiracy led by Bothwell to murder Darnley, husband of Mary Queen of Scots, and after Bothwell's downfall he fled to Orkney. Its elegant staircase, incongruous among such a display of brute force, was probably added by a more aesthetic villain, the notorious Earl Partick Stewart. Open April-Sept weekdays 9.30-7, Sun 2-7; Oct-March weekdays 9.30-4, Sun 2-4. D of E. Admission charge.

Pierowall Hotel pleasant – very reasonable meals, friendly bar – overlooking Pierowall Bay. Regular Loganair and Orkney Island Shipping Co services (see *Getting Around*).

SPECIALITIES

Whisky: two distilleries near Kirkwall. You can go on a guided tour round the Highland Park Distillery every day during the working season, Aug-mid-June at 10.30 and 3. They have been distilling here using same techniques and peaty spring water since 1798. See columned rooms carpeted with thick layer of drying barley, huge wooden vats foaming and fermenting, gleaming copper stills shaped like giant, up-turned French horns, cellars full of barrels where spirit matures for 12 years or so.

Orkney chairs: 19th c photographs and paintings of croft interiors often show these unique chairs with wooden frames and tall backs made from woven straw. Some lovely old ones in Tankerness House Museum (see *Where to Go, Kirkwall*). They are still being made in the traditional way by Robert Towers at Rosegarth, St Ola, Kirkwall, tel Kirkwall 3521. You can watch him at work there. Not cheap – over £100 each – but design has solid, timeless quality that would fit in anywhere.

Food: cooking here may not always be inspired, but with such excellent local raw materials, especially beef, fish and shellfish, we felt Orkney food was better than on a lot of Scottish islands. Look out for delicious pale local cheese – ask for 'farmhouse cheese'. 'Orkney cheese', also good, comes in three flavours, but is factory-made and less special. Lots of unfamiliar kinds of bread rolls eg 'bere bannocks', brown, rather heavy buns made from bere meal, grown only in Orkney. For an ethnic picnic, have bere bannocks and farmhouse cheese and round it off with delicious Orkney fudge in all sorts of different flavours. And don't leave without sampling Scott's smoked salmon and kippers. (See *Where to Go, Kirkwall*).

Fiddlers and weddings: the Orkney Strathspey and Reel Society play enthusiastically for evenings of traditional dancing. Look out for them in local Press. They're often at Ayre Hotel, Kirkwall. Weddings are the great social events here, usually followed by all-night festivities – 'bride's cog', traditional communal cup with tall handles full of fiercely intoxicating mixture, gets passed round and round. Sometimes everyone on an island gets invited to a wedding, including visitors. If you get the chance of going to one, don't miss it.

ACTIVITIES

Fishing: great sport for both sea anglers and trout fishermen. When it's too rough for the open ocean, Scapa Flow provides exciting but sheltered fishing for sea anglers. It's especially good for big skate. Ocean fishing grounds only a short sail from either Stromness or Kirkwall; catch cod, halibut, ling and haddock here. The Stromness Hotel, Stromness and the St Ola Hotel, Kirkwall specialise in accommodation for sea anglers and have boats for hire. Check with Tourist Office for other boats for hire.

Sea trout are an Orkney speciality. The place to catch them is where Loch Stenness empties into the sea. Sinclair's, the tackle shop in Stromness, will give the necessary specialist advice on flies etc.

Excellent trout fishing, with the added bonus that it's free, in scores of lochs scattered over Mainland and islands – only Loch of Skaill is private. The Orkney Trout Fishing Association, who have restocked many lochs, would appreciate it if you joined them: subscription around £3, contact them at Tourist Office. Best fishing of all on west Mainland, especially lochs of Stenness and Harray, both shallow with stony bottoms and full of fine fighting trout. The Tourist Office has published leaflets on sea angling and trout fishing.

Sailing: Clyde Cruising Club, SV Carrick, Glasgow G1 4LN, tel Glasgow 552 2183, publishes invaluable 'Orkney Sailing Directory', from bookshops, chandler's or direct from them. Scapa Flow's enclosed waters are good for cruising and don't need quite as much experience and skill as the open North Sea. Sail Orkney, Orkney Yacht Charters, 11 Broad St, Kirkwall hires out self-sail and skipper-charter yachts.

Beachcombing and Swimming: beautiful sandy beaches on many of the islands, especially Stronsay and Sanday, and lots of secluded bays on the west coast of Mainland, perfect for idly collecting seaweed and shells and peering into rock-pools. Indoor pools at Stromness and Kirkwall.

Walking: fenced-in fields and lots of bulls make parts of Mainland perhaps not quite as good for long walks as most of other islands, but lovely cliff-top walk from Stromness to Brockness and on past Yesnaby as far as Brough Head. Hoy marvellous for hilly cross-country and cliff-top tramps.

Deep-sea Diving: Ivan Owen, landlord of Taversoe Hotel, Rousay, tel

Robert Towers, Orkney chairmaker in Kirkwall.

Rousay 325, a diver himself, organises diving trips, has boat: bring your own suits. Orkney waters very clear and deep, lots of wrecks.

Golf: two 18-hole courses, one near Kirkwall, one in very beautiful setting on edge of sea at Stromness.

FLORA AND FAUNA

Birds: one in six of all sea-birds that breed in Britain nest in Orkney.

Nowhere else are there so many kittiwakes and guillemots, and an increasing proportion of world's great skuas nest here. May till end July best time to see cliffs white and raucous with birds.

Many other migrants increase number of species to be seen – in late July waders like sanderlings and turnstones arrive from far north, in late Sept geese, whooper swans, snow buntings and redwing often fly over,

long tailed ducks and great northern divers arrive in winter, so at any time of year an exciting place for birdwatchers. Look out for birds of prey especially the hen harrier.

The RSPB has six reserves. As well as Marwick Head (see *Where to Go, Mainland*) and Copinsay, Noup Cliffs, Westray and North Hill, Papa Westray (see *Where to Go, Islands*), there are reserves at the Dale of Cottasgarth and at Hobbister – both

A view from the Churchill Causeway, between Glims Holm and Burray.

on Mainland. Both are good for short-eared owls, hen harriers, kestrel and merlin, and even waders at Hobbister.

For more information get in touch with Royal Society for the Protection of Birds, Scottish Office, 17 Regent Terrace, Edinburgh EH7 5BN. The Tourist Office produces a leaflet on birds.

Flowers: profusion of wild flowers. Hedgerow plants once common in England, but now fast disappearing, still grow all over the islands. The many marshy areas at the edge of lochs are good hunting-grounds for rare sedges and water plants. In spring there are masses of primroses and violets, and sea-pinks cover many islands and cliff tops, eg Brough of Birsay.

Orkney rarities include the oyster-plant, supposed to taste like its namesake, blue-green and fleshy, found on stony beaches, eg south shore of Birsay, and alpines which only grow at 2,000ft in Scotland can be seen at 500ft in the Hoy Hills, Rousay and Westray. Orchids, bog-asphodel, sundew and other acid-tolerant plants flourish on the moors. The rarest botanical treasure is the Scottish primrose, *Primula scotica*, found only in Orkney, Caithness and Sutherland – easy to see on cliff tops at Yesnaby. Even if you're not passionate about wild flowers take a good flower book.

Seals: seals, or 'selkies' as they are called here, have always been part of Orkney mythology – the word Orkney means 'seal islands' in Old Icelandic. Common seals and grey seals can be seen all round the islands, though it may take some practice to pick them out. Greenholm and Wait Holm are breeding grounds and in summer there are special half-day boat trips in the 'Jenny Lee' to see the colonies, tel Kirkwall 3691.

The Orkney Field Centre: a good place to stay if you want to learn more about the rich bird and plant life of Orkney. They can put up 20 people in parties or singly – be prepared to share rooms – and run courses on the flora, fauna and archaeology of the islands. House in lovely position near Marwick Head and Brough of Birsay. Programme from Orkney Field and Arts Centre, Links House, Birsay, Orkney.

EVENTS

Agricultural Shows: anyone with a weakness for them should come to Orkney at the beginning of Aug. The county show – livestock, flowers, athletics – is held in Kirkwall at Bignold Park, it's the big day of the year. In preceding week lots of other, smaller shows on several of islands plus East Mainland Show and West Mainland Show. Check dates, in *The Orcadian* or local radio.

Stromness Shopping Week: much more fun than it sounds. In third week of July every year Stromness entertains the rest of Orkney with dancing every night and all sorts of festivities.

St Magnus Festival: annual music festival held mostly in cathedral in Kirkwall third week in June. Inspired by Peter Maxwell Davies who has a house on Hoy – new works by him sometimes performed. Also visiting theatre, mime, puppet companies.

Briefing by Sarah Howell

THE CHANNEL ISLANDS

BY ALEXANDER FRATER

There are four major Channel Islands, a dozen or so minor ones, numerous empty, wind-swept rocks, and a murderous assortment of reefs, each capable of splitting an unwary hull like a hacksaw slicing through melon. Paradoxically, however, the Channel Islands are not in the Channel at all. They run down the Gulf of St Malo and, like great disabled arks, sit beached in the shallows of France; so close is the French coast to Alderney that, over a British gin and beneath the British flag, you can contemplate the evening sun catching the windscreen of Renaults and Citroens hurrying home down the roads of Normandy. Victor Hugo, a longtime resident of Guernsey, remarked that the islands were 'pieces of

Victorian pillar box in the market at St Helier, Jersey.

France which fell into the sea and were gathered up by England', but he was speaking metaphorically. They have never actually belonged to France at all. Instead, they were part of the Duke of Normandy's ancestral estates, and islanders are quick to point out to patronising English visitors that in 1066, when the Duke became William the Conqueror, he merely added England to his existing offshore properties. Over there, England is referred to as 'our oldest possession.'

The Channel Islanders are of Celtic extraction, but the traditional reticence and clannishness of the Celts, once heightened by isolation, is now little in evidence. Fleets of ships, hydrofoils and aircraft make communication easy, plying between Jersey, Guernsey, Alderney and Sark – the quartet of major islands – as regularly as buses, the boats braving the massive 40 foot tides, among the most ferocious in the world, which sweep regularly through the area. Arriving in Jersey I took a stroll before bed along the front, admiring the illuminated lines of Elizabeth Castle, built massively on a rock in Aubin's Bay, its granite ramparts battered by heavy waves. When I awoke at dawn, however, the bay had emptied like a bath, leaving the castle

high and dry in a damp waste-land of sand and mud. The Atlantic had retreated to a distant blue shadow, but after lunch it came back – not insinuating itself discreetly up the beach like a well-mannered English tide, but roaring in like a train.

From the waterfront St Helier, the capital of Jersey, looks faintly disreputable, an assortment of small shops and car-hire establishments where, even on a Sunday, salesmen peer morosely over their Fiestas and Polos at the hydrofoils rushing off to France and the Sealink ferries coming through the murk from England. Cut back a hundred yards, though, and you will find yourself in a town of exceptional charm – prosperous shops, pedestrian walkways, sleepy little squares. Jesse Boot, the pharmacist, lived on Jersey, and the local branch of his empire, built like a bank, is one of the most imposing stores in town. I purchased a box of throat tablets there, and the transaction was completed with the sort of decorum normally associated with booking a funeral.

There is a lot of money on Jersey, though much of it comes from elsewhere. The name is synonymous with beaches, cows and tax havens, and if the number of Rolls knocking about is anything to go by – 60 new ones are registered each year – there are plenty of well-heeled exiles in residence. So highly regarded are they on the island that their houses are pointed out on coach tours. Jersey must be one of the few places on earth where tax-dodging businessmen enjoy the status of stars.

Guernsey has its exiles too, but it doesn't flaunt them and the majority keep a low profile. The locals will tell you, with the waspishness they reserve for commenting on Jersey, that they attract a better class of refugee; the old money comes to Guernsey, they say, while the nouveau riche stuff invariably finishes up across the water.

I had crossed the water myself in a little yellow

St Peter Port, Guernsey: 'an almost Swiss sense of order'.

Trislander of Aurigny Air Services, and it took a mere 10 minutes, howling along at only a few hundred feet as though mounting a pre-emptive low-level strike against the island. Approaching it through a bright, late afternoon sun, it seemed fashioned from crystal, glittering and flashing and dazzling to the eye. What we were picking up, of course, was merely the light bouncing off tomato greenhouses, and a fellow passenger remarked that, until the Guernsey growers entered a distraught plea, Air France was planning to send its Rio-bound Concorde, trailed by a glass-shattering sonic boom, smack across the island.

St Peter Port, the capital, ascends a harbourside hill with an almost Swiss sense of neatness and order. The houses, with the traditional five upstairs windows peculiar to the Channel Islands, are strongly built and smart as paint, while the streets and quays are impeccably tidy; early one morning, in the pretty Candie Gardens, I saw an attendant *hoovering* the paths. There is tourism here too of course but, unlike Jersey, it is covert; visitors are absorbed into a small, purposeful and industrious working town and most seemed to relish this honorary temporary citizenship. I certainly did.

Victor Hugo, a resident for 16 years, loved the place and took its idiosyncrasies in his stride. During his time they were still obsessive about witches, and today lay claim to holding the last witch trial in Europe. That was in 1912, when a woman was given eight days' solitary for putting a spell on the town's chimneys. Piracy was officially and enthusiastically condoned until late in the 18th century, while the proudest boast of the local knitting industry is that Mary Queen of Scots was executed in a pair of their white weather-proof stockings.

One of the charms of Guernsey is the access it affords to Alderney, Sark and a delightful little island with the improbable name of Herm. Alderney, massively fortified by the Germans, takes a bit of getting used to. At first sight it seems just as boring as the Jersey and Guernsey people say it is, but with a little perseverance it grows on one; and a high proportion of Channel Islands regulars name Alderney as their favourite. I had been told that its main export was armadas of empty bottles drifting over to America, its only contribution to mankind a celebrated breed of cow, now extinct. But the people, united by their famous thirst and their contempt for Guernsey and Jersey, will often receive a stranger with a warmth not found on the other islands – particularly if he is willing to risk his liver in the interests of friendship. And once accepted, he is accepted for life. The Alderney folk don't believe in compromise and do nothing

by halves; when the Germans threatened invasion the entire population climbed into boats and left. Not for them the domination of the Reich and, on arrival, the enemy found they had conquered a few dogs and half a dozen old men.

Sark goes in for diminutives, boasting the world's smallest gaol and the world's smallest registered harbour. The visitor is likely to land at the latter, called Le Port de Creux and hewn from

The mailboat from Guernsey sailing past Corbière Point, Jersey.

the base of towering cliffs in 1588, and he is advised to take transport to the village at the top. Since there are no cars, a bloke with a tractor will give you a ride for 30p. The village consists of a couple of banks, several stores and a number of restaurants, and it is a cosy, unworldly little place, not unlike a film set. Since the ban on cars is absolute – a doctor who shipped one in for his practice was allowed to keep it on condition that it was pulled by a horse – the best way to get around it is by rented bike. There are also horse-drawn carriages available for hire, many of them driven by upper-

class Englishwomen with posh voices and an amazing line in blasphemy when their nags are being wayward.

A few of these come for the summers, others have yielded to their affection for the place and settled; and it is not hard to see why. Sark is an unending succession of tiny, deserted bays and winding country lanes. The hundreds of trippers who arrive each day are somehow screened and muffled by the foliage so that, after a few minutes pedalling in any direction that takes your fancy, you experience a rare, heady solitude. Giant

butterflies roost in the hedgerows, gulls wheel high overhead, the scents of acres of wildflowers numb the senses like nerve gas.

The island is run by Michael Beaumont, the present Seigneur and grandson of the legendary Dame Sybil Hathaway, and he and his 600 subjects pay no income tax, property tax, death duty, import or export duty; VAT to them is a brand of duty-free whisky. It's a prosperous little place where, despite the influx of urban British refugees, life still has a solid agricultural ring. Pinned to the wall of the church, for example, is a notice listing the bounties payable for crows' feet, rats' tails and rabbits' scuts, the latter to be submitted in multiples of 10.

A couple of miles away across a stretch of racing tidal water, yet another Seigneur is in residence. Major Peter Wood has no ancestral claim to the pretty little island of Herm, but he is the sitting tenant, following on the heels of Sir Compton Mackenzie and a Prince Blücher von Wahlstatt, now remembered chiefly for the fact that he brought a herd of wallabies with him. Major Wood, who has a military bearing and a brisk manner, is living out a dream but, having a strong practical bent, he is also making his island work. Dairy cows produce milk which is shipped over to Guernsey each morning, a thriving hotel and tourist complex have been built. A week here is the perfect antidote to the rat race. A sandy path circles one of the quietest islands on earth and, strolling along it, taking the Atlantic wind full in the face, I felt a lessening of old, half-forgotten tensions and a palpable lifting of the spirit. There was not another human being in sight, a flock of terns 100 feet up flashed like mirrors as they caught the sun, the sea swished and frothed in the rocks and, just for a moment, the idea of going into permanent exile myself seemed almost irresistible.

ALEXANDER FRATER

BASICS

Jersey is the largest – 45 square miles – and most southerly of the islands, with a high sunshine rate. (Be sure to get a bottle of Modantis sun-cream, made specially in Jersey to combat infra-red rays.) Guernsey, Herm and Sark huddle together some miles north. Alderney is further north still. Circumnavigating them is a challenge to yachtsmen; a tidal rise and fall of 40ft is not uncommon, currents over the plentiful reefs can be as fast as 13 knots. Those stopping off in France take note: animals taken on to French soil even for a walk are subject to Britain's strict quarantine laws on return.

Guernsey is the second-largest island – 24½ miles square – but, like Jersey, measured in local units called vergées. Interior is very built-up – greenhouses seem stacked almost on top of one another – but its triangular shape provides much variety in coastlines, from high rocky crags to low plains.

The islands are divided into parishes (eg Grouville, Trinity on Jersey), used for directions – street names rarely used. Both Jersey and Guernsey have a parliament, flag, currency and a postal system independent of the British Isles and of each other. Both claim to have introduced the pillar box to Britain –

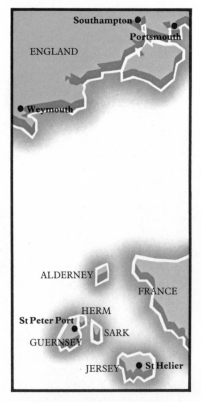

Jersey in 1852 via the novelist Anthony Trollope, who was a PO surveyor at the time, Guernsey in 1853 at St Peter Port. Tourism has erased many native customs but the patois – a rough, corrupt French – is still spoken in Guernsey, Jersey and Sark. Sadly, the language is dying and on Sark it is feared the present generation will be the last to speak it.

With no VAT the islands attract lots of shoppers – the French make day-trips just for bargains. Lovely Continental clothes and other goods, but biggest savings are on perfumes, spirits and tobaccos. Smooth efficiency characterises the larger islands – public telephones work, mainland newspapers are delivered on the day (but cost a bit more). However, attractions are mainly geared to the season, ie April to Sept, or to Nov, if demand is great. Pub hours vary from island to island: Jersey weekdays 9am-11pm, Sun 11-1 and 4.30-11; Guernsey weekdays 10.30am-11pm, closed Sun.

Jersey
WHERE TO GO
Towns

ST HELIER
Jersey's principal town, low and flat. Elizabeth Castle lies over a rocky outcrop to the south-west, accessible by causeway when the tide is out, while Fort Regent, a fortress-cum-leisure centre, looms on the cliffs above. Busy, hustling, and bustling, St Helier is a temple to low-duty

shopping, while The Esplanade, along the harbour, caters for easy holidays, crammed with car-hire firms and island tour companies. Given Jersey's tax-haven status, not surprising that the most attractive buildings are usually banks, embellished with neat white fences or clock towers.

Royal Square: a tree-lined courtyard bordered by dignified buildings. Clustered around a gilded statue of George II are the island's main administrative offices, including the Royal Court House, the States Chamber, and the fine Bibliothèque Publique.

Jersey Museum, 9 Pier Rd: a Georgian merchant's house with four floors of exhibits on Jersey's social and political history, including one on actress Lillie Langtry – known as the Jersey Lily – with a silver-inlaid travelling case thought to have been given to her by King Edward VII. It also houses the separate Barreau Art Gallery showing works by artists with local connections like Millais. Open all year Mon-Sat 10-5 (closed Christmas, Good Fri). Admission charge. Tel Jersey 53823.

Elizabeth Castle on L'Islet, a rock outside harbour: Sir Walter Raleigh, who was Governor of Jersey from 1600-03, named the castle after Queen Elizabeth I. During the Occupation the Germans refortified it. It now contains an exhibition of German weaponry and equipment inside, as well as the Jersey Militia Museum. Picnicking is permitted in the grounds, a ferry runs from the West Park slipway during high season. Open daily end March-Oct 9.30-5.30. Admission charge. Tel Jersey 23971.

Shopping: set aside at least a day for shopping; it's St Helier's main holiday activity. Most shops accept any currency. King St and Queen St are traffic-free and crammed with the latest in fashion and consumer goods. Best for local books are Hilgrove Books, Hilgrove St and Thesaurus in Sand St. Jersey Wool Shop at 2 Charing Cross has balls of strong wool for knit-it-yourself Jerseys. (See also *Guernsey – Specialities*.) For food, visit Central Market at Halkett Place and Market St. It opened in 1882 with 37 wrought-iron beams supporting the roof and over 80 tons of glass in its skylights. Little has changed since: a

Seasonal agricultural workers from Brittany playing a Sunday afternoon game of boules in a Jersey farmyard.

lovely four-tier fountain is centrepiece of stalls laden with home produce, wine, pâtés and French pastries – everything for a picnic. Flowers too. Its red gates are decorated with enamelled cows, grapes and chickens. At nearby Beresford Market fresh fish and seafood are sold. Early closing Thurs, but in summer many shops stay open every day for after-dinner sprees.

GOREY
Ultra-touristy twin towns. Gorey Village is a cluster of neat cottages with lilies blooming in front gardens, while Gorey Harbour is bright with sailing boats and town houses tucked under the dominating facade of Mont Orgueil Castle. Lots of hotels, restaurants and shops in Gorey Harbour, but not a base for those with cars – they have to be moved every 3 hours. Jersey Pottery has a huge car park and pleasant gardens in which to eat seafood salad; their efficient self-service cafeteria amply caters for the hordes. You can watch potters at work in small glass-fronted buildings dotted about the flower arbours or step inside to observe the processes in close-up. Nearby is the Linden Tree Tearoom – formerly Gorey's Catholic church with crosses still on the gates – serving teas with Jersey cream on tables outside. Mont Orgueil Castle is a medieval fortress

built to protect Jersey from French raiders. Tableaux and a small museum illustrate important events in the castle's history, and on a clear day you can see across to Mont St Michel in France. Castle open daily end-March-Oct 9.30-5.30. Admission charge. Tel Jersey 53292. Bicycles – possibly the best way to get around – can be hired in summer from hut opposite the Beach Hotel: tel Jersey 51729, ask for Mrs Heather Levesconte.

BEACHES

St Brelade's Bay, south-west tip: very popular family beach, with cafés and restaurants, tents and windbreakers for hire. Pay car parks nearby. Noisy, fun, and frantic, good for a quick dip. Sir Winston Churchill Memorial park just behind the beach is less crowded.

St Ouen's Bay, west coast: known as the 5-mile sweep, it extends almost the whole length of the west coast. On an islet in the middle of the bay stands La Rocco tower, while all around are vast dunes and mounds. Too huge to get crowded, the bay is safe for strong swimmers only. Atlantic waves roll in to make this a surfer's paradise; national and international surfing competitions are held here.

Rozel Bay, north-east tip: rocky beach backed by wooded hills next to charming Rozel village, all cottages with leaded windows and red fishing huts. Limited parking, can get crowded. Good for a stroll and a drink after dinner.

SIGHTSEEING

La Hougue Bie, Grouville: a major branch of Jersey Museum – really several museums in one – pleasantly situated in separate buildings among fields and trees. Railway, Archaeology and Geology, Agricultural, and German Occupation Museums. La Hougue Bie itself is an impressive neolithic tomb with passage roofed with cap stones leading to a central burial chamber. On top of the burial mound are two charming medieval chapels. Museums open March-Nov Tues-Sun (closed Mon), Spring and Summer Bank Hols, 10-5. Admission charge. Tel Jersey 53823/75940.

Jersey Wildlife Preservation Trust (Jersey Zoo), Les Augres Manor, Trinity: founded by Gerald Durrell, this zoo in 20 acres of parkland has over 1,000 of the world's rarest animals. Controlled breeding programmes are increasing their numbers. Cages are spacious and contain fresh vegetation. You will see from the number of red Dodo plaques, made by Jersey Pottery, that almost every group of animals represents an endangered species. Zoo open daily Easter-Oct 10-6, winter 10-4.30. Admission charge. For more information on the Jersey Wildlife Preservation Trust write to: Les Augres Manor, Trinity, Jersey. Tel: Jersey 61949.

La Mare Vineyard, St Mary: owned by the Blayney family who have been involved in wine-making for 150 years. Cool and welcoming, away from the crowds. Useful tips on how to improve home wine-making. Picnic near old granite farmhouse, children's playground, plus traditional Jersey cider, Clos de La Mare wine and wine mustard for sale. Open May-Sept Mon-Fri 10-5. Admission charge.

Battle of Flowers Museum, St Ouen: everything here is the work of Miss Florence Bechelet, who has won major awards in Jersey's annual Battle of Flowers 34 years out of 36. Huge lifelike animals made entirely from

Dusk at Mont Orgeuil, a medieval fortress built for protection from French raiders.

dried grasses gathered by Miss Bechelet herself – each Clydesdale horse contains 84,000. Open daily March-Nov 10-5. Admission charge.
St Matthew's Church, St Aubin's Rd: also known as the 'Glass Church' because of the simple and beautiful opaque interior work by the French designer René Lalique, whose perfume bottles were all the rage in Paris in the 1920s. There is a glass font, a glass communion table and a 15ft-high glass cross. Even the windows in the church are by Lalique. Close inspection reveals marvellous detail, and the four elongated angels in the Lady Chapel are breathtaking. The work was commissioned by Lady Trent in memory of her husband, originally Jesse Boot, the chemist. Open Mon-Fri 9-7, Sat 9-1, plus Sunday church services when the glass is illuminated. (Other churches worth visiting are St Brelade's, so close to the sea that boats and cars share its park, and St Saviour's, where Lillie Langtry is buried.)
German Military Underground Hospital, St Lawrence: light and sound effects tell the chilling story. Open daily mid-March-early Nov 10-6; Dec-mid-March Thurs, Sun 2.30-5. Admission charge.
Potter's Wheel, l'Etacq, St Ouen: in a pleasant cottage with pots drying in the sun, Eddie Sandham makes and sells decorative vases with cut-out designs, also moule bowls in which to cook mussels – use the deep curved lid for discarded shells. Open all year summer 9-7, winter 9-5.30. Also handmade leathercraft. Tel Jersey 82991.

SPECIALITIES

Ormers (*oreilles de mer*): ear-shaped crustaceans found in rockpools at low tide and highly regarded on the haute cuisine tables of Paris. The shells have iridescent interiors so attractive some islanders use them for garden decorations; buy the shells in fish markets to use as ashtrays. Ormer gathering used to be a great island tradition; the waters have been greatly overworked and strict controls have been brought in to allow for proper breeding.
Giant cabbages: introduced from France as a cattle feed probably late 18th c, these cabbages can grow up to 20ft tall – a big, leafy head atop an incredibly spindly stalk. In Victorian times the stalks achieved great popularity when made into walking sticks. These canes are still made at L'Etacq Woodcrafts, Fair Haven, L'Etacq, St Ouen and you can watch the process.
Day trips to France: Bellingham, 6 Caledonia Place, Weighbridge, tel Jersey 75019, and Summerday, 64 The Colomberie, St Helier, tel Jersey 27841, are two travel agents who offer special excursions to Mont St Michel and towns along the Côte d'Emeraude. For less organised day out, Condor do hydrofoil journeys several times a day in high season to St Malo. Journey takes 1¼ hours. Contact Commodore Shipping Services Ltd, 28 Conway St or Albert Quay, St Helier, tel Jersey 71263. British subjects who don't have passports with them need a 'No-passport Identity Card', valid for 60 hours, which can be obtained from various travel agencies. All others need passports.

ACTIVITIES

Golf: two 18-hole courses by the sea, with bar facilities, clubs for hire to anyone who is a member of a recognised golf club: Royal Jersey Golf Club, Grouville, tel Jersey 51042, and La Moye Golf Club, St Brelade, tel Jersey 43401. Also 9-hole course at Greve d'Azette.
Riding: there are several riding schools. Bon Air Stables, St Lawrence, tel Jersey 63154, are open daily all year. Le Clair Riding and Livery Stable, St John, tel Jersey 62823, have lots of ponies suitable for children. Tuition is available.
Sub-Aqua Diving: visitors are advised to seek local advice before taking the plunge – 40ft tides produce currents as fast as 10 miles an hour. The Jersey Underwater Centre has a school in Bouley Bay which offers individual dives or tuition, tel Jersey 61817, and a shop in First Tower which hires out tanks, wetsuits etc, tel Jersey 32813. They also hire out windsurfing boards.
Surfing: headquarters of the Jersey Surf School at the Watersplash night club on St Ouen's Bay. Tuition fees include use of board and wetsuit. Boards can also be hired separately. Tel Jersey 82886.

Sailing: the two best-known clubs are the St Helier Yacht Club, South Pier, tel Jersey 21307, and the Royal Channel Islands Yacht Club in St Aubin, tel Jersey 41023. Both have facilities for visiting yachtsmen. The Channel Islands Sailing School offers elementary and intermediate courses during the summer: tel Jersey 63286 after 7pm for details.
Walking: there are fine cliff walks along much of the coast – especially nice is the relatively uncluttered north-western tip at St Ouen, where there are exceptional views of Guernsey, Sark and Herm at Grosnez Point, 200ft above sea level. Nearby are the ruins of a 14th c château. 'Walks for Motorists – Jersey' by F. de L Bois is a useful book, (Warne & Gerrard).
Sports and Entertainments: huge complex at Fort Regent, St Helier, with plenty of family-oriented amusements and indoor sports facilities including badminton, tennis, bowls, swimming, table-tennis, squash, rifle and archery ranges and many others. Open daily 10am to 11pm.

EVENTS

Battle of Flowers, 2nd Thurs in Aug annually: breathtaking display of floats made entirely of flowers, worked on for months. After the parade is an evening fête with stage shows and a Gala Ball.
Good Food Festival: every spring Jersey's many excellent restaurants compete. A complete list of winners can be obtained from Tourist Office, St Helier. French, Italian and seafood particularly fine.

INFORMATION

States of Jersey Tourism Office, Weighbridge, St Helier, tel Jersey 78000, has scores of books and pamphlets, including a book with details of access for handicapped people. Also runs room-booking service for personal callers, issues monthly calendar of events. Open May-Oct weekdays 9-9.30pm, Sun 9–12, 7-9.15; Nov-April Mon-Fri 8.45-12.30, 2-5, Sat 9-12.30. *The Jersey Evening Post* is published daily. *The Jersey Sun, What's On in Jersey, Jersey's Weekly Holiday Post* are give-away publications with details of events, activities etc. Available in hotel lobbies and the airport.

Guernsey
WHERE TO GO

ST PETER PORT

Guernsey's capital resembles a sophisticated fishing village. The best view is from Victoria Tower near Candie Gardens – key from the fire station. It's one of three towers which can be seen from the harbour; another is Elizabeth College, a Gothic extravaganza, the third is St James's Church. Residential St Peter Port is characterised by Regency terraced houses, many with distinctive wrought-iron work.

Castle Cornet, the harbour: local shellfish is sold on the causeway leading to the castle, and the circular lighthouse platform is a favourite angling spot. Lit at night, the Norman castle is an impressive sight. Conducted tours daily at 10.45, open daily April-Oct 10.30-5.30. Admission charge. Tel Guernsey 21657. The Noon Gun is fired here every day except Sun.

Town Church, High St: finest church in Guernsey, possibly in the Channel Islands. Chancel is 12th c, south chapel 15th c. Its story is linked more to that of the Duchy of Normandy than of England; inscriptions on the chancel floor are in French.

Guernsey Museum and Art Gallery, Candie Gardens: new and attractive museum of Guernsey history. Many artists, including Renoir, have been impressed by the clarity of the light here, and the art gallery has a good collection of watercolours of the island. In a glass bandstand you can drink tea and look out over lovely Candie Gardens, with its immaculate sweep of lawn towards the sea and gardens with fish-ponds, rock-pools and giant palm trees. A statue of Victor Hugo stands sentry at the top. Open daily mid-March-Sept 10.30-5.30, Oct-mid-March 10.30-4.30. Admission charge. Tel Guernsey 26518.

Hauteville House, Hauteville: home in exile of Victor Hugo, who lived here from 1855 to 1870. Now belongs to the City of Paris. Hauteville has an austere facade and a remarkable interior: a ruby-red drawing-room has damask covering floor, walls

and ceiling; one guest room is all carvings, made out of anything from church pews to chair legs, some carved by Hugo, whose grandfather was a cabinet-maker. The glass-floored look-out at top of the house is where Hugo wrote 'Toilers of the Sea', dedicated to the people of Guernsey. Open daily April-Sept 10-12, 2-4.30, closed Thurs afternoon, Sun and bank hols. Admission charge. Tel Guernsey 21911.

Royal Court, Court Row: granite-fronted late 18th c building housing Guernsey's island parliament, the States of Deliberation or 'the States'. Visitors can listen from the public gallery; the States meet on the last Wed of every month except Aug. Formalities and voting are carried out in French; note the Guernsey flag in front.

Priaulx Library, Candie Rd: old-fashioned public library with chintz-covered chairs, leather-bound books on local history, and a rose garden through the window – perfect for a rainy day. A gift from Osmond de Beauvoir Priaulx who died in 1891. He hasn't gone far; in a small bronze urn by one of the tiled fireplaces are his ashes.

Notre Dame du Rosaire, Burnt Lane: secluded Roman Catholic church has a ceiling built like an upturned boat. On Sundays the Canon, Père Maurice Lecluze, conducts services partly in English, partly in Latin, partly in French. During the summer well-known French musicians play here; check local Press for details.

Shopping: traditional market on

Thurs afternoons in summer with costumes, dancing and local goods, 3pm-sunset. Touristy but fun. Many fine jewellery and shoe shops with names like Béghin's and Machon's, plus all the English chain stores. The High St and its continuation The Pollet are charming small lanes where you can buy fairly inexpensive Continental goods. Buttons Booksellers, Smith St, is best for local books and maps, also tide charts, while Martin's Copper Shop, 2-4 The Pollet, sell fat Guernsey milk-cans. (See *Specialities*.) Most people seem to be buying or wearing Guernseys (see *Specialities*). Thurs market best place for 'seconds' in these.

Shop for food at Market Halls, Market St, like a stately home – all stained glass, turrets and towers. The oldest is the French Halles, originally a meat market, later turned over to the sale of eggs, butter and produce from Brittany – hence the name. Present meat markets date from 1822. All around are fresh fish, especially the giant crab called a chancre, a Guernsey speciality, which can be steamed right in front of you ready for a picnic. To one side of the market is the States of Guernsey Dairy – thick cream and the best milk shakes ever. Early closing day Thurs but in summer shops of particular interest to visitors stay open late every evening.

Eating and Drinking: with wine so inexpensive almost any meal can be a treat. Whistlers Bistro, 3 Lower Hauteville, tel Guernsey 25809, serves steak, seafood and fresh veg from the Market across the road, and a lovely sweet of chocolate and Guernsey cream called 'nearly mousse'. Drinking on Guernsey is basically confined to hotel bars or pubs near the water, popular with sailors and yachtsmen. The Harbour Lights, opposite St Peter Port Marina, serves real ale, and the Wellington Boot, set in the grounds of the Hotel de Havelet in Havelet, has good view of Castle Cornet, floodlit at night.

BEACHES

Locals acknowledge 30 bays around the island. There are others they keep to themselves. The south coast is undoubtedly Guernsey's finest, riddled with private coves and stunning, secluded beaches – hard to find and even harder to invade. The free book-

Victor Hugo's house in St Peter Port, with (left) *the lookout where he wrote* Toilers of the Sea, *and* (right) *the Garibaldi Room.*

let *What's On in Guernsey*, available from hotel lobbies or the Tourist Office, provides an invaluable guide for windy days, detailing which bays are sheltered according to wind direction. There is a machine showing wind direction in the window of the St Peter Port Tourist Office.

Fermain Bay, east coast: popular pebbly beach with sand at half-tide. Go there by launch from Victoria Marina, St Peter Port. Journey takes about 15 minutes. Boatman is an expert on local history; his grandmother used to attend Victor Hugo's Christmas parties.

Cobo Bay, west coast: good for children and great for sunsets. Shores are strewn with rust-coloured boulders which reflect the sun and turn the sea into one huge rosy bath.

SIGHTSEEING

Sausmarez Manor, St Martin's: one of the few Channel Island manor houses open to the public. The de Sausmarez family have been in Guernsey since 1254. Only a fragment of the oldest house remains, additions have been made through the Tudor, Queen Anne, Regency and Victorian eras. The present grey granite facade rather resembles an American colonial house of the early 18th c. One of the most distinctive interior features is a richly carved Burmese teak screen in the hall. Morning coffee, afternoon tea served. Open May-Sept Wed, Thurs, 10-12, 2.30-

5. Admission charge. Tel Guernsey 38323.

National Trust of Guernsey Folk Museum, Saumarez Park, Câtel: museum in stables of an old manor house now used as a hostel for the elderly, reached through attractive gardens and wooded grounds. It consists of several granite buildings set around a courtyard, contains recreations of a traditional Guernsey bedroom and kitchen, dairy equipment and a horse-powered apple crusher. Especially nice are the glassed-in tableaux, eg two ladies dressing for market, made entirely of shells. Museum open daily April-Oct 10-12.30, 2-5.30. Admission charge.

Les Vauxbelets, St Andrew: The Little Chapel, a tiny, shimmering building made entirely of broken glass and china, was the work of Brother Déodat of the Brothers of the Christian Schools order. He wanted to build a grotto like the one at Lourdes, but being penniless had to resort to readily available materials. He began the chapel in 1923. Inside are an altar and small Madonna surrounded by an aureole of ormer shells; the steps were donated by Wedgwood. Be sure to go on a bright day when the glass reflects the sun.

Guernsey Pottery, St Sampson: in a 17th c farmhouse. You can wander round and watch the pottery making, or sit outside and enjoy quiches or afternoon tea. Most of the pottery is stoneware, there are also ash trays and vases in unusual blue and green

shades. Open Easter-Sept daily 10-5.30; Oct-Easter same hours but not Suns. Tel: Guernsey 44282.

Fort Grey Maritime Museum, Rocquaine Bay: connected to the shore by a causeway, the fort was restored by the Ancient Monuments Committee. Devoted entirely to relics of shipwrecks, appropriately enough it is within sight of the notorious west coast reefs responsible for many wrecks, now guarded by Hanois Lighthouse. Open daily May-Oct 10-12.30, 2-5.30. Small admission charge. Tel Guernsey 65036.

Guernsey Tomato Centre, King's Mills, Castel: shrine to the 'Guernsey Tom'. See them, smell them, touch them, even drink them in tomato wine served in adjoining café. Open daily Easter-Oct 10-5.30. Admission charge. Tel: Guernsey 54389.

German Occupation Museum, The Forest: largest display of authentic Occupation relics in the Channel Islands. Open daily April-Oct 10-12.30, 2-5.30. Admission charge. Tel: Guernsey 38205.

Underground German Military Hospital, St Andrew: empty and echoing, the largest structural remnant of the Occupation anywhere in the islands. Very sobering place to visit. Open May-Sept daily 10-12, 2-5, April open Tues, Thurs, Sun 2-5, Oct open Tues, Thurs, Sun 2-4. Admission charge. Tel: Guernsey 39100.

Guernsey Zoo, St Andrew: small zoo concentrating on the smaller mammals and birds. A staff of three aim to help endangered species. Visit and support them; they need the money. Tea barn. Open daily (except Christmas Day) April-Sept 10-6, Oct-March 10-4. Admission charge. Tel: Guernsey 39176.

SPECIALITIES

Guernseys: boatmen, tourists, shopkeepers – everybody wears them, even in the best restaurants in lieu of shirt and tie. Guernseys (never 'guernsey sweaters') were almost certainly developed by the stocking trade which flourished here in the Middle Ages. Knitted without seams, they are virtually wind, spray and snag-proof. Years ago every parish had its own pattern of stitches, given names like 'ladders', 'rope', and 'ripples of the sea'. Guernsey Knitwear, 6 The

One of Guernsey's many bays: What's on in Guernsey *has details of shelter.*

Safe moorings in the harbour at St Peter Port, Guernsey.

Bridge, St Sampson, tel Guernsey 44487, is one of the few shops still specialising in parish designs. Guernseys are available from most fashionable stores all around the islands, but best to buy from shops selling sailing equipment or other utilitarian gear – better quality, more choice and cheaper, too. 'Seconds' on sale at a stall in the traditional Thurs market in St Peter Port.

Milk-cans: lovely hand-made copper cans. The original version came from Normandy in 980AD with the monks who also brought the 'Froment du Léon', ancestor of the famous Guernsey cow. The cans are almost spherical in shape, with a cylindrical neck, designed to use the minimum quantity of metal and hold the maximum of milk. Have them delivered to all parts of the world from Martin's Copper Shop, 2-4 The Pollet, tel Guernsey 21725, or buy them from the Island Craft Centre, Trinity Square – both in St Peter Port.

Water lanes: rugged, picturesque lanes leading to the shore, with a stream running down the centre. The cool water produces ferns of great beauty, as well as nourishing a local plant known as 'stinkin' onions'. Best-known water lanes at Moulin Huet and Petit Bôt.

Vraic-gathering: seaweed provides a cheap fertiliser known locally as vraic (pronounced 'wrack'). Gathered by farmers and stacked so rain washes out salt, the drying piles smell like iodine. Common around coasts. Old photos show horse-drawn carts for the gathering; now modern farm equipment is used.

Day trips to France: Condor operate a hydrofoil service to St Malo. Address: Condor Ltd, Passenger Departures, North Pier Steps, St Peter Port, tel Guernsey 26121. Several travel agencies do excursion trips; inquiries to Picquet House, St Peter Port, tel Guernsey 24677. (For passport requirements see *Jersey, Specialities*.)

ACTIVITIES

Riding: Guernsey Equestrian and Saddlery Centre at Les Grandes Capelles, St Sampson is a British Horse Society-approved school. They have up to 40 horses; also ponies for children. Tuition is available. Rides on the beach before 11am. Open daily all year round. Tel Guernsey 25257.

Golf: only golf course is the 18-hole course on L'Ancresse Common, used by the Royal Guernsey Golf Club, Vale. Tel Guernsey 45070. Bordered on both sides by the sea. Clubs for hire.

Swimming: Beau Séjour Leisure Centre, tel Guernsey 27211, has a 25-metre pool. Four charming salt-water pools near the Aquarium, St Peter Port are best. They catch the sun's rays nicely and have good views of Castle Cornet. Ladies', Gentlemen's, Children's and a Mixed pool. Nominal charge for changing rooms and showers, otherwise free.

Windsurfing: take a 1 or 2-hour lesson on Cobo Bay and learn the basics of this new and exhilarating sport. Tel Guernsey 57417 and ask for Pete.

Sailing: both the Guernsey Yacht Club, Castle Emplacement, St Peter Port, tel Guernsey 22838, and the Royal Channel Islands Yacht Club,

Victoria Pier, St Peter Port, tel Guernsey 23154, offer hospitality to visiting yachtsmen. Beaucette Marina, on the north-east tip of Guernsey, has pontoons with electricity, water and telephone lines. Tel Guernsey 45000 for more information.

Walking: between Havelet Bay, St Peter Port, and Pleinmont Point, Torteval, are 19 miles of paths which offer breathtaking scenery of cliffs, wooded slopes and tiny coves. Jerbourg Point, on the south-east tip, has a magnificent panoramic view. Walks can be planned in sections as there are car parks and bus routes nearby.

EVENTS

Fêtes: the first three Wednesdays and Thursdays of Aug are traditionally given over to regional fêtes, including agricultural shows, stalls and games. Various days in each month are normally dedicated to different regions of Guernsey. Always check local Press for specific locations.

Battle of Flowers: floats made entirely of flowers compete usually on third Thurs in Aug. Occasionally on the fourth Thurs, so it is best to check first with the Tourist Office.

Old bangers knock each other about occasionally on Sun (when tide is out) on beach at Chouêt, near Grand Havre on north-west coast.

Hill Climbs: on Bank Hols motor cycles and go-karts race up steep, twisting Le Valles des Terres hill near St Peter Port.

INFORMATION

States of Guernsey Tourist Office has modern premises at Crown Pier, St Peter Port, tel Guernsey 23552 and can answer questions not only on Guernsey but Sark, Herm and Alderney as well. Their front window contains all sorts of useful clocks and dials showing wind direction, weather reports, temperature which help to plan the day. Open June-mid-Sept weekdays 8.30-8; mid-Sept-end Oct 9-7; Nov-April 9-5. Open Sun April-Oct 10-1, 5.30-7.

The Guernsey coach company is called the Guernsey Railway Co Ltd, having turned to coaches after the

railway folded. Its headquarters are at Picquet House by Albert Pier, St Peter Port – an attractive red and white building rather like a Wild West saloon. Picquet House also acts as Guernsey's main booking centre, offering scores of special island tours, also cruises and boat trips to other islands. Open daily April-Oct 9-6, winter Mon-Fri 9-5.30, Sat 9-1. Tel Guernsey 24678/24677.

The Guernsey Evening Press is published daily, the *Weekly Press* on Thurs. *What's On in Guernsey*, a free booklet, is found in hotel lobbies or given away by suntanned girls at the airport, and includes a monthly list of events, places to see etc.

Alderney

'You either love it or you hate it' is what Channel Islanders say about Alderney – its remoteness from both mainland and more southerly islands produces a rugged, yet engaging character, distinct from the others. Alderney is marginally bigger than Sark and boasts an airport and a large town, St Anne. France rises sharply into focus only 9 miles away across treacherous currents. Pub

hours are based on a loose rota system – each house is open a generous number of weekly hours but they vary according to whim and demand. Many good-natured jokes about locals' fondness for drink – rumour has it that when gales once prevented food ships from landing, aeroplane space was used for booze instead. Good pubs are the Rose & Crown, the Albert, and the Divers, down by the harbour with freshly sanded floors. Strangers don't remain strangers for very long. Young people congregate at the Chez, next to the Chez André Restaurant, and Alderney's oldest pub, the Marais free house, does bar snacks and has restaurant serving full meals lunchtimes and evenings.

Three-quarters of the population live in St Anne. Although buildings around Marais Sq are 18th c, most are 19th c, giving the town uniformity and compactness. Royal Connaught Sq contains Island Hall, once the Governor's House and now Alderney's library, good for books of local interest. Near by is the Folk Museum – curator usually around so just knock – with its room of 'issue' furniture given by the British Government when evacuated islanders returned

Fort Clonque, one of Alderney's twelve Victorian coastal forts.

tidal currents produce dangerous conditions – a challenge to experienced yachtsmen but treacherous to those without local knowledge. Particularly dangerous to those in small craft. Inadvisable to approach Burhou by boat without local consultation first.

No fewer than 12 forts ring Alderney's coasts, built in high Victorian style with moats, towers and private causeways. Some people find them wildly romantic, others stern and graceless, but they certainly distinguish Alderney from the other islands. Fort Raz is a privately-owned oyster-breeding colony. Fort Albert, now fallen into disrepair, commands a stunning view of St Anne and its $\frac{3}{4}$-mile breakwater. Fort Clonque, the most impressive, is rented out as holiday accommodation by the Landmark Trust – write to Shottesbrooke, nr Maidenhead, Berkshire or tel Littlewick Green 3431 for more information. Much accommodation is in hotels or guest-houses although some self-catering is available: write to Tourist Office, States Office, Queen Elizabeth II St, Alderney for a complete list. Tel Alderney 2994.

Alderney would appear to be the final fling for many mainland bangers; newer cars can be hired but the island is so small bicycles are best anyway. Tip: if you go anti-clockwise around Alderney most of the ride is downhill, much less strenuous.

The island's main event is Milk-a Punch Sunday, held the first Sunday in May. Each pub whips up its own punch using milk and rum, dispensing it free to all customers. No one knows how the tradition started – but everybody loves it.

after the 5-year Occupation and found their homes demolished. All over the island occupation relics can be seen: cliffside bunkers now used as flats or store rooms, piles of bricks where a concentration camp stood. There used to be a Russian burial plot on Longy Common; now the sombre Hammond Memorial on the outskirts of St Anne commemorates people of all nationalities who died on Alderney during that period.

St Anne Parish Church is thought by some to be the finest of the Channel Islands' modern churches. With its long drive, undulating cemetery and elaborate tombstones, it looks splendid but spooky when lit through the haze by distant Quèsnard Lighthouse.

The Alderney Sailing Club is open all year round, in summer 24 hours a day, to members of recognised sailing clubs, tel Alderney 2758, and rowing boats or dinghies can be hired from Mainbrayce, tel Alderney 2772. Chandlery and fishing tackle can be bought at the Sail Loft, Braye St. They will also repair sails. There's a 9-hole golf course – on weekdays, tel Alderney 2835. Dave Peacock does round-the-island sea trips, most after-

noons in summer, tel Alderney 2702. These usually take in Burhou Island and the bird colonies. Bays are numerous and pretty – Telegraph Bay in south-west is marked by softly-coloured boulders, worn smooth from the sea and perfect for sunbathing on. In view of the sandy beach is a cave, its outer wall looking like a pink and grey striped beach towel. Les Etacs, in the south, are craggy rocks covered in gannets. Off the southern headland of Longy Bay is the Hanging Rock, in legend the rock formation where a rope would be attached to tow Alderney away – to France, to Jersey, to Guernsey, depending on your source. Some of the coasts' plants are quite rare, and the purple spurge, found in sandy areas, is unique to Alderney.

Burhou is a long, lean island operating as a small bird sanctuary and famous for puffins. Seals can sometimes be seen on the nearby rocks; accommodation is one rebuilt stone hut. Write to Clerk of the States, States Office, Alderney, for details. Lying 1 mile off the north coast, Burhou is separated from Alderney by the Swinge, a passage where the tide flows at a tremendous rate. These

Sark

Great Sark is a rough-diamond shape with Little Sark repeating the pattern: they are joined by La Coupée, a narrow neck of land only a few footsteps wide. Because of its size – 3 by $1\frac{1}{2}$ miles – many think a day is enough time to see the whole island, but with all caves, coves and indentations Sark actually measures 42 miles all round. Best to stay a few days – accommodation is of exceptionally high standard. 'The Good Food Guide' has mentioned three of the six hotels – the Aval du Creux, tel Sark 2036, the Dixcart, tel Sark 2015, and the Petit Champ, tel Sark 2046. The largest on the island is Stocks Hotel, tel Sark 2001. Best to book, or even to arrive, early in the summer when, to paraphrase the postman, the locals are delighted to spy an unfamiliar face; during high season locals are outnumbered by thousands. Write to Tourist Office, Sark, Channel Islands (tel Sark 2262) for complete accommodation list, including flats and cottages for self-catering.

Most of the island's drinking water comes from wells, so if staying in a guest-house, it might be a good idea to buy bottled water to avoid 'Sark tummy'. If you can only spend a day, do what the Serquois do and head for the beaches, like the sweeping Derrible Bay with steps cut into the cliff or sandy Grande Grève. Most beaches are an adventurous scramble to reach, so are fairly empty even during hottest months. Although Sark's attractions are family-orientated – swimming, walking, etc – the inaccessible beaches and favoured transport, the bicycle, lead the Seigneur's wife, Mrs Michael Beaumont, to suggest Sark is best suited for those with children over five.

Over 30 species of butterfly and over 170 species of bird have been recorded on the island, and the road to La Coupée is covered with wild orchids. If you're lucky it's possible to see sea anemones shimmering green, red and yellow on the walls of the Gouliot caves; other caves have names like Heaven, Hell, and Victor Hugo. Caves are best visited with local guidance; persuade a fisherman to take you in his boat or ask the Tourist Office to help.

The present Seigneurie is built on the site of a priory, a rambling granite structure which grew in stages under

Sea view from Sark. In distance, from left, Guernsey on horizon, Jethou and Herm; in middle distance Brechou.

the whims of successive owners from the 10th c onwards. Interior twists and turns, and there are no fewer than 16 flights of stairs excluding those to the windowed signalling tower. The house flag – two Normandy leopards in gold on red – is flown whenever the Seigneur is in residence. Although the house is not open to the public, La Seigneurie's extensive grounds are open every Wed and Fri and include botanical treasures collected by Sark's most famous Seigneur, or in this case La Dame, Dame Sybil Hathaway, on her travels round the world. Near the monk's well is a dovecote, and white fan-tail pigeons roam freely. Dame Sybil is buried in a simple grave in St Peter's churchyard. Note tapestries inside the church, one with a lobster on it. One of these was woven for each of the island's 40 original families.

Sark's mill is immortalised on the Guernsey 2p piece. It was built in 1571 on one of the highest points in the Channel Islands. From here on a clear night you can see lighthouse beacons winking from six different points around the isles and France.

Those approaching La Coupée by bicycle – hired from Jackson's Toystore or from the PO – should have good brakes or a stout heart. This ridge rises a dizzy 300ft above the sea and acts as a natural windcatcher. Passengers in horse-drawn carriages need to dismount, and it's said that children from Little Sark on their way to school had to scale it on hands and knees when the 1811 landslide reduced its width to just a few inches. Sark is for bicycling, or try one of the carriages lined up at the harbour for a moonlight tour of the island. The high-backed victorias are elegant and provide protection in case it rains.

Little Sark is wilder, more melancholy than Great Sark – ponies and horses graze in the sunshine, and abandoned silver mines are silhouetted against the sky. La Sablonnerie hotel, tel Sark 2061, had a licensed tea garden and also does nice lunches with lots of home produce.

Shell Beach on Herm, a conchologist's paradise with millions of minute shells from as far away as Mexico.

Manor House, Herm, lost in the undergrowth.

Herm

Herm lies midway between Guernsey and Sark and is only 500 acres – the sea is never more than a few feet away. On a sunny day it can be seen from St Peter Port harbour, a 20-minute boat ride away. No cars, no buses, no glaring lights and no nightclubs on Herm; it's walking country, basically a Sunday afternoon retreat for the people of Guernsey.

The path from the harbour to the village is lined with hydrangeas and fuchsias, stone cottages are painted pastel shades, and the Argosy gift shop and tiny PO are built in split-level piazza style. Shop does a fine line in Continental goods. The island-made sailing smocks are nice. Herm stamps are sought-after by philatelists. They are on view in the PO, although separate postal system was abolished in 1969.

The island's one hotel – the White House, tel Guernsey 22159 or Herm 83 – offers a sea view from most bedrooms; the diningroom is open to non-residents. There is also some self-catering accommodation. Main meeting spot is the Mermaid Tavern and a few hours in its low-ceilinged bar or grill restaurant should introduce you to everyone on Herm; buy picnic fare in the adjoining snack bar. Only other eating place is the Ship Restaurant, an extension of the White House Hotel.

From the village it's possible to walk all round the coast or direct to Belvoir Bay via a heavily wooded pathway across the centre; this route passes Manor House, an 18th c granite building, now the home of Major Peter Wood. When Major Wood took over the tenancy of the island in 1949 there was no electricity, no roads and it took 3 weeks to find the house in the undergrowth. Current population is 12 families, but in summer day-visitors can number 2,000. Most stick to the beaches, so take a walk instead. Best idea is to stay on Herm, but accommodation is limited. Write to: Administration Office, Herm Island via Guernsey, Channel Islands, for full details. If it's not crowded Belvoir Bay is ideal for family bathing, low and sandy with a beach café and an offshore configuration of rocks called Caquorobert – named after Duke Robert of Normandy's helmet because of its domed shape. Herm's other beach is a conchologist's paradise known as Shell Beach. It is made entirely of bright, minute shells, some washed up from as far away as Mexico.

**Briefing by
Martha Ellen Zenfell**

REVELATION IN THE ROCKS

BY ROBERT MUIR WOOD

Geology knows no boundary like the sea. Islands are no more than hills and mountains whose encircling valleys and cols are all below sea-level. And the sea-level that appears such a permanent geographical base-line is, on the geological time-scale, exceedingly arbitrary; it has risen by well over 100m in the past 20,000 years.

The notion that geology, and therefore rocks, run out at low-tide level is a common one. Before 1970 geological maps always gave the impression that the land was afloat. The 'new geologist' can even be pedantic about John Donne's geographical metaphor validating man's social nature by pointing out that in the sense in which the poet meant it 'no island is an "island"'.

The impetus for continuing the geological mapping underwater has come from the search for petroleum and natural gas. The findings in the waters around Britain were both extraordinary and unexpected. The boundary between land and sea, even among some of the most serrated coastlines and jumbled blocky islands of the north west of Scotland, is not arbitrary. Very often the underwater geology is completely different to that found in the neighbouring islands and coastlines. That familiar profile of a Britain that appears to be falling to bits in the upper left hand corner is no fluke of North Atlantic gales, but a heritage of a period in the past when Britain as an area of continental crust was literally disintegrating.

To understand the individual *raison d'être* of the British islands, it is worth giving a brief history of the region during the last 500 million years – a story rich in geo-political ironies. A little over 400 million years ago the two sides of an earlier Atlantic Ocean came together in a collision along a line that passes between Scotland and England and diagonally NE-SW across Ireland. During the 100 million year build-up to this collision, the northern side had been engaged in mountain building on the scale of the Andes. This union between Europe and America was not well cemented. Major rifts started developing between Greenland and Norway soon after 400 million years ago, and then around 300 million years ago both between Britain and Scandinavia and between Scotland allied with England and Ireland allied with Wales. The latter pair of Celtic landmasses were still firmly bonded to North America. This rifting was propagating from the North; to the South there were a complex series of mountain-building episodes that disrupted much of south-west England and south Wales. Eventually more rifting arrived from the south-west first separating what is now the sunken continent of Rockall (with its single ridiculous 20m high remainder) from Ireland and Scotland, and then about 60 million years ago, opening up a new ocean more or less on the lines of the old one, between Greenland plus North America and Europe. The sense of *déjà vu* in this state of affairs was only broken by the transfer of the Scotland/Northern Ireland package from Greenland to Europe. The North Atlantic continues widening at a few centimetres each year.

Two kinds of information are needed to understand the existence of islands: how and when the fabric was laid down; and when and why this fabric was carved into shape. Sometimes the former dictates the latter; sometimes the two are entirely unrelated.

The most noticeable feature of the distribution of the British Isles is that the eastern side is almost island-free. The most successful of all the rifts that formed around the north-west of Europe is now what is known as the North Sea – a wide tensional basin that is still sinking, dragging such regions as south-east England down with it. On the east coast of Scotland this basin is fault-bounded by a set of fractures that ensures that the

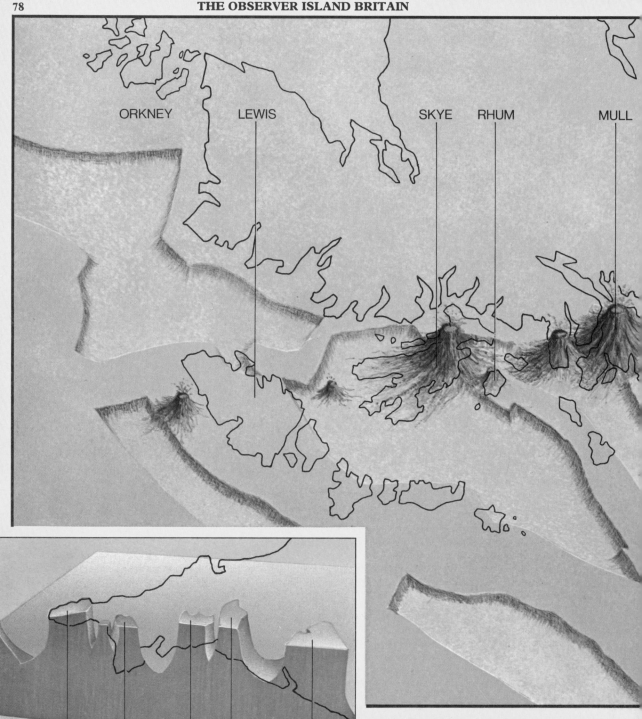

ORKNEY　　LEWIS　　SKYE　RHUM　　MULL

SCILLIES　LANDS END　CARUMENELLIS　BODMIN MOOR　ST AUSTELL　DARTMOOR

The Isles of Scilly. 300 million years ago, an enormous
body of granitic magma oozed to the surface in a series
of giant columns beneath what is now south-west
England. The resistant granite now forms the uplands;
the whole crust later slumped to the west, leaving the
Scillies as a submerged 'Dartmoor'.

REVELATION

Scotland's Islands. 250 million years ago, at a
time when Britain was stranded as a kind of
Mongolia in the middle of a continent made up
of Europe, Greenland and North America, the
crust of Britain began to be stretched apart.
This stretching continued intermittently for 200
million years. Britain became fractured into
blocks – some sections of the crust foundered

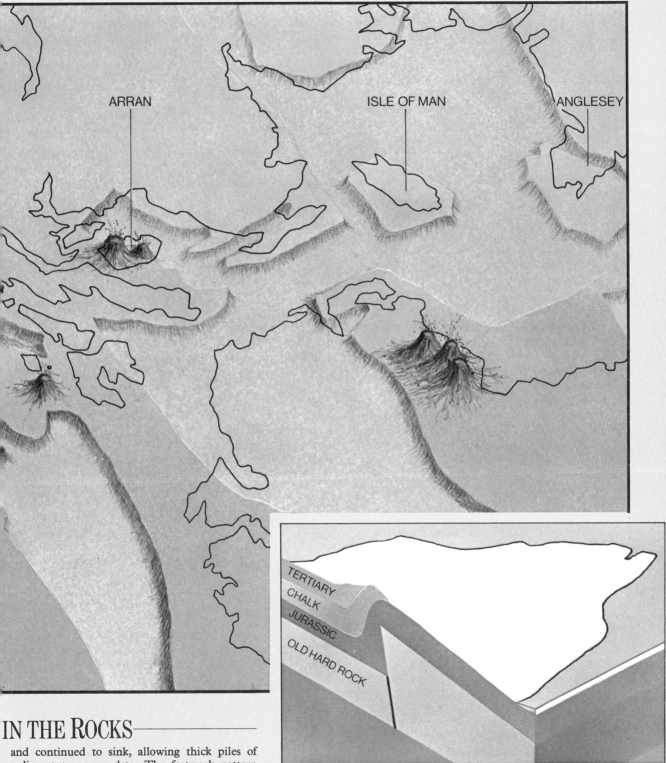

ARRAN

ISLE OF MAN

ANGLESEY

TERTIARY

CHALK

JURASSIC

OLD HARD ROCK

IN THE ROCKS

and continued to sink, allowing thick piles of sediment to accumulate. The fretwork pattern of north-west Britain is a heritage from two episodes: this stretching, which produced the major crazy paving – in this case an exaggerated scarp between high and low blocks, and younger volcanoes (only 60 million years old) with cones eroded away – as at Skye, Mull, Rhum and Arran.

The Isle of Wight. Only 15 million years ago, the south of England was probably as earthquake-ridden as Algeria is today. Beneath the Isle of Wight, Africa's drift into Europe was forcing up the south side of the island along a pre-existing fault to form the Isle of Wight Downs.

land-sea boundary is sudden and unambiguous. Off the English coast – apart from a range of estuarial mudbanks around the mouth of the Thames – there is only a small sprinkling of islands off the north Northumberland coast. These are all associated with the Whin Sill, formed from the solidification of a basaltic magma intruded into the layers of carboniferous limestone to form a hard band averaging about 30m in thickness. The Whin Sill is an important piece of landscape ornamentation inland, where it forms cliffs that reinforce the fortifications along some of the central sections of Hadrian's Wall, and provides the lip of the High Force waterfall in Teesdale. The coastal outcrop has produced the Farne Islands. The sill was injected into this region 295 million years ago as the North Sea crust began to be extended; a large vertical sheet (or dyke) of the same rock is aligned east-west to form the southern boundary of nearby Lindisfarne.

The oldest rocks of the British Isles are found at the margins of the original 400-million-year-old, 'Caledonian' collision. They are all 'metamorphic' rocks that have suffered considerable burial and transformation deep in the crust. Those that make up the Lewisian gneisses of the Outer Hebrides give radio-isotope ages of around 2,900 million years; those from the Icart and Perelle gneisses of the Channel Islands around 2,600 million years. (The Earth itself was born about 4,550 million years ago.)

On geological grounds the Channel Islands are part of France. They have suffered a very complex, but entirely French, history, involving mountain building around 1,950 million years ago, and episodes of granitic intrusion, metamorphism and volcanic activity between 700 and 550 million years ago. They are connected, as if they are hills on underwater ridges, with the mainland to the east, although the island of Alderney is on a rigid block of continental crust that is separated from the block of Guernsey and Sark by an east-west tongue of younger sedimentary formations. The island of Jersey is on yet another block. All three of these blocks survived more or less unscathed a violent phase of mountain-building that was taking place all around them about 300 million years ago. It was during this period that an enormous volume of granitic magma accumulated below what is now the south-west peninsula of England, to form a huge ENE intrusion or 'batholith', at least 200kms long. This intrusion is still buried 12kms underground but some of its magma managed to bulge closer to the surface forming great *cupolas* of granite that rise like towers from the main buried mass. On land these towers reach the surface at

Dartmoor, Bodmin Moor, St Austell, Carnmenellis and Land's End. The granite is hard, and at each place forms rounded uplands. Where the rock breaks surface it is sculpted into piles of bulbous slabs – the tors. The whole batholith and its cupolas has tilted – the western end sunk at the edge of the Atlantic Ocean. The last of the uplands and the last of the visible cupolas forms the Scilly Isles, which with their inlets and sounds, are easy to imagine as an almost entirely submerged Dartmoor.

During the same general period the rocks of Devon and Cornwall, as well as the southern margins of Wales, became deformed into a series of large folds in which rock layers once horizontal are now nearly vertical. Such folds may expose in a small area a variety of rocks of differing resistance to erosion. Along the south Pembrokeshire coast the folds run east-west. Immediately south of Tenby a resistant band of Devonian rocks has protected some softer carboniferous rocks that lie closer to the centre of the 'U' of the fold, and so formed Caldey Island. Further to the west the Devonian sandstones lying at the core of one of these folds have remained to form the island of Skokholm, while the softer, older rocks originally exposed to either side, have been eroded away. Only a short distance to the north, much older (500-million-year) Ordovician rocks are exposed that were deformed during the 400-million-year-old Caledonian period of continental collision and mountain-building. During the Ordovician period this region was a muddy sea through which volcanoes occasionally emerged to pour out lava and so build for themselves islands. Both the modern islands of Skomer and Ramsay are made out of thick piles of volcanic basalts and rhyolites – at Skomer almost 1,000m of them. Both islands probably lie close to their respective volcanoes, but it is a combination of folding and vulcanism that had produced the greatest concentration of hard, resistant volcanic rocks at these two locations. The Skomer Island volcanic ridge follows the line of the fold and emerges further to the west as Grassholm Island and the treacherous reefs of The Smalls.

Many geologists have secretly wished that the island of Anglesey could have been conveniently submerged – so complicated is its geology, and so different to that of most of the rest of Wales. It only qualifies as an island through the work of two small streams that carved themselves narrow valleys during the lowered sea-level of the last glaciation. At the top of the pass between them, now submerged, the Menai Straits are only 12m deep. The two streams employed a line of geolo-

Dun and Hirta. The St Kilda archipelago shows the most sensational offshore geology in Britain.

gical weakness that follows the Dinorwic Fault – last active in 1903 when a small earthquake knocked down a few chimney pots in Caernafon. The bulk of Anglesey is composed of a 10,000m thick pile of coarse-grained marine sandstones that towards the top become interlayered with limestones, cherts and basalts, all deposited at the end of the pre-Cambrian period, about 700 million years ago. The upper part of the pile is extremely badly deformed, with large rock fragments chaotically intermixed within giant underwater landslides, operating as the sediments were accumulating on steep slopes adjacent to an ocean basin. Some of these rocks have been metamorphosed to form schists and gneisses at temperatures high enough to cause rock-melting. All of them have been folded both on a large and a small scale (as can be seen in the cliffs at South Stacks on Holy Island) and intruded by large masses of basalt and serpentinite (resembling ocean-floor crust), and later by granites that provide radio-isotope ages of about 600 million years. To the south of the island there are some high-pressure, low-temperature metamorphics known as blueschists that are characteristic of regions where, according to the theory of plate tectonics, oceanic crust is being dragged down into the upper mantle, as under the west coast of South America and the east coast of Japan. The island of Anglesey is just big enough to tantalise geologists and yet too small to provide an unambiguous history. Parallels have been made

with the modern coastal areas of California, yet telescoped into a much smaller area. Oceans were being created and destroyed around Anglesey 700 million years ago, but exactly how big, or how many they were may never be known.

Having concluded its geological adventures, Anglesey became a region of mountains that during the next 100 million years fed sediment south into Wales and north into a small basin cutting across the Irish Sea. After the 400-million-year collision, granitic magmas collected in great intrusions beneath the central part of the collision zone. These granites are less dense than the rocks around them, and through their buoyancy appear to have raised repeatedly localised parts of northern England, such as the north Pennines and Cumbria. One of these granites lies in the centre of the Irish Sea – more isolated than its eastern cousins, it has still managed to support 620m high Snaefell and the surrounding Isle of Man. The covering sediments are still more or less intact and the granite only peeps through in a few eastern outcrops.

Also following the great collision, various regions of the crust around Britain changed from mountains into sinking basins. The largest of these was in the far north-east. Buried under the thick red sandstones, shales and volcanics of Orkney there is a partly mountainous landscape made out of the hard crystalline Caledonian metamorphic rocks, that only outcrop at a few locations around Stromness. The islands were uplifted and tilted to the east during the opening of the North Atlantic; the streams that began their courses on the highest ground to the west (as is still seen in the island of Hoy) joined to form ESE flowing rivers whose valleys are now all flooded by the sea; the intervening hills have undergone the sea-change into islands.

If the Orkneys resemble a giant tilted paving slab, the Shetlands are a mosaic of intricate lapidary. The British Continental platform is being narrowed to the north by NE–SW faults that mark the edge of the Atlantic and by N–S faults that run down the margins of the North Sea. As the platform becomes pinched out, so it also has risen up to form the Shetlands. The Devonian Old Red Sandstones of Orkney continue northwards under the sea and have been lifted up by the main bulge of Shetland, to outcrop on the tiny island of Papa Stour, and in the far north-west peninsula of Mainland Shetland around Esha Ness. To the east of the NNE trending Melby Fault that forms the boundary to these rocks, the islands have an entirely different history.

Peninnis Head, St Mary's. A fantastic Scillonian outcrop of Henry Moore-like granite.

Throughout western mainland there is a patchwork of 350 million-year-old granites intruded into sediments metamorphosed around 400 million years ago, that have few similarities with comparable rocks from Scotland. To the south of this zone there are Devonian strata that formed in the midst of mountains, and volcanoes and that have suffered considerable folding long after the rest of Scotland had begun to enjoy a period of relative calm. Running down the west side of Sullom Voe there is another major fault – the Walls Boundary Fault that cuts north-south across central Shetland. To the east of it the rocks are different again. An enormous 25 km thick pile of metamorphosed sediments has been tilted almost vertical. Plastered

onto their eastern end in Unst and Fetlar there are huge slabs of serpentinite and metamorphosed gabbro – rocks more typical of ocean crust. The Devonian rocks on top of these formed between mountains to the west and a lake to the south-east. This eastern section of Shetland has a history similar to that found among the Caledonian rocks of Norway. The three separate histories found in an east-west traverse across the islands have become juxtaposed through considerable horizontal movements along the major faults with those regions to the east moving south. The Walls Fault has become linked on many maps with the Great Glen Fault that cuts across Scotland. Such great 'strike-slip' faults are common in modern regions of continental collision and mountain building, such as central Asia.

The final shaping of Shetland came from ice; during the last Ice Age it even had its own ice-cap to compete with the great ice-sheet pouring off Scandinavia. The glacial valleys, now drowned to form the Shetland voes, have often followed the major faults – zones of weakness.

The crustal tension that has asserted itself at odd periods throughout Britain's geological history had its greatest success around 300 million years ago in a phase of rifting that passed down the west coast of Scotland through into the Irish Sea and the Cheshire Basin. The region was turned into crazy paving, defined by the pattern of sunken blocks that even cut through the 2,900 million year old Lewisian gneisses of north-west Scotland. On the eastern side of the Lewisian Outer Hebrides, the Minch Fault marks the boundary of a deep sedimentary basin. A similar fault runs NE–SW on the south-east side of the block that contains Tiree, Coll and a small southern patch of Skye.

Nearer to the zone of continental collision the crust is made from Caledonian metamorphics and intrusives – as in the southern and eastern Highlands. Such rocks have survived in the islands of Colonsay, Islay and Jura, whose shapes are again defined by the surrounding deep sedimentary basins. Apart from Cheshire where the sediments have been uplifted on the shoulders of the neighbouring uplands of Wales and Lancashire, we would never find these sediments exposed at all on land if it had not been for another incident that was taking place underneath Britain a mere 60 million years ago.

As the North Atlantic was about to open, a 'thermal' of upwelling hot, deep mantle material was rising under Western Scotland. As it was rising it began to melt, generating basaltic magmas. These magmas first erupted through great fissures in the sedimentary basins to form up to 2 km of thick basalt lava-flows over wide areas of the regions that are now north Skye, Mull and Antrim, but much of which is still hidden underwater. For some reason, perhaps because the heat was in places melting wide tunnels through the crust, this diffuse pattern of basalt distribution became a centralised process of giant volcanoes. The ruined remains of these volcanoes now make up much of the islands of St Kilda, Skye, Rhum, Mull and Arran. Sometimes the volcano shifted its centre through time, as on Mull and Arran. On several of these volcanic islands it is now possible to walk into the magma chambers, once 1,200°C in temperature and buried deep in the volcano's belly. Great conical sheets of frozen magma indicate sudden explosive episodes of volcanic uplift, and in Skye and Rhum one can trace the internal records of scores of eruptions. The grandeur of the Skye Cuillins has been carved from Skye's very own red-hot magma factory.

Britain then re-entered a new tensional phase. The crust began to split along NW–SE fractures that were being created by high pressure basaltic magma rising from the underlying mantle. These infilled fissures, or dykes, cut across western Scotland, Northern Ireland and run as far as northeast England and north Wales. Around the volcanic centres of Skye, Mull and Arran the presence of buried volumes of high pressure magma caused the lines of relative crustal weakness to deflect and appear to radiate from these centres, like the lines of flux around a magnet. Such a pattern has given the deceptive and entirely erroneous impression that the magma in the Cleveland Dyke of north Yorkshire actually travelled horizontally from the volcano on Mull!

The amount of crustal extension associated with these dykes reaches a maximum of around 7 per cent on the south coast of Arran. The widespread availability of the underlying magma source is shown by the existence of Lundy Isle in the Bristol Channel. The island is made of granite that formed near a basaltic volcano that was erupting at the same time as the volcanoes of western Scotland. The magma chose to emerge along a weakness in the crust associated with the seaward extension of the NW–SE trending Sticklepath Fault of north Devon. The Lundy volcano itself now lies underwater, a little to the north of the island.

After these volcanic fireworks had celebrated the opening of the Atlantic, the region became quiet once again; except to the far south where Africa was busy grinding its way inexorably into Europe. In the south-east of England, sediments had been building up in basins created by downfaulted blocks. As the compression increased further to the south so it began to influence England – the downfaulted blocks started to move up again carrying with them their thick piles of sediments. While Switzerland got the Alps, England grew the gentle folds that formed the Chilterns and the north and south Sussex Downs. The most impressive of all these folds is found in the Isle of Wight where beneath the central Downs a couple of underlying east-west faults run close to one

Prehistoric volcanic convulsions produced the extraordinary rock formations of Staffa, Mendelssohn's inspiration.

another. The Downs were built through the compressional uplift of the southern block by a total of 1,200 m. The movements at depth have created a massive bend in the overlying chalks of the Cretaceous and clays of the Tertiary. The faults swing around to run NW–SE further up the Channel and have suffered less reactivation; hence the Solent Water of Southampton is a south-east-trending drowned river valley. The ridge that is the backbone of the lozenge-shaped Isle of Wight was once connected with the Purbeck Ridge further to the west, but a combination of river erosion and rising post-glacial sea-levels created the island.

The great Ice Age freeze had other cosmetic effects in shaping the British islands. The snow and ice that built up at the base of the perimeter island slopes helped oversteepen them so that many island profiles now present an unnaturally austere silhouette. The vertical chalk layers that form the castellations of the Needles testify to both the island makers: to erosion and to greater earth movements. There cannot be many citizens of the Isle of Wight who realise it is the advance of Africa that they have to thank for the very existence of their peaceful island retreat.

ROBERT MUIR WOOD

THE INNER HEBRIDES

Islay·Jura·Colonsay·Mull·Iona·Staffa·Coll·Tiree

BY JOHN HILLABY

From the Mull of Kintyre to the topmost tip of Skye, the west coast of Scotland has an uncommonly dissipated appearance on the map. The headlands are slashed by sea lochs and studded with a multitude of islands that look as if they've been shoved in like ill-fitting parts of a jigsaw puzzle. Their purpose, you might think, was to protect Drum Albyn, the great ridge of the Highlands, from the ravages of the Atlantic. But the forces that beset the landscape were plutonic not marine. Staffa is the best-known witness to that prehistoric upheaval. There the basaltic columns, like those on the Giant's Causeway in Ulster, are the petrified barometers of enormous heat and pressures deep below the earth's crust.

Plump cherub on a quayside fountain in Tobermory Harbour.

Beneath the corrie and the
    laval flow
I kindled here upon the rocks
The flame of flowers they
    did not know.
The peat rejects my paradox,
My will upon them will not
    grow.

He wrote those lines while cruising for five days without seeing a shark. And then, after getting a signal from the keeper of the lighthouse at Barra Head, he harpooned two between Staffa and Erisgeir to the west of Mull. Instant jubilation. When Maxwell went below to open some bottles of old stuff, I handled a ship's wheel for the first time in my life and headed north in ecstasy, trepidation and golden Hebridean light. Since that memorable occasion, I have seen

What happened is that during the Tertiary period of about 60 million years ago, at least one enormous volcano on the island of Mull blew its top with such violence that the sides caved in, leaving behind a gaping crater, insecurely plugged. Unable to escape in quantity, searing hot beds of lava were squeezed out sideways. In a series of cataclysms, the lava beds were buckled and pierced and the rocks around them baked by volcanic fires that left little or no trace of what the landscape originally looked like. From almost any point around Mull you may see the worn-down wrecks of those convulsions, especially in the bulk of Ben More, usually with her shoulders aloof in the clouds. Mull is very wet.

It seems an age ago since I first saw that louring land mass from the bridge of The Sea Leopard, the launch fitted out for hunting basking shark by the late Gavin Maxwell, that man of many parts, poet, painter and author of best-sellers. But his plans to establish an oil factory on Soay, a little pocket handkerchief of an island close to Skye, were frustrated at every turn. The huge, black, harmless fish were, to say the least, elusive and he ran into marketing problems.

Ben More in all her humours: black and menacing against storm clouds, grey as a dove's wing at dawn and curiously disembodied when mists hang over the Firth of Lorn, effectively isolating Mull from the mainland.

Although the island is only about 30 miles from north to south, it is split up into very different sorts of terrain by the deep sea lochs of na Keal and Scridain. The country to the north of Ulva and Salen is somewhat sniffily referred to as 'Surrey with a tartan fringe' by those who live in austerity on the Ross of Mull. The southerners, in turn, are called 'peat bog Arabs' by incomers who do their shopping in Tobermory rather than Craignure where the boats from Oban come in. The Mullochs, the natives and a distinct minority, seem rather amused by it all. Traditionally the big houses were often in the hands of the English. Certainly the north is more wooded, more gentle and more cultivated in aspect than the rest, but by far the wildest country lies between the two.

A substantial grasp of it can be had from a car trip on (just) passable roads south-west from Salen on the Sound of Mull to the hazardous Gribun and from thence via Glen Seilisdeir and Kilfinichen to

Loch na Keal, Mull, with Eorsa at centre.

Craignure on the seemingly endless ups and downs through Glen More, probably the wildest road on the island. In this way you will have girdled all but the easternmost terraces and screes of Ben More. Passing places are plainly marked and local bus drivers can be relied on for their skill and courtesy. But a word of warning. Unless you are prepared to play Russian roulette with large lumps of basalt that crash down on to the Gribun road from the heights of Coire Bheinn after frosts and heavy rain, ask local folk what conditions are like ahead. Under a boulder bigger than the original building, you can still see the remains of a little cottage. A crofter and his bride died there on their wedding night. On the anniversary of the tragedy, flowers are still placed on the stone, which I take to be as kindly a thought as that of the piper, blind Ronald Dall, who, to keep him in touch with affairs, regularly played for St Michael in his grave.

There is one other geological spectacle that should on no account be missed even if it entails nothing more athletic than looking at the Ardmeanach through field-glasses from the road along the south shore of Loch Scridain, the one that runs down to Fionnphort and the ferry for nearby Iona. To the west of Ardmeanach lies the Wilderness, a headland freaked into savage beauty by the explosion of Ben More. Here you may see terrace upon terrace of grey-black lava which, from the sea or the loch, looks like a gigantic staircase or a petrified waterfall. To reach that desolation on foot entails a 10-mile trudge from – and back to – Kilfinichen Bay or a longer scramble around the headland where you can take in Mackinnon's Cave, thought by Dr Johnson to be the greatest native curiosity he saw on his Scottish Tour.

Ponies wandering along the shore at Leargybreck, Jura.

For the rest, Mull is mostly covered by heather and peat bogs relieved by sage-green bog myrtle and cotton-grass with its blobs like candy-floss. Apart from the dismal corduroy of conifers planted by the Forestry Commission, uncultivated trees are relatively rare. A pity this because, through bad land management, bracken now grows profusely on basaltic soils that should be providing sweet pasturage for those superbly well-adapted beasts, Highland cattle.

Mull, like most of the West Highlands, was grossly depopulated by the evictions of the early part of the 19th century when sheep were accounted far more important than farmers. Sheep can look after themselves. The silent witnesses to that tragedy are piles of nettle-strewn rubble, the ruins of ancient crofts. This is *larach*, 'the place that was', and as some bard sadly put it, 'The world is strewn with shingle from the dwellings of the past.'

The island has sustained invasions for thousands of years. Among the first known inhabitants were an Iron Age people who left behind forts of sophisticated construction called brochs, in shape not unlike modern cooling towers with their pinched-in waists. Today the ivy-covered ruins are tenanted only by owls and redstarts.

Local opinion is that Mull was once divided between Picts and Gaels – Scots from the Irish kingdom of Dalriada – along the natural boundary of Glen More. Opinion is distinctly divided about what the great clan chieftains did or not do for their tenants-in-fee. Strife was widespread and treachery not uncommon. The inter-relationships of the far-flung Macleans resemble in complexity those of the Habsburgs and Bourbons. Their ancestral home, Duart Castle, an outstanding landmark, stands, like much else, on an outcrop of lava.

It's difficult to set down plainly what makes this

group of islands and its thin scattering of local folk different from almost anywhere else. There is first that Hebridean light, which ranges from exceptional clarity to a sort of misty opalescence in which there are no boundaries between the sea and the sky. At such times the clouds come down to earth like the gods of old, and only objects in the immediate foreground such as a broch or a ruined keep mark the shores of creation and void space.

There is more than a hint of this changeableness in the speech of native oldsters, punctuated as it is now and again with unexpected directness, bordering on rancour: a curious trait in people notable for their courtesy. This duality of character seems to be reflected in the Gaelic names of the much-venerated St Columba of Iona, who was called both *Crimthan* – 'Wolf' – and *Colum Cille* – 'the Dove of the Church'.

There are several accounts of why he left his native Ireland in his 42nd year. Some critical biographers say he participated in gross atrocities at the bloody battle of Cooldrevne (561AD) and reached Iona, where he could no longer see Ireland, as an act of penance. Another story is that shortly after he arrived with 12 disciples, Columba declared that human sacrifice was necessary to ensure their success. His old friend Oran volunteered to be put down, literally, and was duly buried alive. Three days later Columba, eager for a last sight of him, or perhaps hoping for a miracle, had him exhumed. Oran did, in fact, open his eyes, but instead of saying something pious he declared: 'There is no wonder in death, nor is hell as it is reported.' Whereupon Columba ordered him to be re-interred immediately, shouting, as his monks wielded their spades, 'Earth, earth on Oran's eyes, lest he blab further.'

The story might reflect a Druidic tradition. It is, however, a matter of fact that, under the guidance of that shrewd man, evangelists trained on Iona not only kept the spirit of the Celtic Church alive, but carried it throughout Europe together with their skills in Celtic art.

Iona is a very small island, but such is the reputation of that saint of royal descent that tourists pour in. Over half a million arrived in 1979. As the majority make straight for the Abbey, the Nunnery and other famous sites near the jetty, those places should be inspected early and the rest of the day devoted to the strangely quiet *machair*, the bright-white shell beaches where blue butterflies dance over sea-pinks, wild asters and blood-red crane's-bills like flickering flames. To the south are lonely beaches where you may find banded agates and sea-green serpentine smoothed by the waves.

Throughout the length of Iona there is scarcely a pool, a well or a landmark without some association with the man who was the wolf of the clans and a dove among the churches. There is the Bay of the Coracle where he landed; the Rock of Erin where, briefly, he looked back; the Place of Angels where he conversed with the almighty ones and that hill, Dun-I (pronounced 'doon-ee'), which he ascended, slowly, to look round the islands for the last time. From that same hill near the Abbey you may still survey outermost Gaeldom.

To the north beyond Staffa and the Treshnish Isle lie Coll and a speck far away which is Barra in the Outer Hebrides. They appeared as fins of basking shark. I turned round to find that Colonsay and the Paps of Jura had loomed up behind the cliffs of Mull whilst to the west no land was nearer than Labrador.

JOHN HILLABY

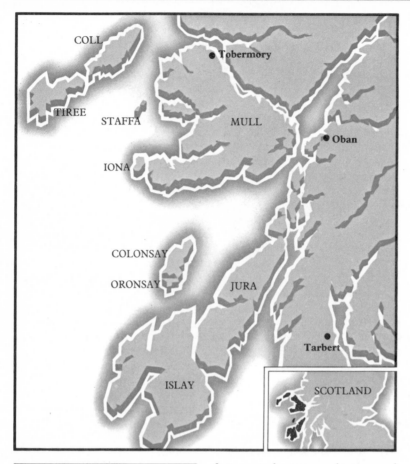

Donald; his grandson Donald of Islay named the clan. Their power in the Hebrides steadily grew. Donald's great-grandson John took the title of Lord of the Isles, and ruled the Hebrides from Islay as a power in his own right, making treaties with England, France and Ireland. Islay passed – like much of the Hebrides – into Campbell hands early in the 17th c. In 1726 it was bought by a Glasgow merchant, Daniel Campbell. As it was not directly involved in the '45 rising, Islay escaped the worst severities of English occupation and punitive clearances, although it had its share of these – to make room for sheep – in the 19th c.

WHERE TO GO

Bowmore: island's administrative centre, with hospital, police station, school, bus depot, off-licence and half a dozen shops. Founded in 1767. Topping the wide main street, which leads down to pier, is Kilarrow Church, built at same time by Daniel Campbell, island's main proprietor, 'for the study of piety, and the culture of truth and honour'. He also built it, the story goes, so that the Devil couldn't find a corner to hide in – it's a round church, whose adjoining tower is crowned by stone octagons, surmounted by a cupola. The distillery here, dating from 1779, has a museum: in summer short tours can usually be arranged twice daily. Four hotels: the Lochside (tel Bowmore 244) includes trout fishing in tariff. For information about local bus service, boat hire, riding and other activities, try, in season (May-Sept), Tourist Office caravan in Bowmore (tel Bowmore 254).

Bridgend: hamlet in wooded, sheltered terrain with a Lowland look, filling station, PO-general store. Bridgend Hotel, recommended, arranges fishing, wildfowling, deer-stalking (tel Bowmore 212).

Port Charlotte: tiny, neat and ultra-tidy, even for Islay: created early last century *ab novo* by Rev Malcolm Maclaurin. Has printers, creamery – where local cheese is made for export – garage, two grocery shops. Port Charlotte Hotel, with its own shooting rights, can arrange fishing trips, offers bar snacks and self-catering accommodation (tel Port Charlotte

Islay

Islay is the most southerly, the most fertile (500 farms), the greenest and yet the most industrialised of the Hebrides. From north to south it is 25 miles: at its widest, 20 miles; but there are some 150 miles of motoring road (most single-track, some roughish going). Area, 235 square miles, much of it trackless peat-bog and moorland. Relatively flat: highest peak is Beinn Bheigeir, 1,609ft. Landscape dominated by the Paps of Jura, Islay's island neighbour. Two huge sea lochs on the west coast – Indaal and Gruinart – are separated by an isthmus 2 miles wide, linking the main Islay with the Rhinns peninsula. Population under 4,000, compared with nearly 15,000 in 1831.

Don't expect the landscape here, or elsewhere in the Inner Hebrides, to be labelled and signposted, if you're looking for, say, footpaths, lochs and antiquities. (Islay preserves the remains of 125 drystone duns – ancient forts – and many curious carved stones. At Trudernish Point is one of best examples of vitrified forts in Scotland.) You'll need local guidebook (variably dependable) and up-to-date ordnance map (indispensable). Don't always be put off by what seems to be a private entrance. Unless there's an uncompromising 'No admittance' or 'Keep out' notice, it may well be the route you want and that you're free to follow.

History: for some 300 years from the 6th c, Islay was part of the Scots kingdom of Dalriada. With the rest of the Western Islands, it fell under Norse rule from c 850 to c 1150. The Norwegians were driven out of the southern Hebrides in 1156 in a seabattle off Islay, when Somerled, king of Argyll, defeated his brother-in-law Godred, Norse King of the Isles. (The Hebrides were finally ceded by Norway to Scotland a century later in 1266.) Somerled, who had been invited by the men of Islay to liberate them, settled in the island and became the progenitor of the Clan

219). There's a comfortable self-service café, the Croft Kitchen. Across the road is the Islay Folk Museum: excellent little historical-archaelogical collection, with reference library, open all year Mon-Fri except Thurs mornings, May-Sept 10-5, Oct-April 10-4.30. Small admission charge for adults. Tel Port Charlotte 358.

Ballygrant: PO, village hall, shop, and modern hotel just beyond the village on the road to Port Askaig. A mile north, invisible from the road, is Finlaggan: a lonely loch with two tiny islands where, once upon a time, the Lords of the Isles ruled their world. The museum guide describes Finlaggan and its ruins as 'possibly the most important place in Islay'. It features on postcards: but be warned – visitors are officially forbidden by the proprietors of the land.

Port Askaig: tiny harbour-hamlet, with a lifeboat station and PO-cum-general store-cum filling station by the Jura ferry. Islay's second port: see *How to get there*. The excellent Port Askaig Hotel (tel Port Askaig 245), dates back to the 18th c and incorporates a 16th c inn. The Dunlossit estate, high above, includes three lochs – Ballygrant, Lossit and Allan, said to offer the island's best trout-fishing.

SIGHTSEEING

Oa (pronounced O): wildest part of 'Green and Grassy Islay', inhabited mainly by birds (including choughs), sheep and wild goats. Peninsula dotted with small lochs, ringed with caves, imbued with a melancholy power of its own. Bumpy road across most of it ends at Upper Killeyan, where a path leads to clifftop monument – on the Mull of Oa – erected by US Red Cross in memory of Americans who died in World War I wrecks here. On a clear day, you can see the Irish coast, which at the nearest point is no more than 23 miles away.

Kilchiaran: ruined 14th c chapel, on west coast of the Rhinns; built on a green plateau, with a path going down to a sandy bay where the Vikings and, some say, St Columba landed.

Kilchoman: a few miles north of Kilchiaran, but you have to get back to the Port Charlotte road if you're

The Jura Ferry by the quay-side at Port Askaig.

driving there. The road ends at the derelict 19th c church, closed to visitors: it's dangerous, like the currents in sandy Machir Bay, below the nearby coastguard's. It's the Celtic cross in the churchyard that draws people here.

Ardnave: the public road stops short of a castellated farm; the loch here contains the remains of a crannog (lake dwelling). From here you can walk freely through the marram grass and sand-dunes, riddled with rabbit-warrens, to Ardnave Point, which pushes out into the Atlantic, with fine views. On the way, down a track towards the sea, you can see Kilnave chapel, with a cross dating from c 750. Here 30 invading Macleans took refuge in 1598: the Macdonalds, enraged by the death of their chief,

set the chapel on fire and burned them alive.

Robert Epps runs combined fishing/seal spotting trips from Ardnave to Nave Island. Tel Port Charlotte 343.

Lagavulin Bay: a mile up east coast from Port Ellen. Now overlooked by the Lagavulin distillery, it was the haven for generations of the Macdonalds' fleet of war-galleys (Nyvaigs) from 12th c onwards. Perched on a rock above the bay are the ruins of Dunyvaig (Dun Naomhaig) Castle, once a stronghold of the Lords of the Isles.

Kildalton: ruined chapel in beautiful hillside setting on the wooded Ardtalla estate, about 8 miles north of Port Ellen on east coast road (which ends 2 miles further on). Set among

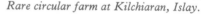

Rare circular farm at Kilchiaran, Islay.

birch and hazel. Rich assortment of carved slabs and effigies, and a tall Celtic cross on a plinth, with carvings of Biblical scenes and animals : ranked with St Martin's on Iona as Scotland's finest.

SPECIALITIES

Birds: about 240 species visit Islay, 110 breed here. Favourite wintering resort of the world's barnacle geese: look for them late Sept-Easter – with greylags, white-fronts and whooper swans – between Loch Gruinart and Loch Gorm. Black guillemots near Port Askaig; choughs and rockdoves in Oa, and the Rhinns west coast; duck of many kinds on Loch Indaal. Terns and eider duck breed on many of the offshore islets. Red-throated divers breed around lochs. Bird list published by Islay Folk Museum (see *Where to Go, Port Charlotte*).

Whisky: eight distilleries have led people to call Islay, admiringly, Whisky Island. Bowmore dates from 1779, Lagavulin even earlier. Together with Ardbeg, Laphroaig, and Bruichladdich, these produce distinctive and delectable malts of the peaty, smoky, husky kind. (The island has also been called the Captains' Nursery, because of the traditional success of Islaymen in the merchant navy; and (by Islaymen) the Queen of the Hebrides.)

Jura

For its size, Jura is the wildest, emptiest and least tourist-oriented of Britain's inhabited islands. It is separated from its southern, lower-lying neighbour, Islay, by a narrow channel. Nowadays, you have to go to Islay first. The ferry from Port Askaig runs about every half hour in the summer: the crossing takes only 5 minutes, but Jura is a world apart from busy Islay.

It is 28 miles long and 8 miles at its widest, narrowing to a mile where Loch Tarbert nearly cuts it in two. Most of its 94,000 acres – divided between five (mostly absentee) landlords – consists of barren hillside, uninhabited moorland and peat-bog, given up to the red deer. These have been Jura's best-known residents since the Vikings and their increasingly profitable slaughter and export has for generations been the main concern of the island's proprietors. 'Everything is sacrificed to the brutes,' said George Orwell, who lived for a time between 1946–8 in a remote croft near Jura's northern tip, and wrote most of '1984' there. Not *quite* everything, today; but they still seem to come first, perforce, in local priorities.

There is little on Jura for unarmed, car-bound tourists to do. But this is an island of unique appeal for those content to enjoy the eastern coastal strip, its beaches and its views, to go fishing, explore the moors and climb the mountains with due care and strict attention to the warnings about departing from the road during the shooting seasons without telephoning *The Stalker*, the nerve-centre of sporting intelligence whose number is displayed on boards along the roadside. For stags, the season runs from mid-Aug to mid-Oct. Hinds are shot Nov-Feb.

Tourists may bring their cars over on the Islay ferry, but they have only one short, single-track road to drive on. Out of the high holiday season, there's so little traffic that you can enjoy walking on it too. It runs for 24 miles from the ferry, through Jura's 'capital', Craighouse, to Ardlussa where – marked Private – it becomes a variably motorable and often very bumpy track. This continues for some 4 miles past Barnhill, Orwell's temporary home – a white farmhouse above a tiny rocky beach – to Kinuachdrach.

From here you can walk along a narrow track, visible most of the way, over hills and moorland to the northern tip: a wonderful walk, when the weather's clear. If it's windy enough, and the tides are right, you can see from here Jura's most notorious sight – the Corrievrechan (Coire Bhreacain) – the dangerous whirlpool in the narrow channel between the northern end of Jura and its uninhabited neighbour, Scarba. It is at its noisiest and busiest when the flood tide going west is met by a gale blowing into the Scarba Sound, and the roar can be heard for miles. On a fine summer day you may see little more than a gentle curl of foam teasing the water. But the perils are real enough: George Orwell and his sister were nearly drowned there in the 1940s. If you want to get a good view, with less effort, you can go by boat. In June and Aug there is a weekly boat trip from Ardlussa pier. In July it goes twice weekly. For details tel: Jura 224.

Jura's trackless and uninhabited western coast may also be reached by boat, if one is available: for details tel number above. Special attractions for persistent visitors include raised beaches of white quartzite shingle, as at Shian Bay and around Loch Tarbert. Here, too, are unusually big

Kilnave Chapel, Ardnave, Islay with eighth-century Celtic cross.

View from Port Askaig, Islay, of the Paps of Jura – legendary lures.

and frequentable caves; in one, Uamh Righ, local historian John Mercer discovered 'over 100 poorly-made crosses' on the walls, and other traces of a clandestine Catholic chapel improvised 350 years ago.

For walkers there is only one map-marked path across Jura to the west. It starts a few miles past Leargybreck, skirts a mountain, Corra Bheinn; a lake, Loch na Fudarlaich; and runs through Glen Batrick to a disused shooting lodge. If you want to see more of Jura on foot away from the road, there are very few beaten tracks.

Craighouse contains Jura's only hotel and only pub, combined in the comfortable Jura Hotel (tel Jura 243). It also has the island's only shop – licensed, all-purpose and among the most expensive in Scotland, according to a recent survey. Plus garage, seasonal café, church, village hall, and – dominating everything – a grim distillery, dating from 1810 and re-opened, after long closure, in 1963. There are two piers (one built by Telford in 1814): once you could sail here directly from the mainland. Most of Jura's population (about 200) live in

and around Craighouse. Nobody has lived on the west coast for years.

The island's legendary lures are the three conical mountains in the south-west known as the Paps of Jura. The highest is Beinn an Oir, 2,571ft. If you're an experienced hill climber, with a day (and a compass) in hand and good weather in view, you can walk over them (they're near-neighbours) by striking up the Corran River from the road and following it to its source in Loch an t-Siob. On a *really* clear day, you're promised a view from the Cuillins to the Isle of Man.

Compared with Islay, Jura is low on wildfowl, because of its geography. Rare plants, noted locally by John Mercer, include alpine meadow rue, yellow and climbing corydalis, frosted orache, starry saxifrage and rat's tail fescue. Recorded antiquities are relatively scarce, although Jura too has its standing stones: the most notable is the Camus Stack, 12ft high, reached by a track off the road between Feolin and Craighouse.

Jura's population reached its peak about 1840, when there were some

240 houses – even a few in the north-west; but this soon began to decline under the pressures of poverty, voluntary emigration (which began nearly a century earlier) and compulsory clearances by the island's owners. Jura once had eight schools; only one survives. For a glimpse of the old Jura, look at Keils – about a mile from Craighouse – where there's a simple, low-roofed thatched cottage, now used as a shed or a byre, beside a modern house and a caravan. About half a mile north of Keils, up a narrow track, is Jura's oldest known burial ground, Kilearndil, the site of an ancient chapel, in a beautiful, secluded oasis under the hills.

If you want to stay on Jura, and the hotel is full, consult the Tourist Office in Bowmore, Islay, open April-Sep (Bowmore 254), or Campbeltown, all year round (Campbeltown 2056). Holiday accommodation is limited, and solo camping isn't permitted on the estates. Prospective deerstalkers should write to the proprietors of the five estates: Ardlussa, Tarbert, Forest, Ardfin and Inver. Cost: about £100 a stag. A 'package' cost quoted by a top mainland agency which handles the letting of some Jura deer stalking – Major Neil Ramsay & Co, Farleyer, Aberfeldy, Perthshire – is 'approaching £1,000' for six stags and a week's accommodation but it does vary from year to year. On Tarbert estate, a week's hind-shooting costs about £225 per rifle. Fishing: the Tarbert figure for brown trout fishing is about £25 a day, including boats.

Colonsay

Colonsay's special attraction for island-fanciers is hard to define briefly, except in negatives. It lacks the mountainous grandeur of Skye and Mull, the wildness of Jura or Rhum, the religious aura of Iona, the rich birdlife and archaeology of Islay. But it also lacks the corrosions of instant tourism, the exclusiveness of a deer park or a nature reserve, and – in spite of its declining population – that mortuary chill of a dying society to be found elsewhere in the Hebrides. Its assets include a wide range of plant and animal life, with 500 species of local flora and 150 birds from the British list – of which the most common is the eider, known as the Colonsay duck. Among its rare plants are rock samphire, blood-drop emlets and slender naiad.

Colonsay has half a dozen lochs full of trout. It has an equable climate, with nearly as much sunshine as Tiree (Scotland's sunniest place) and half the mainland's rainfall, on average. It juxtaposes within a few miles the wild and the tame, pastoral and sporting life, intimations of antiquity and agribusiness. It has at least 12 duns, seven sets of standing stones, six forts, and two hut circles – notably around Kilchattan and Garvard. (The Colonsay Hotel keeps a list.) And it has preserved an unusual degree of social coherence, simplicity and openness: you can walk freely almost anywhere in Colonsay, including the grounds of the laird's house, with their vast, romantic gardens.

The only regular sea route is from Oban, nearly 40 miles to the northeast. (There are strips for chartered aircraft on Colonsay and its neighbour, Oronsay.) Colonsay is 8 miles long, from 1 to 3 miles wide, with about 20 square miles of moorland, woodland, rocky greensward, arable and grazing land, and hill country. By Hebridean standards, it is fairly flat but on the spot, in scale, the hills seem mountainous enough. Craggy Oronsay, about 2 square miles in area, is separated from it by water, except for 2 to 3 hours at low tide. Colonsay's population is about 120 (around 10 per cent that of a century ago). Oronsay's about 6.

There are no organised day excursions, boats arrive only three times a week from Oban, and you usually have to stay three nights on the island. There's no trippers' bait here: just the one – excellent – hotel, the Colonsay (tel Colonsay 316). One small (non-licensed) shop-cum-PO at Scalasaig, Colonsay's port and 'capital', two churches (Baptist and Church of Scotland) and an 18-hole golf-course, make up the amenities.

One reason for its 'unspoilt' condition is the feudal paternalism of one family of (largely absentee) landlords. Colonsay is one of the biggest British islands under the control of a single private owner: the fourth Baron Strathcona, whose great-grandfather, the first Baron – a Scottish-born Canadian financier and statesman – bought Colonsay 75 years ago. Until recently the Strathconas owned not only the island but practically everything on it.

In 1978, Lord Strathcona – who shortly afterwards became a member of Mrs Thatcher's Government – sold the hotel (to Kevin and Christa Byrne, live wires from Ireland who are helping to prevent Colonsay from succumbing to Hebridean sleeping sickness); and, more significantly, the adjoining island of Oronsay (sold to a whisky tycoon). He is now concentrating on trying to make his inheritance pay its way by letting an increasing number of houses as self-catering holiday homes, together with Downstairs parts of his own holiday home, Colonsay House.

Information about Colonsay's past is still relatively scant and shadowy, but research continues: a report on its antiquities is due in about 3 years. Surprisingly, there's no record of compulsory clearances on Colonsay – alone among the Hebrides.

You can drive around the island, stopping to enjoy the views, in under an hour. But you need to walk to savour Colonsay to the full, and the walking is exhilarating and reasonably easy. To the north the road ends at Kiloran Bay, a magnificent stretch of golden sand, where in the 1880s a Viking, his horse and his boat were excavated in the dunes. From here you can walk, along a well-marked track, through a changing terrain of machair and moorland and a horde of rabbits (introduced 200 years ago), under Carn Eoin past the farm of Balnahard to the site of an early Celtic chapel, Kilcatrine, with a well said to have been used by St Columba. This became a convent in the 13th c. Beyond it is one of Colonsay's beautiful, secluded bays.

To the south the road ends at

Garvard, from which – at low tide only, for a limited time – you can cross the Strand, a vast sandy beach, to Oronsay, which holds the biggest monastic building (after Iona) still surviving in the Western islands. Built about 1360 by John of Islay, on the site of a 6th c monastery, this priory was for generations the holiest place, next to Iona, for the interment of the rich and powerful; and its substantial ruins include a medieval high altar, cloisters, a fine stone cross and some 30 carved grave slabs. At the western tip of Oronsay is an islet. Eilan nan Ron, which is a major breeding ground of grey seals: look for them in Sept. Halfway across the

Strand a sanctuary cross used to mark the boundary of Oronsay's holy ground: if you could reach it, and stay on Oronsay for a year and a day, you were safe from your pursuers (*if* they knew the rules).

You can also take a boat to Oronsay from Scalasaig. Finlay McFadyen (Colonsay 333) takes visitors over in his boat, and if weather condition is all right, will also go as far as Jura or Islay. He also does fishing trips. Frank Nicholson (tel Colonsay 354) takes up to eight people, and collects them after about 3 hours. Dougie McGillivray (tel Colonsay 319) takes a boat over once a week in summer, weather permitting. You can also

hire a boat for fishing (takes up to four) from Frank Nicholson. Skin-divers are also catered for.

To play golf, you apply to Kevin Byrne, the club's membership secretary: yearly subscription (no daily rates). Clubs for hire from the hotel by the day.

There's a post-bus service three times a week (a Land Rover visits almost every house), and a mini-bus schedule, tied to the ferry service from Oban. The hotel's London taxi takes its less energetic guests to the start of their walks. You can hire a bike from Archie McConnell. Dinghies, if available may be hired from the Colonsay Yacht Club, through

Calgary Bay, Mull, and Treshnish Point reaching out to the sanctuary of the Treshnish Islands.

Kevin Byrne at the hotel. He also has a list of half a dozen islanders offering holiday accommodation: for Lord Strathcona's list, write to Mrs S. Holmes, 53 Upper Lansdown Mews, Bath. No camping.

Mull

Third largest of the Hebrides, and probably the wettest. But it's the landscapes that matter, and they can look marvellous even in the fiercest rain. Count on wet weather: pessimism pays when the sun comes out – more frequently at some seasons (notably May) than in the south of England. Even more than the other Hebrides, this hauntingly beautiful, empty island is a world of surprises.

From north to south Mull is 25 miles, from east to west 26; but at Salen it's only 2 miles wide, and the coastline is more than 300 miles long – shaped by three sea-lochs on the west. You can drive round a good deal of the coast, but don't leave your fuel supply – or your thirst – to chance. Mull has only eight scattered filling stations, and you can't rely on them all being open, even on weekdays. The only ones open on Sundays are the one in Salen (summer only) and one in Tobermory (mornings only). Inns are just as scarce. Population: 1,600 (in 1821 it was around 10,000), of which an increasing proportion are aging incomers. Mull is scarred with traces of abandoned villages and 'townships' (farms) by the dozen.

In Mull, especially, don't measure signpost distances by mainland time-scales for driving. Nearly all the roads are single-track, with many blind corners, hairpin bends, pot-holes, and some of the most obstinate, unpredictable, suicidal sheep in creation. You *have* to drive more slowly than on the mainland.

Landscapes combine wild and lush, pastoral and barren: green moors, quick streams and waterfalls, high cliffs, meadows, woodland (the Forestry Commission owns 40,000 acres) and mountains. Highest peak, the magnificent Ben More, 3,169ft. Not many fresh-water lochs; the biggest, in the north, is Loch Frisa, which is 5 miles long. Fertile but under-used soil; crofting survives sketchily, and that only in the southern Ross of Mull.

It's a volcanic island; Ben More is highest point in Britain reached by basalt lava. Horizontal lava flows in columnar formation at Ulva, Carsaig Arches and Ardtun.

After Norse rule ended in 13th c, Mull was run by the Macdonalds, later Lords of the Isles (for Hebridean history, see *Islay*). The Macleans of Duart, supporters and relations of the Macdonalds, were Mull's top clan for 300 years till they were ousted by Campbells in 1691.

WHERE TO GO

Tobermory: Mull's main shopping, eating and tourist centre. In the sun, can look surprisingly exotic, with near-Italian touches: blue-gilt cherub on the quayside fountain, and red, gold, blue, green and black facades of early 19th c houses in main street curving round the harbour, full of bobbing boats of all kinds, encircled by steep, wooded hills.

Facilities include a filling station; hairdresser's; launderette; local **Tourist Information Centre** April-Sept, tel Tobermory 2182; tearoom; café; souvenir and crafts shops; Mull's only stationary bank (a mobile office visits the villages). At Brown's, ironmonger's, you can choose from a fine selection of malts, get a ticket for the 9-hole golf course, a permit for fishing several lochs, buy fishing tackle etc. The Back Brae serves take-away snacks, as well as fish'n'chips and chicken'n'chips *in situ*. The Gallery, a handsome decaying bit of Victorian Gothic with a rose window, used to be a church but is now a crafts market selling tweeds, paintings, pottery etc. At the Aros Hall, ceilidhs and dances in the season. Half a dozen hotels. The Macdonald Arms, by the quayside, is a comfortable, small inn, with a lively bar (splendid range of malts): by Hebridean standards, very good food (tel Tobermory 2011). The Western Isles, high above the harbour, is much bigger, more spacious but not expensive, with 50 bedrooms, its own dinghies, golf course, trout fishing (free). Salmon fishing, deer-stalking, may be organised (tel Tobermory 2012).

Don't miss the Mull & Iona Folk-lore Club Museum, in a converted Baptist chapel (1862) by the harbour:

open June-Sept 11-5, small admission charge. A wonderful jumble of local bygones and memorabilia.

Tobermory's prime legend is the Treasure: in 1588 after the Armada débâcle a Spanish galleon, Almirante di Florencia, took refuge in the bay but was later blown up with 350 on board. A century later a hunt for Spanish gold began which has continued, off and on, ever since.

Dervaig: 8 miles north-west of Tobermory by the west coast, near sandy bays, woods and lochs, along a road of frequent hairpin bends and marvellous vistas. Built in 1799 by Maclean of Coll as 26 houses in pairs. Shops include Neil McIntyre, an excellent multi-purpose place for books, fresh coffee, frozen food and Sunday papers (open Sun afternoon). Good small hotel, the Bellachroy (tel Dervaig 225). On the road to Tobermory is one of the most dramatic hill-top graveyards in the Inner Hebrides, Kilmore, site of an ancient chapel. A mile south of Dervaig is the Old Byre Heritage Centre with its 'Scenes from an Island's Heritage'. In summer, programmes every half-hour use hi-fi stereo sound effects to show how crofters lived in the last century, and what the clearances did. Lifesize figures of islanders in reconstructed cottage interiors. Tea room and gift stall. Open daily Easter-Oct, Mon-Sat 10.30-5, Sun 2-5. Admission charge. Tel Dervaig 229.

Craignure: Mull's main port of call. Village has an inn (good bar snacks), filling station, PO-shop where you can buy spirits, fishing tackle, papers, Calor gas etc. Just outside is the island's most modern hotel, the Isle of Mull, opened 1971: 62 bedrooms, all with bathrooms (tel Craignure 351). Craignure's 9-hole golf course has recently been reopened and clubs can be hired through the hotel or village shop.

Salen: neat, pleasant, east-coast village on woody site by a wide bay between Craignure and Tobermory. Two small family hotels, offering fishing, pony trekking, stalking by arrangement. Glenforsa Hotel, about a mile away in isolated woodland site, is built in Norwegian log-style: 14 rooms, with own sea trout and salmon fishing (tel Aros 3779). Grass airstrip adjacent to hotel. Salen has filling station, village hall (ceilidhs and dances in summer), private anchorage, two grocers, crafts-gift shop, licensed restaurant, the Puffer Aground, which serves children's portions and packed meals to order.

Takes its name from the bay, Sailean-dubh-Challum, the deep bay of Columba's church. (For Columba, see *Iona*.) The saint is said to have preached here. A mile down the road to Killiechronan is a stream called Burn of the Sermons because he gave one there. But Salen itself was not founded until 1809, as a model village, by one of Mull's most remarkable achievers: Lachlan Macquarie (1761-1824). The son of an impoverished farmer from the west-coast offshore island of Ulva, he entered the British Army at 15; fought in India, Persia and Russia; rose to

Pennyghael: boasts one of few drinking-places on Mull, between Craignure and Fionnphort – the Kinloch Hotel, with cheap pub food, and a PO incorporated. A few miles down the coast road is one of the best restaurants in Mull, the Clansman, with a public and cocktail bar (draught Guinness). Lobster or crayfish salads can be ordered in advance. Best to book, in season, tel Pennyghael 205.

Bunessan: 5 miles from Iona; PO, licensed shop, tearoom, gift shop, filling station, small harbour and Argyll Arms. Famous fossil beds at Ardtun nearby. Nearer still to Iona, if you miss the ferry, is the highly commended Ardfenaig House Hotel, limited accommodation (tel Fionnphort 210).

inset beside a corridor, of Spanish officers from the galleon sunk in Tobermory Bay – held in Duart's dungeons by Sir Lachlan Mor Maclean. The Sea Room (built 1912) contains a small cannon, one of the few objects ever raised from the galleon's wreck. The Castle's main showplace is the Banqueting Room, with a fine hotch-potch of historical documents, family memorabilia – and family atmosphere. A Crimean Corner includes mementoes of Duart's restorer, Sir Fitzroy, who charged with the Light Brigade as a young Hussar. From ramparts, with luck, a splendid view from three sides. Below there's a tearoom with home baking. Open May-Sept daily 10.30-6. Admission charge. In high season there is a motor launch service direct from Oban Esplanade to the Castle slipway.

Torosay Castle: about one-and-a-half miles from Craignure, on road south. Handsome mid-Victorian specimen of Scottish Baronial, completed 1858 by leading architect of that school, David Bryce, with terraced garden laid out by Sir Robert Lorimer, the Edwardian Capability Brown. Intimate atmosphere. Family portraits and memorabilia make Torosay a pleasant refuge in the rain. The 11 acres of gardens (including plantation of gum trees) deserve to be seen in the sun. Tearoom. Open May-early Oct 11-5 daily, gardens, sunrise to sunset. Admission charge. Miniature railway takes visitors from Craignure Old Pier to within a couple of hundred yards of Castle.

Croig: turn off road about 1 mile south from Dervaig: beautiful tiny harbour. Cattle from Outer Hebrides were landed here on their way to mainland. In season, trips from here to Staffa and Treshnish islands.

Kilninian Church: near Torloisk, on wooded hillside above the road, beside Loch Tuath. Only church in Western Highlands dedicated to St Ninian, 4th c Galloway priest, Scotland's first missionary. Site dates back to early Christian times, once belonged to Abbot of Iona. Medieval gravestones. Rebuilt 1755.

Loch Buie: splendid beach. Follow the drive to Loch Buie House, taking care not to infringe local privacies. Turn to left where road branches just after the gates. To get to the village, go past the lodge gate. Inside the porch

Tobermory Harbour, Mull, with nineteenth-century houses curving round.

be a general; bought an estate in Mull. Later became Governor of New South Wales and has been acclaimed as 'Father of Australia'. Buried 2 miles from Salen, with wife and 'native' servant, George, at Gruline, in a secluded little mausoleum among the woods, down a track, through a farm, off the road to Iona. Unusually for Mull, there's a very clear roadside indicator, put up by the National Trust for Australia, which owns the site.

From Salen, you can see the visitable ruins of Aros Castle – once a stronghold of the Lords of the Isles – a couple of miles away on the north end of Salen Bay.

SIGHTSEEING

Duart Castle: prime sight on the east coast, as you approach Mull from Oban, perched on crag at the end of peninsula. Ten minutes drive from Craignure, on the road south. Stronghold of the Macleans since the 13th c: still occupied by Lord Maclean (27th of his line), the Queen's Lord Chamberlain. But there was a long interregnum. It had been deserted for 150 years when at the turn of this century Fitzroy Maclean, head of the clan, bought back the ruins and rebuilt the castle as the Clan's home.

The Castle's oddly assorted attractions include a Tussaud-like tableau,

Kilmore, Mull, site of an ancient chapel and one of the most dramatic hilltop graveyards in the Inner Hebrides.

of the 1870 church is a Celtic cross, in wall on right. Several stone circles are to be found nearby: notably, one which has nine stones in a circle of 22ft.

Loch Ba and Ben More: about a mile south from the Macquarie mausoleum (see *Salen*), there's – unusually – a signposted 8-mile track along Loch Ba, up a bit of Ben More, and down to Kinloch. You walk past Ben Chaisgidle, all that's left of the double volcano from which, 50 million years ago, poured most of Mull's lava. Loch Ba is Mull's second biggest: for permission to fish, ask the Knock or Gruline Estate Offices. Try climbing Ben More – from Dishaig farm, about 3 miles from Knock Bridge.

Glen More: dissects Mull, with scenic splendour, for 12 miles. Once a boundary between kingdoms of Picts and Scots. Route to Iona of pilgrims – and funeral processions of dead kings.

The Wilderness: 3-mile coastal terrain at tip of the Ardmeanach peninsula, owned by National Trust for Scotland. Rough going for novices: arduous walk of 7 miles via Tiroran, Tavool and Burg. Main attraction is McCulloch's Tree, the cast of a 40ft conifer, possibly 50 million years old, embedded in basalt cliffs at Rudha nan Uamha. Go at half-tide on a falling tide. Easier way of seeing this fossil is to hire a boat, if you can, from Bunessan. Be prepared: it's been severely vandalised by geologists.

Glengorm: 4 miles from Tobermory. Perhaps Mull's most scenic road, worth taking – though it's a dead end – for the views not only of landscapes east and west, but also, at a distance, of Glengorm House, a spectrally extravagant piece of Disney-ish Scottish Baronial perched above. On the way, try the Ardmore Nature Trail through a Forestry Commission plantation.

Antiquities: some 40 duns, including Dun nan Gall, 3 miles west of Ulva Ferry; Dun Aisgean, half a mile from Burg; an Caisteal, between Bunessan and Loch Assapol. Half a dozen crannogs; notably, on Loch Sguabain. Stone circles, notably at Loch Buie and Suie. World-famous fossil leafbeds at Ardtun, near Bunessan, and fossil conifer not far away (see *The Wilderness*).

Treshnish Islands: arc of eight uninhabited basalt islands, 4 miles northwest of Mull, natural bird sanctuary and breeding ground of grey seals (Oct-Nov). Biggest, Lunga and Fladda. Most famous, Cairnburg Mor: history goes back at least 700 years, perhaps to prehistoric times. Macleans made their last stand here in 1691. Taken and retaken in the 1715 rebellion. Islands now owned by Lady Jean Rankin of Treshnish House, who may permit accredited naturalists to land there. Tourist trips (no landing) several days a week in summer, weather permitting, from Croig, Ulva Ferry, Tobermory, Oban.

Erraid: island off south-west Mull, not far from Fionnphort. About a mile square: you can walk to it at low tide. David Balfour in Stevenson's 'Kidnapped' was cast away here; a bay is named after him. Pink granite was quarried here. Now run by members of the Findhorn Community.

ACTIVITIES

Theatre: one of Mull's biggest surprises for a newcomer, driving along the scenic road from Dervaig to Salen through wild moorland, is to see a tiny roadside notice saying simply 'Theatre'. At the top of a steep path in a miniature byre is the Little Theatre of Mull, established in 1966 in the coach-house of a former manse by two astonishing, valiant all-rounders, Marianne and Barrie Hesketh, whose 38-seater is the only professional stage in the Hebrides, and one of the smallest theatres in the world. They act, direct, design and manage it, and in the winter they tour, two-handed, throughout Britain.

They have a splendidly ambitious scheme for a 150-seater and community theatre centre at Torosay Castle (see *Sightseeing*) in disused farm buildings. Tel Dervaig 267.

Loch and river fishing: some hotels (as indicated) organise salmon and trout fishing for guests, most of it in the north. At Brown's in Tobermory you can get daily and weekly angling licences, or hire a rowing boat. Loch Torr, $4\frac{1}{2}$ miles south, is stocked with rainbow trout: has resident population of brown trout. Fly only. Mishnish Lochs nearby have brown trout only. Loch Frisa has small red trout: you can hire boat from Hugh Cameron's stores, Salen. Not Sun.

Sea fishing: from Tobermory and other villages, in summer. For instance, John Bartholomew in Dervaig takes out fishing parties of 10, usually to the Treshnish Islands. For details tel Dervaig 240.

Ponytrekking: Sue Morgan, Ormsaig, (tel Fionnphort 297/8). Mrs Elwis, Erray Estate, Tobermory (tel Tobermory 2052).

Diving: Robert Barlow, Scarba Cottage, Albert Street, Tobermory, tel Tobermory 2107, will supply air and take divers out to good sites around island. Seafare Ltd, Main St, Tobermory also takes divers out, and as well as selling diving gear has limited amount for hire.

Golfing: Tobermory, 9-hole golf course by the Western Isles Hotel. Craignure, 9-hole course recently reopened, see *Where to Go, Craignure*.

Wildlife watching: Mull Wildlife Safaris, leaving Tobermory Mon to Fri at 10, returning about 5, take you by minibus to look at deer, seals etc – 'the most interesting flora and fauna for the time of the year'. Conducted by Richard Coomber. All year, but Oct-March by prior arrangement only. Phone or write to Staffa Cottages Guest House, Breadalbane St, Tobermory, tel Tobermory 2464. Bring own lunch.

Bird-watching: local guide, 'The Isle of Mull' by Norah Turner and Audrey Finlay, lists 60 resident species; 47 summer visitors; 24 winter visitors; 45 migrants; 22 vagrants. (They also proudly list 124 'lesser known' plants and flowers.)

Painting: Julia Wroughton, ARCA, ARWA, runs a Summer School at Inniemore Lodge, Carsaig. Tel Pennyghael 201.

Fishing is still a part of the life of Tobermory, Victorian-built model village.

Iona

For nearly 1,400 years, ever since St Columba died here in the monastery he founded, pilgrims from all over the world have made their way to this tiny green-and-grey shrine-island at the south-western tip of Mull. Before Columba, it seems, Iona was a spiritual stronghold of the Druids, a possibility that has boosted its reputation for unique 'vibes'.

It's consoling to know that this place of marvels is now in public ownership, and cannot be sold for redevelopment. In 1979 it was acquired from the estate of the 10th Duke of Argyll by the National Trust for Scotland, helped by £500,000 from the Hugh Fraser Foundation. But the NTS doesn't own the Abbey and other ecclesiastical sites; and money is still urgently needed by the Iona Cathedral Trustees for repair and maintenance.

Most years Iona is visited by some half a million people, and as it is only 3 miles long and $1\frac{1}{2}$ miles wide, you'd be wise to moderate any expectations in the peak holiday season of tuning in to Druidic, Columban or even Benedictine experience. But most sightseers, spending no more than a couple of hours on Iona, necessarily stick to the $\frac{1}{2}$-mile area between the jetty and the Abbey which includes the island's amenities and main antiquities. So, if you can arrive on an early ferry you should be able to sample, without too much crowding, Iona's silver beaches, wild and boggy moorland, flower-flecked, springy turf and – in good weather – incomparable views.

The purity of changing light and colour here can be unforgettable. You're likely to relish Iona's mini-landscape all the more if you can't drive through it. Tourists are not allowed to bring their cars over on the ferry. (You aren't allowed a car until you've been a resident for 8 months.) And walkers have a better chance than in more mountainous islands of staying dry: Iona's average rainfall is about half Mull's.

After founding several churches and monasteries (including Kells) in Ireland, Columba set off, at 42, to convert the Pictish heathens in the north. In 563AD he landed in Iona with 12 brother evangelists, and created a monastery from which he and other militants took Celtic Christianity into Scotland, northern England and further south. Columba made Iona a place not only of holiness, but artistic excellence (the Book of Kells was started here), learning and political power. Here he carried out the first consecration of any king in the history of Britain, with Aidan of Dalriada, a royal kinsman. Nothing endures of his monastery or church. But you can see the probable foundations of Columba's beehive-shaped cell, excavated 23 years ago, on Tor Abb, the rocky hillock facing the west door of Iona's Abbey. And the

Iona Village, with the twelfth-century Abbey in the distance.

boundary wall of the original monastery runs nearby.

From Kenneth MacAlpin in the 9th c till the time of James VI, many of Scotland's kings, including Duncan and his murderer Macbeth, are said to have been buried here. According to an estimate in 1549, the burial ground, Reilig Odhrain, then contained the graves of 48 Scottish, eight Norwegian and four Irish kings,

a figure still used to overwhelm visitors. Like a good deal of Iona's history, this is open to conjecture. As Dr Johnson wryly said, 'The graves are very numerous, and some of them undoubtedly contain the remains of men, who did not expect to be so soon forgotten.'

It is not *this* dictum, however, that's remembered in Iona; what is preserved in stone, along the path from

the village to the Abbey, is Johnson's celebrated saying, 'That man is little to be envied whose . . . piety would not grow warmer among the ruins of Iona.' Certainly the Reilig Odhrain helped to make Iona a place of pilgrimage; it contained a treasury of astonishing medieval tombstones, now paraded, a bit hugger-mugger, in the Abbey's museum.

Beside the Reilig Odhrain is Iona's

oldest and (for some) most seductive building: the miniature, austere pink granite chapel of St Oran, reputedly rebuilt in the 11th c by the saintly Queen Margaret, on the site of a much earlier chapel.

Between it and the Abbey the stretch of cobbled road is medieval, excavated only in 1962. Not far from the west door is one of Scotland's three great crosses, St Martin's, which has stood here since it was carved more than 1,000 years ago. Before the Reformation, there were supposedly more than 350 crosses on Iona: only three survived the iconoclasts' zeal.

The Abbey itself dates back 800 years to the final collapse of the Columban foundation. It was a picturesque ruin in 1899, when the 8th Duke of Argyll gave it to trustees of the Church of Scotland. In 1912 the Abbey was reopened for public worship for the first time in more than 3 centuries. Now it is open every day throughout the year, with morning and evening services.

The restored Abbey has its eyesores, but there's much to admire in detail: the effigy of the last Abbot, wearing a mitre, beside the sacristy door; the Roy le Maistre picture of Christ crucified in the north transept; the folksy medieval carvings on the south wall piers; the 1959 Lipschitz sculpture in the cloisters.

The Iona Community, who run the Abbey and a youth centre here, restored the monastic buildings between 1938 and 1965. Every week in summer over 100 Christian activists from many countries visit Iona at the Community's invitation to share in 'discussion, worship and recreation'.

Iona's village, by the jetty, includes a PO, café, a multi-purpose chain grocer's, crafts/souvenir shop, and two hotels of different generations, each admirable in its way – the old-established Argyll (tel Iona 334) and the more spacious, modern St Columba (tel Iona 304). Most of the island's 50 houses are in the neighbourhood. One of the island's main roads curves from here around the prime sights – the ruined 13th c nunnery, now a showplace of wild flowers; Maclean's Cross, a powerful, 10ft carved enigma (probably 16th c) near Telford's handsome little 1824 church; the Reilig Odhrain; and the

The Nunnery, best visited early in the day.

Abbey. The road passes the Iona Community's coffee-house, its youth camp and a few houses before petering out into a track just short of Iona's north end. The second road starts from the southern end of the first and crosses the island to the west coast, passing Sithean Môr (pronounced 'Sheean Mor'), the Great Fairy Mound – in fact, a small hillock. The 'fairies' of such mounds in the Hebrides were probably among the earliest settlers.

One of the finest vantage points is Carn cul ri Eirinn ('the hill with its back to Ireland'), in the south-west. East of St Columba's Bay, you may find, with some difficulty, the place where Iona's once-famous marble was quarried until some 70 years ago. The marble on sale today is usually from Connemara. In a nearby bay enthusiasts can still collect multi-coloured stones (Iona pebbles).

The island's best – and most accessible – viewpoint is its highest peak, Dun I (pronounced 'Doon EE'), 332ft, crowned with a cairn built in 1897 to mark the 1,300th anniversary of St Columba's death.

There's a singular absence of organised leisure activity on Iona. There are no bikes for hire, and only one taxi: you *have* to walk. Though there's no blanket veto, camping is very seldom allowed by farmers. You may get one of the island's boatmen (Gordon Grant or David Kirkpatrick) to take you to Staffa or the Treshnish

Islands. But on land, Iona is – as a local says – 'a *great* place for doing nothing but looking and walking, and keeping quiet'.

Staffa

Because of Mendelssohn, this tiny uninhabited island 7 miles west of Mull is perhaps the best-known, globally, of the Hebrides. When the composer saw Fingal's Cave in 1829, after being seasick en route from Oban, it inspired a few bars: it seemed to him 'like the interior of a gigantic organ for the winds and tumultuous waves to play on'. But it was not until 3 years later that he wrote the overture 'The Hebrides', generally known as 'Fingal's Cave'.

The great cave itself, Staffa's prime claim to fame, is at the southern end where the island rises sheer out of the Atlantic to over 130ft and where the extraordinary columnar walls of basalt pillars have helped to make it, for generations, one of Scotland's prime tourist sights. It stretches back 230ft, and its mouth is 50ft broad – like, in Queen Victoria's words, 'a great entrance into a vaulted hall'.

Romantic Staffa – which is $\frac{3}{4}$-mile long – has four other celebrated caves: the Clamshell, the Cormorants, MacKinnon's and the Boar Cave. It has a busy birdlife, rich flora and fine grazing; but nobody has lived there for over 200 years. It has always been hard to guarantee landings, except in calm weather – for that reason, Dr Johnson and Boswell missed Staffa on their travels in the west; and nowadays neither Caledonian MacBrayne nor Western Ferries, both of which run cruises around Staffa, with views of the caves, land any passengers.

However, Turus Mara boat trips do land on Staffa, weather permitting, sailing from Croig, Mull, most days May–Oct, subject to booking. Details tel Dervaig 242. Kenway Travel boat trips also land, weather permitting. They sail daily from Oban, with pick-up stop at Ulva, Mull, mid-May–mid-Sept. Advisable to book a day ahead, details tel Oban 4747. If you're staying on Iona, you might be lucky enough to persuade one of the boatmen to land you on Staffa.

Western Ferries run a Staffa Cruise, departing from Fort William on the Highland Seabird twice a week June–Sept, and Oban three times a week June–Oct. You arrive off Staffa mid afternoon and sail back after an hour. Caledonian MacBrayne's Columba passes Staffa on its way to Iona from Oban, twice a week May–Sept. On the way back it takes a different route.

Coll

Three-and-a-half hours from Oban, beyond the wooded blue-green shores of Mull and Ardnamurchan, Coll's rocky lunar landscape appears, with not a tree or house in sight. 'Getting off here?' ask the Tiree-bound passengers incredulously. But there are signs of life on the fine new pier completed in 1969, and then comes the surprise – tucked out of sight around the corner are rows of neat cottages, trim plots of lupins, violas and parsley, a launderette and tearoom. Dr Johnson commented on the Collachs' gardening skills. Most of the island's population of just under 150 live in Arinagour, the only village. There are a couple of well-stocked stores, PO (but no bank), an eccentrically homely craft shop, and the splendidly situated Isle of Coll Hotel, run by Glaswegian conjuror Alistair Oliphant.

Coll is roughly 12 miles by 3 (and about 7 north-west of Mull). Its forbidding eastern coast belies its curious charm – low peaty hills of heather and gorse, dark lochs filled with lively brown trout, green valleys and a western shore of creamy-white shell-sand bays and rabbit-pitted dunes. The sunshine record is good and the hills not high enough to draw much rain, but it can be windy. The other hazard, as in all this part of the world, is the summer hordes of blood-thirsty midges, some wearing hobnail boots in August.

There are three roads, not linked to form a circuit, and much of the coastline can only be reached by walking, for the most part fairly easy going. The road westwards from Arinagour leads to Breachacha Castle, probably built second quarter 15th c. Home of the Macleans of Coll until 1750 when Hector Maclean, 11th chieftain, moved 100 yards up the field to his ugly new castle, dismissed by Dr Johnson as 'a mere tradesman's box'. The parapet and pepperpot turrets were a 19th c addition. The new castle is now being converted into holiday flats; the old castle, carefully restored, is the headquarters of the Project Trust, founded by Major Nicholas Maclean Bristol to organise voluntary work overseas for young people between school and university, their initiative first tested out on Coll.

Further on, a track leads to mile-wide curving sandy shore of Crossapol Bay and the dilapidated square mausoleum built by Alexander Maclean, 1835, ambitious island proprietor who developed Arinagour and started the population drift from west to east. The Macleans owned most of Coll until 1856. After many clearances, Hugh Maclean sold up to John Lorne Stewart, chamberlain to the Duke of Argyll. He ordered yet more evictions. But since 1964 a helicopter has regularly whirled in 'the Dutchman', new proprietor Dr Jan de Vries, boss of a multinational building and civil engineering organisation. He owns roughly two-thirds of Coll (the two ends have always been held separately); his main interest the island's pheasant and partridge.

The road north forks left at Arnabost to more fine sandy beaches at Traigh Grianaig and Traigh Hogh, and Coll's highest hill Ben Hogh, 339ft, worth the climb for the superb views out to Barra and Uist.

Right from Arnabost the road dips and rises to the rugged north-eastern end, past humbug-striped rocks, secluded sandy coves and the crumbling ruins of 19th c cottages, many being rebuilt by energetic incomers. At the end is Sorisdale – favourite picnic beach and the last thatched croft, home of Hector McKinnon, 82-year-old coastguard with the best TV reception on the island.

There's the excellent hotel, tel Coll 334; Mrs C. Stewart has self-catering cottages and caravans to let, Mrs MacRae caravans in Cornaigbeg – addresses simply Isle of Coll, Argyll. Look out for ads too, in *The Scotsman*. Campers can stay in the field behind the hotel or at either end of the island. Hotel and PO act as general information centres and will help with hiring bikes, taxis (no self-drive car hire), sea-fishing trips for saithe, lythe, flounder and mackerel, and permission to fish in the lochs. Betty MacDougall's excellent 'Guide to Coll' is available locally or from Tourist Office, Oban – see *Information*.

Tiree

'Tiree – south-west by west, 6, 11 miles, 998 rising...' Just a name on the shipping forecast to many, but these forecasts are enough to indicate that it's often windy here. Highlanders reckon you can tell a Tiree man by his 80° gait. But it doesn't blow so much in summer when Tiree usually appears in a different set of meteorological statistics – its sunshine record is exceptionally high, especially in May.

Low, flat and golden – so low (the greater part about 25ft above sea level) it looks as though a wave could wash right over, leaving its three hills sticking out of the water like stranded humps. About 12 miles long and 3 wide, with coastline scalloped by vast curving silvery bays, the island is drenched in a bright white light made even brighter by meadows thick with daisies and buttercups, lochs fringed with iris. The sandy pastures are used to raise lambs and calves, given a daily tablet to prevent 'pine', caused by a cobalt deficiency in the machair grass.

Straggling Scarinish is the capital with hotel, bank, PO etc (Balemartine to the west is a much prettier village), but most of the 800 people (in 1831, 4,450) are scattered over the island in crofts, many in traditional houses with 5ft thick walls and windows like tunnels.

Since 1679 it has been owned by the Dukes of Argyll.

Tiree's earlier settlers chose an enchanting spot when they built the broch at Vaul. A 1st c 30ft diameter tower with galleried 13ft-thick walls is the best of island's archaeological remains. Deep rocky gullies and pockets of white sand make a perfect hide-and-seek bay and, judging by the number of shattered limpet shells,

sea-birds' larder. With countless mad hares (no rabbits on Tiree) and high-pitched yelp of the oyster-catcher, the little loch further along is like a secret pool of the animals.

Best for walking of a slightly tougher kind is the south-western corner. Balephuill Bay, a scimitar of white sand, links Ben Hynish, the highest hill at 460ft, and Ceann a'Mhara, a wild and stormy headland quite unlike the rest of Tiree. Fulmars, kittiwakes and razorbills nest in the craggy 200ft cliffs, wild geranium

and thrift bloom in the ledges. In 1838, in swirling seas some 12 miles offshore, Alan Stevenson (Robert Louis's uncle) began his great Victorian engineering feat, the Skerryvore Light, at Hynish, the signalling tower he built to keep in touch with the lighthouse and model square to house the keepers.

Further on around the coast, the beach of lilac mussel shells at Sraid Ruadh is the place to watch the sun set. Between Balephetrish Bay and Vaul, huge pinky-brown Clach a Choire (if you can find it) is a ringing stone probably brought in on Ice Age ice from Rhum. The eastern end overlooks the rocky island of Gunna, wintering home for flocks of barnacle geese which roost there by night and forage over Tiree and Coll. It also has a grey seal colony, about 50 pups born each Oct. Inland the marshland around the lochs is a perfect winter habitat for snipe, ready to be shot in huge numbers every Jan. Once reckoned the best shoot in Europe.

Tiree has two hotels, the Scarinish (tel Scarinish 410/308) by the old harbour, and the Lodge (Scarinish 353/368) which also has self-catering flats. Balephetrish Guest House (Scarinish 549) is also open to non-residents for meals, tea and coffee. Island House, 18th c residence of the factors to the Dukes of Argyll, can be rented for holidays, details Argyll Estates Office, Cherry Park, Inveraray, Argyll, but self-catering cottages, mostly let to friends of friends, are hard to find. The 9-hole golf course at Vaul welcomes visitors. Tickets for fishing brown trout in the lochs available from Mr Gillis, Gamekeeper's House, Scarinish. The half-dozen stores sell excellent island-baked loaves, so you don't have to depend on 'Glasgow bread' for picnics. Also look out on their notice boards for dances, carnivals etc. Craft shop at Glebe House, near Gott Pier, specialises in sheepskins – open summer 10-1 daily except Sun. Tiree Motor Co, Crossapol, has self-drive car and taxi service. Boat is also available for charter – details tel Scarinish 469. Bikes from Neil MacLean, Crossapol, tel Scarinish 428.

The dramatic falls of Eas Fors, Lagganulva, Mull.

**Briefing by
Richard Findlater
and Pamela Brown**

THE INNER HEBRIDES

Skye·Raasay·Muck·Eigg·Rhum·Canna

BY JOANNA KILMARTIN

Almost tethered to the mainland, the Isle of Skye spreads its wings off the deserted west coast of the Highlands from which its tenuous-seeming lifelines of road and rail reach back over mountain and moorland as far as Inverness and Fort William. After the scale of this intervening wilderness, Skye appears a haven of domestication towards which gossiping islanders cross the Straits of Kyleakin or the Sound of Sleat on the ferries of Caledonian MacBrayne whose timetables govern their lives. (The Sea in the famous lilt, of course, is that of the Minch between the Inner and Outer Hebrides; Skye is the second largest of these islands, with a length of coastline out of all proportion to its size.)

Flower-filled meadows at Pooltiel, north-west Skye.

The majority of travellers leave the mainland either from Mallaig, a small port congested with prawn-boats, for wooded rural Sleat, peninsula of gardens and comfortable settlers, or from Kyle of Lochalsh, taking the short ferry-crossing for the principal centres of Portree and Broadford and the remote northern headlands of Trotternish, Waternish and Duirinish. A few take the small cosy plane from Glasgow to the informal airstrip and perhaps manage to grasp, as never from the ground, the island's bewildering topography of closely-grouped mountains, promontories and penetrating sea lochs: to the observer on foot, these ubiquitous features will appear to shift in relation to one another fast enough; to the motorist, actually to revolve around him.

But the most unusual approach to Skye is on its loneliest side, leaving from the tiny township of Glenelg and following in reverse, as Dr Johnson and Boswell were obliged to do, the route pioneered by drovers who swam their cattle across the narrows of Kyle Rhea before undertaking the gruelling road over the Mam Ratagan Pass. Today, this fine high pass along a precipitous one-track road – a most useful preparation for motoring on

Skye – leads to a small ferry operating only in summer that will deposit you and your car on the island. (Just south of the crossing a lighthouse marks the Sandaig Islands, Gavin Maxwell's retreat, a reminder that you are entering a famous otter stronghold; and behind you, on the empty estuary, lie the ruins of Bernera Barracks, built by the English military commander 'Butcher' Cumberland the better to subdue the Jacobite rebellions whose failure signalled the decline of Skye and the Highlands.)

Above the ferry ramp, a white 17th-century inn is perched on a rock; its twin stands on the opposite bank, below the purplish hump of Torridonian sandstone over which a thread of a road snakes its way to Breakish on Skye. Here, in Broadford Bay, are the first group of satellite islands with which Skye is surrounded, perhaps gale-lashed, perhaps floating like a mirage in sea-green milk after a night's rain, or, on a sunny day, in a sea bluer than the Bay of Naples. The Priest's Island, Pabay, was put up for sale in 1980, its English owner planning a voyage to the Sargasso Sea in order to test a theory about migrating puffins. Nothing surprises the people of Skye – bred as they are to a Celtic culture with its own rich fund of minor myths – about the activities or eccentricities of incomers and entrepreneurs attracted to their island.

One who quickly made his mark – and keeps a sharp eye on others who would – is Brian Wilson, the young Scottish journalist who founded the radical *West Highland Free Press*, published on Skye. Among his first targets was Lord Macdonald, no incomer but High Chief of Clan Donald, now referred to by Wilson almost affectionately as 'Himself'. No sooner had 'Himself', aged 21, inherited the Clan Lands than death duties forced him to sell (he turned, with great good humour, to hotel-keeping). The buyer was a young Edinburgh banker, Iain Noble, whose mission to revive Celtic

---

The Needle, a rocky pinnacle on the Quiraing, Skye.

culture and dignity has much in common with Wilson's concern for crofters' rights and island self-sufficiency. Not one for half-measures, Noble has turned the impressive stone barns of the Great Steading of Ostaig over to a Gaelic College, speaks Gaelic himself for preference and employs in his hotel, farm and cottage-industries only others who can.

Similar recent changes in the north have been less reassuring. Vaternish peninsula, part of the Macleod Lands first sold in 1795, has been bought by a Dutch speculator of notably volatile temperament, while for the inhabitants of the beautiful island of Raasay the strange unfinished story of the absentee proprietorship of fast-decaying, once-elegant Raasay House recalls the bad old days of the last century.

Sheep-ranching on a profitable scale being incompatible with crofting, many Skye families were forced by landlords to emigrate. Poignant traces of populous townships are still visible, especially in the more fertile areas of the north and west: the outlines of runrig field-systems and clustered ruins of 'black' houses – those where the peat smoke rose through a hole in the thatch. Houses belonging to older crofts are identifiable by their rowan tree, talisman against bad magic. The few big houses are confined to the coast: communications on Skye were by sea, not road.

Post Office-cum-shop and Church are the centres of parish life, the one unifying (the postal van is usefully designed as a small bus), the other occasionally divisive, as when a 'Wee Free' minister campaigns against a liquor licence or when, on a Sunday in calm weather, a fisherman risks ostracism by taking out his boat. (If the tourist is not to be taken unawares, he too must adjust to a strictly-observed Sabbath.) Churches are severely simple in design, the oldest of plain stone, wood-lined, with paraffin lamps set above the pews, a long-handled cup for the collection and a huge damp-stained King James's Bible chained to a table. Morning service in winter, when Precentor and congregation chant the psalms in Gaelic, is an awesome occasion.

It's said that visitors either take an unreasoning dislike to Skye or else fall uncritically in love with it, but constant admirers almost welcome the island's secret midsummer weapons – furious weather and infuriating hordes of minute biting midges – that repel unwanted unappreciators. Even in good summer weather the moisture-laden haze can obscure the view, but no one could leave after a typical spring fortnight and not vow to return. Unthinkable never to experience again the cleanness of air that creates a light uniquely pure

and pale, the repeated sight of the Cuillin Hills, veiled or unveiled by cloud, or the moods of the sea lochs, unexpectedly appearing at every turn.

These wild seascapes and landscapes are full of life: the round head of a seal breaks above a travelling swirl, shags suddenly vanish to chase their prey underwater, rafts of eider duck see-saw in the waves. Inland, buzzards, ravens and eagles hunt over huge expanses of heather moorland and scented bog myrtle, herons stand beside lochans where tiny islets are dense with oak, birch, willow and hazel; so too are the rocky stream gulleys: grazing has left few expanses of native woodland on Skye. More and more, though, to judge by Forestry Commission ploughing, the false green of foreign conifers will disguise the shape of the hills.

In northern Skye, where the clear green of the shallows at the base of the sea cliffs is set off by algal-black basalt, lavas are responsible for some extraordinary rock-formations: the sombre, unstable blocks and brittle spires of the Quiraing that tower over a sinister gulch known as the Prison; the Old Man of Storr, the Kilt Rock and the horizontal flows that formed Macleod's Tables;

View from Elgol of the Cuillins, 'a concourse of summits'.

above all, for the island's centrepiece, the Black Cuillins, a huddled range rising magnificently out of the sea to over 3,000 feet. Glen Sligachan separates its jagged weathered profile, streaked with snow, from the imposing granitic pyramids of the Red Hills that cast their shadow over the new road to Portree. The coarse-grained gabbro of the Black Cuillins is a magnet for climbers, and ink-black Loch Coruisk hidden within their glaciated folds a target for tourists, but their sudden sub-arctic weather can be a bitter enemy.

The distinguished Gaelic poet Sorley MacLean, brought up on Raasay from which, perhaps, Skye and the Cuillins look their most enchanted, writes of their 'exact and serrated blue ramparts' and again, in his own translation, as seen from Loch Ainort:

> *A company of mountains, an upthrust of*
> *mountains*
> *a great garth of growing mountains*
> *a concourse of summits, of knolls, of hills*
> *coming on with a fearsome roaring.*

Declaimed in his sonorous Gaelic, MacLean's verse sounds like opera, and the Cuillins are indeed operatic in their grandeur.

The MacLean family history, not uncommon

of its kind on Skye and Raasay, illustrates the islands' principal export: brains. (Another was blood: two World Wars took a disproportionate toll.) Of Sorley's generation, the sons of a tailor-crofter on Raasay, all were exceptional graduates and scholars: John, who already had Latin *before* attending Portree High School, read Classics at Edinburgh, Cambridge and Vienna Universities and had translated the Odyssey and two Books of the Iliad into Gaelic before he died in 1970; Calum became a noted Celtic folklorist, two other sons are doctors in Uist and Yorkshire. Sorley MacLean now lives in his great-great-great-grandfather's house at Braes on Skye, a township where others of his forebears ended up after having been 'cleared'. Braes soon became congested with evicted crofters who, in 1882, fought the sheriff and police officers in the famous Battle of the Braes. Security of tenure was won eventually, but the population declined nevertheless.

Despite the obliteration of cultural identity by the English in revenge for the Jacobite rebellions, despite depletion by clan-fighting, famine and smallpox, the kelp industry had brought the population to a peak of 23,000 by 1841. A history of neglect, bureaucracy and loss of morale has reduced it to just over 7,000 and a dangerous reliance on tourism; everything that is imported, as most things are, or exported, sheep included, must cross not only the sea but the West Highland wilderness.

One of today's Skye children, Innes Morrison, attends a typically tiny primary school on the boulder-strewn beach at Elgol (a beautiful place, from which Prince Charles Edward left Skye). If he's lucky, Innes will go to Portree High School to be taught by Sorley MacLean's son-in-law; the alternative is Fort William School where, inevitably, cultural identities become blurred and aspirations linked to the metropolis. There are few jobs on Skye. Unless he becomes a prawn-fisherman like his father, who also runs boat-trips to Loch Coruisk, eked out by some crofting or winkle-picking, Innes may have to emigrate.

Descendants of older generations who did so return as a special kind of tourist (expatriate Macdonalds to the Clan Donald Centre, for instance), men and women who have kept their culture alive in Nova Scotia, in Texas, in Australia. Once this culture is recognised and supported nearer home for the asset it is, Iain Noble strongly believes, pointing to the undeniable success of the Faeroe Islanders, once Skyemen can take a justifi-able pride in it, then Skye and Raasay will prosper materially as well.

JOANNA KILMARTIN

Skye

BASICS

Big island divided into six peninsulas by intricate coastline of sea lochs. Lochs and peninsulas each have a different character, making Skye ideal for exploring. Staggeringly austere scenery – at its grandest amongst the Red and Black Cuillins or the massive blocks and pinnacles of the Storr or the Quiraing. Central Skye has miles of rolling moorland; in the north, crofting townships with salty close-cropped grazing land; in the south, more sheltered areas around Torrin and Sleat have gnarled woods and are comparatively lush. This variety reflects a complex geology with many unique features. Nothing here ever looks the same two days running. Light and weather rearrange 60 million-year-old features at whim.

Skye has a history of Viking invasion, clan warfare, reprisals for harbouring Bonnie Prince Charlie,

clearances, enforced emigration and crofters' resistance to the withdrawal of their rights. In 1841 there were 23,000 people here, but now there are only about 7,000 who depend mainly on crofting, fishing and increasingly on tourism. Sunday is strictly observed. There is a strong tradition of Gaelic speaking, many people are bilingual. But they rarely use Gaelic if they know it will exclude you from conversation. There is no problem understanding their accent in English, but their wit may leave you standing. People here are very welcoming to visitors. If you go early or late in the season you may find some facilities like cafés and boat trips are not available. Otherwise surprisingly mild dry weather makes April, May and June best times to go. July and Aug have maximum midges and summer rainfall. Skye's dependence on visitors means there are plenty of places to stay at all prices, although during school holidays it is advisable to book ahead. The **Isle of Skye Tourist Organisation** at Meall

House, Portree, is very helpful (tel Portree 2137).

WHERE TO GO

Portree: approaching Portree from south, Old Man of Storr juts in the distance behind terraces of stone houses fringing sheltered bay. Portree is the 'capital' of Skye. The village is beginning to straggle at the edges now, but there's a large central square of solid stone buildings – churches, banks, a hotel, the police station. Tourist office is the oldest building in Portree. It was a jail in 18th c – 5,000 people watched last hanging in Skye here in 1740s. McNab's Inn (on site of Royal Hotel), was visited by Prince Charles and Flora Macdonald and later by Boswell and Johnson. Wentworth St links the square to the top level of the waterfront. From here you go down a steep brae to the most picturesque corner of the village. A terrace of cottages and small shops lines the water's edge up to the pier, where the fishing boats land their catch of king prawns, which are then frozen in the processing station there.

Above Quay St is the Lump – a wooded promontory on which stands the gaunt Highland Gathering Hall. Behind is a marvellous grassy arena cut out of the rock, where the Highland Games are held in Aug. Portree gears itself up for visitors in the summer months, with restaurants, gift shops, boat trips all in operation. There are swimming pool, tennis courts, beach on the other side of bay. But if it rains there is very little to do except shop or drink; even the library is tiny.

Shopping: Mackenzie's bakery in square has a marvellous array of rolls, muffins, scones and pancakes – also excellent shortbread, oatcake and pies. Fraser MacIntyre, the main newsagent, has a selection of books on local topics, as does D. Forsyth on the corner of Wentworth St. All you need for self-catering – choice of butchers: Millar's sells haggis, D. Matheson excellent Skye lamb; greengrocers sell courgettes and aubergines ('I can't imagine who buys them,' said one local), and there is a camping equipment shop in Viewfield Rd.

Eating and Drinking: only pub in Portree is the one used by fishermen on Quay St. Otherwise all drinking is

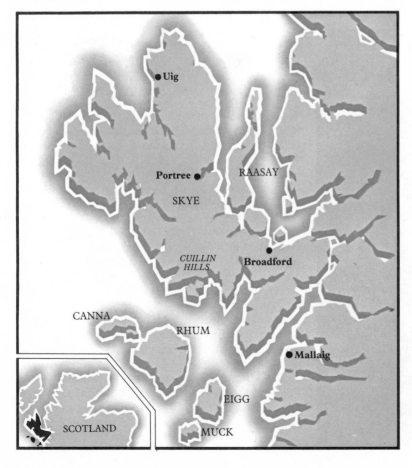

Uig

Portree

SKYE

RAASAY

CUILLIN
HILLS

Broadford

CANNA

RHUM

Mallaig

EIGG

MUCK

SCOTLAND

done in hotel bars – Royal, Rosedale and Portree Hotels have public bars with a local feel. The Cuillin Hills Hotel has comfortable bar with good lunchtime snacks (usually plenty of local salmon) and fine view of Black Cuillins. Best place to eat in Portree is the King's Haven Hotel (tel Portree 2290) which also has pleasant coffee shop. Not many places to eat cheaply – a couple of cafés are open in season and a fish and chip shop in a Portakabin in car park. Fitted out with old chara-banc seats and colour telly, this place is a godsend – it's open late and on Sun. Most places on Skye serve meals early, you'll be lucky to get anything after 8.30.

Outside Portree there are restaur-ants worth knowing about and easily missed – the Three Chimneys at Colbost, near Dunvegan (tel Glendale 258), Macdonald's Hotel at Ken-saleyre (tel Skeabost Bridge 339), the Three Rowans, Kildonan (tel Edin-bane 286), and the Edinbane Lodge Restaurant (tel Edinbane 217).

Broadford stands under the eastern edge of the Red Hills. It is best centre for south end of island, though Cuil-lins more accessible by road from Portree. The village is scattered along an open bay with splendid views of mainland mountains. At low tide, bay is a good place to beachcomb. Broad-ford itself only lines the west end of the bay but joins on to a succession of small settlements. At Upper Breakish School House is the *West Highland Free Press* (see *Specialities*) and just beyond is the airstrip where planes from Glasgow land most days. On A850.

Uig: another small settlement lining an arching, steep-sided bay. From the pier here ferries leave for Outer Hebrides ports of Tarbert and Loch-maddy. There are hotels, guest-houses and B & Bs, as well as shops and a restaurant. Well worth explor-ing the turning to Balnacnoc up Glen Uig where landslips similar to those at the Quiraing have produced a delightful miniature version with, reputedly, 365 small hills, a pinnacle called Ewen's Castle and a sheltered lochan – it's all like a set for 'A Mid-summer Night's Dream'. On A856.

Dunvegan Castle: the only stately home on Skye, ancestral home of the Clan Macleod for 700 years. The castle stands on a rock overlooking

Above: *Sunset at Dunvegan, ancestral home of the Clan Macleod.*
Below: *Re-furbishing a fishing boat in the harbour at Portree.*

Dunvegan Loch which is scattered with small islands. The building has a gaunt, stuccoed early 19th c exterior with much older sections embedded in it. The 14th c keep has been given a sprinkling of turrets, but still contains a dreadful pit dungeon. The old banqueting hall has been altered into a pleasant drawingroom which con-tains the sacred clan talisman: the Fairy Flag. It is thought to have originated in 7th c Rhodes. The legend is that the fairy wife of the 4th chief, who gave it to the clan, endowed it with the power to protect the clan three times from grave danger. It is known to have been used twice. Rory Mor's Horn and the Dunvegan Cup both have fine silver work. There is a

good collection of Macleod portraits including works by Zoffany, Raeburn and Ramsay, and an exhibition of clan and local relics ranging from a Pictish symbol stone to Bonnie Prince Charlie's waistcoat. At the end of the 18th c trees were planted and now the wooded grounds are a marvellous oasis in an otherwise generally tree-less landscape. Dunvegan village at head of loch has hotels, shops, garages, and there is a café in castle car park. (See also *Activities – Swim-ming* for coral beaches nearby, and *Boat Trips* for seeing seals.) Open weekdays early April-mid-May and late Sept – late Oct 2-5, mid-May-late Sept 10.30-5. Admission charge. On A863.

SIGHTSEEING

Armadale Castle – Clan Donald Centre: portions of this 19th c Gothic mansion have been saved from the last stages of dereliction and turned into a centre for expatriate Macdonalds. Once the family seat of the clan chief, Lord of the Isles. An excellent restaurant for teas and suppers in the summer and the best book shop on Skye make up for the fact that there is as yet little to see in the museum. The Victorian wooded grounds are a splendid place to spend an afternoon, laid out with stately exotic trees worthy of Kew – Armadale boasts the finest Wellingtonias in Britain, also woodland walks and nature trail. Open April-Oct weekdays 10-5.30, July-mid-Sept, weekdays 10-8, Sun 2-5.30. Admission charge. On A851.

Flora Macdonald Monument, Kilmuir Churchyard: superbly situated overlooking the sea, this 19th c Celtic cross is inscribed with John-son's tribute to her. Over 25 years after her famous boat trip, Boswell described her as 'a little woman, of a genteel appearance, uncommonly mild and well bred'. Kilmuir is not far from the ruins of Monkstadt House where Flora went for help when she first landed from Benbecula with Bonnie Prince Charlie dressed as her maid, 'Betty Burke'. At Kingsburgh, the lady of the house was appalled to find 'an odd muckle trallup – making long wide steps through the hall that I could not like her appearance at all'

Tarskavaig and the Cuillins, the 'exact and serrated blue ramparts' of the Gaelic poet Sorley MacLean.

until she was let into the secret and they stayed the night. This was only one of the many nail-biting episodes for the Prince during his months of hiding. Flora was imprisoned till 1747. She returned to Skye, married, had seven children, several of which were born in a cottage at Flodigarry, emigrated to North Carolina for a few years but ended her life in Skye in 1790, when 3,000 mourners were said to have attended her funeral here.

Trumpan Churchyard: only the ruins of this small church remain, perched high above the sea at the

desolate tip of the Vaternish peninsula. In 1578 this was the scene of a typical atrocity of clan warfare between the Macdonalds and the Macleods. The Macdonalds, seeking revenge for a massacre on Eigg, drew up their galleys at Ardmore Bay just below the churchyard and set fire to church with the Macleod congregation inside. One wounded girl escaped through a window and warned her clansmen, who gathered with Fairy Flag to retaliate. The Macdonald galleys had been stranded on the beach by the outgoing tide, so that the raiding party was trapped and killed by the Macleods, who toppled a wall down onto their corpses – said still to be unearthed occasionally.

In the churchyard are two reminders of the savage justice of the past. A large boulder with a tiny hole in it was used as a trial stone. The suspect was blindfolded and told to aim at the hole – if he hit it he was innocent, if not . . . The real grave of poor Lady Grange is also here. Two mock funerals had been enacted for her – to disguise the fact that her husband had imprisoned her for life when she discovered he was at centre of Jacobite plot and as a Hanoverian threatened to expose it. She spent years going slowly mad, being moved from one island hideout to another. Track off B886.

Crofters' Cottage Museums: three museums established in old, thatched crofters' cottages to show what living in them was like until fairly recently. They are different in character, however, so it's worth visiting more than one. The Black House Folk Museum, Colbost, is in the earliest type of house with fireplace in centre of the floor and a hole in the roof for the smoke to escape – hence the name. House divided into two rooms – one for people, other for animals. Also an illicit whisky still. Open Easter-Oct. Admission charge (tel Glendale 291). On B884 off A864.

At the Luib Folk Museum and the Skye Cottage Museum, Kilmuir, you can see a later development of the cottage. Both have proper fireplaces, and the second room has become a bedroom. Both also have good collections of local objects and farming implements. The Luib museum has informative displays on local history;

the Skye Cottage Museum includes an old smithy, loom and collection of photographs and documents. Luib Folk Museum open daily Easter-Oct 10-7, admission charge. On A850. Skye Cottage Museum open weekdays Easter-Oct 9-6, admission charge. On A855.

The Black Cuillins (see also *Activities – Walking* and *Climbing*): there are only two places where you can get at all close to the Black Cuillins by road – Sligachan and Glen Brittle. At both points you are only on the edge of the range – to explore further you must be an experienced and fit walker, and eventually climber. The boat trip to Loch Coruisk (see *Sightseeing*) is the only other way to get closer. The view at Sligachan is unforgettable: the symmetrical red granite mounds of the Red Hills on one side of the valley, straight ahead two lonely peaks – red Marsco with black Blaven behind – and, on the right, the Sgurr nan Gillean end of the Black Cuillins. The basalt dykes which seeped between the harder black gabbro have weathered to give the latter their serrated outline. Climbing along the ridge is like going up and down the teeth of a saw-blade, with the rock falling away – often sheer – on either side, and then fanning out into long screes which shoot down into the corries. The highest peak of the Cuillins, Sgurr Alisdair, is only accessible to the walker who is prepared to toil up the most famous of these screes – the Great Stone Shoot (1,500ft).

If you want to walk rather than climb, Glen Brittle is a better place to start from since the main body of the range is accessible from there. Car park in Forestry Commission plantation at head of glen makes good base from which to explore Coire na Creiche, a wide grassy corrie with pools and waterfalls where last clan battle in Scotland was fought in 1601. Bruach na Frithe at head of this corrie is recommended as the easiest summit to get to, with good views – path up from Bealach a'Mhaim. Paths from lower down glen lead up to higher corries. There is a so-called 'Tourist Route' up Sgurr nan Gillean from Sligachan, but be warned – the Youth Hostel Guide to Skye says of it, 'Followers of this return with a sharply enhanced appreciation of

Library and drawing room in Dunvegan Castle, the only stately home on Skye.

what is expected from a Skye "tourist".' Glen Brittle off B8009, Sligachan on A850.

The Red Cuillins: in shape and colour these mountains are a complete contrast to the Black Cuillins. Their appearance changes with the light; some days their red granite screes become a dazzling pale pink. They stretch along the east coast close to the main road between Sligachan and Broadford. Their summit ridge is easily approached from Glen Sligachan. No one has yet equalled the astonishing time for ascent of Glamaig – over 2,500ft – by a barefoot Gurkha soldier in 1899. He took 37 minutes up and 18 back from Sligachan old bridge. Off A850.

Old Man of Storr: 7 miles north of Portree at the far edge of Storr Lochs, a group of black basalt pinnacles tower above the Staffin road. The highest, tilted on its plinth, looks like a giant neolithic standing stone. This is the Old Man. Behind is the great cliff face of the Storr itself, over 2,000ft high; below, the land falls away to the sea. Some of the most interesting arctic/alpine plants on Skye grow in profusion towards the top of the cliffs and on the summit plateau, best reached up the Storr's north-east shoulder, round top of east cliff and up gap in smaller north-facing cliff. (See *Flora and Fauna*.) Off A855.

The Quiraing: at northern tip of the same flow of basalt lava that formed Storr cliffs and the Old Man, the weight of the basalt has caused the shaly strata underneath to give way in one of Britain's most spectacular landslips, the Quiraing. Beneath the cliff face is a jumble of gigantic blocks and pinnacles. Beyond, a series of grassy hills and small lochs fall away to the sea above Staffin Bay. Narrow path leads from car park just under cliffs on Brogaig-Uig road. Follow ridge round to the Prison, enclosed by rock walls, the Needle and beyond to the Table – a grassy pitch on top of a huge block of rock. In more energetic times an annual game of shinty was played there at midsummer. The screes near the Needle are not for the squeamish and some children find them a bit much too, but there are plenty of sheltered spots that make ideal hide-and-seek or cowboys-and-Indians territory. Off A855.

The Kilt Rock: a favourite with the Victorians. The basalt columns and strata of this cliff face fall vertically, resembling the pleats of a kilt. Formation is similar to Fingal's Cave. Viewpoint on the Staffin road, close to where the waters of Loch Mealt fall 400ft into the sea, is a bit over-organised as a picnic site, and newly fenced to prevent people being blown over the edge (it has happened).

Ord road: loops off the main Sleat road between the picturesque little village of Isle Ornsay and Knock Castle and rejoins it again just before Armadale. The island's contrasting scenery can be seen at its most impressive from here. On a rocky promontory on the shore at Tokavaig are the ruins of the castle of Dunscaith. Here Irish Bronze Age hero Cuchullin was said to have been taught the arts of war by Sgathach, the Terrible Queen of Skye, who had a college of arms with five-score warrior women. It was definitely occupied by the Macdonalds of Sleat. Off A851.

Loch Coruisk and the Elgol road: the drive from Broadford to Elgol is one of the most attractive and varied on Skye – the lush Strath Suardal valley, Loch Cill Chroisd, limestone country around Torrin (a pretty village where Skye marble is quarried), round the edge of Loch Slapin with best views of shark-like mountain Blaven and on to Elgol, which has stupendous views of the Cuillins, and its village school on the shore. From here take $\frac{1}{4}$-hour powerboat journey to Loch Coruisk. There's a $\frac{1}{2}$-mile walk up to the loch from the beach. The loch itself is one of the most famous places on Skye, much painted by the Romantics. Sir Walter Scott in 'Lord of the Isles' awards 'this dread shore' the 'prize for desert dignity'. Its still waters lie in a glacial basin 2 miles long, completely encircled and cut off by the black rock walls of the Cuillins. Well worth the trip, weather permitting – telephone Loch Scavaig 213 to find out. Otherwise you can walk along coast from Elgol, as long as you are prepared to negotiate 'The Bad Step' where rock falls sheer into sea and there is a crack to traverse. A881.

Glendale: as you drive over the pass from Colbost this gentle green glen opens out before you with crofters' cottages dotting the hills either side of the river Hamara. But this peaceful community had troubles enough 100 years ago. On the road into Glendale is a monument to the 'Martyrs' of Glendale Land League; crofters here resisted erosion of their privileges – by rent strike and by driving their cattle to graze on landlord's land – with such solidarity that only a Government gun-boat in the bay forced them into token submission. Many other areas on Skye resisted too – and rent arrears on the island were estimated at £20,000 by 1886. But only at Glendale did crofters afterwards come to own their own land.

Down on the shore, where you can look out to the high cliffs of Dunvegan Head and to the Outer Hebrides on a good day, is a small thatched watermill. Now restored as a museum, the mill is 200 years old and was in use until about 50 years ago. Admission charge. Skye Venture Knitwear in Glendale have a range of very covetable garments: speckled shooting cardigans, hand-knitted waistcoats in undyed wool, Aran pullovers. B884. Many other good craft shops in this area.

Niest Point Lighthouse: on the most westerly point of Skye, it stands on a rocky promontory jutting out from Waterstein Head. From here you can look back to the splendid cliffs and to the waterfall where Loch Mor spills over into the sea – and on a clear day you can see across to the Outer Isles. The road ends about a mile from the lighthouse, take the track over the diagonal silhouette of the headland. To arrange a visit to lighthouse, telephone first, Glendale 200. Off B884.

Raasay

Sheltered by Skye, Raasay is a comparatively lush island with woods, hidden arable valleys and overgrown gorges. The ferry from Sconser in Skye crosses Raasay Sound, landing at the southern end of the island. From here to Eilean Tigh, its northern promontory, is 14 miles. A road runs most of the way – made up as far as Brochel Castle and then hand-made to Arnish by a remarkable crofter called Calum Maclean. It took him 8 years.

Brochel Castle, home of Raasay Macleods until 16th c, stands on a rock on the east coast. The Macleods moved from here to the site of the present Raasay House at Clachan. They sent 100 men to fight for Bonnie Prince Charlie at Culloden and also helped in his escape.

In retaliation the English destroyed every house on the island, killed all the animals and destroyed all the boats too. But by the time Boswell and Johnson got there about 25 years later, the houses were rebuilt and the island

restored to its civilised norm – they even had marmalade for breakfast. Raasay House, basically 18th c, was home of the Macleods till 1840s when they had to sell up and emigrate – perhaps because they had never forced their tenants to. New owners rapidly cleared 20 of the island's 27 square miles for sheep and game, forcing at least 98 families to emigrate. The island was later bought by an Englishman who planted shrubberies of rhododendron, fuchsia hedges and acres of mixed woodland. He stocked the moors with grouse, pheasant and deer. The grounds are well worth exploring, look out for dogs' graveyard near the Victorian wing. Churchton House is a pleasant guest-house (tel Raasay 226). There is a Youth Hostel at Creachan Cottage.

The mountain of Duncaan, flattened with a topping of basalt like Macleod's Tables on Skye, dominates the island. The view from the top is worth the climb, but you may not have the energy for the reel Boswell danced on the top.

Apart from a little work with the Forestry Commission, people on Raasay are entirely dependent on crofting. Most of the 150-odd islanders live at Inverarish, where there is a very good shop and PO. There are two churches here, one Wee Free and the other, to which most islanders go, for a group of even stricter dissenters, who broke with the Wee Frees at end of 19th c, led by the Raasay minister. Sunday observance is strict here.

Love of the island is beginning to bring Raasay people who had settled elsewhere back here to a hard life of crofting, but the future is not rosy. At least 40 per cent of the island's population is over 60; and although men can sometimes eke out crofting with other forms of work, there is no work for the young women at all.

SPECIALITIES

Run Rig: the local rock group have effected the difficult marriage between the Gaelic musical tradition and pop and are now packing halls in Glasgow. Watch the *West Highland Free Press* to see if and where they are playing locally.

West Highland Free Press: this unique local paper was started by four graduates of Dundee university in the early 1970s and is still produced and printed by a tiny but energetic staff in the Old School House at Breakish. This radical paper's campaigning vigour has raised a few hackles but it is read in practically every household on Skye and its circulation is still growing on the Outer Hebrides and the mainland. It is *the* place to look if you want to find out not only what is happening each week but also about issues affecting the area. Published Fri.

Gaelic College: Iain Noble has set up this college in the Great Steading at Ostaig to foster Gaelic culture which is still so deep-rooted on Skye. The college has an excellent library

The drive from Broadford to Elgol, one of the most attractive and varied on Skye.

The Sound of Sleat, with Skye to the right.

and bookshop and runs 2 and 3-week language courses in the summer, mainly for those who already have some knowledge of Gaelic. Accommodation can be arranged in Gaelic-speaking households. The college is the venue for Scottish Arts Council cultural weekends, and holds piping, drumming and Scottish dancing classes. For information write to Sabhal Mor Ostaig, Teanga, Isle of Skye (tel Ardvasar 280).

Skye Terriers are bred at the Eileana-Cheo Kennels, Ardvasar (tel Ardvasar 239). These little long-bodied, long-haired terriers were bred for hunting foxes, rats and other vermin until 1930s. Now show dogs rather than working dogs, and too plump to get down fox-holes.

ACTIVITIES

Walking: a great variety, from the most strenuous hill walking (nothing in Black Cuillins is easier than Striding Edge on Helvellyn) to pleasant strolling on springy seaside turf or sandy beaches. Midge repellant is essential in summer. If you want to follow one of the glens, eg Sligachan, which leads through to beautiful

beach at Camasunary – 16 miles there and back, you need proper walking boots, as track is both rocky and famously boggy. Boots are obviously a must for the Cuillins themselves, as is a Scottish Mountaineering Club map (Ordnance Survey not detailed enough) and a compass, which can be affected by magnetism in some parts of the Cuillins. This makes them even more dangerous in cloud. If you are walking or climbing in the Cuillins, local police provide form to fill up and leave with someone responsible, so if anything goes wrong mountain rescue team will know where to start looking – don't forget to fill one in.

From Glen Brittle, Sgurr Dearg and several other summits are accessible to the fit walker. There are fine cliff walks at Waterstein Head and from Orbost along the coast to Macleod's Maidens – needles out to sea at Idrigill. From the Elgol road there are walks to Boreraig – township deserted due to clearances – a shorter route from Kilmarie to Camasunary and a route up Blaven.

The Scottish Mountaineering Club's 'District Guide to the Island of Skye' is invaluable on the Black Cuillins. Hamish MacInnes's recent

'West Highland Walks', Vol 2 covers Skye very readably. There is a useful pamphlet, '14 Walks from Sligachan', by Donald Reid, and SYHA Guide to Isle of Skye is good value.

Climbing: the Black Cuillins are very special: 11 peaks over 3,000ft in a superb situation, rising straight out of the sea in tight formation with narrow crests and steep faces, many accessible only to the climber. The traverse of the 7-mile ridge in one day (12 hours is the average time, 18 if you take in summit of Blaven) is described by Scottish Mountaineering Club as 'the finest mountaineering excursion in the British Isles'. The Cuillins offer a whole range of other climbs from easy beginners' routes to very difficult ones indeed. There are still routes to be conquered here and in the neglected Red Cuillins.

There is a hut at Loch Coruisk which can get cut off, but most climbers use as base the Youth Hostel, Memorial Hut, self-catering cottages, or camp-site at Glen Brittle. People here know the mountains well so ask their advice, check local weather forecasts, fill up police form (see *Walking*), stay within your capabilities, do not underestimate the difficulty or the time you will take. You need to carry water on the ridge. The Scottish Mountaineering Club do two climbing guides and a map.

Cuillin Guides offer a series of 5-day courses and weekends for people with previous hill-walking experience. They range from hill walking and scrambling, through basic and intermediate rock-climbing to winter mountaineering. Contact Gerry Akroyd, current leader of the mountain rescue team, at Stac Lee, Glen Brittle, tel Carbost 289, for details.

Sailing and Boat Trips: surprisingly under-used as a sailing centre considering how beautiful it is. Duisdale Hotel on Sleat offers several sailing boats for hire to guests as well as power-boat trips to Sandaig Island, Loch Nevis for seal watching etc. Also moorings for visiting yachts. Tel Isle Ornsay 202. Strollamus Boat Centre offers everything boaty from charter, sailing lessons, moorings, to water skiing and seal cruises; for details telephone Broadford 596. Mirror dinghies can be hired from Airidh Charnach Sailing and Fishing Centre (tel Broadford 497) and from Charles Barrington (tel Ardvasar 262).

In summer pleasure cruisers from Portree Pier and Kyleakin run a variety of trips lasting about 2 hours. Fishermen sometimes offer trips to tourists in summer – ask at Tourist Office – and there are rowing boats for hire from Portree Pier. On Tues and Fri there are day trips from Uig to Tarbert in the Outer Hebrides.

Fishing: Portree Angling Association, North of Scotland College of Agriculture, Masonic Buildings, Portree (tel Portree 2993), issues permits for a variety of fishing at the north end of the island. Hill Lochs and Storr Lochs with brown trout, Loch Mealt with char, can be fished either from the bank or from a boat. They also have the fishing rights to several rivers. Salmon fishing in Skye is said to be the best in the Inner Hebrides. Many hotels in other parts of the island offer their guests fishing. They will usually offer permits to non-residents. Boats for sea angling can be hired from Strollamus Boat Centre (see *Sailing*), and from Dunvegan and Kyleakin piers. Also from Portree and Camus Moar, near Kilmuir.

Swimming and Beachcombing: several sandy beaches recommended for swimming – Glen Brittle, Staffin, Claigan Coral Sands, Talisker Bay, Camus Ban (near Portree), Balmeanach, Tarskavaig Bay and the fine shingle at Torrin Bay. Although much of the waterline is black basalt rocks or high cliff, the beaches are good combing territory, specially at Claigan near Dunvegan, where the white coral is a great surprise amongst the black boulders and where brightly coloured sea snail shells are well worth collecting.

Pony Trekking: Strollamus Pony Trekking (Broadford 269) and Macleod's, 4 Ullinish, Struan.

Golf: the 9-hole golf course at Sconser on the edge of Loch Sligachan must be one of the most beautifully situated in the country.

Stern, handless mermaid in the grounds of Raasay House.

Dances and Ceilidhs: frequent dances throughout the summer (and at least fortnightly the rest of the year), in the Skye Gathering Hall at Portree (see 'Skye Directory' or *West Highland Free Press* for dates). The ceilidhs held here and in hotels and guesthouses provide a more Scottish entertainment. See *West Highland Free Press* for when and where. Edinbane and Dunvegan hotels have ceilidhs every night.

Flora and Fauna

Flowers: only spot in Britain where alpine rockcress is known to grow is high above Coire na Creiche in Black Cuillins. Other arctic/alpines in isolated patches there. But on Trotternish ridge, particularly at the Storr and the Quiraing, west coast conditions bring a profusion of arctic/alpines down close to sea level. The rarest is the tiny plant Iceland purslane. Mountain avens grow in spectacular cushions on the Durness limestone pavements around Torrin and Ord. The thyme-scented grasslands of Waternish are good place for orchids; there's brilliant heathery moor, and crofting land dotted with ox-eye daisies and corn marigolds. There is a National Nature Reserve at Tokavaig. Skye has rare ferns and many kinds of moss and lichen.

Birds: Skye is probably the place in Britain where you stand most chance of seeing a golden eagle – a considerable number nest on inaccessible cliff faces, some not far from the road. They usually fly silently, unlike the more common mewing buzzard. You should also see hooded crows and ravens on the moors, with luck, ptarmigan and greenshank on or near the Cuillins. Hen harriers are returning to Skye. Forestry Commission plantations have encouraged the return of siskins and other woodland birds. There are few sea-bird colonies, although they winter here – cliffs at north end of Trotternish or at Idrigill best places to look. Fulmars nest at Idrigill; on outlying Ascrib Islands off Waternish there are large puffin colonies. Fishermen will sometimes take you out there. In winter great northern divers in the Straits of Kyleakin; barnacle and white-fronted geese, snow buntings and whooper swans on the freshwater lochs.

Mammals: red deer, blue hares and abundant pygmy shrew. On Raasay a subspecies of vole, the Raasay vole. The otter is comparatively numerous. But when people say, 'Oh, otters – you can see them in the streets of Portree any day,' they are actually referring to one particular otter that used to be seen after dark trying to get chocolate out of slot machines. Three boat trips a day from Dunvegan pier, lasting an hour, to see the colonies of grey seals on islands off the coast. In the summer common porpoises, bottle-nosed whales and occasionally killer whales may be seen off Skye.

Briefing by Jessica York

THE SMALL ISLES

Muck

If the tiny fortunate fertile Isle of Muck has any cross to bear, it is its name. (The present owner, Lawrence MacEwen, tells of the discomfiture suffered by the island's late 18th-century laird for whom, poor man, according to prevailing etiquette, the only polite form of address was plain 'Muck'; and of his efforts, almost certainly unsuccessful, to get his contemporaries to call him 'Isle-of-Muck' instead.) In fact, the word is probably a corruption of the Gaelic *Muc* meaning sea-pig or porpoise, once a common animal around the island's shores.

Although swept from end to end by winter gales, Muck's low profile and small size account for a certain kindness in its climate compared to its much larger, higher, wetter and colder neighbours, Rhum and Eigg, and the easily eroded basalt of its underlying rock for its fertility and greenness: out of 1,600 acres, 100 are cultivated and the remainder high-quality pasture. The volcanic rock is responsible for the jagged sea-worn coastline of caves and cliffs, so difficult to approach by boat; the Gulf Stream for the fascinating jetsam of the tideline. In years when the Atlantic Drift is strong, West Indian beans are cast up and, if chanced upon, kept as a good-luck charm.

On seeing the broad fairways of close-cropped turf, the gentle rises broken by spinneys and hollows, an immediate impression that the visitor has arrived at an exclusive golf-links rather than a large farm appears to be startlingly confirmed by the sight, here and there on the horizon, of small white flags. These turn out to be 'tatter-flags'. Lawrence MacEwen, a progressive and environmentally-conscious farmer, is using this rough-and-ready Forestry Commission system for experimental amenity planting. (A rag attached to a post close to the ground will indicate, depending on how long it takes before it is reduced to tatters by the wind, a site's suitability for a given tree.) Lawrence MacEwen knows each existing tree on his island – and his geologist brother each existing rock – and keeps an affectionate eye on the progress of a eucalypt here (there are three thriving varieties), a Chilean beech there, each plantation carefully screened by conifers and protected by stone walls. (These, such a prominent feature on Muck, are unusual on Skye and the other Small Isles; collected over 100 years ago from the ruins of old crofthouses, they were placed in courses so idiosyncratic that they look strangely top-heavy.) Any natural woodland would have been cut for fuel centuries ago: there's virtually no peat on Muck. In a bad winter, people were reduced to burning furniture, dung and seaweed.

In common with the rest of the West Highlands, Muck's high point of prosperity came during the kelp boom triggered by the Napoleonic Wars. Laboriously netted and dragged on shore, the seaweed was dried and burned for potash to make gunpowder, a labour-intensive industry that, by 1826, had boosted the island's population to 280. With the collapse of demand and the growing interest in sheep-ranching in lieu of crofting, the bankrupt proprietor of Rhum and Muck, Maclean of Coll, evicted the crofters. Like their contemporaries on Canna and Eigg, Skye and Raasay, they sailed for the New World, the majority settling on Cape Breton Island and in Nova Scotia. (Ironically, today Cape Breton is part of Canada's Highlands National Park. The thousands of Nova Scotians who still speak Gaelic find it hard to believe how relatively few Gaelic-speakers remain in the Hebrides.) Muck's population never recovered; today it is 24, with four school-age children.

The MacEwen brothers believe their island could support – indeed must, if the community is to survive the collapse of the fishing industry – at least 50 people, envisaging a kind of collective to which each crofter would contribute his speciality as well as his produce: from pig-breeding to candle-making, baking to whisky-distilling, bulb-growing to lobster-fishing. If this is likely to happen on any Hebridean island, thanks to the energy of these two young men who inherited rather than bought their estate, it will be on the gentle fertile Isle of Muck.

NOTES

There is no transport for visitors on Muck – a road about 1½ miles long runs between the small settlements of Port Mor to the main farmhouse at Gallanach Bay on north side, which faces a sandy beach. Bronze Age burial circle nearby, now MacEwen family grave. Ben Airein, 451ft, is an easy climb offering fine views. Horse Island can be reached at low tide. Visitors can walk anywhere – several safe sandy or shell beaches.

To camp, seek permission from Isle of Muck Farms or at the farmhouse. A large modern guest house (tel Mallaig 2365) has just been completed at Port Mor, with excellent facilities, especially for families. Holiday cottages (limited) can be rented from Isle of Muck Farms. Home-produce available. Craft Shop at Port Mor sells island products and also Lawrence MacEwen's 'A Guide to Eigg and Muck' and the 'Isle of Muck Cookery Book'.

Principal entertainments are the informal ceilidhs, with Scottish and Highland dancing, Gaelic and English singing, to which visitors are invited. They are also welcome to help on the farm.

About 80 birds breed on Muck and Eigg; Manx shearwater nest. Intertidal communities are of special interest for the numbers of southern species carried on the Atlantic Drift.

Eigg

Presided over by an impressive sphinx-shaped ridge of lava known simply as the Sgurr, Eigg is the largest of the Small Isles – roughly nine miles square – and the centre of their scattered communities. The island's seigneur, Keith Schellenberg, also presides: often he's there on the jetty, an amiable casual figure, when the launch returns after transferring passengers from the inter-island ferry, ready to arrange for their accommodation and conduct them personally to his Tea Room.

Sunset lights the windows of Howlin farmhouse, last dwelling on the north-west tip of Eigg.

Since 1975, Schellenberg, a public school-educated Yorkshire businessman, has been Eigg's 'government' and 'civil service' rolled into one. Health, Education, Telecommunications and Religious Affairs seem to be the only portfolios he doesn't hold. He manages his woodlands and hill farms, the island's public transport, a minibus, and the ferrying of livestock, vehicles, supplies and materials to and from the mainland by means of an old-fashioned ferry-boat that also acts as general rescue vessel for the area; supervises the pottery and craft workshops and the letting of a variety of holiday cottages; organises hockey fixtures against the neighbouring island of Muck and the Eigg Highland Games.

The Eigg Games are a typically Schellenbergian invention, with the participation not only of every man, woman and child but also friends from the St Moritz Tobogganing Club with whom he does the Cresta Run. An ex-member of British Olympic winter sports teams, Schellenberg enjoys a combination of endurance-test and speed (powerboat racing is another hobby). He also likes team games; lacking adults, he will assemble children from all over the island to join his own in elaborate contests that range over the large, pleasantly rambling house and lawns of Kildonan Lodge, up the drive lined with palm trees, in and out of the bamboo plantations and down to the Edwardian bathing-hut on the shell-beach.

The Singing Sands near Laig Bay are another favourite playground, where, even when the heights of Rhum opposite are darkened by cloud, the white quartz gives off its own peculiar light. Damp in the wake of the tide, the uniformly-shaped grains squeak underfoot like chalk on a blackboard, and, when dry, emit a continuous moan; a fresh water spring spouting from a cliff-complex of caves and arches mingles with inrushing sea foam; reddish rocks protruding from the sand are patterned by black and white lichens and great fly-whisks of kelp lie about the tide-line. More adventures are provided by the spectacular chain of lochs along the back of the Sgurr, where an islet on which a fortification inhabited by legendary warrior-queens once stood is reached by a hidden causeway and where, in winter, there is skating; and by the many sea caves. In one of them, in 1577, the entire population was suffocated in a particularly barbaric revenge killing between clans: this nasty tit-for-tat was perpetrated by the Macleods on the Macdonalds of Clan Ranald.

The Schellenberg government has, if not an opposition party, then a semi-independent one: the crofting community at the north end of the island manages its own affairs. As police constable and postmistress, the MacKinnons, brother and sister, look after law and order (crime rate virtually nil) and the island's commissariat; a minister and a priest regularly visit. Health is the responsibility of Dr Hector Maclean, whose round also includes the islands of Canna, Rhum and Muck – as often as not in his capacity as piper at the organised ceilidhs held every summer. Education and Telecommunications are provided by the State: a schoolteacher for the nine pupils and, for 20 telephones, a new 100-line, £100,000 automatic radio-telephone exchange, better for emergencies than the pre-1954 system of smoke-signals perhaps, but a much resented piece of bureaucratic extravagance nevertheless.

From 1893 onwards, the long reigns of an arms dealer and two shipping families, the Petersens and the Runcimans, gave Eigg a stability that was shattered by three changes of ownership between 1966 and 1975; now the 80 islanders are keeping their fingers crossed. Everyone who desires to own an island is a romantic, but to be the proprietor of an estate whose boundary fence is the sea and whose tenants are more than usually dependent, you need to be a realist as well.

NOTES

Day-visitors arriving on 5.30am ferry from Mallaig normally have about $4\frac{1}{2}$ hours on Eigg, Sat only, on the Glenuig day trip about 6 hours, on the Arisaig trip about 4 hours (see *How to get there*). A road runs north-south across the island and Eigg Estate runs minibus tours to the Singing Sands, the Kildonan Pottery and craft centre and the Gruline, a ruined crofting township beneath the Sgurr. Nearest sandy beach is Kildonan Bay; a fine beach at Laig Bay in the north. Two sea caves, the Massacre Cave and the Cathedral Cave, a mile from the pier, can be reached on foot by leaving the wide track for the Sgurr and the Gruline by first stile on left after Galmisdale House; candle or torch needed. 14th c ruins of Kildonan Church, beside side road to Kildonan House, are built on the site of St Donan's early 7th c church and contain some carved stones. The Tea Room and craft-shop, also selling books and mugs, are beside the Estate Office at head of pier.

Visitors wanting overnight accommodation or to camp should visit the Estate Office on arrival. Ordnance Survey 1:25,000 map of Eigg essential for walkers. Going always wet, can be rough.

Numerous self-catering holiday cottages can be rented through the

Galmisdale on Eigg, largest of the Small Isles and centre of their scattered communities.

Estate Office, ranging from attractive converted bothies, a woodman's house, a mill-house or a lonely crofter's house on the Gruline to modern bungalows. Fresh seafood and vegetables for sale; other supplies can be bought or ordered in advance from PO shop. In addition, there are independent guest-houses, including Laig Farm (tel Mallaig 82437). Kildonan House is being opened as a guest-house by the Estate Office, and the Tea Room will serve evening meals in summer.

There is a Land-Rover taxi-service. Mopeds and bicycles can be hired from Estate Office, also ponies and Mirror dinghies. There are some television sets, often run off car batteries.

A bird-list is available: red-breasted merganser, golden eagle, sparrowhawk, peregrine and corn-crake nest; sea-birds are found chiefly on the northern cliffs. On the landslip below the basalt cliffs of Bheinn Bhuidhe arctic-alpine plants are abundant in June. Intertidal invertebrate communities, lichens, mosses, ferns are of particular interest.

Rhum

So rum is the island of Rhum (the aspirate is optional), what with volcanic rocks of a nature otherwise found only on the moon, a baronial castle, a mausoleum in the form of a Greek temple and a reputation as The Forbidden Isle, it seemed not illogical that a first glimpse of the stepped summits of Hallival and Askival above the enveloping cloud should have called to mind somewhere as exotic as Angkor Wat.

More prosaically, a drenched mat of moor-grass, heather and bog covers the surface of Rhum, invading once-smooth roads laid down by the island's Edwardian proprietor for the four-wheeled carriages and luxurious limousines which, among other amenities astounding on a remote Hebridean island, he provided for his guests at Kinloch Castle; the latter he built of imported purple sandstone, surrounding it with imported fertile loam.

Evidently nothing seemed impossible to Sir George Bullough, heir to a Lancastrian mill-owner in an age of continuity, complacency and enormous concentrations of wealth. Thanks to an army of servants who attended to every detail, from switching on the stars in the ballroom to feeding the turtles in their tanks, nothing was.

If, for the Bulloughs, Rhum's 26,400 acres were a playground and sporting estate, for the Nature Conservancy, its present owners, the island is a multidisciplinary laboratory for the study of its unique rocks, specialised flora and fauna and island ecology, and for long-term projects: reintroducing the sea eagle, researching the breeding and behaviour of red deer and monitoring the unusual colony of Manx shearwaters – 10,000 pairs of these ocean-roaming birds make their burrows on the tops of Hallival and Askival, eerily cooing and screaming and manuring the summer pastures of the deer.

The Chief Warden also manages a pure-bred herd of Highland cattle, shaggy chestnut beasts on comically dainty trotters, and a stud of Rhum ponies, Garrons, striped like their remote ancestors on back and fetlock, that carry down the culled deer-carcases; by selling venison, the National Nature Reserve earns part of its keep. The balanced grazing of cattle and deer has coaxed from the type of moorland elsewhere grazed by sheep (selectively, thus uneconomically) a highly nutritional pasture (a discovery we may be grateful for in a siege economy), but attempts to grow even native trees on the hills have been frustrated by the searing, salt-laden winds that sometimes gust up to 100 miles an hour.

Ruined dwellings, and goats living wild on the sea cliffs, are a reminder that Rhum was once quite densely populated: in 1828, the last 208 natives were evicted by the Maclean of Coll and put on a boat for Nova Scotia. Since then, Rhum has been inhabited by incomers occupying Kinloch, the small settlement fringed with trees on the sheltered bay of Loch Scresort, and, of course, Kinloch Castle.

This colonnaded, castellated 1901 period piece – used when new as a convalescent home for Boer War wounded and today as a hotel at once slightly shabby and very opulent –

reflects an unashamed taste for display, solid comfort and novelty. Concealed behind the panelling were air-conditioning and central-heating systems and, under the stairs, the vast 'Orchestrium', a busker's dream that still blares out, when the island's hydro-electric power permits, the polkas, waltzes and marches fed into its elaborate maw. A huge hooded bath offers a choice of action, from fizzy sitz to shower wave, before guests dine beneath the electroliers at the long table that seats 16 in swivelling chairs from Sir George's steam-yacht, the 'Rhouma'.

The stars in the ballroom are switched off now, and the present population, fluctuating around 20 in winter, make their own entertainment. They are served by a schoolmistress for the two young children, a postmistress who runs a library and shop, a ferryman who takes them out to the steamer that is their link with the mainland, and a visiting minister, doctor, vet, farrier and piano-tuner.

beside the dunes, and the Bulloughs' picnic pavilion at Papadil, can be reached only on foot: expeditions feasible in the long daylight hours of summer, but where the going – like the weather – can be rough.

NOTES

Day visitors normally have 3-4 hours on Rhum, time to walk the two Nature Trails and to visit the Deer Park, Kinloch Castle and Farmsteadings. The National Nature Reserve booklet can be bought from the PO on Rhum. The lessees of Kinloch Castle often give a conducted tour; or this, and a meal, can be provided by prior arrangment. There is no café on Rhum, but limited supplies available at PO, also postcards and drawings by ornithologist John Love, who keeps a Rhum bird list.

Kinloch Castle, owned by the Nature Conservancy Council, is open as a hotel most of the year, with full-board accommodation in the princi-

Family mausoleum of Sir George Bullough, the wealthy Edwardian proprietor of Rhum.

For the summer influx of visitors who come to explore the odd corners of Rhum there is no transport. Harris Bay, site of the 'moon' rocks, where the mausoleum stands on a raised beach, Kilmory, where the castle sheets were once dried on the turf

pal bedrooms, bathrooms and reception rooms, use of billiard room and library. Special courses – such as an upholstery week to help mend the castle furniture and curtains – are planned. The original servants' bedrooms and halls are used as a hostel where self-service with full board or self-catering accommodation is available. Prices are reasonable and the food excellent; wines and spirits obtained by guests at the PO are served with appropriate ceremony. Details from the lessees, Kinloch Castle, Isle of Rhum, Inverness-shire (tel Mallaig 2037).

Visitors wanting to camp overnight should apply in advance to the Chief Warden at the NCC Reserve Office – sites are limited – and for a longer stay application should be made well in advance to the Chief Warden, The White House, Kinloch, Isle of Rhum (tel Mallaig 2026). Camping confined to foreshore on Loch Scresort; rocky turf, fresh water stream, good bird-

watching. PO supplies may be fully stretched in summer, so advisable to shop in Mallaig, where deliveries can be arranged in advance via the Chief Warden. Films shown once a month in the Community Hall. Conservation Corps Volunteers and school groups to help in the gardens and forestry nurseries are specially welcome.

Walkers intending to go to Harris Bay, Kilmory, Dibidil or Papadil (up to 10 miles there and back) should be well-equipped: there is no shelter. 1:10,000 Ordnance Survey map sheet no. 39 useful. Climbers need permits from their clubs or the Chief Warden, who also sells the NCC's 'Field Guide to the Tertiary Igneous Rocks of Rhum'; parties must be no less than

four in number, no more than 15. Rocks can be unstable after frost; compasses unreliable owing to magnetism.

Some sea fishing and loch fishing for brown trout can be arranged at Reserve Office. Deer population studies are carried out at Kilmory, to which access is limited to Sun to avoid disturbance. Highland cattle with calves can be aggressive. Visiting dogs are not allowed, and the collection of rocks, plants and animals, including cast deer antlers, is strictly forbidden without written authority from the Regional Officer, NCC (North-West), Fraser Darling House, 9 Culduthel Rd, Inverness IV2 4AG.

The island is normally only closed to visitors during the first week of May

Glen Brittle from Sgurr Dearg, high in the Black Cuillins, one of the two places in Skye where a road comes near them.

(deer census), and first week of Aug (stalkers' training).

Canna

Distance giving only a hazy idea of its shape and size, Canna appears to rise and fall on the horizon like the humped back of a whale. The island is still four miles off after the steamer has rounded the shoulder of Rhum, by which time passengers are somewhat frayed after the long outward journey, often in rough weather, that takes in Skye and the other Small Isles. Landfall on Canna is like a homecoming, the shelter and peace of the harbour and the lulling curves of the uplands behind it soothing not only the nerves but the sea.

That others have felt the same is evident from the graffiti – the names of ships painted in letters several feet tall – on the black basalt of the cliffs: a century of ex-votos from fishermen who were forced to run for shelter to one of the few deep-water harbours in the Hebrides, and from the tall round tower of the simple memorial church that overlooks it. In spring, when the eider duck used the bay as a courtship ground, the drakes uttering their loud rhythmic roo-ing, it must be like living in a dovecot; in winter, when Atlantic storms sweep away the footbridge to the Isle of Sanday, the thickets of escallonia that form a tunnel leading to Canna House add to the impression of sanctuary. The unexpected, homely presence of apple, pear and cherry trees in the small settlement is explained by Canna's unusual position, with complete protection from the north winds.

For the past 43 years, Canna House and the fertile, Y-shaped island, six miles long by half a mile wide, have been owned by one of the foremost authorities on the Hebrides, the historian and naturalist John Lorne Campbell. This progressive and most benevolent of lairds met his wife, the American writer Margaret Fay Shaw, when, in the early 1930s, she was living on South Uist, collecting Gaelic folk songs in an isolated community, and when Dr Campbell himself was already known for his pioneer work recording Gaelic stories and work-songs. Their lives have been dedicated not only to Canna but to other islands and minorities as well. In 1981 Dr Campbell transferred the island to the care of the National Trust for Scotland, but he and his wife will continue to live there.

Early in the period of the Highland clearances, the people of Canna were transported wholesale to Canada. Their original township of Cill was situated in a broad valley near the site of the seventh-century St Columba's chapel that stood in a field marked by a sculpted Celtic cross; only this cross, and a strange pink column, standing on a knoll, that may have been a pillory, remain, surrounded by the old burial ground and traces of lazy-beds. Above this touching place, grass-covered cliffs rise in narrow terraces that are threaded with steep burns and culminate in ridges of reddish rock;

in their shelter stand Campbell's fine plantations of Austrian pine and Patagonian beech. From a height of 600 feet, more cliffs pierced with caves and arches fall plumb-straight to the sea. So magnetic are these igneous rocks that three miles out compasses begin to lose their bearings.

Today Canna has only 20 inhabitants, cattle-raising and lobster-fishing crofters who also find work on the estate farm grazed by 1,000 breeding ewes and a pedigree Highland herd. The tiny community is served by a school (for a single pupil at present), a post office and telephone kiosk and peripatetic priest, doctor and piano-tuner (Rhum, Eigg and Canna have two Steinways and a Bechstein between them).

Unlike less fortunate Hebridean islands, Canna has changed hands only three times since 1828 and five times in its history. Before 1560, the island was Church land attached to the Benedictine Abbey of Iona, and it remains one of the Isles where the 'Old Religion' has been preserved: the Roman Catholic inhabitants, who once worshipped in the large church on Sanday built in the 1890s by the Marquess of Bute, now have a lovingly-kept chapel restored by the Campbells. In 1428, the Abbot of Iona petitioned the Pope to excommunicate the pirates raiding the island; these days, peaceful Canna, imprinted with the personalities of its present owners, is disturbed by nothing more alarming than a few day-trippers and the visiting yachts that, in summer, congregate in its welcoming harbour.

NOTES

Day-visitors arriving by ferry normally have about 4 hours on Sat only. Visitors wishing to stay on Canna, which is of particular interest to botanists for its arctic-alpine flora, to bird-watchers for its Manx shearwater and other sea-bird colonies, golden eagle and corncrake, and to lepidopterists for its transparent burnet and belted beauty moths, are allowed to camp. No shop or transport. An Ordnance Survey map of the Small Isles is published; a special map of Canna and Sanday is available from Estate Office, Isle of Canna, Inverness-shire (tel Mallaig 2473).

THE OUTER HEBRIDES

BY DEREK COOPER

It was hotter in the Western Isles in mid-May of 1980 than it was in Casablanca. 'Paradise!' said a visitor marvelling at the burning sun, seas Kodachrome blue. Atlantic breakers foamed gently on the dazzling white beaches of Harris. Beyond the dunes thatched with marram grass, meadows were bright with flowers seldom seen on the herbicidal mainland. Corncrake and cuckoo broke the silence among the buttercups, harebell, wild thyme and speedwell.

Paradise? It ought to be. Remote, unpolluted by industry, lavishly beautiful. But it's a place of paradox too. On a day when the islands shimmer in Aegean warmth it's hard to remember that this can be the cruellest place in Britain – one day in every six

Stornoway – buy fresh fish if the catch looks good.

at the Butt of Lewis a gale is recorded. That's probably why the population is so thin on the ground. The Outer Hebridean archipelago runs in a curve from north to south roughly the distance from Wolverhampton to London. In an area as large as Lancashire, there are so few people that were there to be a shareout of the rocky, treeless land every man, woman and child on the islands could stake a claim to 27 acres.

Just as the wind and rain has inhibited the growth of trees and shrubs so the hostile climate seems to have stunted initiative. It's a challenging place that visionaries have been trying to improve for years. In the 19th century it was Sir James Matheson, the Canton *taipan*, who bought the Long Island with some of the loot from his Chinese opium operations. When he built his castellated mansion in Stornoway soil had to be imported by the boatload to anchor his trees and shrubs. Today the policies of Lews Castle remain the only substantial piece of woodland in the whole of the storm-battered Outer Isles.

Matheson had acquired what a Skyeman once disparaged as 'miles and miles of bugger all' – a wet desert of moorland, barren rock and inland lochs,

most of it uncultivated and to this day uncultivable. Money, as a visitor observed, was poured out like water on the thirsty land. Matheson built harbours, bridges and roads and spent the equivalent of millions trying to reclaim the marshy peatbogs that blanket so much of Lewis. Lady Matheson bought potatoes for the poor and filled the coffers of the Destitution Fund, but at the end of the day it didn't make much appreciable difference. Those who dispense largesse are not always accepted with open arms. This lesson was subsequently learned by the most magnanimous and determined visionary ever to descend on the Hebrides.

Lord Leverhulme, who bought Lewis and Harris in 1918, tried to turn Stornoway into the greatest fishing port in Europe. The land he saw was poor but the seas were teeming. Mac Fisheries was founded, canning factories built, breathtaking blueprints prepared. But crofters bred to a traditional pattern of life – the care of sheep and cattle, a little fishing and weaving, a little marginal sowing and reaping – did not take kindly to the magician from Merseyside. They wanted, sensibly, to conduct their affairs in their own way and in their own time, not at the command of the 'wee soap mannie'. Thwarted, Leverhulme severed his connection with the ingrates of Lewis and moved south to Harris, where the more accommodating natives of Obbe allowed him to rename their township Leverburgh.

But when Leverhulme died in 1925 the dream died with him. The piers, the kippering sheds remained unfinished. You can see the scope of it all today. Enormous iron bollards, never fixed, lie rusting in the sun. The bay was charted with buoys for trawlers that never came. Half a million pounds was spent, but there's little to show for it: a few miles of road, some houses still lived in, and at Geocrab the water turbines of the weaving mill that has lain idle for most of the years since. 'Garry'

Rodel Hotel, South Harris, once the home of Lord and Lady Dunmore.

Maclean, who brought 16 looms here, turned a wheel to show me how there's free power available from the burn. But the mill is closed for reasons which most people find too complicated to explain. Harris tweed itself, woven on unfashionable single-width Hattersley looms, faces an uncertain future. The effects of recession and unemployment make investment in these islands more dicey than almost anywhere else in Britain.

The Western Isles need a heavy financial fix every year just to keep ticking over. Everything here is underpinned with subsidies, loans and grants. The inter-island boats, the air service, agriculture, fisheries, almost every activity is a loss leader. Freight charges, already crippling, have given this low income area one of the heaviest cost-of-living burdens in the country.

But there are paradoxes here too which many people find bewildering. In the same week that the Hydro Board tried to raise an eleven percent levy on all electricity bills it was announced that NATO wanted to spend £40 million extending the runway of Stornoway airport in the interests of defence. The islanders are used to these manic pronouncements. In the same breath that they're told a few hundred pounds cannot be found to repair a rickety pier or bring a piped water supply to a remote community, millions will be made available for some preposterous rocket-testing programme on South Uist.

However, there is public money about. Since 1965 the Highlands and Islands Development Board has played the public role privately assumed in the past by landowners like Matheson, Leverhulme, Lord Dunmore, Lady Gordon Cathcart and others. In the past many proprietors specialised in clearance and eviction. The Board is concerned about depopulation but it is often undermined by the activities of wealthy financiers and speculators. Recently the 62,500-acre Harris Estate was sold by a Northampton landowner, Sir Hereward Wake (sic), to a Geneva-based mystery man whose cronies jet in for shooting and stalking. Tall stories are told on Stornoway of the vast sums of money spent on refurbishing the castle where Barrie wrote 'Mary Rose'. All is hung with silk, they say, a fairy tale come true.

Not so long ago Pabbay was bought by a wealthy young man. In 1980 Eriskay and Wiay were put up for sale. Although the Board has never used its powers of compulsory purchase to prevent land speculation it has injected large sums of money into the peripheral regions. Its budget at the time of writing is £25 million, a fair share of which will go to the Western Isles. The Board cannot state how many businesses which have been assisted have collapsed before repaying their initial loans and grants, but the Western Isles have had their toll of disappointment.

The planting of light industries in rural communities seemed at one time to be a bright idea, especially when the end product was intrinsically valuable but light in weight. But the basic fallacy in such thinking has now been exposed. Asking crofters to sit at benches assembling transistors is about as daft as asking suburban bank clerks to take kindly to the cutting of peats. Many of the ventures to which the Board lent support had a South Sea Bubble feel; manufacturing spectacle frames in Barra proved in the end no more viable than making sunbeams out of cucumbers.

I went to look at Breasclete on the west coast of Lewis, the Board's latest and most trumpeted commercial involvement. Here it has become a partner and major shareholder in a Norwegian inspired fish-drying factory. But before the plant got into its stride half the work force were made redundant, and opinion in the islands sees this as yet another white-hope enterprise cooling to an uneconomic standstill.

'You'll not get a grant unless you talk in millions and are a foreigner,' is how a Lewis man put it to me. Despite local feeling that the Board only gets really enthusiastic when excitingly large sums are involved there is no evidence that this is the case – 45 per cent of all grants given in the last 10 years were for £3,000 or less. But it is the big undertakings that arrest the public imagination – a luxury hotel on Barra won an ecology award but little respect from the islanders. 'It's not a posh hotel we want,' said one, 'but more fishing boats.'

The Board's most exciting venture at the moment in the Western Isles is its encouragement of co-operatives, pound for pound, run by local communities. I was on Eriskay last year when a committee of local people were selecting their first manager. Plans for a shop, renovation of cottages for holiday letting, a revival of the Eriskay knitwear industry, and the knowledge that they were soon to have their first car ferry gave the occasion a pioneering fervour. In other communities scattered up and down the islands there are horticultural projects, schemes for bulk purchasing – anything to make life easier and more attractive in isolated and fragile communities. But again, paradoxically, it is the very lack of improvements and amenities which seems to promote the most evident growth industry in the islands.

The Beaker Folk, Bronze Age incomers to the Western Isles, noted for their stone axes and pottery, have been followed by the Craft Folk, fugitives from the urban south. Craft Man and his

South Uist, island home of the loch-ridden community of Eochar.

often barefoot mate are skilled in the construction of corn dollies, plastic chessmen, decorative candles, macramé and the provision of tea and scones for passing tourists. Energetically polishing pebbles, throwing mud-coloured coffee mugs and hammering pewter, they have created their studios in draughty old crofthouses long forsaken by the more sensible natives for oil-fired pebble-dash bungalows. The Craft People are conservation-conscious, keen to cut peat, collect driftwood, rear goats, weave their own kaftans. A thumbed copy of *New Society* or the London weekly *Time Out* reminds them of the corrupt world they have abandoned for the Gaelic good life.

'I wish,' said one of them, 'the locals were just a *wee* bit more aware of the landscape.' One more paradox; people who live in regions of stunning natural beauty do not necessarily have the outlook of the park-keeper. Rusting cars are abandoned on the skyline; a purple mobile home is carefully manoeuvred to the only spot where it could ruin a perfect view; litter tends to lie where it is left, everywhere is the hand of man, profligate with rubbish. I remember many years ago being driven on a day of sparkling sunshine from Stornoway out into the countryside and remarking on the clarity of the air, the beauty of the day, the glittering as of a million precious diamonds in the grass verges. It was, said my host, broken glass from generations of carry-outs – half bottles of whisky, emptied on the homeward drive and lobbed happily into the Saturday night darkness.

A casual attitude to litter is infectious. This June I walked up to the promontory of Mangersta, where the Ministry of Aviation built a radio station some years ago. The huts are vandalised, full of broken furniture, with shattered windows, doors hanging on their hinges, rusting equipment. Six incongruous concrete street lamps teeter over the site. It has the air of a totter's yard in some city slum. But this is Lewis's equivalent of Beachy Head, one of the most dramatic clifftops in the Hebrides, crowned with rubbish and junk. With remarkable courage, or insensitivity, the man responsible for the radio station (the Chief Telecommunications Officer, CAA, Scotland) has left his telephone number on a faded notice board – in case of complaints.

Of all the offshore islands, the Outer Isles offer the greatest and most surprising contrasts: in

Eriskay, South Uist and Barra a latitudinarian Catholicism, linked to Rome but rooted in the Gaeltacht; in Lewis, the last bunker of Sunday Observance, the heartland of the sternest Calvinist sect in the world for whom most manifestations of modern life including the Papacy are the work of the Devil. These are islands of almost ultimate extremism. Huge areas vote themselves 'dry' and then erect ramshackle drinking *bothans* on the moors to drown their communal sorrows. There are spectacular bouts of Saturday evening boozing before the shuttered retribution of the Sabbath. There are also spectacular reserves of tenacity; a high incidence of iron resolve among the women-folk, men of granite.

And many compensations. A journalist friend of mine who spends a lot of time in the Long Island and plans to move there permanently rehearsed some of the delights for me: 'a constant supply of the best mutton I've ever tasted – apparently it's the heather in the feed that makes it so sweet. Always a bit of salmon, source undefinable. Soup made from the water in which the salmon is poached is exquisite. There's a cow for milk – wait till you try crowdie and cream with freshly-baked scones; they grow most of their own vegetables; free range hens for eggs and eating; a bit of fish now and again . . .'

Paradise? It could well be.

DEREK COOPER

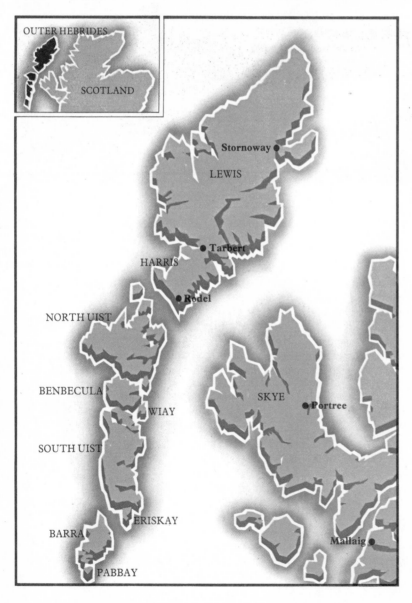

BASICS

Also known as the Western Isles – Gaelic outposts where time stands still; you can drive for miles and see nothing but moor and sea. Excellent for fishing, bird-watching and climbing – organised activities are scarce and most inhabitants seem to prefer it that way. Lewis and Harris are sometimes thought to be separate islands, but are in fact one land mass; North Uist, Benbecula and South Uist are joined by bridges and causeways, and known collectively as 'the Uists'. Islands are much bigger than might be imagined – Lewis and Harris are approx 95 miles in length; adding the length of the others would double this figure. A car is essential, unless you are there for the walking – pubs and restaurants are hard to find and between the two major villages in North and South Uist there is not one public toilet – a distance of 50 miles. Be organised to avoid inconvenience; carry maps (Ordnance Survey maps are available locally, sheets 8, 13, 18, 22, and 31), stout walking shoes, binoculars, repellent for midges, and a packed lunch with whisky to fight off the cold.

On Lewis, Harris and North Uist be sure to stock up on tobacco, food and petrol on Sat, as everything closes on Sun. No pubs open, although if staying in hotel residents can get a drink. Meals in hotels are a little patchy on Sun – no boats so less produce, and limited staff due to strict observance of the Sabbath. Many Lewis women do not cook, hang out washing or watch TV on Sun, so if staying in a guest-house find out ritual beforehand and plan day accordingly.

Although sandy beaches rival the Mediterranean, only the hardy should try swimming and locals rarely bother: Harris temperature averages 55°F in July, only 15° warmer than the average in Jan. Much variety in scenery – barren moorland with not a building in sight, high rocky hills scattered with prehistoric remains, and breathtaking silver bays with footprints of sheep in the sand. Machair is the name given to the sort of flat land that surrounds the west coasts of the islands – the combination of sand and marram grass produces wild flowers of pale and subtle beauty. **The Western Isles Tourist Organisation** operates five information centres round the islands. Headquarters are in Stornoway at 4 South Beach St, tel Stornoway 3088/2941, and if planning a trip to all the islands this should be the first stop. Invaluable and time-saving advice on where to find a pub in the midst of remote moorland, ferry connections etc. Plus the most comprehensive selection of books and maps anywhere in the Outer Hebrides. Office open all year weekdays: May-Sept 9-5.30, and for late ferry arrivals; Oct-April 9-5.30. Centres at Tarbert, Lochmaddy, Lochboisdale and Castlebay are seasonal offices, open May-beginning of Oct. In winter, all queries should be addressed to the Stornoway Centre.

The harbour at Stornoway, the only town in the Outer Hebrides.

Lewis and Harris
WHERE TO GO

STORNOWAY

The only town on the Outer Hebrides – a seaport, a market town and a manufacturing centre for Harris tweed. Tourist office and most hotels stand on a small peninsula where you can watch the boats come in – buy fresh fish for breakfast if the catch looks good. Behind the shopping area are large, gracious houses; many sport wrought-iron finials and one even has an intrepid palm tree in the front garden.

Town Hall, built in the 1920s, is a splendid structure with towers and weather vanes, crowned with a handsome clock tower. Small square which adjoins it has flower-beds and benches overlooking the harbour.

Churches of all shapes and sizes: St Columba's in Lewis St has an attractive bell tower and holds services in Gaelic the first Sun of every month, while St Martin's in Francis St is Stornoway's showpiece – huge clover-shaped windows of stained glass and a rosewood interior polished daily by a lady who loves her work. There is a plaque on outer wall commemorating Sir Alexander Mackenzie, the first European to cross Canada from east to west. He discovered the Mackenzie River. He was born on this site in 1763.

Lews Castle and grounds: mock Tudor building put up in 1847 by Sir James Matheson, a wealthy merchant who embarked on an ambitious land-scaping scheme to change the barren scenery. Lord Leverhulme continued the improvements when he took over in 1917; grounds now owned by Stornoway Trust. Horsechestnuts shelter a picnic area overlooked by a noble fir, streams meander through groves of cherry laurel and silver birch. Grounds are also rich with bird life and wild flowers – partridges and pheasants, as well as wild strawberries and 10 different types of fern. Castle itself is now a technical college and not open to the public, but extravagant facade can be seen from many parts of the grounds.

Shopping: Loch Erisort Woollens is a local concern with three shops in Cromwell St, specialising in island goods – a knitwear store, a bookshop, good for maps, which also stocks a light-hearted Hebridean cookery book, and a craft shop with lots of pottery and several unusual chess sets (see *Specialities*). One has carved pieces depicting Hebridean peasants – a crofter king, a woman carrying peat as queen, and a black house (see *Specialities*) instead of the castle. Buy picnic fare from the Corner Shop in Kenneth St, or hiking boots, raingear and other utilitarian items from Lewis Crofters across street from the Loch Erisort Woollens shops. Early closing Wed, some shops closed all day.

Eating and Drinking: mostly done in hotels. The Caberfeidh is Stornoway's main hotel and serves lobster and other seafood to order (tel Stornoway 2604). The Seaforth takes last orders until 9.45 – good to know if visiting museums over on west coast of Lewis. Tel Stornoway 2740. All hotel bars are open to non-residents every day except Sun when residents only can get a drink. The Criterion Bar in Point St is a pretty cottage-type building dispensing Tennant Caledonian beers, while the low-ceilinged Star Inn, on the harbour, offers a choice of Youngers, McEwans or numerous whiskies.

TARBERT

The Isle of Harris's only proper village, tucked under boulder-strewn hills and blending with landscape so unobtrusively you could almost pass it by. A single terraced street perched above Loch Tarbert with buildings of local stone; few signs or numbers on the shops, locals refer to them by proprietor's surname – MacLeod's or Macaskill's. Each shop sells just about everything – nubby woollen sweaters dangle from wall hooks over meat counters, electric clocks sit on jumbled shelves with perfume, wellies and greeting cards. The local **Tourist Information Centre** is in Pier Rd, tel Harris 2011. Open in season weekdays 9.30-5.30, reopening for late ferry arrivals. There's a vegetable patch in the village green, and roosters strut nonchalantly past sheds selling Harris tweed. Eating and drinking is done in the Harris Hotel, full meals and teas – lounge bar in a separate building (tel Harris 2154), or at the newly finished MacLeod Motel, down by the pier where the ferry comes in (tel Harris 2364). Early closing day in Tarbert is Thurs, some shops closed all day.

RODEL

Charming 'township' (settlement) on the southern tip of Harris – well-kept cottages banked by drystone walls, a large pond ringed by hills where wild irises and mushrooms grow. St Clement's Church is possibly the most ambitious medieval building in the Outer Hebrides, restored to its present state by the Countess of Dunmore in 1873. In a recess behind the tomb of the MacLeod chief who is thought to have built it are elaborately carved panels: fine detail on scenes of the 12 apostles, a stag hunt and an angel and a devil weighing the souls of the dead. Heavy iron key can be obtained from the Rodel Hotel, but church is very spooky if visited after dark.

Rodel Hotel down by the pier, once the home of Lord and Lady Dunmore, was later used by Lord Leverhulme when he moved his canning industry to Harris. Drawingroom is cluttered with comfortable antiques and the view from the bay window is of headlands and lochs; little wooden wash basins in the bedrooms. You can dine on fresh rainbow trout in the diningroom, or fish the lochs for salmon (daily permits available to non-residents) or for brown trout, which is free. Book for lunches, dinners and afternoon teas, tel Leverburgh 210/219. Hotel's most famous lure is a supply of whisky known as 'Royal Household' – every bottle a blend of many whiskies, each at least 12 years old. It slides down the throat like liquid gold. The Rodel is one of the very few places to stock this particular whisky, which it has sold since the end of the 19th c. Royal Household is thought to be a favourite of the Royal Family.

St Clement's Church, Rodel, possibly the most ambitious medieval building in the Outer Hebrides.

SIGHTSEEING

Callanish Standing stones: this great circle rivals Stonehenge in importance. It lies 16 miles from Stornoway on bleak and barren moorland. A circle of 13 stones from 8-12ft high, with the ruins of a chambered cairn in the middle; a double row of 19 stones forms an avenue to the north. No one knows quite how old they are or their purpose, but legends and hypotheses abound – an American professor fed data into a computer and deduced Callanish was for predicting eclipses, others say stones were the site of Viking parliaments or UFO landings. Certainly the site was of great ritual importance. Within a radius of 3 miles are several other stones and circles. A858 west of Stornoway.

Shawbost Museum: former project by the pupils of Shawbost School, this folk museum is housed in an old church. There are looms and furniture, a hand-wheeled bobbin winder, a vivid red and blue farm cart and many old fishing and crofting implements. The students also restored an old Norse mill at Loch Raoineabhat; hand-drawn map in museum shows how to get there. Open March-Nov weekdays 10-6 and at other times by arrangement with the head teacher. Donations welcome. A858, on west coast of Lewis.

Dun Carloway Broch: massive stone tower thought to have been built between 100BC and 300AD as a defensive structure. Remnants of peat ash, hearths and earthenware dishes suggest broch was used by a potter some 300 years after its construction; if so, it is the only Scottish Iron Age pottery to have been found outside Orkney. Narrow stone steps twist and climb up three interior levels, but end abruptly in open space where walls have fallen away – keep an eye on small children. Wonderful panorama from the top: four lochs stretching across the horizon while below the domestic roofscape of Doune Carloway township. Minor road off A858 towards west coast of Lewis, broch on hill can be seen from main road.

Ui Chapel: ruins of a former priory, and the burial ground of the MacLeod chiefs of Lewis – effigy on the south side is said to be that of the 16th c chief Roderick MacLeod, 7th of Lewis.

Stone has been coarsened by rain and gales whipping through the roofless chapel, making Roderick even sterner. Note the drystone wall surrounding chapel, constructed of rich red stones shot through with quartz – looks dazzling after a rainstorm. On Eye Peninsula east of Stornoway, just past modern cemetery.

Toe Head: haven for golden eagles, sheep and hermits, a fat sandy finger of fertile machair crowned by Chaipaval mountain. There are two natural rock arches on the western tip; you can drive through township of Northton to a sandy track which forks right to a glistening beach, and left to the secluded ruins of Rubh' an Teampuill chapel. Sweet smell of clover in the

The standing stones of Callanish, Lewis.

air. You may see the Hebrideans' own form of bumblebee, with the grand name of *Bombus jonellus* var. *hebridensis*. Continuation of A859 west of Leverburgh, south Harris.

Amhuinnsuidhe Castle (pronounced 'Avin-suey'): operated as a private fishing lodge and therefore not open to the public, but road to delightful township of Husinnish runs so close to the castle you can peek into the entrance hall. Whimsical and turreted in pale imported stone, castle was built by the Earl of Dunmore in 1868. Sir James Barrie began his novel 'Mary Rose' here. Manicured lawn and a sleek motor launch contrast with the stony landscape. In July

you can see the famous 'leaping trout' – near the castle, waters from Loch Leosaidh cascade down to the sea in a series of small falls; salmon leap high in the air over a sheer rockface to gain the upper waters. B887 west off Tarbert/Stornoway road.

North Uist

Lochmaddy, the island's only village, is surprisingly sophisticated, with large residential buildings strung along a ridge overlooking a loch. There's a bank, grocery store and the Weehaveit Shop selling crafts, shortbread and warm tartan blankets, useful on cold evenings. Island's doctor, an ex-navy man, flies the flag – you can see it as you come up the hill from the harbour: a Union Jack or the Scottish flag or, if foreign guests are expected, their national flag. Here too is the local **Tourist Information Centre,** tel Lochmaddy 321. Open in season weekdays 9.30-5.30, reopening for late ferry arrivals. The Lochmaddy Hotel controls the fishing rights to over 150 lochs around the island – brown trout and sea trout are specially good. It serves bar lunches and dinners all year round. Tel Lochmaddy 331 for details.

A circular road from Lochmaddy leads round the island. The southern section is sparsely populated, with high barren hills riddled with prehistoric remains. One of the best and most accessible is Bharpa Langass chambered cairn, approx 7 miles south-west of Lochmaddy, hovering high above the main road. Nice to take a picnic up to the top of the hill and enjoy the view. On the north-west ridge of Blashaval hill are three standing stones known as 'Na Fir Bhreige' – Gaelic for 'the false men'. Legend has it that three local men deserted their wives, and a moralistic witch turned them into stone. Scenery to the north of Lochmaddy is considerably softer; lochs widen, with flat squelchy 'steps' of grass leading out towards the sea. Green rolling hills and silvery beaches can be glimpsed in the distance.

Balranald Nature Reserve has a wide variety of bird life in a very small area – there is a high density of breeding waders and corncrakes; large numbers of waders stop over on their way to Scandinavia to forage among the seaweed; migrating gannets, shearwaters and auks pass offshore. Whooper swans feed on the fallen grain in Oct, and in the dense marshes tufted ducks and shovellers breed. Birdwatchers are asked to observe the marsh from a small cemetery on the far hillside, and there's a small blue and white hut with a book for recording new sightings. There is a resident warden in summer who will answer queries and show parties around. Write to RSPB Warden, Goular, Lochmaddy, North Uist.

In a low cottage near the pretty cul-de-sac of Locheport Mr A. MacDougall sells fine Harris tweeds. If he has time between cutting peat and attending to the sheep, he will take you into the back shed where, pumping the well-worn pedals of a 200-year-old loom, he makes the tweeds. In 1923 there were 14 looms in use on North Uist; now Mr MacDougall is the only weaver there, although another lives in the connecting island of Grimsay. His sister, Mrs MacDonald, has recently retired from the business; in 1956 she made a Royal Stewart tartan for the Queen, and presented it during the Royal Visit to the islands. There are pictures of the visit on the shop walls, near all the prizes won at Royal Highland Shows. Mr MacDougall also runs a mail-order service. Write to: A. MacDougall, Pier Rd, Locheport, North Uist, Outer Hebrides, for samples and prices. George Jackson and his wife also run a world-wide mail-order service, of delicious peat-smoked salmon, and visitors can watch the fish being prepared and smoked. It can be deep-frozen or kept fresh in a cool place for 14 days. They will also smoke other kinds of fish if visiting anglers bring along their catch. Write to G & R Jackson, Locheport, North Uist, or telephone Locheport 209.

Benbecula

Connected to the islands of North and South Uist by causeway and bridge over quicksands and shell beaches. Although in Gaelic its name is 'Beinn a' bh-faodhla' – the Mountains of the Fords – Benbecula has only one 'mountain', Rueval, standing 408ft above the main road and offering a fine panoramic view to North Uist and the faraway hills of Harris.

Village of Balivanich, once the site of a monastery, is now taken over by the Army and used as a rocket range. Huge trucks and lunar-scanning devices dominate the landscape, surreal beside tiny stone cottages and the remains of ancient duns. Some of the thatched houses are so old the roofs are sprouting, while occupants of others are entering 20th c resourcefully – using factory-made red bricks instead of local rocks to secure straw to their roofs. Army provides revenue and loans its cinema facilities to the residents, and island attitude to it seems generally favourable. In 1980 lobster fishermen did sail into the missile zone as a protest – but against the import of cheap, subsidised Canadian lobsters. Near the rocket range is Benbecula airport – look out for confusing roadsigns – serviced by Loganair and British Airways.

The small west-coast road runs through flat sandy ground which is awash with buttercups, dandelions, and bright poppies. Their scent catches the breeze and perfumes the whole island.

At Nunton is Culla Bay, a superb beach with safe bathing. In the graveyard is a ruined chapel with a legend attached; chapel was once part of a nunnery but was plundered during the Reformation in 1560 and most of the occupants massacred. A dying nun is supposed to have uttered a curse on the island, saying no priest would ever be born on Benbecula. So far none has. Almost indistinguishable amongst the rugged grey boulders in the island's interior are the remains of shielings – stone cottages to which the residents used to move for a few months a year to give the sheep fresh grazing.

D. MacGillivray & Co can supply a comprehensive range of soft woollen goods – kilt hose, hand-tailored kilts, balls of knitting wool, as well as sweaters, tweeds and ties. Write to: Muir of Aird, Benbecula, Outer Hebrides. Benbecula sports the only restaurant, as opposed to hotel dining-rooms, in the Outer Hebrides. The Dark Island Hotel and Restaurant serves meals, coffee and sandwiches all year round 10-10 (tel Benbecula 2283). If you fancy a drink, the Creagorry Hotel nearby has two lounge bars.

South Uist

South Uist is sausage-shaped, 22 miles long and only 8 miles across at its widest. An island of sharp geological contrasts; to the west is soft machair where flowers grow in profusion and crofting townships nestle; to the east rise inaccessible hills perpetually shrouded in cloud. Bisecting South Uist north to south is the island's only thoroughfare, a single-lane road with frequent passing places but even more traffic; the Army base in Benbecula has added to the overload and driving can be frustrating. Best to explore the island in small sections, preferably on foot. Houses are set far off the road, and front gardens provide a final resting place for abandoned cars and rusting farm equipment, now an integral part of the landscape. Many thatched cottages have straw-roofed byres nearby, all meticulously repaired by the occupants as there is no professional thatcher on the island.

In the loch-ridden community of Eochar stands the Black House Museum, with a genteel display of cotton lingerie and a driftwood dresser stocked with ancient porridge bowls. Mrs MacNeil, the curator, can be reached at 8 Buailedubh, opposite the school, if museum is closed, but a noisy dog next door alerts the neighbourhood to your arrival first. Eochar is the headquarters of a thriving cooperative scheme, sponsoring films, dances, and a handicraft market on Sat, and providing possibly the best snacks on the island in the Talla an lochdair, or Eochar Hall, beside the main road. Nearby is the Hebridean Jewellery Workshop where you can buy necklaces in gold and silver, hand-tooled in traditional designs.

Next to the township of Stiligarry is the 2,500-acre Loch Druidibeg National Nature Reserve, the most important breeding ground in Britain of the greylag goose. Other breeding species include the rare hen harrier, dunlin, black-headed gull and arctic tern. The warden will be pleased to give advice as to where particular species can be found, although you can see a lot from a high wooden platform near the road, or from the small lane which runs east towards Loch Skipport. Tel Grogarry 252 for information, or write to the Nature Conservancy Reserve Warden, Kinloch, Grogarry Lochboisdale, South Uist. For permission to visit during breeding season – approx April-Sept – write to: Mr R. N. Campbell, Nature Conservancy Council, Fraser Darling House, 9 Culduthel Rd, Inverness IV2 4AG (tel Inverness 39431).

The lane east to Loch Skipport is deserted and remote, passing through a plantation of rhododendrons, fir and monkey-puzzle trees to a lonely pier from which, in 1746, Bonnie Prince Charlie was rowed to meet Flora Macdonald. A conical drystone monument to her stands on the site of her home near the township of Milton.

The Polochar Inn is warm and welcoming with Gaelic folk-songs on tape and lots of tales from the landlord, former seaman Don MacNeil. During World War II the SS Politician, carrying 20,000 cases of whisky, ran aground nearby. The story was adapted by Sir Compton Mackenzie in 'Whisky Galore'. Mr MacNeil will

Croft-house at Loch Eport, North Uist.

Ronald Maclellan and Donald Macvicar (right), *sheepshearing on South Uist.*

show you an original bottle salvaged from the wreck, with an unsavoury lump in the bottom, consisting of solidified whisky and the diesel oil which seeped in from the wreck. Pub is well situated at the tip of South Uist with fine views of offshore islands and a solitary standing stone on a single headland. 'Pollacharra', from which the Polochar Inn takes its name, is Gaelic for 'Bay of the Standing Stone'.

Lochboisdale is the island's only town, a cluster of functional modern buildings where most requisites can be bought. The Lochboisdale Hotel (tel Lochboisdale 332) has exclusive fishing rights to all the fresh water lochs, where sea trout up to 14lb have been caught. Hotel's comfortable residents' lounge has a wonderful guest book dating from 1882 full of quaint remarks. The Askernish Golf Club is the only course outside Stornoway, with a 9-hole course and clubs for hire. Tel Lochboisdale 301 during the week, or turn up at the club in person at weekends. All other queries answered at the local **Tourist Information Centre,** Lochboisdale, tel Lochboisdale 286. Open in season weekdays 9.30-5.30, reopening for late ferry arrivals.

Barra

Planes to Barra land on a runway washed twice daily by tides – a 2-mile beach known as Cockle Strand. You get a seagull's view of the island from the 8-seater planes – it's only 14 miles around and encompasses every aspect of Hebridean landscape, from tall desolate mountains to smooth green pasture, cattle nibbling the flowers, to good-looking council houses on the outskirts of Castlebay, Barra's village.

Castlebay, Barra. Kiessimul Castle, ancient MacNeill stronghold, sits on the islet.

Cockles play an important role in the island's economy – in the 1880s cockles were sent as far as London, while now island does a thriving business in 'harl,' the coarse, grainy mixture of shells and lime used for exterior house walls. Sir Compton Mackenzie wrote 'Whisky Galore' here, in a white house near the cockle beach.

Bicycles are the best way to travel, you can hire them from PO, or from the Isle of Barra Hotel on island's west coast. This hotel has just won an architectural award from the EEC, given for designs which blend with the environment – its smooth creamy

walls with high pointed eaves look just like sand dunes tossed by the wind.

Kiessimul (Kismul) Castle sits on a small islet in the harbour at Castlebay. Visit it on Wed or Sat afternoon (May-Sept) and be rowed across by a hard-working boatboy. Fare includes entrance fee. The castle was the ancient stronghold of the MacNeils of Barra who died out in the direct male line in 1863. It had been uninhabited for over 200 years when it was cunningly restored in the late 1930s by the late Robert Lister MacNeil, a distant relation who became chief of the clan. He was also a talented architect. Contained within the ancient circular walls is an ingenious modern apartment complex, with chapel and courtyard. A seal frequents the harbour, bobbing up among lobster boats and the ferry from Oban bringing bread, milk and fruit. If you need these items, best to be in the shops the day ferry arrives, as there is little home produce on the island. George MacLeod of the Castlebay Hotel charters his private boat for sea angling trips and visits to the neighbouring islands, tel Castlebay 223, while the Barra Knitwear company has a small workshop specialising in Shetland wool and supplying Fair Isle jumpers to Harrods. Help in climbing steep Heaval hill in the form of walking sticks from the Skallary craft shop; for a less energetic experience visit the small perfumery in Kinloch which produces musky scents with local and evocative names. The local **Tourist Information Centre** is at Main St, Castlebay, tel Castlebay 336. Open in season weekdays 9.30-5.30, reopening for late ferry arrivals.

SPECIALITIES

Harris Tweed: 'made from virgin wool, spun, dyed and finished in the Outer Hebrides, and handwoven by the islanders in their own homes'. It is exported to more than 50 countries and used in the first-class lounges of the QEII. Its distinctive label has trademark of an orb with a cross on top. Each of the crofter-weavers can produce $2\frac{1}{2}$ tweeds a week, a 'tweed' being 80 yards of material $28\frac{1}{2}$in wide. They are self-employed, buy their own looms and bobbins and maintain their own equipment. Although most often associated with the warm coarse

cloth of huntin' and shootin' jackets, Harris tweed can also be a lightweight material of surprising elegance. Many Stornoway shops sell it at a much lower price per yard than you can buy it elsewhere in Britain – a man's jacket takes $4\frac{1}{2}$yds – but there is no tailor on the islands. Miss Marion Campbell of Plockropool, Drinishader, Harris, demonstrates the way the 'clo mor', or 'the big cloth' used traditionally to be completed, from spinning the raw wool on a wheel to colouring it, using dyes from vegetables, lichens and roots, to weaving on a loom. The Western Isles Crafts Guide, available from tourists offices, gives a list of craftsmen and weavers around the islands.

The Lewis Chessmen: almost four sets of ancient chessmen were found in Ardroil, parish of Uig, Lewis, in 1831. Thought to have been buried in 12th c by a shepherd after the murder of a merchant sailor whose ship ran aground in Uig Bay. The stocky, robust carvings portray actual warriors, kings, queens, and bishops seated on ornamental thrones, rooks as armed foot soldiers and knights mounted, ready to do battle. Thought to be of Scandinavian origin, they are carved from walrus tusks, one side stained red. Originals can be seen in the National Museum of Antiquities of Scotland in Edinburgh, or the British Museum in London. Replicas on sale in Western Isles craft shops.

Ceilidhs: spontaneous social gathering with much storytelling, dancing, singing and drinking. Traditionally each village had its own 'tigh ceilidh' or gossiping house, now ceilidhs are held in hotels. Check with tourist offices for the next one.

Black houses: abandoned, oblong windowless thatched cottages which seem older than they actually are; many were built this century and in 1960 nine black houses in village of Arnol, Lewis, were still occupied. Traditionally they had only one room, animals and people lived together, although later models had byres separated from main house by a passage. There was a peat fire in the middle of the room but no chimney – it was felt smoke enriched the thatch and made it better for the soil when used as fertiliser later on. Black houses – so called after mainland-type cement and mortar 'white' houses appeared – are best seen in Arnol, where one has been preserved by the D of E as a museum, complete with furniture and peat fire. Open weekdays April-Sept 9.30-7, Oct-March 9.30-4. Small admission charge.

ACTIVITIES

Fishing: usually free for brown trout, tourist offices can advise on permits, but rights to the lochs for salmon and sea trout fishing belong to lodges and hotels. Some allow non-residents to purchase permits. Little equipment for hire, as it is thought enthusiasts will have their own. Lochs around the parish of Stornoway are for public use, contact the Factor of the Stornoway Trust, tel Stornoway 2002. The season for salmon fishing is later in the Outer Hebrides than in other places – from July-Oct. For permission to fish on the Lacasdale Lochs around Tarbert in Harris, contact the Harris Hotel, tel Harris 2154. Little fishing on Benbecula; for North and South Uist see text under individual island; on Barra contact the Isle of Barra Hotel, tel Castlebay 383, or Castlebay Hotel, tel Castlebay 223. Costs vary depending on hotel.

Golf: 18-hole course in Stornoway where clubs can be hired. Course is laid out deep in Lady Lever Park with wooded and hilly areas providing a challenge. Closed on Sun. Tel Stornoway 2240. Well-kept 9-hole course in

South Uist is situated beside the sea. Contact South Uist Estates Office, Askernish. Tel Lochboisdale 301.

Walking: with so few roads the islands make ideal walking country – both the North and South Uist tourist offices publish lists of recommended walks, available direct from offices. The 14-mile coastal route of Barra could be walked in a day. On Lewis, walk the enchanting nature trails around Lews Castle in Stornoway, or for a more bracing experience try the remote parish of Uig with its fine scenery of hills and lochs. Isle of Harris caters for everyone – the west coast has magnificent beaches and pockets of wild flowers, the east coast is rocky and full of unexpected, but delightful townships.

Climbing: North Harris presents the best opportunities, with eight summits exceeding 2,000ft. Uisgnaval More rises to 2,392ft and offers some short faces and particularly splendid views.

FLORA AND FAUNA

Flowers and plants: most widespread is heather – it's even used to prop up piles of drying peat. Most common species is the ling heather, purple and spiky, although two others are also found, the cross-leaved heather in bogs and the bell heather, which grows in stumpy shrubs in dry areas. Hare's tail cottongrass is also

abundant; the small downy tufts on top of a long spike were once used for stuffing mattresses. Royal fern is one of the Hebridean specialities, much desired by collectors. It grows mostly in damp, acidic soils. Also throughout the Hebrides is lovage, with shiny leaves and greenish flowers; it can be used as a flavouring for stews. There are also dainty marsh orchids, yellow irises, plus masses of poppies, daisies and primroses and fields of meadow buttercups.

Deer: stags and hinds in North Uist, and on North Harris. Deer can sometimes be seen on the main Stornoway/Tarbert road especially in winter.

Seals: grey Atlantic seals are so commonplace locals fail to point them out to visitors. If taking Donald Campbell's boat to Barra, be on the look-out, the Sound of Barra has plenty. There is also a colony in Stornoway Harbour, best studied as the seals tread water near the quayside waiting for the fishing boats.

Birds: best place to see the famous golden eagle is high in the hills, as for example in the parish of Uig, Lewis, or Toe Head in Harris. There are Hebridean sub-species of the twite, wren, dunnock and song-thrush.

Reserves: Monach Isles, several tiny islands plus rocks and reef, approx 6 miles west of North Uist, are wintering grounds for barnacle and white-fronted geese. Permission to land from North Uist Estate, Lochmaddy, North Uist, and from warden of Loch Druidibeg Nature Reserve, Kinloch, Grogarry, Lochboisdale, South Uist (tel Grogarry 252).

North Rona and Sula Sgeir Reserve, 46 miles north of Butt of Lewis, notable for large breeding colony of grey seals. Sula Sgeir has a large colony of gannets. Permission to land from Barvas Estates Ltd, c/o Smiths Gore, The Square, Fochabers, Moray. The Regional Officer of the Nature Conservancy Council must also be informed; he can advise on how to get there or to the Monach Isles. Write to Mr R. N. Campbell, Nature Conservancy Council, Fraser Darling House, 9 Culduthel Rd, Inverness IV2 4AG (tel Inverness 39431).

**Briefing by
Martha Ellen Zenfell**

Wildflowers on a hill-side in Lewis.

A SEABIRD SPECTACULAR

BY JIM FLEGG

The offshore islands of Britain hold some of our most spectacular sights, sounds and smells of birds. There is no question that Britain and Ireland, and especially the offshore islands, are the European centre of excellence for seabirds.

Some seabirds are extremely adept at coexistence with man. Prime amongst these are the various members of the gull family—and this is very much the century of the gull. Almost unknown at the turn of the century, gulls are now as much a part of farmland as lapwings, and as much a part of urban life, on playing field or rubbish tip, as blackbirds or starlings. The change has not been confined to inland areas. Gulls, especially the herring gull (which remains with us all year) and the closely related lesser black-backed gull (which migrates south for the winter) have risen in numbers over the last few decades because of an ability to exploit man, his works and his waste.

Sadly, man's own population explosion and affluence (in terms of free time and mobility) have put summer recreational pressures on many islands off the south and west coasts of England, causing greater disturbance than most seabirds could tolerate. Add to this the high levels of chemical and oil pollution in the Channel and its approaches, and the relative lack of the more genuine seabirds is easily understood. So on most of these islands now the great majority of the breeding seabirds are herring gulls, which prefer relatively inaccessible nest sites anyway; with occasional pairs of greater black-backed gulls (often preying on the offspring of their smaller relatives); and colonies of lesser black-backed gulls on sufficiently secluded cliff-top swards. And all this despite a considerable amount of gulls egg collecting for the table.

In the west and north, some things are different. The increase in gull populations has been no less dramatic, forcing them increasingly into conflict

with other seabirds and with conservation bodies concerned with seabird protection. As well as scavenging from man, gulls are no less opportunists as predators; unguarded eggs or chicks fall easy prey, and as the auk family in particular seem notoriously negligent as parents, gull predation can become a major problem.

Greater black-backs can develop into birds of prey – siezing an unfortunate puffin as it emerges, temporarily blinded by the light, from its burrow, and quickly despatching, skinning and eating it. On occasion, greater black-backs will fly down puffins, falcon-like, grabbing them in mid-air and even devouring them while still in flight. Others are more subtle in their approach. Herring gulls will often loiter among the burrows, waiting for the landing of a puffin circling anxiously offshore with a beakful of small fish for its nestling. Puffins are *not* masters of the air, and find delicate manoeuvring extremely difficult. On a windy day, the added harassment caused by a waiting gull often leads to misjudgment and a crash-landing. In the head-over-heels melee, the fish are dropped, to be picked up by the gull at leisure after the puffin has beaten a retreat.

In other cases, sheer pressure of space caused by rapidly expanding gulleries has forced long-established tern colonies to leave their island beaches. To protect other species, some conservationists believe that there should be counter measures to limit the increase in the gull population. This may be relatively simple when the need is to eliminate a few pairs of rogue greater black-backs, but can be a considerable problem when perhaps several thousand pairs of herring gulls are the source of trouble.

Just what is it that makes our islands so special that some 70 per cent of the *world* population of the razorbill nests on them? Most good seabird islands are girt with precipitous cliffs, providing natural

—A SEABIRD SPECTACULAR—

1 Guillemots. 2 Skua. 3 Tern.
4 Great black-backed gull eating puffin. 5 Guillemot and egg.
6 Kittiwake. 7 Gannets. 8 Puffins.

Stac Lee : the St Kilda archipelago has more seabirds than any other island group in Britain.

nature reserves with little need for fencing. They are further guarded by treacherous and almost always rough seas – or so it seems to those trying to land to observe the seabirds. Some of the cliffs and stacks are gigantic and magnificent, rising 1,000 feet or more from the sea. But for seabirds it is important that the rock is of the right type, with strata and fractures producing a habitable terrain. Caves provide sites for black guillemots, smaller crevices places for the razorbills and puffins to lay their eggs. Boulder screes house more razorbills and puffins, with petrels and Manx shearwaters for good measure. The cliff ledges, which need to be more or less horizontal to be of use (hence the importance of how the rock fractures), provide a home for gannets, guillemots, kittiwakes and fulmars.

Most razorbill colonies are relatively small, and often interspersed among other auks. Because the nest is hidden, observation and counting is difficult, but the razorbill is perhaps the most handsome of our seabirds. The plumage is immaculately contrasting black and white, the black offset by elegant white trim on the beak and in a fine white line of tiny feathers running from beak to eye – suggested by some to be a sighting device when hunting underwater.

Structurally, the razorbill and the other auks are part-way, as it were, to penguins. They lead a split existence, partly in the air, partly on land, and partly on or under the water, but their major adaptations are for swimming. Their wings are reduced in size and stiffened–approaching penguin flippers – which gives poor flight but excellent underwater propulsion. The head and body are streamlined, the eyes deep-set, for underwater movement, with the extended webbed feet serving like control fins on a submarine. The body is purpose-built for deep diving, with an immensely strong ribcage. The ribs are fused, through projecting spurs, to each other and to a rigid backbone and breastbone, forming a rigid box protecting the vital organs from the crushing pressure of the sea.

A recent census suggested that the guillemot population exceeded the half-million mark in Britain and Ireland, and they seem to be holding their own in the modern environment, despite their all-too-often tragedies when caught up in oil spills. A glance at photographs of the seabird stacks of St Kilda or the Farne Islands confirms this, with guillemots packed tight on the tops and ledges, standing upright and looking much like a month's uncollected deliveries of milk bottles. Each new arrival, trying to find a space to land, causes noisy confusion as he blunders among his fellows.

The guillemot has one of the simplest of all nests: it just lays its single egg on a ledge, with no nest foundation, not even a few sprays of seaweed for decoration. The egg that allows such simplicity is a masterpiece of evolutionary design. It is large – four or five inches (10cm) long – and tapered sharply like a pear. If knocked accidentally (as often happens in such crowded conditions) it rolls in a tight circle but stays on the ledge. In similar circumstances, the normally-shaped razorbill egg would have as much chance of survival as a breakfast egg rolling off the kitchen table: so razorbills tend to be crevice nesters.

There are other differences, too. Razorbills, like puffins, bring fish to their young in beakfuls, often of ten or more but sometimes up to 50 sand eels or small fry. The guillemot usually comes home with a single, much larger, fish for its youngster. In the crowded circumstances of colony life, even feeding must be circumspect. To exclude neighbours' greedy offspring, the guillemot extends its wings like an umbrella, surrounding its chick, and then transfers the fish headfirst, so that it can be easily swallowed. When the chick is very young, not all the fish may get in at first attempt, and replete guillemot chicks are a common sight with several inches of fish tail dangling from their mouths. Digestion is astonishingly rapid, however, and a couple of hours later the chick is clamouring for more.

Some guillemots, particularly in the north, show a peculiar white ring round the eye, with a bar stretching back, looking like a pair of spectacles. They were once known as a separate species, the bridled guillemot, and just what the function of this plumage variety is, nobody knows; nor why it becomes more frequent as you travel north.

Guillemot and razorbill chicks leave the nesting cliffs before they are fully fledged: usually they are about two-thirds grown. They have plenty of warm down, covered by a layer of water-repellent body feathers so that they can swim safely. The 'wings' are mere bristly stubs at this stage. Their early departure from the nest is amazing: they jump off into the sea, which may be several hundred feet below! Despite their inability to fly, feathers and fat combined apparently have a sufficient cushioning effect to allow them to bounce off any projections on the way down without harm. The operation is often made more hazardous by taking place at night, but at least this allows the chicks a better chance of escaping marauding gulls. Once off the cliff, the chick swims with its parents – often in a group with other families – out to the open sea to complete its development away from the gull menace ever-present on the cliffs.

Much scarcer than its larger relative, the black guillemot is particularly a bird of the islands of the northwest. It is jet black, save for bold white wing patches and bright vermilion feet – so bright as to be visible underwater even at long range. The black guillemot is a cave nester, usually in colonies of only a few pairs. Strangely, unlike its auk cousins, it lays two eggs and often manages to rear both young. Off-duty birds occasionally roost in buoys, emerging in a black cascade when their roost is rocked by the wake of a passing vessel. The solemn note of the bell-buoy is then joined by their improbable whistling tinkle of a call. Another improbable feature is its change to winter plumage. The other auks become generally greyer, but the black guillemot emerges almost as the photographic negative of itself in summer: the body white with contrasting mainly black wings.

*The guillemot has one of the simplest of all nests –
and a suitably adapted egg.*

The puffin, perhaps more than any other bird of sea or land, has the ability to arouse the enthusiasm and fascination of man. Often described as 'like little men in evening dress', perhaps it is the upright stance of the puffin, and its busybody enthusiasm to observe and participate in all the social functions of its neighbourhood, that most endears it to us. For all its handsome charm and its popularity, the puffin is most difficult to study. Its comings and goings about the colony are notoriously fickle, despite the spectacle when a whole large colony decides to indulge in an evening 'flypast'.

When the Kearton brothers, the Victorian authors and pioneer bird photographers visited the huge colony on St Kilda, they recorded a fly-past big enough to darken the sky and force them to allow longer exposure times. Being well prepared, they had with them umbrellas, not, as you might expect, to protect themselves from droppings, but to fend off the shower of feather parasites that pattered down like rain from the wheeling hordes above!

The puffin is a cavity nester, choosing tunnels in boulder screes or evicting rabbits from their burrows in cliff-top thrift and turf. Where rabbits are absent, as on St Kilda, puffins will excavate their own nests with the needle-sharp claws that arm each orange foot. Deep in this burrow lives the single chick, as drab in its sooty black down as its parents are colourful. The beak, too, shows dramatic differences. The harlequin-coloured parrot-like summer beak of the Puffin is a temporary horny ornament, of use only during courtship and the breeding season. Part of the colourful outer sheath is shed in late summer, leaving a drab but functional beak of more normal proportions. In the chick, the beak is smaller still and darker, rather like a miniature razorbill.

Over much of its north Atlantic range, the puffin has decreased in numbers, sometimes drastically in recent years. In the south, this is perhaps to be expected as the puffin seems relatively intolerant of disturbance by people, but in the north-west it is more worrying. Here, some colonies have been estimated in the past as millions strong, and obviously formed a major natural stronghold for the species. Operation Seafarer, mounted in 1969 by the Seabird Group to census our seabird populations, came up with a total of about half a million pairs: a *grand* total less than that for several individual colonies mentioned by Ronald Lockley and James Fisher only 30 years previously. Despite extensive research, no clear reason for the decline has emerged, which is perhaps most worrying of all. We can only take comfort in the fact that recent surveys indicate that the situation has apparently stabilised.

That such a decline should occur in the middle of the 20th century is the more remarkable when the past persecution of the puffin is taken into account. Up to the turn of the century (and in some cases beyond) remote island communities depended heavily on seabirds, and their eggs and young, as a year-round food supply. Eggs were collected

Puffins on Staple, one of the Farne Islands – summer nesting haven of countless sea-birds.

and stored in ashes for later consumption, and adult and young birds were caught by fowlers using nets or nooses, and either dried or salted. Expert fowlers were invaluable to the islanders' well-being, and the toll they took was often enormous. On St Kilda, where the community never numbered more than a few hundred souls, even in Victorian times the annual catch of puffins alone (adult birds from the breeding population) often exceeded 100,000. Salvation lay in the evolution of the annual toll – better described as a harvest. It was strictly regulated at levels that past experience had shown to be tolerable by the seabird populations, and there could be no excesses, because the colonies had to be 'cropped' in succeeding years.

Kittiwakes, avian master-builders, nest on the tiniest ledge.

Such a harvest is still taken on many of the Faeroe Islands, and even on our own Sula Sgeir, where the island crofters are allowed by law an annual harvest of the young gannets, called 'gugas'. The gannet is one of the avian success stories of the past 100 years. It is strictly a remote island breeder, and many new colonies have been founded. Existing ones have also grown. Boreray, part of the St Kilda group, and its two gigantic stacs, houses the largest northern hemisphere gannetry (perhaps the largest in the world) now numbering about 100,000 pairs. At a distance, the towering cliffs are so gannet-crowded that they look like a giant iced cake, snow-white with birds and guano.

The colony itself must rank as one of the visual wonders of the bird world – hundreds of gannets plunging, often from 100 feet or more, headlong into the sea in pursuit of a school of fish. How there are not more collisions is difficult to understand, as birds are plunging in from all directions at high speed, then bouncing back to the surface, heavily laden with fish, for a laborious take-off across the waves. Some mental arithmetic on the daily catch

of fish when the colony is in full swing indicates that about 200 tons of fish a day are needed to supply it.

The fulmar, superficially similar to a gull but far more a master of the art of efficient gliding, has capitalised on the changing practises of the whaling and the fishing industries (in particular gutting at sea). Most of our islands, and the mainland coastline now have fulmar colonies, although in 1870 St Kilda held Britain's only fulmar colony. Fulmars nest on cliff ledges. Where these are absent – as in parts of southeast England – they will nest even on nuclear power station windowsills. They are able to defend themselves by spitting the oily and extremely smelly contents of their stomachs at any intruder.

Windowsills, cliffs, old jetties and even seaside piers are used by the other recent seabird success story, the kittiwake. The kittiwake is the avian master-builder, an oceanic gull coming to the land only to breed. On its island colonies, it chooses the tiniest projections (often under formidable overhangs) on which to cement its nest of flotsam, jetsam and seaweed. As the nest is plate-sized, often with only air beneath it, the kittiwake chicks are amongst the best-behaved of young birds: one false step in the excitement of greeting a parent returning with food would be one too many. Kittiwakes call their name, and are deservedly popular, seeming from the safety of such inaccessible nests, not to mind birdwatchers who are fascinated by the noisy comings and goings.

This, then, is a kaleidoscope (and far from complete) picture of the role islands play in the life of our seabird populations. They are often natural fenceless nature reserves. They can be the undisturbed home of countless thousands of seabirds, where the birds (as for centuries past) get on with their lives unmolested by man and in harmonic balance with their natural surroundings. And for small land birds, islands can be salvation. Many a tired migrant blown off-course by unfavourable winds or grounded by heavy rain or cloud, owes its survival to them.

In some, though, there has been an ominous change. Our northern seas are lit at night by the lights and flares from oil platforms. This oil demands terminals, with their attendant hazards. The recent spillage at Sullom Voe, Shetland, is a warning that we must guard this island heritage and its wealth of seabirds jealously: for ourselves, for a balanced environment, and so that our children and grandchildren may also know and enjoy the spectacle of the raucous turmoil of life in a seabird colony.

JIM FLEGG

SCILLY ISLES

BY PATRICK HERON

Physical scale – this is always the greatest mystery. With your feet in a rock-pool, looking down, you suddenly read promontories, lake, islets, bays and fjords into the minutely ragged edges of the pool's surface as it eats into the granite, imagining yourself looking down from a jet 30,000 feet up. And of course, there really is an *exact* relationship between the most minute geological manifestations and the coastlines on a map: the calligraphic linear patterns patent in the smallest surfaces of a granite pebble do precisely coincide with western coastlines on the Ordnance Survey map. The design is the same whether the jagged or rippling contour is contained within a yard of the rock-pool's edge or extends along 100 miles of coast. Smaller suggests bigger. And vice versa.

Ship's figurehead in Valhalla, Abbey Gardens, Tresco.

All of which, perhaps, is a commonplace. With the Scillies, though, there is an altogether new and, as far as I know, unique complication in this matter of the confusion of scale: this fabulous archipelago of between 200 and 300 separated rocks and islands seems at all times, and in all lights, totally to defy identification as to actual sizes and distances.

At one moment you feel, as you look from one of the larger islands to the others, across a sound that is streaked with long low miniature 'islands' of rock (surfacing like semi-submerged submarines), that half the Aegean is in front of your eyes, so majestic seem the misty spaces between one rocky profile and the next. A moment later you realise it is five human figures which are punctuating the crest of a nearby island, so miniature is its scale. Yet, at the same time, it is an island which makes a shape, in profile, as grand and imposing as a small mountain in any other climate or place.

Despite this grandeur of effect, the Scillies are actually very low-lying. Of the five inhabited islands only one small area on the largest, St Mary's, rises to just over 150 feet, while St Martin's, Tresco and Bryher achieve little more than 100 feet at their highest points; and St Agnes is lower than that. Yet the great variety of shape in the profiles these islands present against sea and sky, and the fact that they reach out for more than 11 miles (from rocks north-east of St Martin's right down across the entire archipelago, south-west to the Bishop Rock) produce an overwhelming feeling of space – of a far-flung and essentially horizontal, panoramic immensity that itself never fails to exhilarate, with its sense of the enormous ocean all but washing over these sharp and eaten-away fragments and particles of solid land.

How is it, one wonders, that the great Atlantic storms do not sweep everything away? For instance, why do the 50-foot waves of the winter gales not wash the small houses of Hugh Town, capital of the Scillies, off its isthmus of sand on St Mary's, itself barely 10 feet above high-water mark? Anyone who has been there in a gale knows the answer: a complex system of semi-submerged rocky ledges, lying down to the south-west towards the Bishop, serves to foil the huge seas, which explode on them in gigantic fountains of spray, each perhaps 100 feet high. The central sound which separates St Mary's from Samson, Tresco and St Martin's is thus protected by all those unseen encircling reefs.

There is no doubt about it, small islands set in great oceans (and if the Scillies don't feel like the furthest end westwards of the vast Eurasian land mass, what does?) exert a hypnotic spell over the mind. They symbolise a security of isolation; they are a manifestation of self-containment, of self-sufficiency, which has mesmerised man for centuries. D. H. Lawrence's short story, 'The Man Who Loved Islands' was an exploration of the impulse to look for an ever-smaller and remoter island sanctuary – until the subject of the tale finally retreats to a mere slab of rock (the smallest of all his islands) and gets swept clean away.

Naturalised narcissi on Bryher: the white ones are first to show.

Whether or not the fascination of islands should be dismissed as a form of escapism, one thing is certain: one has only to spend a few hours on the Isles of Scilly to be virtually brain-washed by a very special kind of physical space and remoteness. One's whole mode of awareness changes dramatically. One's senses seem liberated. All visual perception appears to be more concentrated and, furthermore, quite effortless. One is aware of one's surroundings to an unusual degree, from the sea-washed twig amongst the wrack cast up at one's feet on the silver-white sand (tiny flecks of mica gleam everywhere in that sand, like minute silver mirrors) to the Day-glo pinks and yellows of the papery petals of the flowers on the mesembryanthemum which sprouts from the salty turf at the beach's edge. And, surely, the clarity of the whitest light in Europe plays its part in all this.

The central lagoon separating Samson, Bryher, Tresco, and St Martin's from St Mary's is so shallow that its sandy bed – only a few feet below the surface – causes it to turn a brilliant turquoise on a sunny day, a turquoise beyond which the deep ultramarines and indigo of the open sea outside the encircling islands dramatically signify the deeper ocean. Crossing and recrossing this shallow sound, the open launches (the only transport between islands) deftly weave changing courses, according to the state of the tides; and no one heeds the bump and swish of the boat's bottom as it passes over banks of seaweed. And it is on these short trips between islands, from open boats, that one enjoys one more of the almost baffling spatial experiences of Scilly – namely, the sight of the rapidly changing silhouettes of rocks and islands which one thought one knew as one moves over the water between them.

No sooner has one learnt to identify the vertical pile of rock which is Men-a-vaur, looking like the west front of a Gothic cathedral when seen from Crow Bar, than one finds oneself consulting the map, as one walks over the high flattened heath of the north end of Tresco, in order to disentangle and name that isolated mass of rocks which seems so surprisingly far out beyond Round Island. Men-a-vaur again! As for Round Island itself, it is always identifiable only because of its beautiful white lighthouse (the lighthouse that casts a hypnotic beam of deep rose light all night long).

But perhaps this almost total transfiguration of identifying outline most frequently occurs in the case of all those major uninhabited islands which, in a sense, are simply great rocks. And what names they have! Hanjague, Great Ganinick, Little Ganilly, Nornour, in the Eastern Isles; Mincarlo, Great Minalto, Great Crebawethan, down towards the distant Bishop Rock, with its half-seen vertical shadow, the column of the pencil-like lighthouse, floating but constant in the haze. It is the first light in the approach to Europe, coming in from America.

The Scillies are the most southerly fragments of land in the entire British Isles, their climate the most temperate, if one is speaking of air temperature and forgetting the ravages which violent horizontal airstreams – ie the ferocious Atlantic gales – can visit on any landscape. All of which means that, on the Scillies, if you put up a barrier against the wind, you have a most benign climate, favouring any number of sub-tropical plants, trees and bushes. But the windbreaks have to be established.

On St Martin's, the island itself is little more than a long spine of land with its backbone just over 100 feet above sea level, acting as a windbreak against the north. And along its flat top, as in the bays and coves of its northern coastline (nowhere are they on the scale of cliffs), the wind does not permit more than shallow beds of heather or the occasional low thicket of gorse. But its south-facing edges could not be in greater contrast, consisting almost uninterruptedly of gigantic arcs of white sand beaches.

At the western end this great beach rises in a wave against the island; and this wave has long been cultivated. Succulents and cacti abound in the hedges here: and crops of nerine lilies, or narcissi, or iris, according to the season, are grown in long strip-like enclosures between 20-foot evergreen hedges, all clipped and pruned into a rigid wall-like windbreaking structure, as formal as any yew hedge topiary. But these living walls are of escallonia or pittosporum; as they trace their parallel rippling lines up the small slopes they may be so close together that from certain angles one cannot see the long thin slabs of yellow (daffodils) or purple-red (anemones) enclosed between them.

On the sunny side of St Martin's, where these bulb enclosures run at right angles to the shore, only the odd large umbrella pine, or a small hillock culminating in a crest of rocks, disturbs this pattern of windbreaker hedges on that raised beach. If the climate enclosed between these green walls can be compared to that of the Cap d'Antibes, that prevailing a mere 80 feet higher, on the heathery flat top of the island, must differ little from the

Gweal Hill, Bryher: 'small islands set in great oceans exert a hypnotic spell over the mind'.

Orkneys. In other words, on St Martin's a mere drop of 80 feet, by cheating the gales, may be said to compress nearly 2,000 miles on the European map. Where else could one find this?

St Mary's, by far the most populated, seems nearer in scale to the mainland of Cornwall, and thus less exciting. But it is still remarkable. The wind-stunted pines, matted together in a small wood on the Garrison hill, are a scented paradise, full of large thrushes which flash out on to the beautifully formal, low fortifying wall which entirely encloses this headland. St Mary's southern coast contains a series of exquisite miniature coves and bays (for instance Old Town Bay, where a couple of farmhouses look bigger than the headlands themselves). Beginning within a few hundred yards of Hugh Town, the outcrop of pink granite rocks known as Peninnis Head can be seen down to the left of Porth Cressa Bay; in Sir John Betjeman's second 'Shell Guide' to Cornwall this collection of grotesquely carved and worn-away rocks is described as 'Henry Moore-like', and that is right: the formal complexity of this fantastic outcrop is unsurpassed. Clambering or sitting amongst the uninterruptedly undulating surfaces of this world of granite forms on a cloudless day – only a backdrop of pure cobalt and ultramarine sky and sea – is almost a surrealist experience.

The island containing the greatest contrasts is Tresco: its northern end unbelievably bleak, a high, flat moor of heather in gritty granite subsoil without a bush or tree of any kind; its centre as lusciously sub-tropical as anything in the British Isles, the result of decades of expert gardening by the Dorrien-Smith family. The gardens of Tresco Abbey nestle under the protection of groves of immense pines, which begin as a frieze for two large inland lakes. Part of Tresco's magic lies in this geographical paradox – a small island itself containing islands of water. However, it is the outlook *from* Tresco that mainly fascinates me: the southern half of the island is virtually surrounded by an unending ribbon of white sand, in a succession of mile-long scimitars or arcs, linking the minute granite points but backed mainly by duneland. To walk right round these lonely beaches from Old Grimsby in the east to New Grimsby in the west is to have the entire archipelago wheeling itself round into view for you, from St Helen's, Tean and St Martin's in the north and east through the Eastern Isles, then the great mass of St Mary's followed by St Agnes, Annet, the jagged teeth of western rocks, the Bishop and finally, to the west, uninhabited Samson followed by Bryher seen close in across Tresco Flats.

PATRICK HERON

BASICS

Five inhabited islands and more than 100 rocks and islets sit out in the Atlantic Ocean, about 28 miles south-west of Land's End. All belong to the Duchy of Cornwall. Centre is St Mary's, the biggest island but still only 3 miles at its widest and a pleasant day's amble (about 10 miles) round the entire coast. The rest are known as the off-islands.

Fertile source of romantic theories – are these the remnants of the lost land of Lyonesse? Are they perhaps the Cassiterides, the unidentified islands which traded for tin with the Phoenicians? Huge number of Bronze Age tombs on the islands has led to suggestions that they may have been centre of funeral cult, with ships sailing from the mainland to bury the dead here.

Lilliputian landscape with narrow lanes, tiny cottages, flowers everywhere. Flower farmers have imposed distinctive pattern of small strip fields, hedged with high shelters of pittosporum introduced from New Zealand. Early potatoes, harvested in May, are the other chief crop – apart from visitors, the most lucrative of all.

Water very cold, but staggeringly clear. Popular with divers because of the chilling series of wrecks round these islands.

Population now about 2,000 of whom all but 300 live on St Mary's.

St Mary's
WHERE TO GO

HUG TOWN/OLD TOWN

Hugh Town is chief centre with a smaller scattering of houses at Old Town, the original settlement, mostly rebuilt in the 1960s. Streets narrow, many buildings of great granite blocks like the dour Victorian PO (1897). Chief focus of activity is the Quay built out to Rat Island. The ferry docks here and all boat trips and launches for off-islands leave from this spot. Town Beach here is where locals keep their boats. Not much room between mooring ropes for swimming or sandcastles, but good for beachcombing.

Fascinating details of finds from

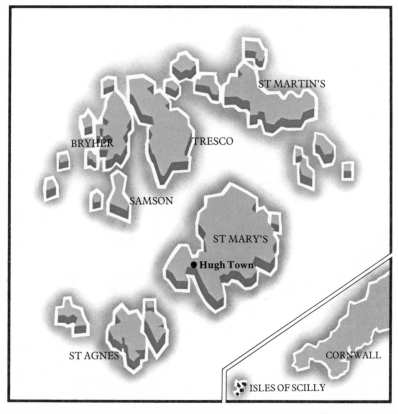

local wrecks are posted outside Customs & Excise Office on quay. From the Dutch East Indiaman Hollandia, wrecked 1743; '1 part tortoiseshell fan, 1 silver teaspoon rat-taled, 3 gold buttons'. Also finds from the Colossus which sank in 1798 with Sir William Hamilton's priceless collection of Greek vases. Salvage started in 1975, 8,000 fragments of the vases have been brought up.

Isles of Scilly Museum, Church St: excellent small museum in ugly modern building. Exquisite bronze and enamel brooches, mostly Romano-British, found on Nornour in the Eastern Isles, and nautical pictures embroidered by Thomas John Pender, a local shipwright, in the 19th c. Good shipwreck display, including cannon from the Association and many finds from the Hollandia. Downstairs is fully rigged gig, Klondyke, seafaring gear and smugglers' tools. Museum publishes some useful pamphlets, especially one on Nornour finds). Open Oct-March Wed 2-4; March-Oct weekdays 10-12.30 and 1.30-4.30. Extra evening opening June-Aug 7.30-9.30. Admission charge.

The Garrison: small fortified island, the Hugh, joined to St Mary's by the neck of Hugh Town. Entrance through fine stone gateway carved with the initials of Abraham Tovey, Master Gunner, who arrived at the beginning of the 18th c to brush up the island's defences. Handsome houses inside. Road leads up to Star Castle, now a hotel, built by Francis Godolphin who leased the islands from Queen Elizabeth in 1570 for £10 a year. Very bizarre shape, an eight-pointed star with outer ramparts, intended to protect the approach against any sneaky designs by the Spanish Armada. Last Royalist stronghold in England to fall to the Parliamentarians, when Sir John Greville surrendered with honour in 1651. Pretty walk past old signal station and along ancient grass-topped battlements around south of island.

Old Town Church: short walk from Garrison along Porth Cressa beach and over Buzza Hill to church at Old Town. Church heavily restored in 1890s, but door possibly Norman. Very small and simple, on superb terraced site overlooking Old Town Bay. Churchyard dominated by two enormous pinnacles, one to memory of Augustus John Smith who for 38 years until 1872 was Lord Proprietor of Scillies. The other commemorates a young American girl, Louise Holzmaister, who drowned in the wreck of the *Schiller* 7 May 1975. More than 300 died that night on the Retarrier Ledges and 100 of them are buried here. Spirit and sound of sea fill this churchyard.

Road from Old Town leads back to Hugh Town passing on right the box always referred to locally as 'The Wilson Residence'. Remarkable only for its barrenness. Comment of one passing American: 'Our President's *lavatory* is bigger than that.'

Shopping: about two dozen shops, mostly clustered in the area around Hugh St. The Sandpiper sells pottery, jerseys and Scilly T-shirts. Very little local craft in evidence, though Isles of Scilly Knitwear sell home-knitted woollen jerseys and a good range of pull-on hats. Will knit to order. Two local potteries, Newman House out on Garrison Point and John Bourdeaux in Airport Lane. Isles of Scilly and Cornish Stone Co sell pretty jewellery made of local stone, pendants and brooches of cornelian, rose quartz and agate.

Eating and Drinking: Atlantic Hotel on Hugh St favoured place for coffee and lunchtime snacks; Shipwreck Bar has balcony built out over Town Beach with good view of the bay. Coffees and lunches also at the Inn Place Grill Bar next door or with the obliging owners of the Galley, a fish and chip shop with a small restaurant upstairs. Posh food at the Pilot's Gig Steak Bar or the Good Companion, both at The Bank. Mermaid, popular pub by the quay also looking on to Town Bay, is sandbagged against high tides. Bishop and Wolf pub in Hugh Town sells heavy Hicks Special beer. If you're out walking, oases for coffee and snacks at the Rendezvous at Telegraph or at the Garden Café, facing Old Town beach, where you can get excellent lunches.

Sightseeing

Essential to take one of Vic's tours round the island. His bus is a 1952 model in vintage Odeon cinema style. Times of tours (variable) chalked up at departure point in The Parade,

Hugh Town. Delivery splendidly laconic; information the sort you won't get in local guidebooks – the saga of the incinerator, the life history of any inhabitant who happens to pass by. One of the few locals to play unashamedly to the tourist gallery.

Bant's Carn Burial Chamber and prehistoric village site is about $1\frac{1}{2}$ miles from Hugh Town near the tiny hamlet called Telegraph. Chamber about 40ft across, roofed with massive stone slabs, rough stone passage leads inside. Foundations of ancient houses close by are later, used during Roman times. Stone querns for grinding corn found in field nearby are now in local museum. Two smaller Bronze Age

Garrison Gate, inscribed with initials of Abraham Tovey, Master Gunner.

burial chambers at Innisidgen (good Celtic place name, Innis-i-Geon or John's Island) and a fourth on Porth Hellick Down, very well preserved. D of E booklet (HMSO) very good on these, also on other Scilly monuments in their care.

Porth Hellick: rough stone memorial here to Sir Cloudesley Shovell whose body was washed ashore and buried in this bay after the disastrous wreck of the Association and her sister ships in 1707. He thought he was on Ushant latitude but sailed straight on to Gilstone Ledge. 2,000 men were lost. Body later disinterred and buried with great honour in Westminster

Abbey – odd how the English treasure a really monumental mistake.

Rocks: extraordinary shapes, sculpted by wind and sea. At Porth Hellick is Dick's Carn, known locally as The Loaded Camel. Best collection on Peninnis Head, most southerly tip of island where granite soars and curves with wild abandon. Just northwest of lighthouse here are great basins of Kettle and Pan Rocks. Tooth Rock on headland is more than 30ft high, reckoned by geologists to be best example of vertical decomposition of granite in world. Pulpit Rock, standing out to east of lighthouse, has done the opposite, weathering horizontally. Two 'faces', Laughing Man and Old Witch; to see both requires a bit of squinting and a lot of imagination. Logan Rock, south-west of lighthouse, weighs about 300 tons and moves. Delicate rocking balance upset by World War II bomb nearby, but it's said that if you put a matchstick under the side nearest Peninnis Head you can move the rock enough to snap the matchstick. There are quicker ways.

Tresco

Second largest of the islands, but even so, only a mile wide by 2 long. A manmade landscape of almost unreal beauty. Whole island leased from the Duchy by the Dorrien-Smith family, now fifth generation since Augustus Smith took over in 1834. Scarcely a gorse bush grew when Augustus arrived and started to build his house close to ruins of Abbey. Throughout the island he planted sycamore, elm, ilex and Monterey pine shelter belts, marked out field boundaries and then began to make a terraced garden of bizarre New World plants round the Abbey, now famous for its rare exotics. Tree planting continues. Two and a half thousand *Pinus contorta* put in this year.

Tourism infinitely bigger business than flowers or potatoes. High proportion of island's houses are let as holiday cottages and there's also very de luxe accommodation at the Island Hotel (tel Scillonia 22883) or at the friendly New Inn (tel Scillonia 22844). Less sense of community here than on other off-islands, but much greater variety of things to see and do.

Tresco: the Abbey Gardens, lushly sub-tropical; and Cromwell's Castle – 'right but revolting'.

Wonderful beaches, backed by feathery tamarisk trees at Old Grimsby, dunes at Green Porth. Tiny white cowrie shells sometimes to be found, especially at Pentle Bay, but beach-combing rewarding on most beaches. Amazing variety of settings: lane that runs between the two harbours, Old and New Grimsby, also marks off wild northerly end of island, Castle Downs, scrubby heath with shiny gravel – superficial Pleistocene deposits which excite geologists. Shallow pits made by tin prospectors in the 1700s, humps are Bronze Age burial chambers. Southern part lush, with splendid walks, either on beaches, or past Hansel and Gretel cottages of Racket Town wood. Supreme for bird-watchers, Great Pool and Abbey Pool provide habitat for waterfowl and waders. Some strange migrants pass through in spring and autumn, golden oriole, Lapland bunting, red-breasted fly-catcher and vagrants from across the

Atlantic and the east. Landing fee for day visitors.

Abbey ruins are almost smothered by luxuriant growth of garden. Fine arch and outline of nave and chancel remain. Tresco monks were bosses of Scilly in Middle Ages, trading with worldly expertise and squeezing Rachman-type rents from anybody using the harbour. Guide book cheerfully says: 'Rather gruesome gardening anywhere near the old Abbey. If one digs too deep, up comes somebody from long ago.'

Abbey Gardens: many of plants and trees are totally unfamiliar. Twelve acres in all plus rudimentary tea hut. Huge, showy *Echium* straight from Disney's 'Fantasia' bloom in startling blue; great succulents called *Aeonium*, and agapanthus in July and August. A very un-English garden – few lawns – but fascinating. Roman altar carved in granite with axe and sword at west end of Long Walk.

Valhalla: collection of ships' figure-

heads, restored to their original brave colours, on the sea edge of the gardens. All cast up from wrecks in these islands. There's a lady absentmindedly clutching her breast, from the *Primos*, wrecked in 1871. Only survivor drifted with his arms wrapped round her neck till he was rescued off St Martin's Head. Admission charge to Gardens and Valhalla.

King Charles's Castle: built in Edward VI's reign when Scillies became strategic defence point. Unfortunately defenders discovered after it was built that guns could not be angled down sufficiently from this site to command the New Grimsby Channel. 'Also,' wrote Francis Godolphin to Queen Elizabeth, 'which is worst, it is of so weak form as it cannot be defended.' Black mark to John Killigrew, Surveyor. Perhaps he was distracted by the amazing view. **Cromwell's Castle:** below on rocks at water's edge is damnably efficient Parliamentarian version. Tall round tower built of irregular rubble stone, with original entrance through doorway still visible high up on south side. Splendid vaulted stone roof to main tower room. Platform added by Master Gunner Abraham Tovey in 18th c with guns (now on replica trolleys) firing over low parapet.

Tresco Church: built by Richard Chudleigh and his son, Thomas, masons, and William Nicholls, carpenter, in 1877. Nicholls, more used to ships than churches, apparently tackled the roof as if it were an upside-down boat. Island family names thick in the churchyard here: Pender, Hicks, Tregarthen, Jenkins. Some wildly romantic Christian names. Tameyzaina Ellis echoes the Tamazina Nance in the churchyard of neighbouring St Martin's.

St Martin's

Glacial deposits of flint and greensand chert, especially on Chapel Down, brought men to this island in prehistoric times, flints being rare in West Country. Electoral roll now shows 66 people, though no Nances, once one of the leading island families. It was Arthur Nance who started the local kelp industry in 1684, burning seaweed in pits to provide an alkali which was shipped to the mainland to make glass. Old kelp pits still visible, especially on White Island. Watch out if you go to look at them – connecting sand bar is cut off at high tide.

Scillonians tell you that St Martin's has the best beaches of all the islands: Higher Town Bay, Lower Town and St Lawrence's in the south, Great Bay in north. But, on a first visit anyway, this is the least prepossessing of the inhabited islands. Three small settlements, Lower Town, Middle Town and Higher Town, where chickens scratch about in the sand of the foreshore next to the quay. Lane leads up to little green and The Rock, a pile of granite that's a sort of focal point and meeting place for the island. Good look-out point. Turn left for the PO and Stores, with brass ship's clock and good stock of guidebooks and paperbacks. Breakaway sells fruit and vegetables, also organises the St Martin's Sailing Centre (1-hour lessons or courses, tel Scillonia 22872).

Glenmoor gift shop and art studio has pictures for sale by I. W. Turner, who lives locally, and his 'St Martin's Sketchbook'.

Chapel Down and north of island is barren heath, eroded by wind and sea and stripped by generations of peat cutters. Stripy daymark on the down put up in 1683 as a shipping aid by Thomas Elkins, steward to the Godolphins. Second-highest point in the islands, 160ft. (Highest is Telegraph on St Mary's, 187ft.) Cliffs falling sheer to the sea are home for colony of kittiwakes. Wide grassy path leads over The Plains to modern Seven Stones pub at Lower Town. Serves coffee and snacks.

Lower Town quay on the south shore of St Martin's.

St Agnes

Enchanting island with an almost tangible air of self-reliance, the result perhaps of its being the most physically isolated of all the inhabited islands. Very deep water between St Mary's and small quay here at Porth Conger. Good beaches on the bar, but bathing dangerous when it's covered at high tide. Odd little neck of the Gugh is then completely cut off. Two barn-like houses and many megalithic remains on the Gugh, scattered unmarked among bramble and bracken. 9ft monolith Old Man of Gugh is easiest to find.

Lane runs from quay to Middle Town, then on to church and old lifeboat station on west side. New pub with old name, the Turk's Head, now

sits just above quay. Very useful lookout for boats and an excellent place for pizzas. Name comes from old nickname for Agnes people – the Turks. Tresco men were Caterpillars, Bryher men were Thorns, St Mary's men were Bulldogs and those on St Martin's Ginnicks.

Chief landmark is old lighthouse, no longer in use though kept gleamingly white by Trinity House. Built 1680, second-oldest in Britain. First light was from coal fire lit in brazier inside lantern. Possibly a bored lighthouse keeper made maze on cliff edge at Troytown in 1729; it is also argued that it dates from Bronze Age. Nature Conservancy worried about number of replicas made by holidaymakers, ruining turf. Biggest settlement round lighthouse, best earth must be here too – tiny fields with high hedges crowd together in this centre part. Very pretty walk to church down narrow deep lane, so protected that for an instant one forgets about the sea.

Church done out in glossy brown paint right on the sea's edge at Periglis, where islanders keep their boats. Simple, gaunt building with toughness and drama of many coastal churches. Fitting place for lifeboat citations. Station opened in 1890, closed 30 years later, and in that time rescued 206 people. William Thomas Hicks was lost trying to save the Thomas W. Lawson of Boston in 1907; the Hicks are still the chief island family, 15 out of 50 or so people.

Comprehensive PO and shop with board outside giving details of boats and trips. Barn Shop has sophisticated collection of gifts. Unfortunately there doesn't seem to be a lot of local stuff to sell. St Agnes Bulb Store at Troytown Farm sells packs of agapanthus, lilies and local narcissi like Soleil d'Or – probably the best souvenirs of all. Guest-house run by Mrs Peacock at Downs Cottage with room for about 10 (tel Scillonia 22704).

Bryher

Tough, independent little island, looking out over New Grimsby Channel to its sleek neighbour, Tresco. Bryher men enjoy making comparisons between the two. Most of houses tucked together on the sheltered eastern side of Watch Hill. West open to full force of Atlantic. Chilling, spiky, angry landscape. Northerly section well dubbed Hell's Bay. Splendid walk on springy heath over Shipman Head Down.

Watch Hill has stone marker on top and small stone shelter possibly once used as look-out by gig crews hoping for rescue work. It's a relief to get down away from this savage side to foreshore of Town Bay. Kath Nicholls does excellent tea, coffee and home-made cakes at Harbour View Café. Churchyard full of Jenkinses, the founding family. Still eight on the

electoral roll. Vicar is rowed over from Tresco for services, weather and tide permitting. Very pretty little beach on southern tip called Rushy Bay. Bright white sand with intricate maze of tiny, hedged bulb fields behind. Metallic, spiky sea holly fringes at beach edge, flowering July-Aug. Biggest event for years was decision to build Hell Bay Hotel (tel Scillonia 22947) which opened this year.

Off-island boatmen, on whom all life depends, based on Bryher, with launches Commodore, Faldore, Falcon and Sapphire, stubby, tough, open wooden boats that they handle with silent coolness. Can be hired for special trips, diving parties or sea fishing. Phone Leonard Jenkins (Scillonia 22828) or David Stedeford (Scillonia 22886).

Samson

Finest of the uninhabited islands, a child's dream, with a great curve of white beach looking north towards Bryher. Boatmen will drop you off here but there's no quay, so be prepared for a jump, a wade, or a dinghy scramble. Daunting megalithic tombs on North Hill face the angry Atlantic, seething over Mincarlo and Buzza Scud. Lived on till mid-19th c when all the able-bodied men, 19 of them, were drowned going out to wreck. Women and children lived thereafter in desperate poverty, eating little but

limpets, until they were all shipped to St Mary's by the autocratic Augustus Smith. Remains of their cottages on South Hill romanticised by Sir Walter Besant in his novel 'Armorel of Lyonesse'.

St Helen's

Once a place of hermits and monks. Ruins of early granite church remains, service held once a year in Aug. Boats leave from St Mary's, St Martin's, Tresco and Bryher. Pest House set up in 18th c for detaining people with infectious diseases. Later the commander of guardship moored at St

A gig race, with Tresco/Bryher gig Czar, built 1879, in centre.

Greath Porth Bay, Bryher: above the beach high ledges form wall-like windbreaks against the Atlantic gales.

Helen's Pool during the Napoleonic Wars made a garden on island. Mesembryanthemum and Hottentot fig escaped and naturalised.

SPECIALITIES

Flower industry: started by William Trevellick of Rocky Hill Farm, St Mary's, who made collection of Scilly's wild narcissus in his garden. Sent an experimental batch of Soleil d'Or off to Covent Garden in 1879, packed in a hat box. Astounded by generosity of cheque, he and three friends settled down to exploit mainland market for their 'weeds'. Season lasts Nov-April with Sols and Paper White the first to show. Old abandoned fields of flowers make islands shimmer; they climb up hillside of Gugh, poke through rusty prams on Tresco tip. Terminology confusing. High hedges round little fields are here called fences; stone walls are hedges. Bulbs are called roots and daffodils are lilies. You can buy bulbs in small packs from many local growers or wholesale from Tresco Bulb Gardens, Tresco, Isles of Scilly. Varieties of narcissus include Ice Follies, Crescendo, Brunswick.

Wrecks: only Scillonians could have objected to building of lighthouse because it would rob them of 'God's grace' – shipwrecks. R. L. Bowley (see *Information*) quotes splendid tales of cows left wandering on the coast with lights tied to their tails and of vicar who positioned himself at church door before announcing news of a wreck, saying 'This time we all start fair!' Graveyard inscriptions, ship's bells in school towers, the ghosts and remnants of shipwrecks haunt all the islands.

Gig races: every Fri May-Sept. Strong inter-island rivalry with Tresco/Bryher gig, Czar, top of the league in 1979, her centenary year. Rousing account of her life by Alf Jenkins in *Scillonian* magazine posted up at New Grimsby, Tresco. Long, narrow boats, six-oared, originally used to

Grimsby Harbour, scene of medieval Rachmanism practised by the monks of the now-ruined Abbey.

race local pilots out to passing ships (first man aboard got the job) or for salvage and life-saving in shipwrecks. Times of races posted on all islands and trips organised to follow the boats.

ACTIVITIES

Fishing: John Poynter of St Mary's, skipper of twin diesel catamaran White Hope, is available for hire for shark fishing or sea angling. Tel Scillonia 22583. Boatmen are, quite rightly, unwilling to hire boats without themselves as well – too many dangers. Fishing off rocks and quay brings in mackerel, pollack, wrasse. Local angling club organises competitions. Contact D. Metcalfe, 31 Porthcressa Rd, St Mary's.

Sailing: not for novices, but if you want to bring a boat, contact Harbour Master at St Mary's (tel Scillonia 22768). If you are staying on Tresco, Estate Office has a Wayfarer, two sailing boats with outboard and 14ft runabouts with outboard. Channels not marked. Manoeuvring can be tricky on the falling tide.

Windsurfing: hire and instruction at South'ard Sailing, St Mary's Quay (tel Scillonia 22837).

Diving: wonderfully clear water and a graveyard of wrecks make this a popular centre, but nearest decompression chamber is 120 miles away at Plymouth. Some sites protected, others privately owned. Details of local facilities from Underwater Centre, Warleggan, Church St, St Mary's (tel Scillonia 22563) and the Marine Study Centre, Pelistry, St Mary's (tel Scillonia 22415). They don't like spear-guns.

Boat trips: at least twice daily throughout summer from St Mary's. Tickets on sale at kiosk on quay. Bishop Rock round trip to lighthouse taking in seals and puffins en route. Watch out for ruins of cottage on wild Roseveare, built to house wretched lighthouse builders. Mon evenings May-Aug Golden Spray does local history cruise, about $1\frac{3}{4}$ hours, with castles, burial chambers, smuggling.

Walking: an unparalleled pleasure and the only way to get about on the smaller islands. For wildness and a hint of savagery, keep on the outside of the ring of islands, the west of Samson, Bryher, St Agnes, the north of Tresco and St Martin's, the east of St Mary's. Tresco has most variety, though its beauty is curious, in aspic almost. St Agnes also a delight – good walk past St Warna's Well round Horse Point and back by Beady Pool (Wingletang Bay). Beads from shipwreck 300 years ago still sometimes found here.

Swimming: cold but safe anywhere except high tide on bar between St Agnes and Gugh and bar between St Mary's and Toll's Island. Beaches are glorious with white, quartzy sand that makes mermaids out of wet children. Pentle and Green Porth both splendid on Tresco. Par Beach, Perpitch, Great Bay and others equally empty on St Martin's.

Golf: 9-hole course on St Mary's, open to visitors. For temporary membership, apply to Steward.

Tennis: hard court on the Garrison, St Mary's. Small charge. Hiring done through Douglas the Chemist, Bank, St Mary's.

FLORA AND FAUNA

Birds: variety of seabirds notably storm petrels, terns, auks, nest happily in the Scillies, especially on uninhabited islands like Annet and Mincarlo. Regular boat trips to Annet and Western Rocks, leaving St Mary's or Tresco/Bryher. Puffins in Annet are a delight. Great black-backed gulls, ruthless predators, patrol higher rocks.

Black birds diving more likely to be shags than cormorants. Shags have easy-to-see crest during breeding season. Local Royal Society for the Protection of Birds man gives useful tip (not infallible) – cormorants are loners. All stand hanging their wings out to dry like miniature petrified witches. Terns are summer visitors from Africa and two sorts nest here, the common and the roseate. Sites often roped off (as on Castle Down, Tresco), as they are shy birds. Don't intrude. Islands attract many off course migrants in spring and autumn, such as pectoral sandpiper from America, warblers from the east; skuas are regular, preying on the terns.

Inland pools like those on Tresco and Bryher provide different habitat for waterfowl and waders, moorhen, coot, mallard, mute swan, sedge warbler and gadwall. Chinese geese on Tresco are descended from birds which escaped from the clipper Friar Tuck, wrecked in 1863. Tresco Estate Office will hire binoculars plus bird book to anyone staying on island.

Scilly expert is local David Hunt who does regular 'Sea and Shore Bird Specials' leaving from quay at St Mary's. Full weekly programme of excursions, including guided walks from David Hunt (Holidays), St Mary's, Isles of Scilly.

Seals: breed on islands near Bishop Rock lighthouse, usually included by boatmen on Annet trip. Pups have white coats for first month. Can be seen Sep/Oct, best at low tide. Inquisitive seal faces often pop up in other areas too, like the rocks between Tresco and St Martin's.

Flowers: man has actually helped a bit here as uncommercial throwouts from bulb fields have naturalised everywhere, not only daffodils and narcissi, but agapanthus and belladonnas too. Amazing on Tresco in late summer to see huge clumps of

Above: *wild garlic, St Mary's*. Below: Carpobrotus, *Tresco*.

witchy belladonnas pushing through bramble and bracken.

Wide range of habitats means wide range of wild flowers too. Yellow horned poppy in the dunes and sea-pinks everywhere, especially staggering on Annet, full bloom in May. Gnarled ling on the downs. Three-cornered leek and yellow oxalis grow over stone walls in spring. Catchfly

and whistling jacks (a wild gladiolus) also found.

Ken Johnson, who lives on Tresco, does an excellent island ramble with his family on Saturdays. He's a bird buff – his daughters handle the flowers. Meet at Timothy's Corner, Tresco, donation to RSPB funds.

Briefing by Anna Pavord

ISLE OF MAN

BY RICHARD ADAMS

People are never neutral about the idea of living on an island. Either they find it uncongenial – 'miles away from everything, cut off from all the people and events that really matter' – or else they are attracted by the notion of seclusion. One would expect the latter group to include both creative artists and retired people, but it is perhaps more surprising that a great many young Manx either choose to remain on the Island or else come back to it after a year or two 'Across'.

The Isle of Man is 30 miles long and about 12 miles across, with a present population of 63,000. It has only one sizeable town, Douglas (20,000), and six smaller towns scattered round the coastline. There are no inland towns and little industry, for there are no longer any mineral deposits, the former copper, silver and lead seams being long worked out. (The old mine buildings, gaunt and deserted, are still to be seen in remote places, relics of the Island's industrial past.) Today the principal sources of income are farming, fishing, holiday trade, motor-cycle racing and the money brought in by investors, and by 'come-overs' attracted by the leisurely pace of life and the low rate of income tax (20 per cent).

Visually, the Island gives a first impression of a cross between Northern Ireland and the Lake District: the bare, heathery, unfrequented hills, on which blue- or red-marked sheep wander and graze unattended; the plain, blunt, friendly shepherds and farmers, most of whom don't mind where you walk as long as they can see that your dog's under control and you can be trusted to behave properly over things like gates and matches; the sudden snow storms in winter, sometimes bad enough to cut off farms and disrupt electric supplies and telephones; the relatively high rainfall; the gulls, magpies, hooded crows, jackdaws, curlews; the low, white-walled cottages with their fuchsia hedges; the endearing and very proper preoccu-

Lady Isabella Water Wheel, Laxey, built in 1854.

pation of most people with local rather than national affairs. Lilliput if you like, but a serene, beautiful Lilliput, where people don't get pushed about, can hear themselves think, have little to fear from robbery or violence and are free to take things at their own speed. *Traa dy-liooar*, in fact.

Traa dy-liooar? The Manx coat of arms, as everyone knows, carries the Island's famous three-legged emblem, with the motto '*Quocunque jeceris stabit*': 'Whichever way you may throw him, he will stand.' This is appropriate enough to the dogged Manx character, but equally so is the Manx catch-phrase '*Traa dy-liooar*' (pronounced 'Tray d'*loo*ar'); 'Time enough'. No one should interpret this sardonically, on the lines of the Irishman smoking his pipe while the roof lets in the rain. Most Manx are hard workers: but they are not given to flapping and they are not to be hurried.

Manx nationalism has a quiet but very real strength. Unlike Welsh or Scottish nationalism, it is not vociferous or aggressive. Rather it resembles the quiet ticking of a clock, of which you become conscious only when you have been in a room for some time: but once you *have* become conscious of it, you can't cease to be aware of it and it continues to underlie all you hear. The Manx are courteous and pleasant; many, even forthcoming. Yet they retain withal an arcane, esoteric, spiritual core, a strong if mostly silent conviction that the Island belongs to them and not to just anybody who happens to have come over to live there. This is a matter on which they can be understandably touchy, especially if provoked. The Manx, a united community, all know each other – the Quilliams, the Quayles, the Kneales, the Skillicorns, the Clagues, the Cregeens and the rest. They've known each other and intermarried for centuries. If you go to Lonan and visit the tiny Old Church standing lonely in the fields, you can see the Clagues laid out

Douglas, largest town and capital of the Isle of Man.

in rows, back to the 18th century. It would be a great mistake to try to force yourself upon the Manx, let alone push them around, just because they don't push you. You'd meet a brick wall. There's a great deal to be learnt about the Island – by anyone who wants to learn it. Otherwise you can stay in your house (for which you probably paid more than many Manxmen can afford, because it's the likes of you that have inflated prices) and drink yourself silly. Some do, and never learn anything. They just die after a bit. (Somebody once nicknamed the Island 'God's waiting room'.)

Well, and how do you learn? In delightful ways. By drinking the excellent local beer in pubs and talking. By walking over the hills, through the glens and along the beaches and cliffs. By watching sea-birds in lonely places, such as the grassy patch above the sea under the west face of Cronk ny Arrey Laa (Hill of the Rising Sun), near the ruins of the little *keeill* (chapel or hermitage), built long before the Norman conquest, from which one looks out across the Irish Sea. On a clear evening the Mountains of Mourne, 50 miles away, are plain against the sunset.

Neither the Romans nor 1066 mean anything in the Isle of Man. The Romans never got here; nor did the Normans; nor, for the matter of that, did St Augustine. The Island was Christianised by Irish missionaries during the latter part of the fifth century, more than 100 years before St Augustine landed in Kent. The remains of their little Celtic Christian *keeills*, dating from the sixth century onward, are still to be seen in lonely spots. The Celtic Manx were overrun by the Vikings early in the ninth century, but rulership remained a free-for-all until in 1079 Godred Crovan, a Norwegian, conquered and united the Island. That was the Manxman's '1066'. In 1266 the Island passed to the Scottish crown and not until the middle of the 14th century did it become an English possession. Through all these vicissitudes, its essentially Celtic character has endured to the present day. *Quocunque jeceris stabit*. This is not England, or Ireland, or Scotland. It is Man – an autonomous realm under the Queen.

Douglas is a graceful, largely late 19th-century seaside town, built round the two-mile bay between Douglas Head and Onchan Head. The town rises fairly steeply from the bay, so that from many of the quiet, residential areas inland there is a clear eastward view across the sea to the hills of the Lake District, 40 or 50 miles away. Some of the quiet, stone-built squares and terraces resemble those of Bristol's Clifton in style and elegance. The Gaiety Theatre remains a Victorian jewel, its

décor unaltered since the 1880s. The museum is a model of what a provincial museum should be.

But it is in its solitudes that the Island's greatest fascination and character are to be found. Late one winter afternoon, on a high, lonely moor west of Snaefell, near the centre of the Island, I saw three ravens come flying out of the gathering darkness and alight, some way off, on an open patch among the heather. It was like 'Macbeth'. Sometimes, on that moor in winter, you can hardly stand against the wind. Again, I remember a bright, clear, April afternoon on the North Barrule ridge, and snow lying. You could see not only the Ulster coast, southern Scotland and the Lake District; you could also see Snowdon, and distinguish its gleaming features. On a May morning in steep, ferny Dhoon Glen, the scent of gorse drifts from above and the stream – which includes an 80-foot cas-

Sulby Glen, one of the most beautiful of Man's many coastal and mountain glens.

cade – chatters down through the ferns until it reaches the 'port', where it flows across a stony beach into the sea. (The common Manx name 'Port' So-and-So doesn't necessarily denote a harbour. Port Erin and Port St Mary are 'ports', true enough, but Port Grenaugh, Port Cornaa and several others are nothing but sheltered, lonely coves. Their names recall old smuggling days.)

The path along the western, slate cliffs from Peel to Glenmaye, some 350 feet above the sea, is literally the most beautiful walk I know (and I've walked a good deal, in various countries). In summer you can lie on the grassy cliff-top and watch the cormorants (which the Manx call 'jinny-divers'), the fulmars, puffins and guillemots below. Further north, the beaches are sandy and open, and here is the place to see terns (including the not-very-common little tern), oyster catchers, ringed plovers and offshore gannets. In the south, down by the Sugarloaf rock in Bay Stacka, the razorbills breed in summer, and this is as good a

spot as any to look out for the red-legged chough, that splendid maritime bird which has become less common since the days when Shakespeare put it into Edgar's 'Dover cliff' speech in 'King Lear'. Choughs in flight sport and tumble in the air in a most attractive way. Or if you fancy something a little more sheltered and secluded on a windy day, you can walk along the disused railway line, down the valley of the river Neb from St John's, among wild currant bushes, horsetails and meadowsweet, past the ruined mill to Peel harbour, with its fishing boats moored in the lee of the medieval castle on St Patrick's Isle.

At the churches of Maughold and Kirk Michael there are two marvellous collections of Celtic-Viking stone crosses; strap-decorated, rune-carved, adorned with figures of Sigurd, Odin and the dragon (the same Norse myth as Wagner's 'Ring'). At Cashtal-yn-Ard and at Cregneish you can see the ruins of prehistoric stone burial chambers; and it is in these places, I think – especially on winter

afternoons – that one experiences most strongly a sense of that solitude and remoteness that must have enwrapped the Island, lonely, wild and sea-girt, long ago.

There are ghosts and goblins in the Island – and plenty of people who retain what one might call a half-belief in them – or perhaps rather more than that. On the inside of many a front door is fixed the cross-kern, renewed each 30 April: a cross of rowan bound with sheep's wool, to deter malicious fairies. On that night, too, horns are blown on Peel hill to scare evil spirits away. On Tynwald Day (in July), most Manx people, from Members of the House of Keys downwards, wear a sprig of the bollan vane (*Artemisia vulgaris*) to ward off evil, and the rushes strewn along the green path to Tynwald Hill serve the same purpose. Wise precautions. The *Moddey Dhoo* (Black Dog), the *Lhianan-Shee*, the *Buggane* – I would not care to meet them.

To get to know the Island requires perseverance, tact, respect and also, perhaps, a certain feeling of affinity with its lonely character and rather strange – indeed, unique – history. For someone with the time and will, the effort's more than worthwhile.
                                        RICHARD ADAMS

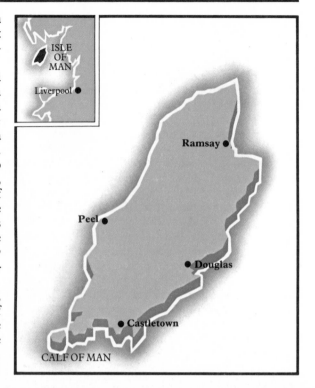

BASICS

Population increases by about 500,000 visitors each summer. Manx people are friendly and helpful. ('We're easy to tell – three legs and no tail.') Most actually seem to like the summer invasion. During the winter they give themselves over to societies and social clubs. Perhaps a quarter or more of the people on the island are 'come-overs' rather than native-born, possibly attracted by tax-haven status: everyone expresses amused contempt for the Weneyes, a tribe of vaguely-retired folk who start every conversation 'When I was in . . .' Taxation is light, with income tax at 20 per cent and no surtax, capital gains tax or death duties: those on the lower end of the wage structure say the highish cost of living cancels out any advantage. Offshore finance, with something like 25 banks in Douglas, is one of the three main industries, along with light engineering and tourism. Man has its own coinage, including a 50p note and £1 piece, and its own stamps – UK stamps are not accepted. Early closing day for most places Thurs.

Constitutionally not part of the United Kingdom but a self-governing dependency of the Crown. Lieutenant-Governor, usually appointed for 5 years, is personal representative of the Queen, who is Lord of Mann; Lt-Gov has considerable authority but his personal 'rule' tempered by agreements with UK administration, EEC commitments and the elected representatives who form the executive. The people of Man elect 24 members to the House of Keys; the Legislative Council consists of the Bishop, the Attorney-General – who has no vote, however – and eight members elected by the House of Keys, often from among their own members. Tynwald is Keys and Council together, presided over by the Lt-Gov, and ratifies laws and appoints the administrative boards.

Manx language is a form of Gaelic. Older people can still remember listening to ordinary conversations carried on in Manx. Nowadays the language survives through the efforts of '*Yn Cheshaght Ghailckagh*,' the Manx Gaelic Society, and '*Aeglagh Vannin*,' the Youth of Man, whose members encourage each other to learn Manx. Some 60 people are fluent speakers, a few hundred more have some knowledge of the language and it may be accepted as an O-level subject. For those intrigued by accents, Manx English is probably at its most distinctive in Peel.

Isle of Man Tourist Board main information bureau is at 13 Victoria St, Douglas, tel Douglas 4323. Good source of useful leaflets about places and activities. They produce a detailed leaflet on the many sporting facilities – from angling, golf and pony-trekking to roller-skating, yachting and sub-aqua diving.

WHERE TO GO
Towns

DOUGLAS

Largest town and capital since 1860s when Government moved from Castletown in response to growing commercial importance of Douglas. Set on wide curving bay with harbour to south, under Douglas Head, and 2 miles of promenade lined virtually from end to end with hotels: one of the most impressive, Castle Mona, was originally residence of 18th c Governor. Shopping and residential areas run into each other, but it's developing a hint of citified centre. Lively shopping area along narrow Duke, Strand and Castle Streets, just behind promenade, recalls tight-packed 18th c layout. Older Inner Harbour still the place for fishing boats to berth, making for an interesting wander along North Quay. Main holiday playground along the front. Horse-drawn trams run length of promenade. Manx Electric Railway Terminus is at north end of promenade – lines from Douglas to Laxey were first laid 1894-1900.

House of Keys/Legislative Buildings: in Bucks Rd, with chambers for the three 'parliamentary' bodies: House of Keys, Legislative Council, Tynwald. Ask at Inquiries about taking a look at the (empty) chambers, usually possible during office hours. More interesting is a visit to the public gallery during a working session.

Manx Museum, Crellins Hill: archaeology galleries display history of Man from Stone Age until end of Norse period around 13th c, model of Viking warship, maps, natural history including island birds and so on. The folk-life galleries are particularly jolly with a dairy, fisherman's shed, small shop and a full-size reconstruction of the kitchen of a Manx 'quarterland' farm. Open weekdays 10-5.

Entertainment and Sports: look for Gaiety Theatre, only live theatre on island, converted from music hall by architect Frank Matcham in 1900, stages Manx Amateur Drama Federation Festival of Plays at Easter and family variety shows during summer. Villa Marina, vast indoor and outdoor complex, stages variety shows. Palace Lido has dancing and cabaret as well as shows. Palace Casino and the Whispers night-club are both in Palace Hotel. Teenybopper ravers head for the MGM Disco in Duke St.

Aquadrome has Olympic-size main pool plus shallow teaching/children's pool. Also sauna, Turkish, Russian and ordinary baths. Summerland is all-purpose leisure complex (refurbished after 1973 inferno). Piazza floor on upper level provides bars, sun-room, facilities for children and staged attractions. Open daily May-Sept 9am-11pm. Admission free. Lower level offers superb sports facilities, squash, badminton, gymnasium and so on. Open daily all year 9am-11pm. Admission charge, family

membership could be a bargain for the sporty.

Eating and Drinking: Crow's Nest Restaurant in Sea Terminal Building, tel Douglas 5009, closed Sun, and Inner Mann Restaurant, Nelson St, tel Douglas 3646, for seafood, closed Oct-Easter. Cannell's Café, Duke St, does good cakes that would make a slimmer whimper. High-class cuisine at Boncompte's, outside the town at Onchan, on a hill overlooking sea, tel Douglas 5626 (closed Sun).

Pleasantly lively drinking available at New Strand, Strand St; Victoria Tavern, also known as the Dog's

Above: A horse-drawn tram on Loch Promenade in Douglas, the capital.
Below: Ceiling of the Gaiety Theatre, converted by Frank Matcham in 1900.

Home, just round corner in Drumgold St; the Grosvenor Hotel, Athol St; or the British Hotel, North Quay, plus any number of other jolly pubs. Main Manx night out seems to be Fri.

CASTLETOWN

The capital from 15th c, under the Stanleys who later became the Earls of Derby, to mid-19th c. Older houses, harbour works and wonderfully preserved Castle Rushen are built of local limestone that has weathered to a lovely blue. Set on beautiful bay, although a difficult anchorage for ships.

Relaxed mix of narrow streets and spacious areas round harbour and castle. Grander buildings include 19th c Church of St Mary and Old Parliament House, a strong square Georgian edifice, 19th c meeting place of the House of Keys and now the offices of the Castletown Commissioners. On the other side of harbour inlet, red and white Castletown Brewery, as beturreted as the castle, spreads a hoppy aura.

Viking Hotel, Station Approach, is a free house with good pub lunches,

Castle Arms (also known as the Glue Pot), a super little panelled bar.

Castle Rushen: in near-pristine condition. The Vikings probably took over a wood-palisaded Celtic fort, raising a square, stone keep: the last Norse king of the island, Magnus, died here in 1265. 14th c extensions, influenced by Edward I's castle-building in North Wales, raised the height of the keep, added towers and flung a fortified curtain wall round about. Later the castle became a prison and then a lunatic asylum: court sessions are still held in the Outer Gatehouse. Open May-mid-Sept weekdays 10-6, Sun 10-1; rest of year Mon-Fri 10-5, Sat 10-12. Admission charge.

Nautical Museum, Bridge St: across harbour inlet from Castle Rushen. Sailmaker's loft, models of deep-sea sailing ships and local fishing boats, whole cabin of Nelson period, ship's biscuit machine and so on. Displays centre on The Peggy, $26\frac{1}{2}$-ft long, schooner-rigged cannon-carrying yacht constructed around 1790. Open mid-May-Sept weekdays 10-1, 2-5, Sun 2-5. Admission charge.

PEEL

Western port and fishing base, sometimes called Sunset City – the warm red of the local sandstone used for castle and most of older buildings makes this doubly appropriate. There's a sweep of sandy beach inside breakwater; the harbour, lined with smaller fishing boats, stretches back up inlet to River Neb.

Old town hunkers down behind prom: narrow twisting streets were planned that way to keep out driving wind and spray. Try Charles St for a real taste of the early 19th c: just a dozen or so terraced sandstone houses on either side, but a narrow entrance and exit plus a couple of kinks cut you firmly off from any later influences. Shops strung along town centre streets include the newsagent's at 24 Michael St where Fred Palmer still prints a cut-down version of the *Peel City Guardian*, the weekly paper his grandfather took over in 1895. Marine Hotel, Shore Rd, epitomises the seaside bar.

Down by the quay, the Fisherman's Association, in the old railway station, sells warm and waterproof clothing as

Castletown, the capital of Man from fifteenth- to mid-nineteenth century.

well as heavy-duty fishing boat gear. Further along the quay, in the town's industrial area, the fish processors have their kippering works. Despite what some guidebooks say, you aren't allowed round.

Peel Castle and **St Germain's Cathedral:** impressive ruins covering a small islet, connected to the shore by a causeway, and encapsulating much of the early history of the island. The earliest remaining fortification is the 10th or 11th c Round Tower, a splendid refuge from Vikings. Simon of Argyll, a 13th c bishop, began the cathedral on the site of an even earlier church. Still in use up to 18th c but fell into ruins during 19th. Castle and cathedral open May-Sept weekdays 10-5, Sun 2-5. Admission charge.

RAMSEY

A sheltered, sunny town in the northeast with two vast sand and shingle beaches set either side of working harbour which leads back, under swing bridge, to Sulby River, largest on the island. A straggly place with new buildings along front, attractive older houses behind – take a look at a particularly fine row at the top of Parliament St. Mooragh Park has boating lake; amusements; plenty of pubs; youngsters' disco at the Plaza; terminal for electric railway. Harbour Bistro, East St, tel Ramsey 814182, provides some delicate cooking – try the Queenies Isabella; there's Italian food at Casa Siciliana, Parliament St, tel Ramsey 814493. Pubs all over the place, with the loucher-looking elements frequenting the harbour-side hostelries.

The Grove Rural Life Museum, Andreas Rd: the Misses Janet and Alice Gibb, grand-daughters of a 19th c Liverpool ship-owner, made over well-preserved house, out buildings and contents shortly before they died, both aged over 90, as a domestic museum. Costume displays, agricultural gear, horse-drawn threshing mill. Open mid-May-Sept, Mon-Fri 10-5, Sun 2-5 (closed Sat). Admission charge.

Millennium Way: a one-day waymarked walk from just outside Ramsey, round Snaefell and down through Baldwin and Garth to Castletown – can be split into sections by less ambitious ramblers. Manx Mountain

Cashtal-yn-Ard, south of Maughold, a classic megalithic tomb.

Marathon, for the more energetic, follows the ridge tops to Port Erin. There are many other walks and footpaths on island often signposted and waymarked. Mist can come down very quickly on the high moorlands so take a map and compass.

Villages

Jurby: just two or three houses at a crossroads in north-west but with a fine airy church set on a low rise out towards the shore with a generous view of the northern flat-land; 10th c crosses in the church porch illustrate the Viking story of Sigurd slaying the dragon Fafnir for its gold. Jurby beach is a 10-mile stretch of lonely sand and shingle accessible from the road at only half a dozen points.

Kirk Michael: largish village spread along road; church has one of the earliest Viking crosses on island, carved in interlaced pattern by 10th c sculptor Gaut Björnson; Philip Morrison's Church View House Antiques has some attractive pieces. Mitre Hotel reputed to be oldest inn on Man.

Laxey: spread-out village running up glen from sea. Lower Laxey has promenade, sandy beach with pebbles, tiny harbour tucked under headland. From a corner workshop opposite the Shore Hotel, Fred Osborne Printers (actually Derek and Elsie Saunders) make an intriguing contribution to island life by producing very nearly all the posters required by

the many societies: set in original 19th c type, these are pulled up by hand, by Elsie, on a museum-piece 1830 Albion press.

Upper Laxey, expanding along the Douglas-Ramsey main road, has shop and cafés, an extensive electric railway depot, and continual reminders that this was one of the island's two main 19th c lead-mining centres. (The other was Foxdale.) Most impressive lead-mining relic is the Lady Isabella Water Wheel, one of the largest in the world, built 1854 to pump water out of the mines and named after the wife of Lt-Gov Charles Hope. For a splendid view you can climb the tower that delivers drive water to the top of the wheel. Open daily May-Sept 10.15-5. Admission charge.

Mines Trail heads up the glen to the old workings. Every day during the summer, a minibus runs from Brown's Café on Dumbell's Terrace (known to locals as Ham and Eggs Terrace) up to the Wheel and down to the beach. Mines Tavern, near station, is cosy 'tram' bar with photos of old mine workings, plus snacks, the Bridge Inn has smart bars, Ye Olde Coach and Horses games and folk-singing.

Port Erin: most resort-like resort on the island, set down on south-west corner: classed as a village but feels far more like a low-key town, and is still developing. Enclosed, almost urban, bay, with safe bathing from curve of sand. Edwardian hotels march along upper promenade, white cottages tucked between beach and grassy 'cliff' recall fishing village origins. Arts Centre, in converted church, home of fortnight-long Mananan International Festival of Music and the Arts in June and triennial competitions for viola, double-bass and harp in Aug. It's the terminus for steam railway. Aquarium, part of Marine Biological Station, beyond the Lifeboat House, researches ways of keeping up fish and lobster stocks. Open Mon-Fri 10-5, Sat 10-1.

Impressive views from Bradda Glen and Bradda Head – the tower commemorates 19th c Liverpool safe-maker William Milner who planned the (now ruined) breakwater, and feasted the fisher folk on roast bullock and beer after the foundation stone was laid in 1864. Lively drinkers today should look for the Eagle Hotel and Bay View Hotel, both on Promenade, or the Station Hotel, Station Rd.

Port St Mary: smaller version of nearby Port Erin (and still with memories of inter-village rivalry). Attractive cottages set around small harbour; yachting centre with Isle of Man Yacht Club, deep-water berths and slipway; sheltered from south-west and, it is claimed, one of the island's warmest spots – though sometimes the wind seems to come from every direction. Barn Restaurant, The Quay, tel Port St Mary 832064, offers roast lamb, beef and so on, unlicensed so take a bottle, closed Sun, Mon.

SIGHTSEEING

Antiquities: Cashtal-yn-Ard, south of Maughold, is a classic megalithic tomb. Once covered by a mound of earth, it now stands as a gallery of stone burial chambers with a crescent-shaped forecourt of standing stones. King Orry's Grave, near Laxey, and the Meayl Stone Circle, in the far south-west, are equally impressive. In addition, there are a number of cairns and, from a later era, more than 200 *keeills*, tiny Celtic Christian chapels that were often built on sites already considered sacred. Many of these places are worth a visit just because they were so carefully placed within the landscape. The churchyard at Maughold (St Maughold founded a monastery here around the begin-

ning of 7th c) contains the remains of two *keeills*, as well as a haunting array of Celtic crosses.

Chasms: scenic area on south-west coast, high up above some of the island's most impressive cliffs with views across to Calf of Man. Part of the attraction – and a reason for taking great care – comes from the vertical rifts where the slate has split apart. They go 200ft deep, running right down to sea level – it's as if the edge of the island were cracking off. Yet many are narrow enough for venturesome souls to jump across. Most promising area on island for rock-climbers.

Cregneish: small village in south-west with open-air folk-museum which gives good idea of 19th c Manx crofting life. Open mid-May-Sept weekdays 10-1, 2-5, Sun 2-5. In 1928

Alfred Hitchcock shot scenes here for his last silent pic 'The Manxman', based on the Hall Caine novel.

Foxdale and Beckwith's Mines: reminder of 19th c 'Lead Rush'. About all that's left at Foxdale are the waste heaps and a grandiose clock-tower celebrating Queen Victoria's jubilee; at Beckwith's, 3 miles away in the hills, an attractively eerie desolation with a precarious boiler-house chimney or two set amid spoil tips. Foxdale Hotel is a pleasant drinking spot.

Glens: many of the most beautiful coastal and mountain glens are specifically open to the public, admission free, with walkways, bridges and so on maintained by the Forestry Department. Glen Maye, south of Peel, is like something out of a Tarzan

movie, fern-covered rock-face dripping water, waterfall, deep pool and even, so it is said, a water sprite. Glen Helen, 4 miles inland, has lots of mildly exotic trees, planted in the 1850s, plus an Alpine Ballroom and Bistro. There is a lovely drive through Sulby Glen, one of the most beautiful; Dhoon Glen, north of Laxey, has magnificent waterfall and views.

St John's/Tynwald Hill: in central valley between Douglas and Peel; scene of Tynwald ceremony held early in July. Tynwald comes from the Norse for 'field of the Thing' (assembly), and this open-air court at which the ruler gave out the law dates from the 10th c. Man celebrated 1,000 years of Tynwald in 1979. Tynwald

Old stone bridge spans the stream at Sulby Glen.

View from Rushen: Port St Mary on right of the bay, a smaller version of nearby Port Erin.

Herds of the four-horned Loghtan sheep can be seen on Calf of Man and elsewhere.

National Park (and newly-planted arboretum) open daily 10am-sunset.

Snaefell: highest mountain (2,036ft), a rewarding 5-mile walk from Laxey or a pleasant ride by electric railway. Summit somewhat cluttered with wireless masts but superb views – on clear days – of the Mull of Galloway, the English coast and the Mourne Mountains in Northern Ireland.

Ayres Nature Trail: a waste of sand, sea-holly, wild thyme and bent in the north, beyond the village of Bride. From the Ayres Visitor Centre, a one-room mini-museum (open May-Sept, Thurs, Sat, Sun 2-5), the trail wanders out on to the beach and back through dunes and heath to a picnic site; chance of seeing seals, gannets.

Calf of Man: small island separated from south-west point of Man by narrow tide-tipped channel; bird sanctuary, with thousands of birds, particularly puffins, packed into its cliffs and grassy heights. Herd of four-horned Loghtan sheep. On calm days, in latish summer, can be visited by boat from Port Erin or Port St Mary.

Curraghs Wildlife Park: 1 mile east of Ballaugh, set in marshland nature reserve; all sorts of animals and birds including deer, flamingos and the four-horned Loghtan sheep. Pair of pumas for big-cat watchers and impressive group of otters. Café.

Sea lion feeding times 11.30 and 3.30. Open daily Easter-Sept 10-6. Admission charge.

SPECIALITIES

Motor-cycling: end of May-beginning of June is super-hectic fortnight for Tourist Trophy, with thousands of enthusiasts coming to watch the professionals whiz round the 37¾-mile circuit of ordinary roads closed off to traffic. Amateur riders get their chance later in the Manx Grand Prix. Start and finish at the Grandstand in Douglas, overlooking the cemetery: some vantage points, Quarry Bends for example, a fast left, right, left just before the Sulby straight, you have to reach before the roads are closed off and can't leave until the race has finished. The day of rest between practice week and race week is called Mad Sunday, as blokes with bikes try to emulate their idols. TT practice last week in May or first week in June, races first or second week in June, Manx Grand Prix practice last week in Aug, races first week in Sept.

Drinking: a beer-person's dream, the pubs stay open all day and the island beers are singularly good, usually served unpressurised. Week-day licensing hours from Thurs before Good Fri to the end of Sept are 10.30am-10.45pm; during the rest of the year 12-10, with an extension to 10.45 Fri, Sat; Sun, throughout the year, 12-1.30 and 8-10. A 19th c pure-beer law means the island's two breweries, Okell and Castletown, use only malt, hops and sugar in the brew. Okell, based in Douglas and the larger firm, won a Bronze medal for their bitter at the 1980 brewers' exhibition. Many pubs are part of an inn or hotel and often provide good bar snacks. A bonus for pool players is the seriousness with which the game is taken: pubs often have a separate poolroom.

Eating: Manx delicacies include local lamb, queenies or small scallops, and local cheese. Breakfast menus nearly always offer Manx kippers: Devereau's in Strand St, Douglas, will send some home for you, but be warned – one or two other fishmongers have given up the service after finding out what summer postal delays can do to half-a-stone of kippers. Manx ice cream (Manx Ices) is real dairy produce, richer and creamier than mainland ices.

World Tin Bath Championship: takes place in Castletown harbour every July. About 60 people in tin baths paddle madly round and round in heats and finals. It's more a matter of staying afloat than getting up speed.

Little People: Manx folk-lore still lives. White-painted parapets at Ballaglonney on the main Douglas-Castletown road mark out the Fairy Bridge across the Santon Burn: when Manx people drive across the bridge they raise a hand to greet the Little People who throng around the area. As well as 'good little people' and 'bad little people' there are giants, who tend to be obstreperous. Other tales tell of creatures such as the '*Moddey Dhoo*', or Black Dog, of Peel Castle. One intriguing oddity, for those who like these things, was the 1930s haunting of Doarlish Cashen, a lonely farmhouse on Dalby mountain, by Gef the talking mongoose.

Manx cats: tail-less, of course, and said to be even more cattish than ordinary cats, friendlier and yet more independent. See them at the Cattery in Nobles Park, Douglas (small building opposite aviary), set up to keep the breed going.

**Briefing by
Humphrey Evans**

ISOLATION OF SPECIES

BY TONY SOPER

With the exception of seals and, in the far north, otters, most mammals have found their way to Britain's offshore islands as a consequence of human activity.

In prehistoric times, men brought sheep and cattle to islands to take advantage of the summer grazing – at the same time helping themselves from the abundant supplies of birds and eggs. More recently, the export of island-fattened livestock has flourished because of the prime quality of the animals. The problems have always been those of transport and wintering.

In the St Kilda group, there have been Soay sheep for at least a thousand years, their ancestry directly relating to the Neolithic root-stock of domestication. Small, goat-like and dark choco-

late-brown, they are the most primitive of breeds, but they are able to endure the harsh winter without assistance. They owe their survival in such unchanged form to the benefits of island isolation – no fresh blood disturbing their genetic flow. Soays may also be seen in Ailsa Craig and Lundy, and there is a thriving flock on Cardigan Island, though the animals which were introduced to the Pembrokeshire islands of Skokholm and Skomer no longer exist. I remember the wild frustration of trying to capture these sheep on Skokholm, when Ronald Lockley wanted to establish a flock at his embryo Field Centre at Orielton. However we tried, there was no way of herding them; they dashed in all directions and then found sanctuary on impossible cliff ledges. Unlike the currently fashionable domestic breeds, these Soays are very much at home on fearsome cliff-slopes.

On North Ronaldsay, the most northerly of the Orkneys, there is a breed of small short-tailed sheep that lives largely on seaweed, their meat being dark and rich with iodine. Under the auspices of the Rare Breeds Survival Trust, a flock nucleus was shipped to the tidal island of Lihou, off Guernsey, some years ago. They flourished on a diet which

consisted of one third grass and two thirds seaweed and now there are about a hundred of them. Every day, as the tide drops back, the sheep pick their way over the slippery boulders to graze the rich meadows of wrack and kelp.

Goats have wrought more havoc to the islands of the world than it is possible to imagine. Released by generations of island colonisers or passing mariners to multiply and provide milk and flesh on demand, they have taken to the feral life with gusto, reducing many a paradise to a barren slum. It might have been better for us all if these creatures, first domesticated thousands of years ago, had been left undisturbed in their rocky fastnesses in the far corners of Europe and Asia. But apart from their usefulness as a provider of milk, they have served sheep farmers in a curious manner. By eating the choicer grass, which is to be found on the most awkward cliff ledges, they reduce the incentive for the less agile sheep to try to emulate them – thus reducing the shepherd's losses.

On Lundy, in the Bristol Channel, feral goats were abundant, but the last survivors of a large herd of white goats were killed in the late nineteenth century. The Trinity House lighthouse keepers re-introduced them, for milk, in the late twenties. As on so many previous occasions on numberless other islands, some individuals soon escaped. At one time there was a wild population of some 200, though there are fewer today.

Broadly speaking, the same is true of red deer. Once ranging the greater part of Europe, they have been progressively exterminated by the destruction of their forest habitat and, on islands, by persecution. In the nineteenth century they were re-introduced to the Scottish islands in the name of sport. As the years go by, the scramble for prize 'heads' has been overtaken by the more logical and ecologically acceptable concept of management, where the annual cull, though it may well

ISOLATION OF SPECIES

1 Otter. **2** Dolphin. **3** Common seal. **4** Goats. **5** Grey seal.
6 Scilly shrew. **7** Rhum ponies. **8** Red deer.
9 Icelandic ponies. **10** Soay sheep. **11** Rabbits.
12 Shetland pony. **13** St Kilda mouse. **14** Orkney vole.

be exercised by sportsmen paying large fees for the privilege, is nevertheless aimed at maintaining a healthy population. The victims are selected not for the excellence of their antlers but in order to leave behind a balance of age groups representing the healthiest stock. So the yearly harvest leaves the herd in good shape. On the island of Rhum, in the inner Hebrides, the re-introduced red deer are farmed by the scientists of the Nature Conservancy, whose object is to study the biology and management of the species. Though the native stock was exterminated in the eighteenth century, there are some 1,500 of these magnificent beasts on the island today.

As part of the management programme the island also supports a couple of dozen Rhum ponies which serve as pack animals bringing in the deer carcasses from the hills. These small horses, never higher than 14 hands, are the product of Arab sire and west Highland mares. Kept free of Clydesdale or similar heavy horse blood, they are typical of the saddle and pack animals which serve remote island communities. Big enough to do the required work, they have small appetites, fending for themselves throughout the year; though mares in foal, and foals and yearlings get some extra feed. The Shetland pony is a triumph of selective breeding, less than 11 hands high, by comparison with the Shire horse's 17. But the Icelandic pony is the typical form of light Celtic horse, one of several subspecies deriving from the original pre-historic European stock. Good load carriers but frugal eaters, some of them can subsist to a certain extent on a seaweed diet.

Like the sheep and goats, rabbits were brought to islands by farmers in search of an honest profit. While rabbit warrens were first established on the mainland, in the Middle Ages, the species could have been designed for islands, with their lack of ground predators. Rabbit meat and rabbit skins were long regarded as luxuries, fetching a high price. In 1324 the Earl of Pembroke held the rights to Skomer Island. At that time the pasturage was valued at £2.75, the annual return from rabbits was £14.25. So a pattern of farming was established. Through the winter ferreters worked the warrens. In spring the seabird eggs and, later the fat chicks were collected. Then the grazing was enjoyed by summering cattle and sheep. Arable farmers arrived around 1700, building a farmhouse and exporting high quality seed corn. The Skomer farm flourished till the mid-twentieth century, when labour and transport problems brought it to an end.

Through the centuries the warreners' rabbits have escaped, times without number, to set up feral populations and increase mightily. It seems incredible today to consider that at the turn of the twelfth century the tenant of Lundy was permitted, by privilege, to take 50 rabbits only in one year.

In 1955 myxomatosis wiped out the major part of all rabbit populations in the islands, as on the mainland, but the inevitable recovery took place and, while the disease is well-established, rabbits have come to terms with it. On some remote islands black rabbits, selectively bred for their fur value in ornamental trimming, can still be seen.

The influence of the rabbit on island pasture is clear – continuous nibbling produces a close-cropped turf which is springy and pleasant to walk over. The constant cropping encourages the spread of ground-hugging plant forms. Because the rabbits enjoy grasses, sea-pinks have room to flourish and decorate the cliff slopes. In fact the cliffside vegetation is held in equilibrium by their activities. However, it is true to say that where there are no rabbits there is a more luxuriant growth of more species of plants.

While the sheep, goats, cattle and rabbits were brought intentionally by island-colonising Man, other less welcome mammals arrived unintentionally. The mainland wood mouse, shrews and the brown rat were transported along with the fodder for the domestic animals. Some of these creatures have undergone an island-change through the thousands of years in which they have been isolated from their original mainland stock. As living proof of the effects of ecological isolation we have the Rhum mouse, the St Kilda mouse, the Orkney vole and so on. Skomer is famous for its vole, an island race of the familiar bank vole, and it also has a field mouse of distinction. Although neither of these animals is a separate species in the strict scientific sense, since each can breed with its mainland cousins to produce fertile young, they nevertheless have distinctive features resulting from their adaptation to island life.

The Scilly shrew represents a creature with no counterpart on the mainland. One of two species on the British List, it has white teeth, unlike all mainland shrews which contain a red pigment. The white-toothed shrews, Crocidurinae, live only on Scilly and the Channel islands; possibly descendants of a mainland population which was wiped out after the last glaciation or, more probably, the result of introduction by Man, since they are common elsewhere in Europe. On Scilly, the animal has foxy ears and long silky bristles on its tail. Its hunting ground is the tide-tossed kelp on the strandline of exposed beaches. Indeed the strandline is a happy hunting ground for other

Seals loll about in dozens on the half-submerged rocks of Knivestone, Farne Islands.

mammals, as well as insects and birds. Apart from treasure-hunting beachcombers, rats and mice tunnel into the weedy piles searching for sand-hoppers and carrion.

In the Scottish islands, and round the coast of Orkney and Shetland, otters are relatively common, leaving their webbed footprints in the sand. While they are retreating and sadly decreasing in England, their numbers are much healthier in the north, where they are more marine in character, fishing for sea fish and crustaceans close inshore. In areas where they are undisturbed they are to be seen during daylight hours, but otters are masters at concealment, and you need to cultivate your local contacts if you are going to see one.

The most typical seashore mammal of our islands is the seal. Grey seals tend to prefer the remotest and most isolated beaches and caves and storm-wracked west-coast islands. They are sea-going animals, completely at home in wild waves and on thunderous beaches. Common seals, while overlapping in distribution with the grey in Scotland, tend to go for tidal sandbanks, sheltered lochs and ledges, on the eastern side of the country.

Seals are in their element as divers, able to work hard and remain underwater for long periods. They are perfectly able to chase and capture fish in murky conditions; recent research shows that they use a form of echo location similar to that of bats. They are sociable animals, gathering close together in large numbers, sometimes several hundreds at a time, in assemblies before and after the breeding season. Away from the breeding beaches, you are likely to see a seal either basking on a comfortable rock, close to or in the water, or surfacing between bouts of fishing. If you are lucky, you will see one treading water while he deals with a fresh-caught fish, holding it with forepaws while tearing the flesh with his powerful teeth. It is conventional to say that you identify the bull grey seal by his greater size and his convex head profile – the roman nose, while the cow has a straight profile, but it is not so easy in the sea. Much the best method is to observe the tonal contrasts of the pelage, no matter what the general colour of the animal, which can be any combination of greys, browns and russets. If the seal's coat has light patches and spots on a dark ground, then it is a bull; if it has dark splotches and spots on a light ground, then it is a cow. This solves the problem of sexing the young bulls, which lack the roman nose, and old cows which have a marked convexity of profile.

Seals have been much persecuted by fishermen who resent their habit of sampling fish in nets, and sometimes damaging the nets themselves, but there's little evidence to suggest that seals damage fish populations as a whole.

Grey seals drop their pups well above high-water mark in caves or at the back of a beach away from the reach of storm-driven tides, and the young seal normally stays put until he is a month old. Fed with super-rich milk by his mother, he grows from a skinny white-coated pup to a barrel-shaped grey-coated moulter in the space of 21 days. At this point his mother abandons him for good. When he is hungry he finds his own way to the sea, perhaps subsisting on crabs and whatever he can find till he perfects an inborn skill for pursuing more rewarding prey. In his first year he may wander, travelling as far as France or Norway, but in due course he returns home to a sedentary and enviable life on the home coast.

The other mammals which you may see from an island vantage point are porpoises, dolphins and larger whales. On occasion quite large numbers of porpoises and dolphins may come close inshore to take advantage of a shoal of mullet or mackerel. Mostly all you will see is a dorsal fin rolling over and disappearing in slow rhythm. Very occasionally one of them may leap right out into the open and hang suspended before falling back with a mighty splash. Killer whales and pilot whales are sometimes seen round our coasts, but on the whole the chance of seeing them is small, and the chance of being eaten by one is even smaller.

TONY SOPER

THE PEMBROKESHIRE ISLANDS

BY CHRISTOPHER WORDSWORTH

Like first love, there are islands that are better left to the glow of memory than encountered again with the risk of disenchantment. But time and change have been lenient to the northern trio of Pembrokeshire islands, Ramsey, Skokholm and Skomer, and the lonely outpost of Grassholm. The remotest acre of Wales was always immune, apart from a few lobstermen who baited their pots with puffins from the huge colony that has long since vanished.

Iron Age Celts, Norsemen and Normans have all left their mark on the islands and men have fought salt-bitter winds and inaccessibility to farm them until defeated. Today a few of the dry-stone walls have crumbled a little more, and truceless war between bracken and heather has progressed another stage, some species of birds have prospered, others like puffins and razorbills declined.

On a clear day in late spring the islands look as though you can reach out and touch them through a haze of bluebells. But they belong now and perhaps forever to the sea-birds and seals who owe their undisputed possession to the six-knot 25-foot tides, fanged reefs like Ramsey's hungry Bitches, and the careful guardianship of the Nature Conservancy Council. Skomer is only three-quarters of a mile away from the mainland, Ramsey one mile, Skokholm three, but the short seas that can brew up suddenly when the tide meets a head wind are a matter of more than local folklore. And rough as the crossing can be, it is nothing to the problems of landing from small boats on rocky shores in a heavy lop. 'If a northerly wind is forecast the trip will be cancelled,' says the guidebook on Skokholm, and 'landing arrangements on Skomer may pose difficulties, especially for the elderly and people with young children.'

Once ashore, looking back at the peerless Pembrokeshire coastline with its stratified shades of rock and lichen, you are in another world, the turf,

View from Ramsey of the Pembrokeshire coast.

hollowed into catacombs by generations of shearwaters, puffins and rabbits, is marvellously springy, and in May carpeted with a bright harmony of colours – campion, squill, scabious, samphire, bluebell, celandine, vetches, and rusty bracken turning to delicate green. Fulmars glide below you from crevices in the 400-foot cliffs, great black-backed gulls, the swaggering villains of the piece, pass derisive comments, puffins on Skomer and Skokholm, where rats have not got at their underground burrows, quiz you like painted clowns, a seal dreams of pollack.

On a calm day the water seems mysteriously and uniquely pellucid, 'the dragon-green, the luminous, the dark, the serpent-haunted sea'; and if there are no serpents plenty of big conga come up writhing and barking in the lobster pots – but far too few lobsters nowadays, the fishermen complain. Dressed crab, is their standby, less lucrative, more tedious and time-consuming. One lobster per pot used to be a fair average; five lobsters and four crayfish from 38 pots was the last catch I witnessed, plus some three dozen crabs which paid for the boatman's time and fuel (less one £10-pot lost) but left him muttering that the life was going out of the sea. 'Dead man's fingers,' was his term for a particular patch of seaweedy bottom that was once prolific. Granted that pessimism is part of a fisherman's code of supersition (salmon net-men will leave a few old fish-scales in the scuppers for luck), it's the same old story almost everywhere.

Under the aegis of the Royal Society for the Protection of Birds there is better news of the avian world. Surface oil pollution has hit the swimmers and divers like guillemots and razorbills; peregrines no longer nest on Ramsey, where Henry II regularly obtained them after seeing one of the island falcons make mincemeat of the Royal goshawk when he was in those parts; there are fewer buzzards on Skomer, which 20 years ago had

The old red sandstone rocks of Skokholm.

the largest population density in Britain. But puffins, after tragic depletion, and kittiwakes seem to be holding their own. For the gulls of course, those supreme pragmatists, it's a continuing success story; thousands of lesser black-backed now nest anomalously among the Skomer bluebells, and the whole tribe learned to exploit tourism long before the locals. Rare and exotic strangers like golden orioles can be seen, though few as exotic as ex-King Ferdinand of Bulgaria who visited Skockholm when that Crusoe of naturalists, R. M. Lockley, established the first bird observatory and bird-ringing station in 1933.

CHRISTOPHER WORDSWORTH

Skomer, largest of the Pembrokeshire islands.

Skomer

At 1⅛ square miles, Skomer is the largest of the group, a National Nature Reserve leased by the Nature Conservancy to the West Wales Naturalists' Trust. A plateau in swirling tides with some quite hazardous cliffs, it is one of the seabird showpieces of Western Europe with as many as 100,000 pairs of that remarkable mini-albatross the Manx shearwater, with the unearthly cry, that visits its underground burrows only on moonless nights to escape the murderous great black-backed gull. Also, but not after August, puffins, second only to the Asiatic hornbill as natural comics, and other rarities like the short-eared owl. Pheasants call, an unexpected sound in a marine habitat. There are no snakes, no rats or mammalian predators to keep the rabbit population in check. A warden is in residence from March-Oct.

No dogs, no accommodation or facilities for visitors (limited to 100 per day in the season). Landing trips (20-min crossing) from Martin's Haven (approx 15 miles from Haverfordwest). For weather queries etc, telephone St David's 241 between 8-8.30am. Also from Dale Slipway (1-hour crossing, tel Dale 349). Organised parties from Solva (tel 387, and worth it for the visit to Solva's charming little recessed harbour like Boscastle), full day trip, also visiting Skokholm and Ramsey, for party of 10, costs about £6 per person.

Skokholm

First British bird observatory, following Heligoland example. 240 acres, leased to and administered by the West Wales Naturalists' Trust. The Trust provides accommodation, male and female warden mid-April-September and runs week-long ornithological and other courses, board – single or double rooms or dormitory – provided for up to 15 persons.

Separated from Skomer by the rip-roaring Broad Sound, Skokholm is a smaller edition of its neighbour but with dramatic red sandstone instead of grey cliffs – one is thankful for its dry pumice-like foothold at the rather challenging landing stage. Here R. M. Lockley lived for 13 years, married and made pioneer studies of puffins, shearwaters, rabbits (introduced by the Normans). Alice, the figurehead from his wreck is mounted

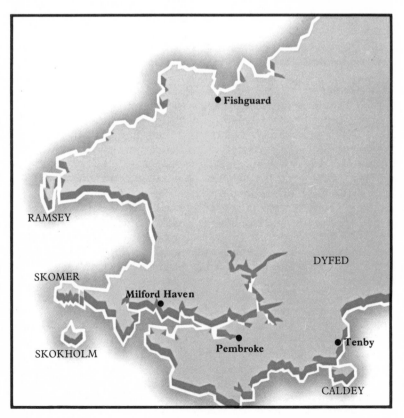

on the rocks, the snug cottage and Wheelhouse refectory testify to the good use he made of the salvage. Look out for purple-quill, heart's ease, bog pimpernel, a lighthouse manned by three, and – the Crusoe touch – a few feral goats descended from domestic milkers.

£57.50 per week, blankets and pillows provided. Change-round on Sat. Beware of delays on A40 at Carmarthen if travelling by car in midsummer. Full information from West Wales Naturalists' Trust, 7 Market St, Haverfordwest (tel Haverfordwest 5462). Boats leave from Dale, Dale Sailing Co, tel Dale 349 Easter-mid-Sept. Also read 'The Island' by R. M. Lockley (Penguin).

Grassholm

A 22-acre hump eight miles out from Skomer, Grassholm has the second largest concentration of gannets anywhere around our coasts with 20,000 breeding pairs. They first arrived mysteriously over a century ago, it is thought to escape persecution on Lundy. From the mainland one sees them as a huge snowcap on the north side. A visit – for which you will require a wise boatman, some agility, and permission from the Royal Society for the Protection of Birds – is an overwhelming experience, almost a taste of heaven and hell. From four miles or so downwind the fishy stink

of guano can undo most stomachs on a choppy crossing; closer, it is like the fumes of hell itself. At the vortex of activity over the island it is shattering and exalting to be enveloped by wild cries and beating of wings as the splendid birds circle and plummet.

'The Brothers', by L. A. G. Strong, tells how some Scottish fishermen with an illicit whisky still executed a suspected informer by setting him afloat with a herring fixed to his cap for a diving gannet to split his skull. Watching them sheath their six-foot wingspan and peel off into a Stuka dive, it is easy enough to credit.

No landing before mid-June, thereafter several boats a week. No dogs, no facilities. Contact Dale Sailing Co (tel Dale 349); and they arrange the necessary permission from the Royal Society for the Protection of Birds.

Ramsey

Ramsey (650 acres) is privately owned and up for sale because of those persistent island problems for its one family – winter crossings, school, a growing only child. There is a clause (how binding?) that the next purchaser must continue to observe the interests of conservancy. Atlantic seals breed here – about 400 pups at the last count – and on Skomer (not on Skokholm, though they frequent it).

Unlike the other islands Ramsey's coastline runs parallel lengthwise

with the mainland, the plateau is more irregular, a swayback of deep bracken, rabbit-bitten fields and heather pitched between two tor-like outcrops. Red deer, from Woburn, provide the cash crop; calving is in June, when casual visitors may be courteously restricted. Stags on a distant skyline make a brave change from the maggot-like sheep they have replaced.

Ramsey is the richest of these islands in history and legend; Justinian, St David's confessor, is said to have withdrawn here with his monks who registered their protest at his austere discipline by murdering him, a reminder that islands are by no means all sweetness and light.

There is a small society of choughs, smartest and rarest of the *corvidae*, an attractively renovated old white farmhouse, a bijou landing cove with natural rock archway – the harbour wall is a feat of engineering. No smoking, dogs, photography, some prohibited areas. Win the pools and buy yourself a dream!

By boat from the Lifeboat Station at St Justinian, which is 2 miles north of St David's. One daily excursion, weather and new owner permitting, from May-Oct (not weekends). Tel St David's 438 for details of times. Several other boats do round-the-island trips (no landing), daily May-Oct. They take about 1 hour and there's never any need to book.

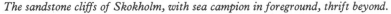

The sandstone cliffs of Skokholm, with sea campion in foreground, thrift beyond.

View of offshore islands, seen from Ramsey. Calluna Hummocks in the foreground.

Caldey

South round Pembrokeshire's elbow opposite Tenby, that picturesque, now slightly blowsy, dowager Welsh resort, Caldey is different. Its 449 acres are sheltered, fertile, wooded, farmed, rabbit-free; it has sandy beaches, gift shops, ice cream, summer crowds, dogs (on leads). It also has seals, an offshore islet with Britain's largest cormorant population, sweeping views (including distant Lundy), tranquillity, a fascinating ancient and recent history that was not always so tranquil.

It made news in 1913 when its Anglican Benedictine Order turned to Rome after the vaulting ambition of the first spendthrift Abbot brought it near to ruin. The Abbey, on a hill at the end of a verdant valley, with its rash romantic neo-Tyrolean turrets and cupolas, is only the first fruit of great things planned by this strange megalomaniac who ended by making a humble oblation of his life. Belgian Cistercians of sterner stock took over.

Today's community, vegetarians and modified Trappists, farm the bulk of the island on up-to-date lines. They export their famous perfume, make chocolates and real Jersey ices for the multitude, provide a livelihood for 30 boatmen with the boat fleet that shuttles across daily in season, conduct a brisk running battle with Tenby Council about needs and dues, and offer a period of retreat and dialogue to all denominations. There is an automatic lighthouse on the open headland, a restored Norman priory church with crooked spire, a conducted tour of the monastery for men only.

The island is open from the third week in May to mid-Sept, Fri-Mon inclusive. It is a heartening example of how to compound with God and Caesar in this day and age. No trouble with boats in Tenby, only with queues and parking. Last boat back 5.30pm.

ST KILDA

BY DEREK COOPER

Until 29 August 1930 St Kilda was the remotest inhabited island in Britain. When I circumnavigated it aboard the 14,000-ton Uganda, on a National Trust tour of the northern isles, the huge ship was plunging like a toy duck in the turbulent waters of a Force 10 gale despite its stabilisers and massive bulk. Rolling in the enormous seas, we stood off Hirta as giant waves crashed against the tallest and most dramatic sea cliffs in Europe.

Nowhere round offshore Britain is there another sight like this. Here is the largest gannetry in the world, an outpost of ocean wildlife without equal, a sight to dazzle bird-watchers: 100,000 pairs of puffins, 40,000 pairs of fulmars, 20,000 pairs of guillemots, 12,000 pairs of kittiwakes.

Stac Lee, 540 feet high, summer home of thousands of gannets.

There are shearwaters and petrels in abundance, razorbills, gulls, shags and skuas.

It was the birds that enabled man to keep a foothold on St Kilda for some 2,000 years. Corn could be grown, hay made and sheep and cattle kept, but it was the flesh and eggs of sea-birds that provided the staple diet. For a large part of the year mountainous seas would cut the islanders off from the rest of the world. Passing boats might heave to, but time and again landing was impossible.

During the summer in Victorian times tourists from Oban would occasionally, on a calm day, come ashore to patronise the natives and photograph them, much as you might visit the zoo on a Sunday afternoon. The St Kilda Parliament, the daily meeting when tasks for the day were discussed if seldom executed; the skill and daring of the St Kildan fowlers who at the turn of the century were slaughtering 12,000 birds a year; the appalling toll of infant mortality brought about by tetanus infantum; the rigours and hardships of St Kildan life, became a subject of universal curiosity.

The islanders themselves, with little immunity to infection, were prone to the 'boat-cold'. Visitors brought diseases which would sweep through Village Bay and prostrate the island for weeks. It was a close-knit, inbred society without money, without a doctor, without any of the amenities which had become necessities on the mainland. The island was owned by the Macleod of Macleod who lived in distant Skye and the St Kildans relied completely on his beneficence. Annually the factor came to take away fulmars' oil, feathers, salted sea-birds, fish, sheep and tweed, and in return he brought the seed and supplies needed for survival.

By the end of the Great War the St Kildan population had declined to less than 40, of whom many were elderly. The average weekly income of each family was about 10 shillings and it was apparent to the very competent nurse, Williamina Barclay, that it was really only a matter of time before everyone would have to leave. But where would they go? Who would assume responsibility for them?

The winter of 1929–30 was disastrous, there was hunger in every family. On 10 May the missionary, with the approval of his fellow islanders, wrote a petition to the Government requesting that they be evacuated and resettled elsewhere. Several of the abler men had already decided to seek employment on the mainland; that meant that all would have to go. The petition was passed to the skipper of the first trawler that called at the island.

Then the dilemma of the islanders was dramatically highlighted by the death from tuberculosis of 21-year-old Mary Gillies. The lighthouse vessel *Hesperus* was unable to land a boat to take her off and no doctor could ready her. Despite devoted nursing by Miss Barclay she died on 21 June. It was an event which sealed the fate of St Kilda.

On the morning of 29 August 1930 the Fishery Protection vessel *Harebell* and the ancient steamer *Dunara Castle* were moored in Village Bay with

Soay and Hirta with (below) *a detail of Hirta's northern coast.*

steam up ready to complete the evacuation. The day before had been spent ferrying out personal possessions; the sheep had been taken off. At eight o'clock anchors were weighed; one or two of the old people openly wept. 'The loneliest of Britain's island-dwellers,' wrote Alasdair Alpin Macgregor who witnessed the evacuation, 'have resigned their heritage to the ghosts and the sea-birds; and the curtain is rung down on haunted homes and the sagas of the centuries.' Strong stuff! But it was the very moving end of an incredible story of endurance on the edge of the world.

Fifty years later the Army maintains a presence on St Kilda, assisted by an oil-fired power-station, frozen food, helicopters and landing craft. In their million-pound missile-tracking station they are on St Kilda but not of it. The island archipelago – Hirta, Soay, Boreray and Dun with its attendant skerries and inaccessible stacks – remains the most sensational piece of offshore geology in Britain. In storm force winds, lonely in the waste of the Atlantic, St Kilda is a spectacle that reduces one to silence.

DEREK COOPER

SALT ON THE PETALS

BY ANTHONY HUXLEY

Britain's islands stretch all the way from well north of the mainland in Shetland to well south of it in the Channel Islands, and their flora reflects the very considerable climatic change between those two extremes. This alone makes it difficult to present a short, coherent account of their flora, just as it would be almost impossible to do so briefly for Britain as a whole. And apart from climate, which is the most important influence on plant distribution in the British Isles, there are many other factors affecting the plant life.

For these reasons this chapter can only discuss some of the botanical interest revealed by island floras and mention some of those plants remarkable for rarity or other reasons. I have used English names almost exclusively; these names, which have been bestowed on virtually every British plant, have achieved wide currency either in *The Wild Flowers of Britain and Northern Europe* by Richard and Alistair Fitter, or in the standard *Flora of the British Isles* by Clapham, Tutin and Warburg.

When numbers of species on a particular island are stated, these refer to flowering plants (including grasses, rushes and sedges) and ferns. Precision in such totals has not been attempted since it depends on different views of what constitutes a species and also on the acceptance of microspecies such as are discussed later; my totals do not in principle include the latter.

First, it is a general rule that islands, unless they be very large, have fewer different life forms on them than the nearby mainland – this applies to animals and birds as well as plants. But while islands, especially isolated oceanic ones, become important centres to seabirds and sea mammals like seals, which may breed there in immense numbers, no such effect occurs with plants, and the flora of even relatively large islands is likely to be reduced compared with a similar area of nearby mainland.

A large number of Britain's islands are close to the Scottish mainland, where vast areas are covered by heath, peat, bog and rock which carry relatively few plant species, so the chance of rich floras is diminished in comparison with those such as Anglesey and the Isle of Wight, where the nearby mainland has numerous species. Many of these northern isles are exposed to very severe weather conditions which, by reducing the possibilities of tree and shrub cover, further diminish the numbers of potential plants.

This climatic austerity does not apply to islands like sheltered Gigha and Arran, which also enjoy the warmth of the Gulf Stream, nor those further south – Man, Anglesey, Wight, Scillies and Channel – which become increasingly mild. Indeed the last three are rich in unusual plants, and the most interesting islands overall for botanists and flower-lovers to visit; they are dealt with towards the end of this chapter.

Some species survive in relatively difficult climatic conditions. The few rocky acres of the half-mile-long gannetry of Sula Sgeir has seven species of plant. North Rona, at 300 acres, carries some 43 or 44 species. Hirta, the largest of the St Kilda group, has around 140 species in 1,575 acres. The Shetland archipelago, totalling some 550 square miles, is a great increase in area but only boasts some 450 native species, plus around 150 aliens which have become naturalized – meaning that they have 'gone native' in terms of reproducing themselves outside their original artificial habitat. Very many of these introductions, as they may also be called, are 'garden escapes' or hortals to use a botanist's term, but some arrive as a result of commerce and travel. Naturalised aliens become increasingly numerous as we go south, mainly because an increasingly comfortable climate makes it more attractive to garden extensively and possible to grow an ever-increasing range of exotic plants.

SALT ON THE PETALS

Top row, left to right: Silverweed, Clover, Birdsfoot trefoil, Wild pansy, Yorkshire fog, Globe flower, Purple saxifrage, Mountain sorrel, Lesser meadow rue.

Second row: Avens, Four-leaved allseed, Cretan tree mallow, Adder's tongue, Three-cornered leek, Corn marigold, Gladiolus, Bermuda buttercup, Bee orchid.

Third row : Autumn lady's tresses, Autumn squill, Sand crocus, Lundy cabbage, Shetland campion, Royal fern, Scottish primrose, Whitebeam, Wood calamint.

Fourth row : Fly orchid, Hare's-tail, Broom, Dune helleborine, Irish ladies, Jersey lily, Lizard, Early spider, Guernsey Lily.

Thus, in more favourable conditions in the south, species per square mile number very many more – the Isle of Wight has over a thousand, including introductions, in 147 square miles; the Scilly Isles 687 species on 6.3 square miles, and the Channel Islands 1,700 species in 75 square miles. These figures must be compared with Britain's overall total of 1,511 native species (excluding micro-species) and at least 625 naturalized aliens, a total of not less than 2,136 species.

In general, Britain's islands are too close to the mainland for another feature of isolated islands to be much apparent, that of endemics – species known only in that place. However, interestingly enough, one of Britain's very few truly endemic plants – there are not more than 20 in all – is found only on cliffs on Lundy, not an island otherwise notable for flora. This is the Lundy cabbage (*Rhyncosinapis wrightii*), a close relation of the smaller-leaved, smaller-flowered Isle of Man cabbage which is also found locally on various mainland coasts.

There are a few other island specialities, most of them only sub-species differing slightly from the basic species, which have evolved in a relatively short time due to the island's isolation. Shetland is the home of a large number of endemic hawkweeds, but this is a special case: the only reason there are so many is that hawkweeds, like brambles, reproduce apomictically, which means without pollination. Therefore every time a mutation occurs it is carried on in the seeds of the plant concerned, which produce offspring of the same mutated type, and many different, often very small, populations arise. These are examples of micro-species, and only the ardent hawkweed specialist will spend time on them, though in mass these colourful golden and orange flowers are a feature of Shetland's rock ledges.

More generally interesting plants can produce sub-species, for instance orchids. Thus the spotted orchid (*Dactylorhiza maculata*) has a unique sub-species on Rhum, which replaces the species there. The common spotted orchid (*O. fuchsii*) has a sub-species *okellyi* mainly confined to the Isle of Man; while its sub-species *hebridensis* is almost entirely confined to islands – Shetland, Outer Hebrides, Skye, Coll and Tiree.

In most of the islands man has undoubtedly had a massive effect on the plant life. Many of the Scottish isles are rich in peat, and the practice of digging peat for burning, without replacing the more fertile top layer, has effectively scalped the land in places, leaving bog or more often bare stone. In islands like North Rona, seals, wallowing in the mud in their breeding season, have prevented scalped turf ever re-establishing itself.

Some of the islands at least became forested after the Ice Ages; pollen analysis suggests that even gale-swept St Kilda had birch and hazel scrub. When he arrived, man cut the trees for building and fuel, and only in the last century or so has replanting shown that trees *can* thrive on various hitherto bare northern islands. Finally there is grazing to consider as a shaper of vegetation – on Shetland for example intensive grazing, and accompanying burning of scrub, have gone on for an estimated 5,300 years.

On all Britain's islands the botanist can interest himself in comparing the flora with that of the nearby mainland. Very often islands miss out, and this is rather a mystery. One might, for instance, look at essentially maritime plants which seldom grow inland, and form perhaps the only well defined group of species one might *expect* to see on islands where coasts are extensive relative to area.

The British Isles have, very roughly, some 80 maritime species (excluding rushes and sedges). Yet only about one third of these are to be seen on most islands. These ever-present species include stalked scurvy-grass, sea rocket, sea campion, sea sandwort, sea pearlwort, the sea spurreys, samphire, parsley water dropwort, the coastal form of wild carrot, sea aster, sea mayweed, thrift, sea milkwort, common centaury, buckshorn and sea plantains, annual glasswort and annual seablite, saltwort, and creeping willow. Among ferns, sea spleenwort, royal fern and tiny moonwort and adder's-tongue are frequently seen. Scottish lovage, essentially northerly, is characteristic of most northern islands, and sea bindweed and wild beet, basically southerly plants, on most southern ones.

A relative poverty of species does not necessarily mean lack of pleasure or surprise for the flower seeker. One of the pleasures is to see great masses of flowers, sometimes acres of a single kind – something seldom possible on the mainland with its intensive agriculture and use of weedkillers. What is more, these are often more brilliantly coloured than their mainland representatives – and this is not something in the eye of the beholder but represents local races which are genetically different: on Shetland for instance in sheepsbit, bush and tufted vetch, while the Shetland red campion is a distinct sub-species.

In Orkney, plants which make extensive drifts are birdsfoot trefoil, white clover and eyebright behind the sand dunes, while the unusual blue-leaved oyster plant (mertensia) is often profuse just above the shoreline. In the generally desolate moorland of Lewis, kingcups grow in spectacular quantity in June, followed in the same wet places by yellow flag. Thrift often carpets the ground by the tideline or on cliff edges; Lundy is a positive rock garden of thrift.

In terms of floral spectacle the machair is un-rivalled. This is the Gaelic word used for the short springy turf growing on stabilized sand just inland from the dunes on the beach-fringed Atlantic coasts of a large proportion of all the northern islands. It is particularly well developed in the Outer Hebrides, nowhere more so than on north and south Uist where large areas of machair are amazingly colourful.

Machair is often cultivated on a shifting system, as on Uist, and once left fallow displays a succession of different dominant species, each appearing at first in great sheets of colour, acres at a time. First come daisies, pink when closed in rain or white when open in sun; then buttercups of several com-mon species; third silverweed, as pretty in silvery leaf as in its golden blooms. It is sobering to recall that the thin though fleshy roots of this plant were once a famine food in the Highlands and Islands, and before potatoes were introduced the plant was even sometimes cultivated: the roots were boiled, roasted or eaten raw, or ground into meal for bread and a kind of porridge.

After the silverweed come white clover, birds-foot trefoil, kidney vetch, lady's bedstraw, the grass Yorkshire fog, and the wild pansy, in the outer islands a clear pale yellow. Sometimes there are low dense tufts of bright yellow pepperwort, patches of golden corn marigold now so seldom seen on the mainland, or of scarlet poppies.

Other machair species include the northern marsh orchid, whose spikes dot the turf in hundreds in June, followed by the less prominent frog orchid. July sees red clover and rich purple tufted vetch standing out among greens and browns.

In adjoining marshy slacks the unusual bogbean blooms in May, giving way to spotted and lesser butterfly orchids which may occur in quantities; here and there ragged robin is thick on the ground in an extra-vivid pink, together with dark red marsh cinquefoil, and the clustered thin green spikes of mare's-tail are sometimes dominant. Where marsh gives way to water, amphibious bistort with its pink spikes, lesser spearwort, water lobelia and white waterlilies spangle the lochans (yellow waterlily or brandy-bottle is found only sparingly in the Outer Hebrides, Skye and Mull). By the lochans too, especially on islets where sheep and cattle cannot reach it, the stately royal fern grows in quantity; later, when it fades, its rusty colouring can dominate the autumn landscape.

The machair, especially in the Outer Hebrides, is well defined, as one can clearly see from an air-craft, as a green strip on the western edge of these

Eoligarry, Barra, bright with thrift.

Bogcotton and peat on Leorin Farm, Kildalton, Islay.

islands. The eastern coasts are rocky, and in between there is mostly peat and rock, showing brown and grey. Here the botanist will find little besides sphagnum moss, sedges, grasses and heather – cross-leaved, ling and bell heathers.

The Inner Hebridean islands have a very complex geology, as the chapter on island geology shows. This causes all kinds of surprising variations in the flora, often between neighbouring islands. Skye's limestone pavements, for instance, hold many rare ferns and Sleat has a large wood dominated by ash. Most of the island's other thickets, of beech, hazel, oak and willow, are in the safety of lochan islets. In marked contrast the basaltic pinnacles so popular with climbers hold an assortment of 'arctic-alpines' – plants which are known from the sub-arctic zone and recur in the European Alps. As in Scandinavia and western Ireland, they also descend here to sea level. Skye is the only British habitat of the alpine rockcress; other alpines to be seen are the handsome globe flower, mountain sorrel, catsfoot or mountain everlasting, lesser meadow rue, purple saxifrage, cushion-forming moss campion, the glaucous tufts of roseroot and sometimes in sheets, mountain avens with its

large white, gold-centred blooms. Arctic-alpines like these are also to be found on Mull, Orkney and Shetland, and a few on St Kilda.

Volcanic rocks often give rise to rich soil, as on Muck and Canna, resulting in good grazing and the earliest potatoes in Scotland. The most varied geology occurs on Raasay and Rhum, both of special interest to the keen botanist (Rhum is a nature reserve) and also Mull.

Colonsay and Oronsay have a basis of sandstone which often provides excellent soil as well as sedge and heather moors between their coastal sand dunes, rocky beaches and low cliffs. It has been said that these islands are 'an epitome of the West Highland world in its full range of Atlantic exposure and sheltered mildness.' Despite the exposure, there are natural woods, including birch, hazel, oak, rowan and willow, while the lochans are fringed with royal fern and covered with water-lilies. The prevailing humidity, as in many of the western isles, encourages a rich growth of lichens and mosses on the trees, and encourages ferns like the filmy fern and prickly buckler fern. It is interesting that some exotic trees and shrubs, like acacias, ceanothus and escallonia, grow much better than the native trees because they enjoy the humidity more.

One particularly interesting geologically controlled habitat is on Unst, Shetland's northernmost island, where serpentine rock and severe exposure from weather have, in the Keen of Hamar reserve, created a pocket of rhacomitrium-heath and fell-field – technical names for examples of 'relic' vegetation from the late glacial period such as can be seen in the Cairngorms. In Shetland, this is the only area where the island's most famous endemic, the Shetland mouse-ear chickweed, grows. Its close relative, the arctic mouse-ear, is a Scandinavian and Icelandic species, like the Norwegian sandwort which also grows here. Here too are arctic-alpines, including black bearberry and the tiny 'wild azalea' (*Loiseleuria procumbens*), otherwise only found in Britain on Orkney and in north-western Scotland.

Some of the more northerly islands do have their own specialities, and I have already mentioned some of them. Here are some others to be sought. The charming little purple-flowered Scottish primrose inhabits Orkney and Shetland, apart from a few localities on the extreme north of Scotland. Equally charming, the white-flowered dwarf cornel, local on the mainland, only exists on Orkney and Foula. Pale Butterwort, a lusitanian plant, inhabits Orkney, the Outer Hebrides and Isle of Man. The northern knotgrass, if you are into this rather weedy group, replaces the tall common knotgrass in Orkney and Shetland – its main habitats range from Canada to Scandinavia. There are some unique eyebrights on the northern archipelagos also, as well as the arctic-alpine hawkweeds already mentioned. The insignificant annual Iceland purslane (koenigia) exists only on Skye and Mull – two localities each: this mainly arctic plant is found also in central Asia and Tierra del Fuego. Alpine saxifrage, very rare in Britain, is only found on Rhum. On Arran live two whitebeam relations (*Sorbus arranensis* and *S. pseudofennica*) known only from that island. An exciting, relatively recent discovery is the Irish lady's tresses orchid, primarily a North American native and known from a few Irish localities: in 1939 it was discovered on Coll and a little later on Colonsay. Since then it has been found on two further Hebridean sites, some in Scotland and one unexpected one in Devon.

Some of the naturalized plants of the northern islands are rather unexpected. The pinkish-purple *Iris versicolor*, a North American native, has colonies of unexplained origin on Harris and Iona, while another North American, *Lupinus nootkatensis*, blue, white or yellow, is found on Orkney. The yellow Pyrenean lily grows very freely in Shetland gardens and has not surprisingly become naturalized, as it is on Mull and in Devon. Both Shetland and Orkney have large colonies of a tall white daisy-flowered plant, *Senecio smithii*, native of Chile and the Falkland Islands; apparently Orcadian shepherds used to spend some time working on the Falklands and presumably one brought the plant, or seeds, back as a memento. Another Chilean, the white irish relation *Libertia formosa*, and South African red hot pokers, have also formed colonies beyond Orkney gardens.

Now to turn our attention to more southerly islands. First on the way south comes the Isle of Man with roughly 720 species of plant in 220 square miles – the mild climate has increased the floristic level, and allows gardeners to grow sub-tropical plants, some of which have become naturalized. This is the first island southwards on which we can find bee orchid and autumn lady's tresses, wallflower and the Mediterranean annual sweet alison, and – apart from Ailsa Craig – tree mallow. The unusual blue form of scarlet pimpernel is shared with the Scillies and Channel Islands. One remarkable recent discovery (1969) is of the insignificant dense-flowered orchid, previously known only from the Burren in western Ireland. But the flora is not a remarkable one overall, though attractive enough with plenty of western gorse, bird's foot trefoil, kidney vetch, marsh cinquefoil, alexanders, cross-leaved and bell heather, harebells, bluebells and royal fern. The herb sweet cicely grows here,

which has been recorded by one authority as 'popularly believed to blossom at midnight on old Christmas eve.'

Anglesey is not much bigger than Man at 275 square miles. The flora, which runs to about 785 species, is distinctly more interesting in many ways, though it is in general very similar to that of Caernarvonshire just across the Menai Strait. Massed colour comes from luxuriant gorse, foxgloves, bluebell-packed woods, moorland with cross-leaved and bell heather. There are legions of rose species and bramble relations for the specialist.

Naturalised narcissi on Bryher, Isles of Scilly.

Rarities for which Anglesey is the only island locality include hoary rockrose, Irish marsh orchid and dune helleborine (the last only on four other British sites). It is the only island with meadow saxifrage, petty whin, the handsome aquatics arrowhead and flowering rush, and lax-flowered sea lavender. Common sea lavender is shared with Jersey, and other plants found only, among islands, on one or other of the Channel Islands, include the very rare annual or spotted rockrose, very rare cottonweed, rare sea stock, orpine or livelong and dropwort. The very large wintergreen occurs otherwise only on Orkney and Jersey among islands. Other plants seldom seen on British islands are maiden pink, wild madder, the once troublesome cornfield weed corn cockle, Solomon's seal (an introduction), wallflower as on Man and Lundy, and fly orchid, also on the Isle of Wight.

The Isle of Wight is really a detached chunk of southern England, or more precisely Hampshire. In 147 miles there are well over a thousand species, reflecting the profuse mainland flora and a relatively mild climate. Across the island stretches a ridge of chalk with the rich flora typically associated with it, such as orchids, 22 species in all including lizard and early spider orchids found on only a few mainland sites, and the always local man orchid. The chalk sea cliffs here include new maritime species compared with the list given earlier, such as yellow sea poppy, Portland spurge, sea radish and alexanders.

Greater or wood calamint with its large purplish-pink flowers, which goes as far abroad as north Africa and Syria, is in its only British locality here. Other unusual plants include a centaury, *Centaurium capitatum*, which was first described from an I.O.W. specimen; hoary stock in probably its only natural British locality; the very local *Arum neglectum*, sometimes called rare cuckoo-pint and distinct from its mainland near-relation *A. italicum*; the rare parasite purple broomrape, also on Guernsey; and purple cow-wheat, described by one expert as more permanent here than in any of its few other British localities. Seeds of this handsome 'poverty weed', as it was locally called, made wheat ground up with it bitter and unmarketable, hence its rarity. Less rare, but still uncommon, are the endemic English monkshood (here an introduction), green hellebore, columbine and Deptford pink.

Once again, however, we are up against mysterious absences of plants common in Hampshire a few miles away – nearly 150 species including milkwort, field mouse-ear chickweed, round-headed rampion, ground pine and musk orchid. Conversely there are about 20 species found on the Isle of Wight but not on the neighbouring mainland, which is even more surprising. A number of rare plants are now known to be extinct in the Isle of Wight, including mezereon and venus's looking-glass; the Mediterranean *Gladiolus illyricus* has probably gone too.

The Scilly Isles, off Cornwall's western tip, are remarkable in many ways, and botanically very rich for their size – there are 687 species in a mere 6.3 square miles comprising about 140 islets and rocks. A very high proportion of these plants, however, are introductions, garden escapes which have become firmly established. Here of course, as with the Isle of Wight and Channel Islands, we are dealing with land which was never glaciated in the Ice Ages so that the plant life has had millenia in which to accumulate.

The native flora is actually likely to be much reduced from what it may have been a few thousand years ago, for even in Bronze Age times, large areas between the islets were dry land. Bronze Age inhabitants used the land extensively for grazing; from the Middle Ages man carried out intensive arable cultivation of all ground capable of this; and since just over a century ago the vegetation has been influenced on the larger islands by the flower-growing industry, concentrating almost entirely on bulbous plants.

The main influences on the native flora are first of all that of the sea and the gales that so often rage around the islands, sometimes creating waves 100 feet high, and sending salt spray right across even the largest islands. Although this allows some saline plants to exist on high ground inland, like sea spleenwort and Danish scurvy-grass, the overall effect is a limiting one since relatively few plants can stand salt, while the wind stunts and deforms any woody plant – on the tops of Samson's two low hills no plant grows more than $1\frac{1}{2}$ inches tall!

The smallness of the isles means also that some typical plant habitats are virtually absent – stream, freshwater and bog habitats barely exist, there is no salt marsh, and the only trees, arisen from planted introductions, are low copses of elm growing from suckers, and of willow originally grown for hurdle and basket making. In the distant past native oaks, hazel and ash are known to have existed.

These factors no doubt explain the absence of some species quite common in Cornwall but not found in Scilly, such as greater stitchwort, herb robert, meadowsweet, kidney vetch and heath pearlwort, the last two abundant at Land's End Conversely, the Scilly flora's affinities with the Mediterranean and the Azores gives rise to a number of species not found, or only rarely, on the mainland. Among these, smaller or Cretan tree mallow, hairy bird's-foot trefoil, western clover and shore dock are abundant in Scilly and rare on the mainland, while dwarf pansy, orange birdsfoot, four-leaved allseed and the very rare least adder's-tongue fern (*Ophioglossum lusitanicum*) are Scilly plants absent from Cornwall.

Some of the last are doubtless encouraged by Scilly's almost complete absence of frost, and this is certainly the reason for the persistence of so many of the aliens, many of which are succulents of the fig-marigold family. These are almost exclusive to South Africa and were planted in gardens, notably of course those of Tresco Abbey. One owner of Tresco was indeed in the habit of carrying a pocketful of these ready-rooting plants to push into the ground wherever he walked. The large, handsome-flowered Hottentot Fig, which is also found on southwest mainland coasts, owes some of its habitats to seagulls who use pieces of its growth to make their nests.

Another Scilly curiosity arises from the burrow-making seabirds, puffins and Manx shearwaters. These usually erode the surrounding ground completely, but a few maritime plants, like sea beet, sea mayweed, sorrel and orache grow to enormous size on the birds' rich droppings.

Besides the South African succulents, Tresco Gardens act as a centre for many other plants which reproduce from seed, including cabbage palms, olearias, pittosporum (used extensively for windbreaks), gazanias, tree echiums, agapanthus and New Zealand flax.

The other source of alien plants is the bulbfields, where the light shallow soil encourages growth from winter to late spring and dryness in summer, which is exactly what Mediterranean annual weeds enjoy. One of the more unusual is the shoo-fly plant, *Nicandra physalodes*, with its large blue bell flowers, while the corn marigold grows so abund-

Tresco Abbey, Scilly, behind the lush sub-tropical Gardens.

antly and to such size that growers have on occasion marketed the flowers. The relatively infrequent cultivation given to these bulbfields has also encouraged bulbous weeds including Spanish bluebells, star-of-Bethlehem and the yellow Bermuda buttercup (actually a South African oxalis) which is such a pest of cultivation in Greece.

Several introduced onion relations are common, including the attractive rosy garlic, Babington's leek, which increased remarkably quickly from its first recording in 1939, and three-cornered leek, known on Scilly as white bluebells, probably first introduced in the 1890's, which has spread like an epidemic: like the Bermuda buttercup it is virtually impossible to eradicate.

Escapes from the bulbfields and in some cases from ancient monasteries are also frequent, notably the narcissus Cheerfulness. A particularly handsome escape is *Gladiolus byzantinus*, once cultivated as a cut flower and known in Scilly as whistling jacks because children use the leaves, placed between their hands. to whistle.

The commonest wild plants on the Scilly Isles include thrift, a showy feature in May on headlands and all over the small islets, and other maritime plants like sea campion, sea bindweed and the pungent samphire. Perhaps the most frequent plant inland is bracken, usually associated with brambles. Bracken reaches over 6 feet high by July and then, to quote botanist J. E. Lousley, 'visitors become painfully aware that there is an understorey of *Rubus ulmifolius* invisible beneath the fronds and ready to gash their flesh and tear their clothes.' This bracken/bramble association often includes figwort, hogweed, foxglove and red campion, and lower plants which flower early before they become choked, including bluebells which are very abundant, ground ivy, lesser celandine and cleavers. Sometimes the bracken and bramble link up with thickets of gorse. Royal fern is frequent on St. Mary's and in the late summer the white daisy flowers of common chamomile dominate much of the landscape.

In marked contrast to the Isle of Wight, only three orchids exist on the Scillies, two very rare; the only abundant species is the pretty little white autumn lady's tresses.

Our final island group, the Channel Islands, are botanically the richest of all British islands, with approaching 1,700 species in a mere 75 square miles comprising Jersey, Guernsey and five smaller isles. This includes about 700 aliens which are naturalized. This last figure, provided by enthusiastic local botanists, exceeds that already quoted as the grand total for all Britain: the criteria for considering an alien to be well established vary somewhat. But the figures show how rich the flora of these islands is, with over three times more native plants per square mile, let alone aliens, than the average for Britain as a whole.

Clearly, alas, one cannot in limited space begin to do justice to such a range of plants which owe their profusion to an exceptionally mild climate, adequate rainfall, moderate exploitation of land and no air pollution. In geographical terms, of course, the Channel Islands have much more affinity to France than to Britain, while the flora is more of a Mediterranean type than that of adjoining Normandy and Brittany. Even French botanists find much to surprise them there.

One reason that the flora is much richer than that of the Scillies is the greater range of habitats in a much larger area. The only type of substrate missing is pure chalk, but even so, limy soils are present and support some chalk-loving plants.

There are some sumptuous massed displays to be seen on all the islands, especially perhaps Guernsey and the barely exploited smaller isles. Primroses, violets and a wide range of ferns fill the lane-sides in spring. Then, too, the cliff-tops and commons are covered with carpets of thrift and sea campion, thickets of gorse and broom (including a beautiful and uncommon prostrate form), drifts of bluebells, sheepsbit, ox-eye daisies and red campion, together with bell heather in rich purple. The keen-eyed may spot colour variations of the last worth propagating and indeed four varieties found in this way are now marketed commercially. The heather is often in flower in winter and indeed the cliffs are colourful all the year round thanks to the mild climate.

Jersey has some of the highest tides in the world, and shoreline plants have to be able to stand drenching with sea water. It is noticeable how plants like sea beet, rock samphire and Danish scurvy-grass have extra-thick leaves in this 'drench zone,' while sea spleenwort is extra fine with fronds up to two feet long.

Many of the less common plants grow in the short turf on the dunes, including bee orchid, autumn lady's tresses, tiny 'sand crocus' (*Romulea columnae*), autumnal squill, charming variegated catchfly, and dwarf pansy already mentioned from the Scillies.

Rarest of all is Guernsey centaury, a tiny pink-flowered annual not known elsewhere in Britain; its relation the slender cicendia has its only island habitat on Guernsey.

Partly because of the absence of chalk downland, orchids are not as numerous here as in the Isle of Wight, but the ten species that do exist are often in large numbers. The only sites for lizard orchid and

Alderney, home of many Channel Island specialities.

marsh helleborine have, alas, recently been destroyed. Jersey and Guernsey have their own British orchid speciality, the Jersey orchid, a tall, slender-spiked plant carrying many crimson-purple flowers. Alas, the elusive summer lady's tresses, early spider orchid and lady orchid are known to be extinct here.

Other Channel Islands specialities mostly not found on other British islands, and often very local, include asparagus in the wild prostrate form, butcher's broom, so-called Deptford pink, sea stock, annual or spotted rockrose, autumnal squill, and the very scarce if less spectacular Cornish moneywort which occasionally carpets moist banks (it is also known on Lewis). Guernsey also has drooping star-of-Bethlehem, snowdrop, wild narcissus, and mistletoe in its only island habitat. Tiny purple spurge is only known from Alderney, and there is an endemic buttercup, *Ranunculus paludosus*, on Jersey.

It is impossible to dwell long on the hundreds of naturalised aliens. A charmer from the dunes is hare's-tail grass, a Mediterranean plant. It was introduced to Guernsey at least 200 years ago and first sown on Jersey in 1877. Now it is used there in enormous quantities to create exhibits for the Battle of Flowers, and covers many coastal areas in large tracts.

A sand crocus from South Africa, the onion-grass (*Romulea rosea*) exists in one large Guernsey colony in an albino form, its origin a mystery. In both islands there are literally millions of natural-ized narcissi in at least 50 kinds cast out from culti-vation over many decades; the historically-minded narcissus fancier can find varieties a century old or more in this living museum. *Gladiolus byzantinus*, another outcast from cultivation, can form large colourful swathes. The so-called winter daffodil, *Sternbergia lutea*, has one large colony near Gorey Castle on Jersey.

The 'giant rhubarb' gunnera (it is actually no relation to rhubarb) is undoubtedly self-sown in many places; so is spectacular giant echium from the Canaries, while Guernsey boasts greater herb robert (*Geranium rubescens*) from Madeira, a stately three-foot relation of the common wild plant. One very unexpected naturalized plant is apothecaries' rose (*Rosa gallica* 'Officinalis'), fully established on a gale-swept headland. As in the Scillies, Bermuda buttercup and three-cornered garlic are profuse, and also the non-oniony, fragrant Honey Bells (nothoscordum).

A final word for Lily Langtry's emblem the Jersey lily, the South African *Nerine sarniensis*. It is often recounted that bulbs floated ashore following the shipwreck, two centures ago, of a ship from Japan. The truth is slightly less romantic. A ship – from South Africa – did run on shore but was refloated, and the sailors gave some bulbs to the helpful local landowner. Some of these originals became naturalized abundantly, but this striking pink flower is now difficult to find except in a few gardens.

ANTHONY HUXLEY

LUNDY

BY JOHN EARLE

On some days Lundy lies like a low blue line on the horizon. Very often nothing at all can be seen of this mysterious little island from the mainland. At other times it stands up so sharp and clear you can see the shape of the cliffs, the Old Light and the church of St Helena gauntly pointing into the blue sky. On those days the old countrymen of North Devon gob at a gull and say that it is going to rain.

Eleven miles from Hartland Point and 24 from the harbours of Ilfracombe and Bideford, Lundy lies where the Bristol Channel becomes the Atlantic Ocean. On the map, it looks as if some giant hand has wrenched a piece out of Woolacombe Bay and pushed it west into the sea.

All islands seem mystical, magical places, but Lundy, for me, is the best of them all. Childhood memories flood back: paddle-steamers pounding and churning over from Ilfracombe on those pre-war days – always sunny – great granite cliffs with gannets wheeling like knives in the blue sky; whiskered grey seals poking inquisitive heads out of a sparkling sea to watch a little boy's delight at setting foot on an 'unexplored' island for the first time.

Lundy does have an exciting and romantic history. Early Christians were here in the Dark Ages. The Vikings raided and wrote about Lundy in the 'Orkneyinga Saga'. Indeed, the name Lundy itself comes from two Norse words, 'lund' meaning a puffin and 'ey', an island. The Normans came to Lundy and left; William de Marisco, the owner, was hung, drawn and quartered by Henry III, who then built Marisco Castle in 1243, to prevent the island ever again falling into the hands of his enemies. Then came a turbulent time of pirates, refugees from justice and Royalists; the island was held for Charles I – the last bit of Britain to surrender to the Roundheads. But it is the pirates, the wreckers and, of course, the innumerable wrecks that dominate its history until the 19th century.

The Constable Rock, petrified Cornish giant, and the North Light.

For most of the 19th century, the Heaven family owned Lundy; the Rev. H. G. Heaven built the incongruously urban Victorian church of St Helena. After the long, rough and dangerous sea crossing to Lundy to consecrate the new church, Bishop Bickersteth remarked that now he knew of the difficulties one had to face to reach the Kingdom of Heaven! The island now belongs to the National Trust, which has leased it to the Landmark Trust for 60 years at a peppercorn rent. The latter hopes to carry out extensive rebuilding, and keep maintenance at a reasonable level so that it can hand the island over when the lease expires as a self-supporting concern.

So what of Lundy today? You won't find candy floss and fish and chips; you will find peace and tranquillity. Lundy is never crowded, except perhaps on the Landing Beach when the day visitors arrive by ship, some 600 of them, and surge ashore to pant and gasp their way up the steep track to the hub of the island where the church, the Marisco Tavern, the shop and café stand. Some get no further. Walkers – and on Lundy you must be prepared to walk – can be on their own within minutes.

Lundy is about three miles long and half a mile wide. On the west, 400-foot granite cliffs take the full fury of the Atlantic storms; the east of the island is gentler, with trees, rhododendrons and little hanging valleys. The main part is a rolling moorland plateau, most of it over 400 feet in height. As you walk the track over the moor on hot spring days the air vibrates with the songs of larks and curlew, while lapwings fall about the sky, swooping within a few feet of your head, uttering strangled, plaintive cries if you get too close to their nests. Lundy is an ornithologist's paradise, though sadly the puffin that gives the island its name is now rare here. However, the 400 different species of bird recorded over the years will keep most bird-watchers happy. A golden oriole was visiting when

The Devil's Slide, Lundy's most celebrated climb, amid towering granite cliffs.

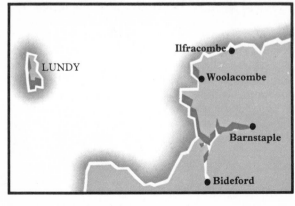

I was there. Grey seals, Sika deer, wild goats, Soay sheep and the Lundy ponies all add their own enchantment. The Lundy Field Society, 17 Furze-field Road, Reigate, Surrey, runs courses and excursions for those interested in wild life.

The island is a graveyard of ships of all sizes and all epochs. The most famous wreck is the battleship HMS Montagu that hit the Great Shutter Rock in 1906. Divers can still find much of her, including gun-turrets, lying off the south-west corner of Lundy in water which is often gin-clear. Europe's first underwater marine reserve is being established here, with an underwater nature trail. Information

The Landing Beach and South Light, Lundy.
Top right, *Millcombe Hotel, 1835.*
Above, *Marisco Castle, built in 1243.*

about diving on Lundy from Bristol Channel Divers Ltd, 21 Millers Lane, Stanstead Abbotts, Ware, Hertfordshire.

The towering granite cliffs and outcrops offer exciting climbing of all standards with routes over 400 feet long. The most famous climb of all is perhaps the Devil's Slide, but there is still a chance, even now, to put up new climbs. ('Lundy Island Climbing Guide' by Bob Moulton is excellent; it is published by the Royal Navy Mountaineering Club and available from most climbing equipment shops.)

But Lundy is not just a place for doing things. Part of its charm is the marvellous opportunities it offers to do nothing but wander and look. Almost every building, ruin, wall or rock has a story. The Constable Rock at the north tip is said to be a Cornish giant who came to Lundy to get rid of the snakes and was then turned to stone – somewhat unfairly; there are indeed no snakes on Lundy. There are legends galore attached to Marisco Castle, the Devil's Limekiln, Queen Mab's Grotto, Jenny's Cove, Brazen Ward, Benson's Cave – enough to keep you wandering, reading and looking, for weeks.

JOHN EARLE

ARRAN

BY RICHARD FINDLATER

Lochranza, near Arran's northernmost point, guarding the entrance to the huge sea loch.

If you are sailing from Kintyre to Arran, on the Claonaig-Lochranza route, the dark peaks of this spud-shaped island in the Firth of Clyde loom up with spectacularly sombre, menacing grandeur: the place looks from the sea like another, lonelier Skye. If you land in high summer at Brodick on the eastern coast from the Ayrshire port of Ardrossan, you will find yourself among thousands of instant holiday-makers in a bustling commercial suburbia. Like many islands, Arran has a schizophrenic personality, but its two faces are more conspicuously distinct in landscape, mood, and social geography than elsewhere in offshore Britain.

On the east coast, it is the most holiday-oriented and organised of Scotland's offshore islands, with scores of hotels and boarding houses, roadside bed-and-breakfast signs, public seats for view-gazers, marked parking places and well-signposted footpaths.

But Arran also preserves a proud, intact, Hebridean wildness in its glens, moorland and mountains – it has 11 peaks over 2,000ft: Goatfell, the highest, is 2,866 – and you're more likely to enjoy the views free of mist and rain than in the Hebrides. It's both Highland (in the north) and Lowland (in the south). And while the east coast is dotted with seaside resorts, the west coast belongs to farming Arran: black-face sheep and Ayrshire cows grazing on green fields, white farmhouses, clipped hedges and pastoral peace.

Arran is 19 miles long, 10 miles wide, with a 60-mile coastline, most of it edged by the main road, giving marvellous sea vistas. There are two other roads in the south. By the roads, much of the land is fenced in, often electrically – signalled by red warning notices. There are 14 villages, all close to the coast. For nearly 500 years much of Arran was owned by the Dukes of Hamilton. Thence, at the century's turn, that land passed to the family of the Duchess of Montrose. Members of her family still keep large chunks of it. But the National Trust for Scotland owns 7,000 acres of mountain and glen around Brodick, as well as Brodick Castle and Goatfell; and the Forestry Commission owns about 15,500 acres. A popular hunting-ground for geologists, ever since James Hutton's pioneering work nearly two centuries ago, Arran also offers much to amateur naturalists, antiquarians, archaeologists and romantic historians, as well as families on traditional holidays.

RICHARD FINDLATER

Lush farmland, a contrast to the stark Highlands of the north.

WHERE TO GO

Brodick: Arran's main port of call, shopping and tourist centre. Hotels, shops and houses line the road between the pier and the site of the old Brodick village at Cladach, below Brodick Castle (see *Sightseeing*). High above is the towering, dramatic summit of Goatfell. Near the garage is the Arran Pharmacy, which sells books, china, practically *everything*: even pharmaceuticals. Other shops include Alexander's, another good all-rounder (try the very Cheddar-like Arran cheese); and David Hadley's Wholemeal Hot Bread Shop, where fruit, veg and fresh cream cakes may be had. Early closing Wed. Two real-beer hotels – the sea front Kingsley and the Ormidale, with conservatory-cum-greenhouse bar.

Tourist Information Centre, The Pier (tel Brodick 2401), is open all year. It bristles with guides, leaflets and tourist aids of all kinds.

Whiting Bay: popular resort, with small-scale seaside suburbia, boasting wide, sandy bay. Several hotels, bars, cafés and shops. Vic's Kitchen for fish'n'chips. Nearby sights include Glenashdale Falls (see *Sightseeing*) and King's Cross, where Robert the Bruce embarked for the Ayrshire coast in 1307 and where a Viking's grave was once discovered. Craft workshops are thick on the ground between main seashore road and Knockinkelly. The Gallery, in converted church, sells local handspun wool (not to be confused with Irish Aran wool), ethnic hand-knitteds, including Scottish Inca bonnets, hand-printed stationery etc. Courses on spinning, natural dyeing and weaving are available – details from Silverbirch Workshop, The Gallery, Whiting Bay, tel Whiting Bay 232. Further on up the hillside are a couple of jewellers, an enameller, soft toy-maker etc. (Booklet from Tourist Information Centre gives details of all Arran's craftsmen.)

Lamlash: holiday resort dominated by Holy Island (see *Sightseeing*): also Arran's administrative, educational and medical centre. Marvellous natural harbour was an anchorage for Vikings and a rendezvous for the pre-1914 North Sea Fleet, when Lamlash was a naval base. Takes its name from St Molios of Holy Island. High School

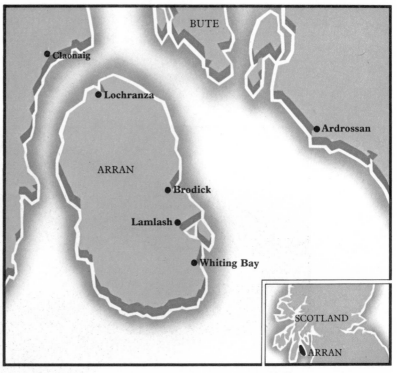

is on the land where Arran's world-famous seed potatoes were produced, between 1908 and 1947, by Donald 'Tattie' McKelvie. Now no longer grown for export, because of high freight charges. A tavern, tearoom, restaurants, bars, off-licence, chemist's. Memorial recently erected to some of 19th c victims of clearances. Craft shops outnumber all others, but there's a tempting antique shop in the Boathouse on the pier, and Carraig-

Mhor Eating House serves good home-cooked food – soups, salads, delicious creamy puddings at lunchtime, fish, steaks etc in the evening. Best to book for dinner, tel Lamlash 453.

Lochranza: port of call for ferry from Claonaig, Kintyre, April-Oct. (See *How to get there*, p. 243.) Once centre of herring-fishery. Pier Tea Room is pleasant 1940-ish café, serving the usual chips cuisine. Near island's

The ruins of Lochranza Castle, probably mainly sixteenth-century.

northernmost point, Cock of Arran, and Glen Chalmadale – with superb views of the northern mountain-cluster. Picturesque, very ruined castle probably built 16th c, but incorporating fragments of 13th-14th c building. Stands on spit of sand guarding entrance to huge sea loch circled by dark hills. Open April-Sept weekdays 9.30-7, Oct-March 9.30-4, Sun from 2. Key from Croft Bank, near village shop-PO.

Corrie: still the prettiest of Arran's holiday villages, with tiny harbour and a crafts shop open 7 days a week in season. The Corrie Hotel has a seashore pub-garden. Daniel Macmillan, Supermac's grandfather, was born in a farm on the hillside near here in 1813.

Tiny harbour at Corrie, still the prettiest of Arran's holiday villages.

SIGHTSEEING

Brodick Castle: red sandstone palace, towering above Brodick Bay, among woods and splendid gardens, notable for rhododendrons (flowering Jan-Aug, best in early May). Architecturally, impressive combination of 13th c, 16th c, 17th c and Victorian revised Scots Baronial. On site of earlier castle, twice captured by the English. Seat of Dukes of Hamilton until 1895. Acquired by National Trust for Scotland in 1958. Treasures include part of William ('Vathek') Beckford's collection; sporting pictures and trophies (no Stubbses – but some charming Rowlandsons of pugilists); 90 stags' heads (the only non-Arran one is Hungarian); a restored Victorian kitchen; portraits by Clouet, Van Dyck, Kneller, Winterhalter, de Laszlo; an appropriate amount of Chippendale, Hepplewhite, Sheraton, Sèvres, Meissen, Chelsea and Chinese porcelain. Plus small exhibition about work of early 20th c botanist George Forrest, whose plant collections from Tibet and China helped to inspire the gardens. Head gardener and deputy give fascinating guided tour of gardens May-Sept Tues 2.30, starting from main entrance gate. Castle open Easter weekend and May-early Sept 1-5, gardens all year daily 10-5. Admission charge.

Brodick Nature Centre: fascinating collection of displays and exhibits arranged to stimulate awareness and interest in the environment, with

Head gardener at Brodick Castle, giving guided tours of the gardens.

especial appeal to young visitors. Features nature diary kept by naturewatchers on holiday, recording in detail sightings of eagles, deer, buzzards etc. Weekly nature trails include trip to Holy Island and a couple of geology and seashore trails. Centre has items on local history, notably the clearances. Useful bookshop. At far end of Brodick from pier, in Cladach, site of old village and its jetty. Look for plaque marking arrival of Edward VII and Alexandra: they first set foot on Scottish soil here after their coronation in 1902. Open daily Easter-

early Oct 10-1, 2-5 (tearoom all day). Small admission charge.

Rosaburn Heritage Museum: small but enlightening local history display housed in part of 18th c croft on the northern edge of Brodick. Includes a smithy (a school 200 years ago), where shoeing is demonstrated in summer. Three-room cottage is furnished as it would have been in early 1920s. Latest addition is perfect 4,000-year-old earthen vessel from nearby Bronze Age burial chamber. Open mid-May-Sept Mon-Fri 10.30-1, 2-4.30. Admission charge.

Holy Island: brooding offshore presence at Lamlash, looming above beaches. On western side is the Cave of St Molios, Irish missionary of royal blood, who gave his name to Lamlash. He made two visits to Rome, and was abbot of Leinster when he died in 639. Runes, crosses and somewhat later graffiti may be seen. Summit reaches 1,030ft. Site of 12th c fort and St Molios's Well, thought to be a cure-all for centuries. Wild goats, Soay sheep and lots of tourists in high season. Boat regularly ferries passengers to and fro, daily Easter-Oct from 10am, Lamlash Pier.

King's Cave: mile along coast from Tormore, near Drumadoon Point (Iron Age fort): the legendary refuge of Robert the Bruce – and his lessons from the spider – before he set out to reconquer Scotland in 1307. 100ft long, up to 50ft high, with almost obliterated engravings. Kirk Session meetings held here in 18th c: an adjoining large cave became local school for many years. Reputed birth-place of the legendary Gaelic hero Fingal.

Glenashdale Falls: highest of Arran's waterfalls, in two leaps of 100ft and 40ft, reached by foot from Whiting Bay (about 1½ miles). Nearby are the Giants' Graves, the grossly misleading name for some remains of chambered cairns (there are 17 on the island).

Machrie Bay: stone circle at Achan-gallon, overlooking the Bay. Accord-ing to legend, these 15 blocks sup-ported Fingal's cooking pot while it boiled. More dramatic in early morn-ing or at sunset.

Kildonan: series of sandy beaches on southern tip of island, segmented by natural breakwaters like rocky fingers stretching out into the sea. The best place to see basking seals. Looks out on to the little offshore island of Pladda, and in the distance, Ailsa Craig, conical rock usually sur-rounded by a flurry of gannets.

Lagg: pretty, almost sub-tropical spot dripping with greenery, where coast road suddenly dips away from sea views through a wood. The Lagg Hotel has a pleasant garden with palms (not true palm trees but *Cordyline australis* – the New Zealand palm lily). Short walk along bluebell-wooded path leading to Torrylin chambered cairn and sandy beaches.

The Ross: the Ross road from Lam-lash to Sliddery tops a dramatic val-ley of green folding hills – usually a deserted area, even in the height of summer. There's a pleasant but toughish walk over to Urie Loch, with colonies of nesting gulls.

ACTIVITIES

Walking: Scottish YHA guide gives plenty of routes for hikers (and cyclists). Among the best and not too strenuous is 1-hour walk up to Coirein Lochain – a dramatic little loch fringed with white shingly beach which appears suddenly over ridge when you've nearly given up hope (signposted just north of Pirnmill). It takes a good deal longer to reach the top of Goatfell, from Corrie or the

The dark peaks of Arran viewed from Claonaig on the mainland of Scotland.

Fishing at dusk from an Arran pier.

grounds of Brodick Castle, but it's a popular exercise. Or try North Sannox to Fallen Rocks, a dramatic craggy landslip dating from second oldest geological era, the palaeozoic. If you carry on up to Laggan, there are some 18th c salt-pans near the tiny harbour (salt tax was so high it was worth boiling off the water), and on the beach, if you can find them, 280-million-year-old fossilised tracks of giant 3ft centipede *arthropleura* – there's a replica of the creature at Arran Nature Centre. On the hillsides here are poignant remains of 19th c clearances – ruins of clachans, small farming communities that practised the system of communal agriculture known as runrig. (At Glen Sannox is charming little church completed by the local people just before setting sail for Canada.) You can carry on round the Cock of Arran, northernmost point, to Lochranza – complete walk takes about 5 hours.

Angling: apart from Machrie River, fresh water fishing is controlled by Arran Angling Association – best rivers, the Sliddery, Rosa, Cloy and Sannox. Brown trout are small, but there are plenty of sea trout and the occasional salmon from early July to Sept/Oct for Sliddery. Permits from PO, Sliddery; others from Tourist Information Centre; Arran Sea Angling Centre, Shore Station, Brodick; Gordon Bros, Ship House, Lamlash; Kilmory PO. Machrie River is good for salmon and sea trout – details from Strathtay Estate Office, Boltachan, Aberfeldy, Perthshire or from the Water Bailiff on Arran, tel Machrie 241.

Sea fishing for cod, mackerel, flat fish, haddock. Boats for hire at Brodick, Corrie, Lamlash, Kilmory, Whiting Bay and Lochranza – detailed list from Tourist Information Centre.
Sub-Aqua Diving: visibility surprisingly good, especially in winter when water is warmed a little by the Gulf Stream. Plenty of wrecks to explore, lots from early 1880s and World War II. The Old Pier Shop, Lamlash, sells air and has limited amount of equipment for hire.
Pony Trekking: Glen Rosa Farm Stables, Brodick, tel Brodick 2380; Cloyburn Trekking Centre, tel Brodick 2108; Kelvinhaugh Trekking Centre, Whiting Bay, tel Whiting Bay 424; Cairn House, Blackwaterfoot, tel Shiskine 256. Corrie Pony Trekking, tel Corrie 669. Isle of Arran Riding Centre, Shedock Farm, Shiskine, tel Shiskine 261.
Golfing: Arran has seven courses: 18-hole at Brodick, Lamlash, Whiting Bay; 12-hole at Blackwaterfoot; 9-hole at Corrie, Lochranza, Machrie. Details, Tourist Information Centre.

FLORA AND FAUNA

About 2,000 red deer in the hill country. Golden eagles may be seen in the north. Birds of prey of all kinds – buzzards, peregrines, kestrels, harriers etc. Other birds include oystercatchers, shelduck, mallard, heron, redshank, curlew and ring ouzel. Basking sharks occasionally, in early summer. Grey seals. Red squirrels (no grey, yet).

Nature Conservancy Reserve in Glen Diomhan, near Catacol. Here may be seen two service trees peculiar to Arran – *Sorbus arranensis* and *Sorbus pseudofennica*, akin to the rowan. Look for carline thistle and fleabane near Struay Rocks at Bennan Head; for oysterplant at Drumadoon Point; seaside convolvulus near Blackwaterfoot.

Consult Arran Nature Centre (see *Sightseeing*).

THE KINDLY LIGHTS

BY DOUGLAS B. HAGUE &
ROSEMARY CHRISTIE

The earliest island lighthouse off the mainland of Great Britain is that built early in the 14th century on Chale Down, at the extreme south of the Isle of Wight. With the exceptions of the Roman Pharos at Dover and the 13th century Hook Tower at Waterford, it is the oldest lighthouse structure in Britain or Ireland. St Catherine's Point, below Chale Down, was the first land to be sighted by those engaged in the wine trade from Bordeaux in the Middle Ages. Many ships were wrecked at this point and some questionable practices were known to have taken place. Indeed, one incident precipitated the building of this tower: a ship laden with wine had run aground and fortunately the crew managed to get ashore.

Also, fortunately for all concerned, it was found that a great deal of the cargo was safe and an agreement was made between the crew and Sir Walter Godeton, the local squire, and his men to recover it. Because the ship belonged to a French monastic house, Sir Walter had to appear before a Papal Court in 1314 to answer for his disposal of the cargo. Its ruling was that he was to build an oratory, endow it, provide for a priest to say masses for the souls of those lost at sea and to provide a lighthouse. The oratory did not survive much after the Dissolution but the tower stands to this day, and the creasing, or 'imprint', of the oratory roof can still be seen. This building, which rather resembles a rocket on its launching pad, is unique. The lantern set at the top of the octagonal stone tower was two-thirds solid stone on plan and it requires little imagination to see that the efficiency of a primitive cresset lamp or candle displayed 770 feet above sea level and 1½ miles from the coast was of a very low order. An illustrated map of 1544 shows what appear to be bundles of faggots or wood drying for a bonfire, which was one of the most effective and popular methods of displaying a light from the earliest times. In the 18th century a low circular

tower, now known as the Pepper Pot, was built nearby, but this was often obscured by fog and in 1838 the present tower at St Catherine's Point was built on lower ground, this in turn being lowered further to its present height in 1875 after a serious list had developed.

The importance of the Isles of Scilly as the first sight of England on the voyage from America is obvious, and the first light on the islands was displayed from a fine tower on St Agnes, built in 1680 by Hugh Till and Simon Bayly, two Brethren of Trinity House. Not only is the surviving tower interesting architecturally, it is one of the very few for which specifications have been preserved, having survived fires and other disasters at Trinity House. Originally the light was provided by a coal fire in a cast-iron brazier, one of which survives in the famous gardens on Tresco. Oddly enough this brazier stood on an insulated wooden floor with a lead-encased wooden lantern which survived until the present cast-iron lantern was fitted in 1809. Another unique feature of this tower is the gunports which were a defence against Barbary pirates who roved the western seas. The St Agnes light was replaced by the famous Bishop Rock in the 19th century, but is kept a gleaming white as it is still used as a daymark.

The eastern seaboard of Britain has, since medieval times, been busy with maritime trade from the Low Countries and the Baltic. These North Sea waters also carried large fishing fleets and heavy coastal traffic, notably bringing coals to London. Although the coastal scenery of the east coast is not as ruggedly spectacular as that of the west, the navigation is notoriously dangerous, and islands such as Coquet and the fiendish scatter of the Farnes, whilst daunting in daylight are deadly in the dark.

The Farnes consist of a dozen or more low islands or rocks extending for about three miles

THE KINDLY LIGHTS

1 St Catherine's, the medieval tower, at the extreme south of the Isle of Wight.
2 The High Light on the Calf of Man.
3 The Skerries light, the site of which cost Trinity House £444,984 in 1836.
4 The now-disused Old Light, Lundy, with cavity walls of native granite.
5 St Agnes, Scilly, 1680, with gun-ports for protection against the Barbary pirates.
6 A restored drawing of the original Brownsman.
7 Bardsey lighthouse, with original 1821 bellied-out railings.

off the coast. Although from the 16th century the Corporation of Trinity House was empowered to build and maintain lighthouses, its monopoly was not upheld by the Crown who profited from the sale to private individuals of patents for the collection of dues. Also the Corporation itself was glad to farm out its responsibilities to those who were prepared to take them on, naturally with profit in mind. In 1669 the entrepreneur Sir John Clayton, without consulting Trinity House, erected several lighthouses, including one on the top of the medieval pele tower of St Cuthbert on the Inner Farne. It was to have been illuminated by a coal fire, but indignant opposition from Trinity House thwarted his plans and it was not until 107 years later that Captain John Blackett obtained a lease from the Corporation and erected two lights. The coal light on the old tower was reinstated and a small neat cottage lighthouse lit by oil lamps was built on Staple, or Pinnacle, Island. This still stands to eaves level but it had presumably been ill-sited and in 1791 a tower for a coal fire light was hastily erected on nearby Brownsman Island. The remains of this rude masonry building of undressed beach pebbles and wooden floors can still be seen.

Complaints from mariners led to the building in 1810 of the present Inner Farne lighthouse, the only English tower to retain its original lantern and balcony. At the same time a new tower, the stump of which still remains with adjoining cottage, was built on Brownsman. It was in this cottage that Grace Darling was born, one of the nine children of

A zig-zag of steps leads down cliffs and over a suspension bridge to South Stack Lighthouse, Anglesey

William Darling, the lighthouse-keeper. The engineer of Trinity House, Daniel Alexander, designed these oil-burning towers, which were built by Joseph Nelson. This little-known character designed the Longstone, the tower which replaced the Brownsman, erected in 1826 on the most northerly of the Outer Farnes. From here the heroic rescue of the crew of the *Forfarshire* by Grace Darling and her father was carried out.

The 18th century and the beginnings of the Industrial Revolution saw the rise of Liverpool from a small, undistinguished seaside town on the wide flat banks of the Mersey's mouth to one of the best equipped and largest ports in the world. In its heyday at the end of the last century, the emphasis of trade was to America and the west, and the need to provide lights on the Welsh coast became urgent. The vital point where ships changed course from the Irish Sea to Liverpool Bay was the Skerries, a small island and rocky reef off the north west tip of Anglesey. The Skerries light, built in 1714 by private enterprise, is unique in lighthouse history because it brought about a major change in the law. Excessive lighthouse dues were having a harmful effect on international trade. By an Act of 1836, all private lights were taken over by the three lighthouse authorities: Trinity House, The Commissioners for Northern Lighthouses and The Irish Lights. Compensation was paid to those whose lighthouse leases were taken over, but legal difficulties were encountered when a lease had been granted in perpetuity – as in the case of the Skerries, whose astute and avaricious lessees fought a rearguard action and succeeded in obtaining £444,984, which translated into modern values might be around £11 million. Having paid such a vast sum, Trinity House felt that any modernisation and improvements must be done on a style commensurate with its value. The architecture of the ancillary buildings has great charm. Fortunately the attractive little crow-stepped gabled keeper's cottage of the early 18th century has been retained as a store. As it stands the present tower is much as it was when built by James Walker who encased and heightened the tower of 1759. It has the solid, crenellated parapet he favoured, which can also be seen at Trwyn Du, St Catherine's and the Needles.

Of Anglesey's lighthouses the best known is the South Stack. It occupies a site of dramatic grandeur on the 100-foot summit of a small island about 50 yards offshore and ten miles south of the Skerries. Since it was erected in 1809 the scene has attracted many artists, photographers and geologists inspired by the fantastic and flamboyant folds of pre-Cambrian rocks in the 400-foot cliffs. The engineer and builder of the South Stack light were Daniel Alexander and Joseph Nelson. The tower is more austere than Alexander's later towers, most of which have very heavy and elaborate base moulds. South Stack had two highly unusual features: an inverted fog-bell and a clockwork-operated mobile lantern which was lowered on a railed incline to within 50 feet of the sea where it could often be seen when the lighthouse was obscured by fog. Only the incline survives.

Two other lights in Anglesey qualify for mention. The very attractive Salt Island Holyhead tower designed by John Rennie in 1821 as a terminal for the Irish packet, had a matching tower at Howth in Ireland. Although now disused, this elegant, tapered structure retains its original lantern and curved railings and is the oldest lantern in Wales. The other, Trwyn Du, set in the narrow strait between Penmon and Puffin Island, is the first wave-washed tower designed by James Walker and completed in 1835. Not a very distinguished structure, it can claim to be the first to house a primitive and rather unsatisfactory water-closet.

Bardsey, like Lundy and several Scottish islands, is better known for its birds and its early Christian settlement than for its maritime associations. As it stands on the route of migrating birds, Bardsey's powerful light dazzles them and great numbers have been killed by flying against the tough glass of its lantern. Trinity House, in conjunction with the Royal Society for the Protection of Birds, has carried out a number of experiments to avoid the excessive casualties; the latest is the flood-lighting of an area of gorse near the tower, where the birds are attracted to roost.

The Bardsey lighthouse is the tallest square tower in the British Isles and was designed by Alexander, with Nelson as builder. Fortunately when the present lantern was fitted in the mid-19th century it was found possible to keep the original bellied-out railings of 1821 as preserved at Salt Island Holyhead and the Inner Farne. There is a blocked and never used directional low light which had a small external hood in the style of those at Lundy and Harwich.

Although Ramsey Island does not support a lighthouse, its presence, and a villainous scatter of islets and rocks to the west, is marked by the South Bishop lighthouse. This and the earlier Smalls, ten miles to the south, were vital aids to the navigation of the Irish Sea. Its rock is high, and landing is difficult, but quite commodious accommodation was provided by James Walker when he built it in 1838. Its original lantern is still in use and its contemporary and rather spidery gallery railings

are a unique design. Unfortunately this attractive station is being converted for unmanned use and some of the buildings are being demolished.

Skokholm lighthouse, built in 1916, is one of the last to have been constructed of brick and masonry in the traditional pattern, although its design, with its 58-foot tower incorporated into the two-storied keepers' dwellings, is of a style commonly used in Scotland and America.

Bardsey Lighthouse, tallest square tower in the British Isles.

Lundy, set almost malevolently across the misty mouth of the Severn estuary, has for centuries claimed hundreds of ships bound for the ancient port of Bristol. Five miles long, of uncompromising granite, with formidable 400-foot high cliffs, it is surprising that mariners had to wait until 1820 before Daniel Alexander built the now abandoned High Light. It is unusual in many ways, being built of the native granite, but with cavity wall construction, a method of weather-proofing usually associated with modern flimsy domestic building. It also had a secondary low light displayed 37 feet below the main light. These two lights were to enable mariners to differentiate between Lundy and Mumbles and Flatholm, further up the estuary, which displayed single lights. This same arrangement of a hooded lower light was also used by Alexander in his nine-sided brick tower at Harwich, where it provided a directional beam. However, the Lundy lower light was not a success; the great height of the tower often resulted in the upper light being obscured by fog, or alternatively it was found that at a distance they merged into

View from Merchant's Point, Tresco, of the Round Island Lighthouse, Isles of Scilly.

one. Largely with this in mind, a lantern was devised at the foot of the tower, but even this did not help. The keepers' dwellings of 1820, connected to the tower by a corridor, were built with supreme confidence; a massive gable faces full into the prevailing winds, with the kneelers, or base stones, of the copings carried on detached granite columns, a gesture without parallel in British architecture.

To provide a good fog warning it was decided to build a battery near the foot of the western cliffs. This remarkable roofless building, with its magazine and cottage for the resident gunner and his family, can still be reached by a long zig-zag flight of steps. Eventually the whole station was abandoned in favour of two separate lighthouses with fog warning systems at north and south ends of the island. The northern one is now unmanned.

Scotland is not well endowed with early lights, the Isle of May being the obvious exception, but Pladda, set on an islet beyond a promontory of the Isle of Arran, was established in 1790, and was one of the first ten towers built for the Northern Lights by their first engineer, Thomas Smith. He was step-father to the well-known Scottish engineer, Robert Stevenson, who also worked with him on many other lighthouses. The station now has two towers, but a year after the completion of the earlier and taller one, it was found necessary to add a lower lantern, as was done later on Lundy and Harwich. No details of this have survived, neither has it left any scars where it was fixed, but clearly it was not a success because by 1831 the second squat tower had been built. Both are fitted with the most beautiful cast-iron lattice gallery railings, a feature of so many Scottish lights of the first half of the nineteenth century. The low level of the later building makes it easy to examine and appreciate the sensitive detailing of this lantern with its delicate cast-iron floor and decorative panels. The lantern of the taller tower was replaced by a larger 'double balcony type' in 1901, which has in no way marred this delightful site.

North Unst, or Muckle Flugga, in the Shetlands is rightly renowned as the most northerly lighthouse in the British Isles, but it can also claim other historical credits. It was erected in 1854 as a direct consequence of the Crimean War, to aid the Navy's movements to the Baltic. The speed at which the temporary iron light was built in 26 days must be a record. It is precariously situated on a knife-edge ridge 260 feet above the sea. The present sturdy masonry tower was completed in 1859, and despite its height it is frequently covered by green seas which sweep up the great inclined rock face.

The Isle of Man is well endowed with a number of major lights of great distinction and it has a considerable number of lovable and charming harbour lights. In 1818 Robert Stevenson designed three of his finest towers for the island. The tallest, 99 feet high at the extreme north end at Point of Ayre, is still operational and had a new large lantern fitted in 1890. Fortunately the original railings were kept.

On the Calf of Man, Stevenson built two, an upper and lower, which, when in line, warned ships of Chicken Rock situated three quarters of a mile to the south-west. Both these, alas, with their fine attached dwellings are ruined, having been abandoned in 1875 when the Rock itself was provided with the 143-foot high tower designed by David and Thomas Stevenson. This was badly damaged by fire in 1960, and two years later it was repaired

The Old Light, Lundy. Built of native granite in 1820, it is now disused.

and converted to a lower powered unmanned light, and a new lighthouse with a square lantern, built of artificial stone, was erected on the Calf.

Lighthouses on islands are now almost all classified as 'rock stations' and have no married quarters. Gone, too, are the days of silently operating lanterns lit by vaporizing-oil lamps and resplendent with polished brass gears; on even the most remote rock tower, electricity has taken over.

DOUGLAS B. HAGUE
& ROSEMARY CHRISTIE

BUTE

BY PAMELA BROWN

Scanning the island-riddled map of Scotland's western shore, you hardly notice Bute: it's tucked so neatly into the fingery maze of peninsulas and lochs where the Clyde runs into the Atlantic. Tilt the map, and it sits in the Cowal Peninsula like an egg in an egg-cup, the northern half separated from a bowl of heathery hills by a few hundred yards of scenic waters, the celebrated Kyles of Bute. Roughly 15 miles long and 4 wide, and almost divided by the Great Highland Fault running along Loch Fad from Rothesay to Scalpsie, like neighbouring Arran, it has two quite distinct sides to its landscape – wild moorland in the north, trim farmsteads, bright greenery and palm trees in the south.

As soon as the ice had melted, this mild little island began to draw the travellers. Prehistoric dwellers were followed by coracle-paddling missionaries of the Celtic church, looking for a green and pleasant spot to found a monastery. Hot on their heels came the Vikings. Bute was like a Piccadilly Circus of the medieval sea lanes. After 600 years or so of relative quiet, apart from occasional Campbell raids and the customary heredi-tary feuds, came an onslaught from a different direction. Glasgow had grown into a teeming city, and here was Bute so handily placed at the mouth of the Clyde, the perfect holiday island. With the early 19th-century vogue for sea bathing, wealthy Glasgow merchants and tobacco barons acquired yachts and grand houses along the southern shores past Rothesay at Craigmore, Ascog and Montford. Ardbeg, at the north end of the bay, was, like the wrong side of Hyde Park, for the not-quite-so-wealthy.

As the holiday idea spread and moved down-market, Victorian seaside villas sprouted along Rothesay Bay as thick and fast as Benidorm skyscrapers and the sea lanes were busier than ever. During the island's heyday – about 1880 to 1910 – 30 to 40 paddle-steamers a day plied

Mr Ritchie's son Neil smokes fine salmon in Rothesay.

the Firth of Clyde laden with passengers and, more often than not, a German band to entertain them. And the jour-ney was very nearly the most exciting part of the holiday. From 1840 to the turn of the century, there was terrific rivalry between the ships' captains. Sometimes they completely mis-sed out scheduled stops along the way in the now legendary races to make the fastest time to Rothesay, and were occa-sionally fined for reckless navi-gation as a result. There were also cruises galore – musical cruises, mystery cruises, torch-light evening cruises. On the most extravagant of them all, in 1901, the Kyles of Bute rever-berated to the sound of the Berlin Philharmonic.

The golden era may have passed, the paint-work peeled a little on the hotels with their curlicued balconies and curious cast-iron coro-nets, but come July and August, Rothesay still brims over with visitors, especially during Glasgow Fair. An air of faded gentility per-vades. Holidaymakers eat high tea served on paper doilies and tiered cake stands, and after-wards stroll along the prom to watch the sun go down over Rothesay Bay. In the Athletic Bar in Gallowgate, they join in the fun and sing-along with Hilda and Victor Zavaroni (Lena's mum and dad) – 'Victor on the accordion and "you" at the mike'.

But like the two sides to Bute's landscape, there are two quite distinct sides to its character. All the commercialism and trappings of the tourist trade have been concentrated into one town, Rothesay, leaving the rest of the island with its sandy beaches, Celtic chapels, gentle hills and well-ordered farms, bluebell and primrose-covered banks and hedgerows, completely unchanged and unspoilt.

PAMELA BROWN

Rothesay, destination of the now legendary paddle-steamer races.

WHERE TO GO

ROTHESAY

For many Glaswegian holidaymakers and day-trippers, a name more familiar than that of Bute itself. Capital and only town on the island, with Ascog, Craigmore, Ardbeg fused into one, huge bay is fringed with Victorian hotels and guest-houses. Submarine, lone survivor from 1950s when Rothesay was important naval base, often lurks incongruously in front of Esplanade with its well-tended flower beds, palm trees, putting-green and chinoiserie-inspired Winter Garden. Charming examples of Victorian cast-iron work round every corner – ornamental street lamps, brackets etc: even the drain-pipes outside the tenements in Russell St have a barley-sugar twist.

Rothesay and Isle of Bute Tourist Organisation, The Pier, (tel Rothesay 2151) has useful leaflets on walks, cruises, entertainments etc.

Many of the shops are of the sea-side-gift variety. Bread and cake shops are good, but Ritchie's, Watergate (tel Rothesay 3012) is Bute's gastronomic pinnacle. Jane Grigson, the *Observer Magazine*'s cookery correspondent, thinks there is none to match Mr Ritchie's 'Authentic Bland Cured Salmon', smoked in the shavings of whisky barrels. His Loch Fyne kippers are equally delicious, but only available June–Nov when they're 'in the pink of condition'. Salmon all year. Mail order service.

Eating out, however, isn't Rothesay's strong point. Apart from the odd Chinese and Indian restaurant, the staple diet is fish and chips, pie and chips, haggis and chips etc, and in the slightly posher hotel restaurants, gammon and chips. There are several tearooms – one of the nicest on the old pier at Craigmore. Pubs are plentiful. The Golfers' Bar, East Princes St, has some splendidly old-fashioned fittings – friendly patrons sing-along with Max on the TV which stands in the middle of huge art nouveau bar. The Paddle Boat Bar, in the basement of Bute's grandest hotel, the Glenburn (overlooking bay on southern side of Rothesay), is much more trendy. Early closing Wed.

Rothesay Castle: massive structure dominating centre of town. Great circular curtain wall with four round

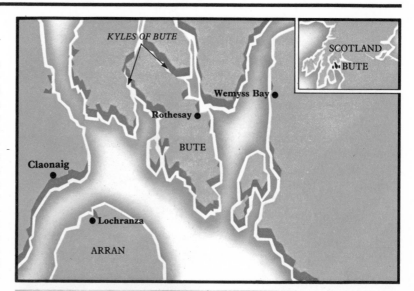

towers, surrounded by wide moat, dates from 13th c. Twice taken by the Vikings, eastern side shows signs of breach perhaps made by them in 1230. A favourite residence of Roberts II and III in 14th and 15th c and in 16th c of strategic importance to James IV and V in their Hebridean campaigns. After being burned by Earl of Argyll's men during 1685 rebellion, it remained a ruin until repaired in 19th c by 2nd and 3rd Marquesses of Bute. Open April-Sept weekdays 9.30-7, Sun 2-7, Oct-Mar closes at 4. D of E. Small admission charge.

Natural History Museum behind Castle in Stuart St: stuffed birds, sea shells, jam jars filled with the wild flowers of the month gathered by schoolchildren, help city visitors identify Bute's flora and fauna. Another room shows its history; exhibits include Stone and Bronze Age finds, reproduction of William Clark's charming watercolour of the 1840 Regatta of Royal Northern Yacht Club showing early yachting scene in fine detail, and fascinating old photographs of the Clyde steamers, trams etc. Open daily April-Sept weekdays 10.30-12.30, 2.30-4.30, Sun 2.30-4.30 only. Oct-Mar 2.30-4.30 only. Small admission charge.

Ardencraig Gardens, Eastlands Rd: municipal gardens with cascade, cockatoos, budgies and greenhouses where Bute's summer bedding and more exotic plants are raised. Also tearoom. Open May-Oct Mon-Fri 9-4, Sat-Sun 1-4.45.

St Mary's Chapel, High St: remains of a little chapel, probably built c 1300, in the pretty hillside churchyard of High Kirk of St Mary and St Bruoc. Inside are two rather grand medieval canopied wall tombs of a lady and a knight, perhaps Robert II or his father Walter the Steward. The churchyard also has mausoleum of the Marquesses of Bute and gravestone of Stephanie Bonaparte, Napoleon's niece, who died here in 1885.

PORT BANNATYNE

Tiny fishing village more or less joined on to northern end of Rothesay. A couple of rows of old stone houses and brightly painted shops look out on to Kames Bay, favourite yachting haven especially for bigger craft. Sleepy atmosphere. There are a couple of bars to quench yachtsmen's thirst, and tearoom selling delicious home-made tablet (hard Scottish version of fudge). Also a junk shop.

SIGHTSEEING

Kerrycroy: 19th c estate village originally designed by wife of 2nd Marquess of Bute. A model of English rusticity with black and white timbered cottages surrounding one side of oval green complete with maypole, the sea on the other. South of Rothesay, on edge of Mount Stuart estate. Mount Stuart itself lies hidden behind a jungle of rhododendrons and greenery. Private home of the Marquess of Bute (who still owns most of the island), it is not open to the public and can only be seen from the sea on one of the boat trips.

St Blane's Chapel: in enchanting setting in a hollow among ash and elm trees overlooking the sea, remains of Celtic monastery founded by St Blane c 570, ravaged by the Vikings c 790. A little Norman church was built 300 years later around the ruins of the chapel. Evidence of the early monastic buildings clearly visible. According to legend, the baby Blane was set adrift in a coracle with his mother Ertha, because she couldn't explain his birth. They landed in Ireland, where he was educated; he returned (surprisingly after such a send-off) to his

The lights come on in Rothesay, a nineteenth-century Benidorm.

native Bute many years later, to found the settlement. There are two burial grounds, said to be segregated with men in the upper one, women in the lower. His own grave is said to be just outside the wall of the church. Off A844 past Kingarth.

Dunagoil Fort: most impressive of Bute's prehistoric sites – perched on craggy promontory by shore of Dunagoil Bay, remains of vitrified Iron Age fort. At narrow seaward end you can still see portion of the fused wall – fused by the heat of burning wood in the timber-laced structure (probably accidental, rather than a deliberate method of strengthening the walls). Would have enclosed settlement of wattle and daub huts and iron and bronze smelting equipment, roughly 200BC to 200AD. Almost opposite St Blane's Chapel.

Kyles of Bute: narrow straits separating Bute from Scottish mainland. Celebrated beauty spot. Cattle used to swim the 400 yards from Rhubodach to Colintraive on the long drove to the Falkirk Trysts. Road gives view over eastern side, but best way to see the Kyles is by boat (see *Activities – Clyde Cruising*).

Woodend: Edmund Kean took a fancy to this secluded spot halfway along the shore of Loch Fad while on tour in Scotland in 1822 and built a house which he used regularly as a retreat over the next 10 years, especially when audiences' reactions to his private life became too much for the temperamental actor. In 1825, when Greenock theatre-goers booed his Richard III, he stomped out between acts and sailed for Bute still wearing humpback, crown and medieval hose. House has retained magnetic and mysterious aura, but it is not open to public; take a long glimpse across water from A845.

Straad and Inchmarnock: the village of Straad is greatly diminished in size and importance since last century, when it was a thriving fishing community. Just a few farmworkers' houses now, with PO in one of the back rooms. Track leads down to huge, curving St Ninian's Bay, a good place to watch wading birds, especially shelduck. Short walk, crunchy underfoot with cockleshells (which used to be collected to improve Bute's lime-deficient farm soil) leads around peninsula to remains of Celtic chapel. Overlooks the bird-haven island of Inchmarnock, where donkeys were sent for summer grazing, and habitual drunks to sober up. About 2½ miles long and ½-mile wide, island has remains of another monastery, 7th c. Lignite necklace from about 1500BC which was found here is one of Rothesay Natural History Museum's prized exhibits.

ACTIVITIES

Walking: Buteshire Natural History Society has put together excellent series of Nature Trail booklets, covering the best walks. Full of detail, they tell you every flower, tree, bird, rock to look out for on the way, along with sites of neolithic burial cairns and local Victorian murders. On sale at Natural History Museum and Tourist Office. About the nicest walk is around Garroch Head, the southern tip of island, from Kilchattan Bay to St Blane's Church. Walking in the north is a different kettle of fish. Wild lonely moorland inhabited by feral

Thirty or forty paddle-steamers a day once plied the Firth of Clyde.

Gentle, unchanged corner of Bute's coastline.

goats, buzzards and kestrels – take care not to get lost in summer thigh-high bracken. Circular walk from Rhubodach leads up around Bull Loch to Buttock Point, the northern tip, and along coast past red and white striped Maids of Bute, rocks that look like two tiny sedentary ladies.

Clyde Cruising: The Waverley, last sea-going paddle steamer in the world, carries on the tradition with various trips to Tighnabruaich, Tarbert, Dunoon, Langs etc, mid-May-end Sept. Details of times and dates of her cruises, also those of MV Prince Ivanhoe, from Tourist Organisation or Waverley Excursions Ltd, Waverley Terminal, Stobcross Quay, Glasgow, tel Glasgow 221 8152. Caledonian MacBrayne's Glen Sannox runs excursions daily except Sat, May-mid-Sept, details Caledonian MacBrayne office or Tourist Office, The Pier, Rothesay. Gay Queen sails most mornings and afternoons in summer; details posted at the slipway, opposite The Pavilion, Rothesay.

Swimming: nice unspoilt sandy beaches on western side. Scalpsie Bay – reached through a field – is the prettiest. Gulf Stream takes some of the chill out of the water. Ettrick Bay has pleasant tearoom much favoured for its home-baking. St Ninian's Bay is better for shell-collecting.

Yachting: waters sheltered by the hills of Cowal, a popular place with yachtsmen. In grander days, the Prince of Wales, the Kaiser and Thomas Lipton raced in the regattas. Both Rothesay and Kames Bays are good anchorages. Isle of Bute Sailing Club, West Bay, Rothesay, has monthly membership for visitors, will hire out dinghies and give some tuition. Scotia Island Chartering Ltd, 13 Pointhouse Crescent, Port Bannatyne, tel Rothesay 2870, and Isle of Bute Charter, Albert Place, Rothesay, 2865, both hire yachts for sailing holidays.

Angling: coarse fishing in Loch Ascog with pike, perch and roach in large numbers, in Sept-Oct pike of 20lb and over. Trout fishing in Lochs Fad and Quien – fly fishing only. Boat on Loch Quien can be booked in advance from Bute Estate Office, High St, Rothesay, where permits are available.

Sea fishing for cod, haddock, whiting and flat fish. Plenty of day fishing trips mostly from pier – details from Tourist Organisation. MacLeod Marines, 5-9 Montague St, Rothesay, tel Rothesay 3950, and Mr G. Pellegrotti, 17 Bishop St, Rothesay, tel Rothesay 3625, both charter boats for longer trips but they need to be booked well in advance.

Pony Trekking: pleasant and varied riding country. Couple of schools – Rothesay Riding Centre, Little Barone Farm, tel Rothesay 4718, and Ettrick Bay Trekking Centre, Ettrick Bay, tel Rothesay 2473. Both will also arrange inclusive holidays.

Golf: 18-hole course at Rothesay, 13-hole at Port Bannatyne, 9-hole at Kingarth. Clubs can be hired at main Rothesay course.

LINDISFARNE AND THE FARNE ISLANDS

BY VERONICA HEATH

Stand on the shingle of Lindisfarne, look south to the rocky isles of Farne and west to the mainland, and you are transported back centuries in time – nothing, here, has changed since Christianity was born. Six miles south of Berwick-on-Tweed, and six miles north of Bamburgh, Lindisfarne is England's most northeasterly land, jutting out as it does from the mainland of Northumberland into the North Sea, island and peninsula. The climate is something special: part island and part mainland, gales and rain in plenty, but idyllic days too. The light is so strong sometimes that the glare from sea and sand reflects like sunlight off snow.

As a child, I remember crossing the causeway to Lindisfarne

St Cuthbert's Chapel, Farne, completed in 1370.

with my father, a great naturalist, who took us there frequently. It took ages, jolting along in a pony and trap or in a battered old taxi. In an old manuscript I discovered this charming verse which exactly describes the place:

For with the flow and ebb, its style
Varies from continent to isle;
Dry shod, o'er sands, twice every day,
The pilgrims to the shrine find way;
Twice every day the waves efface
Of staves and sandalled feet the trace.

Now the causeway is metalled, and visitors drive over in the comfort of their own cars when the tide is low. A safety box has been constructed halfway across for foolish travellers to retreat to, should the tidal notices go unheeded.

The original name, Lindisfarne, probably derived from a brook called Lindis which flows into the sea near Goswick on the mainland and from the Celtic 'fahren', a place of retreat. Earliest Christian records begin with the arrival of the pilgrims on the island in 635AD. The original community, under Aidan, must have existed in a gaunt austerity quite unimaginable to us. The

modern name, Holy Island, was used at the re-foundation of the priory soon after the establishment of the Benedictine monastery in 1082. The priory is now roofless and ruined, but the beautiful arches and half-arches of dark sandstone framing the sky and sea give a feeling of great serenity and peace.

Pilgrims travelled to Lindisfarne from all over the western world and it became a centre of spiritual, evangelical and intellectual activity, unparalleled in the history of the English church. Christians still visit Lindisfarne in memory of this golden age. There is much to see and to find here, too, for historians, geologists, naturalists and other travellers.

My daughter and I walked the length of Lindisfarne's shore last spring. We met two local children searching in the shingle for Cuddy's beads, the fossilised stalks of the crinoid or feather star, a primitive marine creature. (Cuddy derives from St Cuthbert, 7th-century Bishop of Lindisfarne.) I remember doing the same many years ago: customs die hard on Holy Island. With our two dogs we explored the rocky promontories, coves and long sandy stretches. My daughter, a keen botanist, discovered a cornucopia of wild flowers and an abundance of interesting sea shells. In his book 'A Naturalist on Lindisfarne' Richard Perry lists 250 species of bird on Holy Island. We noted 19 and I jotted them down on a postcard while she checked them in our bird book. We were particularly pleased to see a rock pipit in residence.

The castle, built on Beblowe crag on Lindisfarne, can be seen for miles from the mainland. There are some picturesque fortifications along this north-east coastline – Tantallon, Bamburgh and Dunstanburgh – but this romantic pile, seen through mist or sea fret, is like something out of Grimms' 'Fairy Tales'. It was constructed as a harbour defence in the 16th century. In 1900 Edward Hudson, founder of *Country Life* maga-

---

Lindisfarne Priory, a place of pilgrimage in the Middle Ages.

zine, and Sir Edwin Lutyens discovered it un-occupied and recognised its potential. It was rebuilt by Lutyens, an inspired choice as architect, and the castle is an outstanding example of his work. It is now owned by the National Trust.

Leave your car in the car park by the harbour (only room for six cars) and climb the short, steep, cobbled track to visit this gem with its dramatic use of irregular levels and angles, glimpses of grass, sea and sky contrasting with stone. When visibility is good you can see immense distances from the upper rooms of the castle: the whole of Holy Island with St Abb's Head to the north, Bamburgh Castle massive in the south; due west are the Kyloe hills with the Cheviots in the distance. Eastward lies the grey North Sea, with the islands of Farne jutting whale-like out of the water. Explore the village below the castle and taste the local Lindisfarne mead, produced from a centuries-old recipe and a small industry on the island. There is a small community of 200 souls here; though tourists are now the life-blood of the place they have in no way destroyed its atmosphere.

Lindisfarne Castle, rebuilt by Sir Edwin Lutyens, was a harbour defence in the sixteenth century.
Left: *Inner Farne, visited by St Aidan and St Cuthbert.*

To get to the Farne Islands you must travel six miles via Bamburgh to Seahouses. The Farnes lie off the coast of Northumberland, about one and a half miles from Monks House, the nearest point on the mainland. These islands were originally called Faréna-Ealande or 'islands of the wanderers', whence the modern name clearly derives. They are appropriately named, for they are the summer nesting haven of countless seabirds which travel thousands of miles between their annual breeding visits. And they are also home throughout the year for a large colony of grey seals.

The first person known to have visited the Farnes was St Aidan, who made a custom of

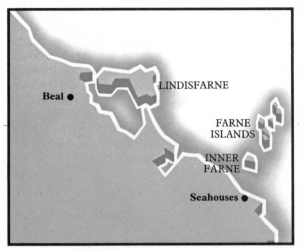

retiring there to pray. St Cuthbert lived the life of a hermit on the Inner Farne from 676 to 684AD and, after two years as Bishop of Lindisfarne, returned there to die in 687. The chapel dedicated to him was completed in 1370. It now houses a memorial to Grace Darling and some fine 17th-century woodwork.

A visit to the Farnes is a real adventure, quite unspoilt with the passing of the years. The boats used are motor cobles, sturdily built craft which can weather heavy seas. The Seahouses fishermen who take visitors to the Islands every day are fine men and good naturalists, and a day spent in their company is an education and a pleasure. They are genuinely interested in the bird life and extremely knowledgeable. We telephone before setting out, to be sure that weather conditions are favourable for the two-mile crossing. Binoculars, wellington boots and warm clothing are always essential, and even on the calmest day spray breaks over the bows

of the open boat. Immediately outside the harbour, we begin to see eider, guillemots and puffins.

The eider duck has a romantic link with the Farnes; St Cuthbert tried to guard it against human plunderers (it was the first bird in Britain to be protected), and locally the bird is sometimes referred to as Cuddy's duck. Throughout the year, the eider is accompanied by the shag, the cormorant, lesser black-backed gull, herring gull and oyster-catcher.

In due season, non-residents such as the arctic, roseate, common and sandwich tern, kittiwake, guillemot and fulmar may be seen, as well as that delightful comic the puffin, with his huge multi-coloured beak and yellow clown's feet. Razorbills are now occasionally seen; we saw two that spring day. At the right tide level, the boat is brought close up to the marvellous nesting sanctuary on the Brownsman and amateurs can photograph the nesting birds. As the boat approaches Big Harcar, Staple Island and the North and South Wamses, grey seals bob about in the water, rearing up to inspect it, and loll in dozens on half-submerged rocks. The colony is now so big that annual culling has to be undertaken to protect the fishermen's rights.

The most interesting island on which to land is the Inner Farne, where a Nature Trail has been laid out and a good brochure provided to explain flora, fauna and bird life. In May and June, the best months for visiting, the route is carpeted with white-flowering scurvy grass, replaced late in June by pink thrift. Sea campion flourishes over large areas, and a golden-yellow lichen covers much of the rock. Eider nest all over it; the different species of tern inhabit holes in the ground and can be seen, and photographed, at very close range.

VERONICA HEATH

Keeper tending the light at Longstone Lighthouse, and sea-birds clustering on the cliffs of the Farne Islands.

FROM GIGS TO SIXAREENS

BY JOHN LEATHER

Islanders are a naturally sea-conscious people with a preference for a craft suited to their own waters. In the past, inhabited British islands had many types of boat, each with distinctive features of hull form, construction, rig and arrangement. This reached a peak during the latter half of the 19th century and lasted until shortly before 1914 and in some places rather later. With the acceptance and installation of engines in many fishing and cargo boats, there was a rapid decline of oars and sail; both being relegated to an auxiliary role and eventually discarded. However, characteristics of hull form and arrangement remained or were modified to suit power propulsion, often leading to new styles of shapely

and seaworthy vessels; a process again upset by the arrival 20 years ago of standard-hulled craft produced in glass reinforced plastic, leading to a dreary similarity, often ugliness and occasionally unsuitability, particularly in hulls which are primarily used for fishing.

In the heyday of sail and oar the people of the Isle of Wight used small sailing craft called wherries for communication to and from the mainland and for tending on ships in the Solent, a strait that can be amazingly rough when strong winds oppose the fierce tides.

Their principal work was carrying officers, baggage, stores and provisions to warships and other vessels lying in Spithead or in St. Helen's Roads, off the eastern end of the Isle of Wight, in company with many similar wherries sailing from Portsmouth. These also often carried passengers, light general cargo and livestock between the Isle of Wight and the mainland. In slack times they might fill in with fishing, or assistance to ships with unlicenced pilotage, or go sweeping the anchorages with a rope on the bottom to raise lost anchors. Many first class wherries were used to smuggle from Cherbourg and Barfleur and these

had a reputation for speed and as sea boats.

A naval officer serving in a sailing-line battleship during the 19th century recalled his having to anchor to the east of the Isle of Wight with her sails blown away and shoals close under her lee. The ship was plunging in a heavy sea. An hour later the anxious deck watch saw a scrap of sail making towards them, tumbling from sea to sea. It was a wherry which ran close under the great warship's stern to read her name and then she plunged off to windward to beat back to Portsmouth and report the ship's danger.

A typical boat was 34 feet 6 inches overall length by 9 feet beam by 5 feet 6 inches depth from the top of keelson to the sheer. Draught forward was 3 feet and aft 4 inches more. The hull was very fine in form with hollow waterlines at bow and stern. The pointed stern was only slightly fuller than the bow and the amidship section was very easy and almost semi-circular in shape. Wherries were clinker planked, usually of oak, copper-clench fastened to sawn frames which were fitted when the planking was completed; a light construction, but they were long-lived.

Apart from the forward and after decks wherries were open from gunwale to gunwale, but side benches were fitted for passengers and crew and a wide thwart for the helmsman. A cuddy cabin was contrived under the foredeck with a stove and at its after end some locker tops for sitting and sleeping. Three or four tons of pig iron ballast were stowed under the cockpit sole and there was some shifting ballast which was shoved up to the weather side in a strong wind, to aid stability.

The wherry's rig was, from forward, a staysail set to the stemhead and locally termed a 'jib'; a sprit foresail on the foremast which stepped through the foredeck. A spritsail was of quadrilateral shape, with its peak spread by a spar known as a sprit and set up by a purchase of blocks and rope at its heel and a spritsail mizzen aft, set on a mast immediately forward of the short after deck. The sprit foresail was fitted with rope brails which drew it to the mast like a curtain when anchoring or going alongside a ship, when the boat's short masts allowed her to lay close alongside, under the lower yardarms.

In calms the wherries were rowed with long oars known as sweeps. In strong winds their fine lines got them to windward in the short seas around the island. When the warships boats were hoisted in, wherries cruised around the fleet looking for a job; taking an officer ashore or posting a letter. By the 1880's steam launches were rapidly reducing the wherries' work and only a handful of them remained by the 1920's.

The present equivalents of the sailing wherries of Spithead are the fast launches used by watermen and ships stores suppliers to tend ships in the West Solent, Southampton Water, Spithead and the approaches. These sleek, blue-hulled 40 and 44-footers have hulls of plastic construction and twin diesel engines which at full power enable them to achieve speeds up to 30 knots, though most are content with a maximum between 19 and 23. Many similar craft are used in the area and in other countries as pilot boarding launches. The local boats are based at Ryde, Cowes and Yarmouth to serve the pilotage of ships of all sizes which trade to the mainland ports of Southampton and Portsmouth.

The birthplace of these seakindly craft is Bembridge, the home of the Thornycroft family, noted as designers and builders of fast vessels of many types from mid-Victorian steam launches to large destroyers. They were amongst the earliest designers and builders of fast launches for many purposes in their various yards on the mainland. One of the family, Commander Peter Thornycroft, maintains this tradition from his design office in the village and specialises in fast launches, besides designing small fast ships up to corvette size. These round-bilged, purposeful looking craft have well flared bows and a sweeping, flush sheerline. Cabin tops and wheelhouse are carefully designed for functional use and also to blend in with his concepts of seakeeping efficiency.

Peter Thornycroft's long process of evolution has resulted in international acclaim and the functional elegance of his craft has also attracted yachtsmen who like a seaworthy motor boat. However, he gains most satisfaction from the faith that pilots and other round-the-clock seafarers have in his boats and their acceptance in many countries as the right boats for the job.

ISLES OF SCILLY

In the Scilly Isles, rowing and sailing gigs were used for many purposes from pilotage to salvage, and in fine weather they were sometimes used to carry potatoes and flowers to Penzance. Some were built by Samuel Tiddy, who was apprenticed at Peters' yard at St Mawes, near Falmouth and afterwards established himself in the islands; a tradition of craftsmanship that is continued today by Tom Chudleigh in his St Marys workshop, where fine-lined gigs and other craft take shape under his hands for local rowing and sailing enthusiasts.

Several six-oared gigs worked with the pilot cutters which cruised from the islands near the Bishop Rock lighthouse to put pilots aboard ships which were to await orders at the Scillies for destination of their cargoes. The Scilly gigs also landed pilots from outward-bound ships and there was generally considerable rivalry amongst these gig crews to get jobs.

Similar gigs were used from Penzance, Newlyn, Falmouth, St Mawes, on the south coast of Cornwall and from St Ives, Hayle and Padstow on the north coast. Most were owned by pilots, others by ship chandlers and runners who provided men for ships crews, or by outfitters seeking business amongst the ships in the anchorage of Falmouth.

The Scilly Isles gigs were in working use for many years until after the 1914–18 war. Some very old ones survive for regatta racing in the islands and on the mainland. A typical gig averaged 26–32 feet length and from 4 feet 9 inches to 5 feet 6 inches beam. The dimensions, particularly depth, varied for the type of work for which the gig was likely to be used. Those likely to be working at salvaging goods from ships stranded around the islands were beamier and deeper than the pilot gigs. Weight was as light as possible consistent with strength, though some gigs in the Scillies were very light so that a seven-man crew could carry them to launch or when beached.

The planking was usually English elm in long lengths and $\frac{1}{4}$ or $\frac{3}{8}$ inch thick. Timbers were oak or Canadian rock elm and keels of oak or pitch pine. All members were carefully put together and well fastened. These long, narrow boats flexed but rarely leaked seriously. Oars were 16–18 feet long, of ash or clear pine, working in thole pins of oak or iron, or in rowlocks in later boats.

The gigs could set a dipping lug foresail and, in the Scilly Isles, a triangular mizzen. Gigs are fast on a reach or with the wind aft. They will sail to windward but a centreplate is rarely fitted in them. They are slow to tack and when coming about the

Isle of Wight sailing is for pleasure now, not commerce.

bow oar is usually used to pull the head round, through the wind. When on a windward leg, the lee bow oar was often kept slowly pulling to keep the gig's bow to windward.

When used for smuggling, the gigs were usually rowed, so a lowest profile was exposed. If chased, a gig would usually row directly to windward as fast as possible, much faster than the revenue cutter could turn to windward, and many escaped by this method. Occasionally the Scilly gigs were used to row across the English Channel to return with contraband goods; a considerable feat in an open boat with little beam or freeboard. Arrival at the islands was usually timed in darkness.

The traditions of the Scilly gigs have remained vigorously alive, and besides renovating very old craft for competitive use by youthful crews, new gigs have been and are being built at St Marys by Tom Chudleigh, the islands' boatbuilder, for the summer gig races, where hard-trained crews row in fierce competition, gig against gig, against crews from other islands in the group. Gigs also come over to compete from the Cornish mainland ports of Newquay and Falmouth.

The Scilly Isles gigs look well set to be rowing, and occasionally sailing, under their large dipping lugsail and leg of mutton mizzen, into the twenty-first century.

THE CHANNEL ISLANDS

The fleet of fishing craft registered at the island ports of Guernsey and Jersey a century ago num-

bered 72 first class, 583 second class and 147 third class boats. Pride of the fleet were the powerful cutter-rigged smacks, which were mostly built at Gorey, not only for islanders but also for owners in England. They were principally used for dredging the deep sea oysters and scallops in the English Channel and the North Sea. Many were sold to north-east Essex fishermen and my great-grandfather owned one which was by all accounts a well constructed and noble cutter which was fast and would stand much bad weather. Speed was often a feature of craft built in the Channel Islands, particularly the Guernsey boats. For centuries, islanders usually mixed smuggling with fishing. And poaching on French fishing grounds was common – another reason why speedy boats were necessary.

Besides the sleek cutters, Guernsey boatbuilders turned out small schooners which were bold-sheered, three-masted open boats from about 26 to 40 feet long, the largest having a beam of about 12 feet and a draught aft of 6 feet. The long straight keel rose to a draught of 3 feet forward and these boats were remarkably quick in turning, like most craft from the islands. The schooner rig had boomless gaff sails on the fore and main masts and in many boats a standing lug mizzen was also stepped, sheeted to an outrigger. A large jib could be set on a long bowsprit and in fine weather, topsails were set above the fore and mainsail. The schooners were fast and were occasionally raced in summer regattas. They had a chunky boxiness in appearance and generous freeboard which kept them dry in the

FROM GIGS TO SIXAREENS

1 Manx 'Nickie', *c.* 1865: based on the Cornish lugger, these large sturdy craft were ideal for drift net fishing.

2 Scottish fishing smack: this cutter-rigged boat, with its double-ended hull, shows clearly its Viking ancestry. It fished and traded between Scottish islands a hundred years ago.

3 Guernsey fishing boat, *c.* 1850: between 32 feet and 40 feet long, these luggers carried a crew of six and were good seakeeping boats.

4 Spithead wherry, *c.* 1860: widely used in ship-to-shore work, especially for the Navy.
5 Shetland sixareen, *c.* 1860: there was a lot of the Viking about this boat, the name of which, in Norse, meant 'six men rowing'.
6 Coble: these shapely boats are ideal for launching from exposed beaches and are still used in the Farne Islands – but with motor instead of sail propulsion.
7 Scottish motor drifter: a classic of fishing boat design. Boats of this type can be seen in all the island ports of Britain, and its lines have even been copied for private yachts, called Motor Fishing Vessels.

short seas raised by the fast tides of the rock-strewn waters surrounding the islands.

A crew of five manned these stoutly built schooners and their principal work was drift net fishing for mackerel during the summer, about 10–30 miles from the islands. A herring fishery kept locals busy in winter, along with oyster dredging, until the herring suddenly disappeared. They also used trammel nets, trawls, lines and beach seines and caught lobsters, crabs and crayfish in pots laid on the bottom.

Fishermen from Jersey generally used smaller boats but, even so, managed to carry and lay about 100 pots at a time. However, most Jersey fishermen shipped in larger schooners, which each spring voyaged across the Atlantic to fish for cod with lines on the north-eastern American banks off Newfoundland, returning each autumn, when they fitted out their own small boats for local fishing through the winter.

Fishing for lobsters, crabs and crawfish still goes on in the Channel Islands and there are many small modern fishing vessels working from the harbours. The wooden ones are as powerfully formed as ever, with characteristic high freeboard forward, a sweeping sheer, flaring bows, hard, full bilges and broad decks.

ISLE OF MAN

During the 19th and early 20th centuries, the Isle of Man was a centre of herring drifting. Small open boats of the Manx fishermen developed to cutter-rigged craft by the beginning of the 19th century. Appearance of the venturesome Cornish drifting luggers in local waters during the 1860s led the Manxmen to copy these more able, decked craft which could more quickly sail to what were then the local fishing grounds about 40 miles from Port St Mary. Their finer lines and towering lugsails enabled them to return more speedily with their catches in good condition and commanding a higher price.

These copies of the Cornish luggers were powerful and fast craft known as 'nickeys', reputedly because of the frequency of Nicholas as a christian name among Manx fishermen. Most nickies had the same pointed stern as the Cornish originals but some later boats had a counter to improve deck space for working gear. The Manx luggers tended to be larger than the Cornishmen and in the 1880s, a foresail was added, in addition to the jib, which was set on a long bowsprit. The resulting rig was known as a 'nobby', no one now knows why. The nobbies needed less crew than the nickies, which were generally smaller than the new breed of boats.

Besides fishing around the Isle of Man, the nobbies ventured as far away as the Shetland Isles, sometimes also reaching the North Sea to work out of ports on the north-east coast of England in the herring season. Many also fished from the west coast of Ireland.

Generally their crews of up to seven men and a boy were ill rewarded for their hard work and like most fishermen of the days of sail, and some of today, they were paid on a share system divided in proportions from the proceeds of the catch, giving shares to the owner, the boat, the nets and the crew as individuals.

The nickies and nobbies are long gone, and motor fishing vessels have sailed from Manx ports for 70 years. As in many places, these are now a mixture of modern and not so new craft, with many wooden-hulled Scottish-style seine netters and small trawlers. Others are the similar looking scallop boats, and there are some glass-reinforced plastic boats, but the whole fleet amounts to only a tenth of that which once fished under sail.

FARNE ISLANDS

The North Sea may lack the long, swinging ocean rollers of the west and south-west coasts of Britain and Ireland but in strong winds, particularly when these oppose its tides, it has short, vicious waves which pound and smash at the coast and can make the north-east coast of England a fearsome place for craft and men. 'Whom the North Sea hath dyed in grain, he shall neither shrinke nor strayne' ran the medieval sea rhyme, which remains true today.

Between the river Tweed, just south of the Scottish border with England and the mouth of the river Humber in Yorkshire, many small communities launched open sailing and rowing boats known as cobles. These put out from beaches and harbours to set long lines, to drift-net for herring and set pots for crabs and lobsters. When motor cobles were introduced after 1919, some men also commenced trawling. In some places a remnant of this once great number continues to fish with powered cobles, using hydraulic haulers and coilers to handle gear, and tractors and winches to haul their cobles up the surf-ridden beaches. Sail and oar are gone, but the proud coble shape remains; an exaggeratedly shaped sheer, bright painting of the hull, which is planked clinker fashion (with overlapping seams) of larch on sawn oak frames and an oak 'ram plank', which in a coble replaces the more conventional keel, an oak stem and a well raked transom stern. Cobles evolved as beach boats to suit the surf of this coast. The deep forefoot, flat after sections and generous forward freeboard enable them to launch or beach with bow to surf on what is often a lee shore.

Before the introduction of motor power, about 26 feet was an average length for many sailing and rowing cobles. The rig was a square-headed dipping lugsail which had four or five rows of reef points to reduce it in strong winds. The mast was stepped at a rake and could be shifted to several positions to suit sail area and wind strength. When the coble was rowed in a breeze the mast was usually laid in the boat to reduce windage. As cobles did not have a centreboard, they relied when sailing to windward on the lateral plane offered by the deep forefoot and also partially on the deep and narrow rudder blade. The rudder was unshipped when in shallow water and cobles were usually beached under oars. In fine weather a jib might also be set on a short bowsprit and larger cobles in some fisheries also set a mizzen, which could serve as a storm sail.

The men of Holy Island, in the Farnes, were noted coble sailors. In 1838, ten cobles, each about 26 feet long, were fishing from the island and many of the men were pilots for ships navigating the coast to Newcastle. Island men also owned 30 foot long, lug-rigged open boats called 'keel boats' because of their more conventional construction and hull form. These set a single dipping lugsail on a mast stepped in the eyes of the pointed sterned hull. They fished mainly for herring in season, from the Firth of Forth to the Tyne. The islanders also manned a lifeboat, for much merchant ship traffic passes that coast.

The physical harshness of this coast and its fisheries was reflected in the often stark poverty of its fishermen, particularly before railways and improved distribution of fish enabled the markets of many large northern industrial towns and cities to be reached quickly. The fishermen's wives and daughters usually shared their work, gathering bait for line fishing, clearing, baiting and coiling lines.

The hardships and spirit of the coble fishermen are well expressed in the writings of the late Leo Walmsley who lived and worked alongside them when motors were introduced. The motor did much to relieve the toil of the coble men and since the 1920s motor cobles and the similar, pointed-sterned 'surf boats' have evolved to a fine type of inshore boat, well understood by their owners but still seeming strange to other seafarers. The hull form retains its characteristics except that the propeller is fitted well under the hull aft, often working within a shallow semi-tunnel to protect it when beaching. In some boats it is capable of being drawn up close to the bottom by a lever. Hauling up is now aided by a tractor or a motor winch but it remains a strenuous way of earning a living.

Cobles are still built by small yards in Northumberland and Yorkshire. Cobles are still built in larch and oak by small yards such as J. and J. Harrison at Amble, Northumberland and others in Northumberland and Yorkshire. Others are produced in glass reinforced plastic for pleasure sailing, sometimes fully-rigged with a dipping lugsail; a use which would have puzzled their crews in the days of sail and oar.

SHETLAND

The small boat heritage of the Shetland Isles leans towards Norse origins. Nowadays the islanders use motor boats, still often with the fine, pointed stern of their rowing and sailing ancestors. Larger wooden and plastic-hulled craft are used for fishing further afield and for pilot duties to serve the increasing numbers of large tankers coming to the island's oil terminal.

Perhaps Shetland's most distinctive boat was the sixareen, literally 'six men rowing'; a pointed-sterned, clinker-planked open boat in which, until the end of the 19th century, hardy Shetlanders fished with lines in the deep and often stormy waters around their islands and sometimes ventured almost in sight of the coast of Norway in the search for fish.

There were also the smaller but similar 'Fourareens'. Shortage of useful timber in the islands resulted in the early boats being constructed in Norway and then being dismantled, to be imported in 'knock-down' form until the 1830s. Later the timber from which planking could be cut was imported unworked, and the boats were built in the islands, often by their owners, who led a composite life as fishermen-crofters.

The sixareen rowed and sailed to distant banks to fish by line for cod and ling. The boats might be at sea for several days in fine weather, the crew sleeping on the bottom boards wrapped in the sail. This venture was known as the 'Haaf fishing'.

In summer the boats fished from the 'Haaf stations'; stone huts roofed with turf and sited at landing places around the islands where the sixareens could be laid off to anchor in a comparatively sheltered bay or cove. Each day the boats were rowed and sailed to the fishing grounds and set long lines which might have over a thousand hooks. A good day's catch might be as much as one and a half tons of fish, so the boat's stone ballast would have to be jettisoned to enable her to carry it.

The fully developed sixareen of about 1890 was around 36 feet long and had a keel length of about 22 feet. The beam was about 8 feet 3 inches. The stem and sternpost raked gracefully forward and aft and the hull form was light and buoyant, with a gull-like sit in the water and modest draught which, coupled with fine lines at the ends helped her to sail well. The hulls were planked in eight or nine strakes of $\frac{3}{4}$ inch larch and widely spaced sawn oak or pine frames were fitted after this was completed. The overlapping lands of the planks were clenched together with soft iron nails. These boats were only expected to last for five years before being replaced. The most unusual feature of the sixareens was the rig; a close-winded squaresail. The mast was stepped almost amidships. The mainsheet, controlling the set of the squaresail, led from the clew of the sail, through a hole in the gunwale on either side, back through a thimble on the clew and returned to the helmsman's hand. The yard at the head of the sail was set at an angle and this jaunty and powerful squaresail, which resembled the dipping lug much favoured by the Scotch and East Anglian fishermen in appearance, was flattened when sailing to windward by a rope called the bowline, which led from the luff and tack (the forward edge and lower forward corner) to make the sail set better and enable the sixareen to point higher into the wind. Reefs were often needed in these boats where the hull form lacked stability under sail in strong breezes and reef points were provided at the foot and, unusually, at the head and down the leach of the sail, allowing for considerable progressive reduction in area.

A wooden pump was fitted close to the helmsmans hand and one or two wooden scoops were

Peter's Port on Benbecula, a paradisaically remote spot.

used to fling out the considerable quantities of spray and wave crests which came aboard in strong winds.

Fishing in a sixareen under sail and oar was amongst the most physically demanding ways of earning a meagre living and the hardy islanders realised the deficiency of the sixareen when they tried to turn them into craft for herring drifting, in imitation of the vast numbers of bluff bowed Dutch 'Bomschuits' which, like the 'busses' before them, had for centuries sailed to the Shetlands to set their miles of drift nets through the herring season. By the mid 19th century numbers of east-Scottish luggers known as Scaffies, or Fifies, were working the fishery and gradually these craft were bought by Shetlanders and were eventually built in the islands. By the beginning of the twentieth century, some Shetland fishermen were venturing, in collectives, to own the then new steam herring drifters, large numbers of which were then being built and owned on the east coast of Scotland and in East Anglia. A boom in steam herring-drift fishing lasted until 1914 and recommenced in modified form between 1918–1939 with steam and then motor drifters. It revived in 1945 but died during the 1950s when herring stocks dwindled rapidly, aggravated by overfishing with mid-water trawls by European vessels.

Meanwhile, the descendants of the sixareens remain in the smaller sized boats used for pleasure sailing in the islands. Few of these now set the Shetland squaresail, their owners preferring the tall and efficient gunter lug and foresail rig for regatta racing.

WESTERN ISLES

In the western isles of Scotland a variety of lugsail rigged craft were principally used for herring fishing. Popular among them were pointed stern skiffs, known in some localities as 'nabbies'. Many of these were about 42 feet long and had a well-raked stem and sternpost and a short foredeck with a cuddy in which the crew of three or four lived. The mast was heavily raked aft and a large standing lugsail was set, with a jib on a bowsprit. Small open skiffs from about 16–24 feet long, rigged with a single lugsail and sometimes a jib were also used to fish for crabs and lobsters, and for herring in season.

Until late in the 19th century the carriage of goods and occasionally also passengers to and from the islands and to the mainland was principally by small sailing vessels known as either 'smacks' or 'gabberts.' The smacks were strongly built, round bottomed craft with a counter stern and were about 60 feet long. These carried 20–25 tons of cargo in a hold amidships. The rig of gaff mainsail, foresail and jib could be supplemented by a topsail in light weather. They were sailed by two men and a boy who lived in a small cabin aft, though sometimes the boy lived in the fo'c'sle along with the stores and gear. These able little vessels were fast sailers and could face bad weather.

The usually chubby and often pointed sterned gabberts were mostly rigged as ketches in later years but earlier examples were cutters. Length averaged 65 feet and many were built to pass through the Crinan Canal. The ketch rig with its divided sail plan enabled them to be sailed by a crew of three.

All these craft were strongly built so they could be loaded or discharged while grounded in harbour or on a sheltered beach, which was frequently done.

These boats were displaced by more efficient small steam coasters about 75 feet long known as 'puffers', from the early form of their puffing, non-condensing engines. These continued to distribute cargoes among the islands until recent times.

ORKNEY

The inhabitants of the Orkney Islands, which are separated from the north-east tip of the Scottish mainland by the turbulent Pentland Firth, found most of their living from their crofts and only went afloat for subsistence fishing or for inter-island communication. They used a pointed stern, clinker planked open boat known as a 'yole' or 'jol.' These beamy and deep boats were built from timber sent over from Norway, as there are so few trees on the islands.

The yoles were usually planked in ten strakes on each side between keel and sheer, laid on sawn oak or pine frames notched over the plank lands. A typical yole was 19 feet long overall and 14 feet on the keel, with a raked stem and sternpost. The rig was two masted with a lugsail set on each. The fore lug was boomless and sheeted abaft the mainmast. The mizzen lug had a boom. A jib was set on a light bowsprit and the boats were often rowed. The yoles of the south Orkney islands were rigged with two spritsails, in similar fashion to the wherries of the Isle of Wight.

Yoles built for inter-island transport and passenger work had a beam of half the length and were full bodied to load up to about two tons of cargo.

The pointed stern hull form remains in the fully powered successors to the yoles, but not in the new plastic-hulled lobster boats and other craft recently built in an Orkney yard.

JOHN LEATHER

ANGLESEY

BY CHRISTOPHER WORDSWORTH

Apparently as shallow as a soup plate against the breathtaking jaggedness of Snowdonia, a mere 200 yards off-shore at the narrowest part of the Straits, and regarded by many as just a platform for the A5 to Holyhead, Anglesey to the uninitiated may seem an open and rather dull book with little of the romance normally associated with islands. 'Hideous. All garages,' said one person canvassed for his impressions. 'Perfect for holidays when we were children, but I shouldn't bother too much with the rest of it,' volunteered another. Don't be deceived. Having experienced the legions of Paulinus and Agricola in its day and given Edward I a run for his money as the granary of Wales keeping resistance in the mountains, Anglesey

Fisherman with a 10lb cod caught off harbour wall, Amlwch.

offers an inscrutable Druid's smile to outsiders but has learned to keep itself to itself. The Roman Mona is the Mona Lisa of islands, her charms impenetrable to the Volvos of August, her secrets safe from the casual eye.

Away from the ring road there is more for the patient seeker than a variegated coastline of wide bays, safe sandy beaches and precipitous coves. Thrill to dramatic cliffs and lighthouses like South Stack with its teeming sea-birds. Explore Holyhead for its layers of history under the latter-day huddle. Brood over the Iron Age traces at Din Lligwy and note how the massive adjacent neolithic burial chamber in its parochial railings looks as absurd as a mammoth in a hen coop. Visit Amlwch with its whaling tradition and Shell Terminal above the tiny crevice-harbour which the rich deposits of Parys Mountain, now a lunar wasteland, once made the busiest copper port in the world.

Salute the memory of the first Marquess of Anglesey, Wellington's cavalry commander at Waterloo ('By God, sir, you've lost your leg,' said the Duke. 'By God, sir, so I have'), for his perspicacity in setting up house at Plas Newydd with its

marvellous prospect of the Strait. Climb the Anglesey Column for the panorama. Buy if you must the longest platform ticket in the world at the defunct Llanfairpwllgwyngyllgogerychwyrndrobwllllandysiliogogogoch. Deplore the inevitable building-eczema at resorts like Benllech. (But for a nation that could perpetrate such infamies at Valley Crucis, Llangollen, Anglesey's caravan parks are reasonably discreet.)

Then, having discharged your obvious scenic duties and north of the Newborough Warren Nature Reserve enjoyed one of the finest coastal walks in Europe, take to the by-lanes, the veins of the secret heart; low white-washed cottages, the shells of old Celtic churches remote from any hamlet, boggy fields enclosed by turf banks, rocky outcrops, reedy lakes (when the guidebooks say 'good trout fishing' they usually only mean 'trout fishing', but for once they are right). A private land, where you may sometimes hear the booming of that most private bird, the bittern. Or even see a pair of flamingoes, exotic truants from an aviary.

There are no clues to this other Anglesey and nothing could be more deceptive than the entry. Seen from Telford's suspension bridge – with Stephenson's tubular railway span, one of the great sagas of pioneer engineering – the treacherous straits look as placid as a river between their wooded banks. Menai is pure English Victorian, with a charming Museum of Childhood (the Welsh don't keep their nostalgia in museums). The approach to Beaumaris might be the Boscombe Undercliff. Beaumaris itself (*Bew*maris, echoing Norman pronunciations), except for the unrivalled view of the Caernarfonshire escarpment, is as un-Welsh as possible; Tudor frontages in the high street, yacht club and pier, Victorian terraces overlooking the Green, the dependable comfort of the Bulkeley Arms Hotel, where the olde Englishe custom of throwing hot pennies from the balcony

Menai Bridge on the A5 : Telford's octagonal toll-houses can still be seen.

to the peasants is perpetuated, for tourists, by the local hunt. The castle, the masterpiece of military architecture in its day, and the massive presence of Caernarfon Castle opposite, are a statement of alien power.

For the abiding spirit of place, take the shoreline road to the sixth-century Penmon Priory, sacked by Vikings and rebuilt with walls as thick as a breakwater. Or stand on Penmon Point opposite Puffin Island, formerly Priestholme. The priests are gone, the puffins are going, and the clang of the bell in the unmanned light sounds like a knell when Thermoses and sandwiches are out and the mists are swirling.

CHRISTOPHER WORDSWORTH

The dovecot at Penmon.

BASICS

The Welsh Môn Mam Cymru, Mother of Wales, perhaps because the island once grew enough corn for the whole Welsh mainland. Overall, agriculture is main source of income and island interior is still pastoral, but more money earned at the huge aluminium works, at Wylfa nuclear power station, Amlwch oil terminal and Valley airfield than from corn.

There are 125 miles of coastline with a ring road joining up the beaches all round the island.

Main cross-country route is Telford's road from Menai Bridge to Holyhead, now the A5. Last public turnpike in the country. Telford's octagonal toll houses still stand along the way. If you leave main roads you'll need a large-scale map (Ordnance Survey sheet 114) as the land is scored with more lines than a waffle iron and there are few natural barriers to prevent an endless proliferation of tracks and lanes.

Roughly 21 miles long by 19 broad, population about 68,000. In 1961 75 per cent of the people spoke Welsh. Now the figure has dropped to 59 per cent.

Highest point is Holyhead Mountain (Mynydd Twr) right over on the westernmost tip, and that's only 710ft. Difficult to compete with magnificent backdrop provided by Gwynedd, the other side of the Strait. Anglesey doesn't need its own mountains when it can borrow these.

Isle of Anglesey Tourist Association has small office at Coed Cyrnol, **Menai Bridge** (tel Menai Bridge 712626) with stacks of information on where to go, what to do, where to stay. They publish excellent official guide. There is another **Tourist Information Centre** at **Holyhead,** open Easter to end Sept, Marine Sq, Salt Island Approach (tel Holyhead 2622).

WHERE TO GO
Towns and Villages

BEAUMARIS
A place well used to visitors. 18th c travellers commended it as a watering place and paddle-boats from Liverpool used to bring Victorian holiday-makers to promenade upon the Green. Cast up now by the high tide of progress, it is a quiet, almost elegant place. The best beaches aren't here, but the best sailing is.

Main street, Castle St, has splendid

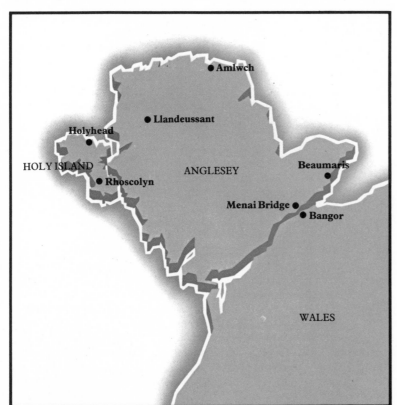

range of buildings, with openings on south giving sudden glimpses of glittering Strait. Big bonus of Beaumaris is show-stopping view of mountains across the water, misty and infinite on hot days, close and cloud-brimmed when it's not. Always superb. Grand houses built in the last century high above the route to Menai Bridge have exotic, profuse gardens of rhododendron and azalea, turning the coastal road into something more like a carriage drive.

Chief hotels are Bulkeley Arms (tel Beaumaris 810415) on the front, hefty in a gentleman's club sort of way, and Ye Olde Bull's Head Hotel (tel Beaumaris 810329), beamy and ancient. Commandeered by General Mytton in 1645 when he was laying siege to castle, a Royalist stronghold. Pretty entrance to coaching yard in Rating Row.

Lots of gifte shoppes, mostly along Castle St, the Quarterdeck, Cottage Crafts, Welsh Crafts, Mona Gift Shop, selling different combinations of Welsh wool, tapestry and slate.

Tudor Rose Antiques claims to be oldest house in town, but popular George and Dragon pub (1410) runs it a close second. Coffee, home-made cakes and biscuits at All Things Nice, Church St. Morris Fishing Tackle is here too and in a courtyard off Church St there's the Farm Shop, selling good waterproofs and eight different sorts of welly boot – useful if weather really bad. Hobson's Choice restaurant is smart, pretty eating place in Castle St, offering local scallops. Gwalia Supper Bar on corner of Rosemary Lane does fish a cheaper way, with chips.

Beaumaris Castle: built by Edward I after conquest of Wales. He started in 1295, the year after good old Madoc ap Llywelyn had burnt down Caernarfon, the other side of the water. Never finished though 400 masons, 2,000 labourers and 30 smiths and carpenters were employed in its construction. The Welsh Office, who look after it, say it is 'the most perfectly symmetrical example of the concentrically planned castle in Britain'. Very pleasant walk all around the cobbled battlements, moat partially restored below. Open mid-Oct-mid-March, Mon-Sat 9.30-4, Sun 2-4, mid-March-mid-Oct 9.30-6.30, Sun 2-6.30. Admission charge.

Courthouse: opposite the castle with pretty Gothicky windows. Built 1614, final assize held in 1971, but still used as magistrates' court. Splendid untouched interior, flagstone floor, pegged beams. Separate entrances for all involved. Jury in balcony sit far higher than judge. Standing room only for public. Open daily 10-5. Admission free, donations welcomed.
Gaol: built 1829 by Hansom (of the cabs), but closed before the century was out. Now a grisly museum. Children love it. Prison cells, punishment cell, wooden treadmill and exhibition of 19th c prison life. Open daily May-Sept 11-6. Admission charge.

MENAI BRIDGE (PORTHAETHWY)

Exotic drive from Beaumaris along wooded coast road to Menai Bridge, 4 miles to south-west. Wild Gothic extravaganza on shore like Dracula's Castle is Plas Rhianfa – no vampires, but holiday flats.

Museum of Childhood in Water St has six rooms packed with clockwork toys, old tinplate cars, trains, music boxes, magic lanterns. Selection of musical toys set off on the hour at 11/12/2/3/4/5 o'clock. Rocking horse rides on the landing for under-fives and penny-in-the-slot dramas from Brighton Pier: 'Burglar' or 'King Tut's Tomb'. Also a splendid melodious Polyphon. Open Easter-end Oct weekdays 10-6, Sun 1-5. Admission charge.

Tegfryn Art Gallery, Cadnant Rd, shows work of North Wales painters. Open daily 10-1 and 2-6. Big fish and chip shop in main street open lunchtime until 11 at night.

From car park at Tourist Office you can walk down through pungent pine woods to promenade along shore of Strait, built by Belgian refugees in World War I. Causeway leads out to tiny church of St Tysilio, founded 630AD. Valerian and columbine sway over monumental slate graves, sadly vandalised. Church locked. Windows smashed. While in Menai, worth slipping out to look at splendid menhir in a field beside the Llandegfan road.

MOELFRE

Small village of character on northeast coast (pronounced 'Moyelvruh'), tucked into valley with steep pebble beach. Good beaches to south at Traeth Bychan and to north at Traeth Lligwy. Mackerel fishing from shore, past lifeboat station. Dickens stayed here in 1859 and based a story in 'The Uncommercial Traveller' on Moelfre lifeboat's rescue of the Royal Charter returning from Australia with sheepskins and gold-diggers.

Kinmel Arms overlooks beach, sells Robinson's Ales. Ann's Pantry nearby does tea, coffee, home-made cakes. Superb craft shop up the hill towards PO, called Moelfre Crafts (open daily summer 10-10, thereafter weekdays 10-5), sells fine and intricate jewellery,

View of the mainland from Penmon.

Telford's suspension bridge over the Menai Straits to Anglesey, opened in 1826.

also smocks, glassware and much else. Very good coffee shop behind, which does salad lunches.

Short distance to the west in rolling, wooded country are the three splendid Lligwy monuments, a burial chamber (neolithic), a hut settlement (4th c AD) and a ruined chapel (12th c). All in the care of Welsh Office. Worth buying their 'Ancient Monuments in Anglesey' as they have 23 on the island. Chapel roofless, but charming, surrounded by low stone wall. Ancient village (badly signposted) is some distance away, southwest of chapel, across field and through iron gate. Worth persevering because it is spectacular with enclosing walls, 4-5ft thick, of huge limestone slabs, infilled with rubble, Inside are two circular and seven rectangular huts, some with doorsteps and tall stone entrance posts. Best is beautiful round one in western corner, with slabs perfectly fitted together. Trim clipped yews in the garden of Plas Lligwy over the field contrast primly with this rugged settlement.

BEACHES

A great string of popular ones along north-east coast from the enormous sweep of **Red Wharf Bay** (Traeth Coch) to the remote **Porth Wen,** reached on foot by farm track. Watch the tide at Red Wharf if you are crossing the sand. Pretty whitewashed pub here, the Ship Inn, with benches outside. Also café, Y Gegin Fach, which does coffee and sells beach gear, spades, fishing nets. **Benllech** has depressing hinterland of bungalows, but fine, if crowded, beach, good waves, donkeys, all the Bournemouth razzmatazz. **Traeth Bychan** is a much more muscular place, for doing rather than idling. Boats, dogs, purposeful. In the south the great sweep of **Llanddwyn Bay.** Massive conservation programme here to try and stabilise the dunes by planting marram grass. **Cable Bay** (Porth Trecastell) is pretty, rocky inlet between Aberffraw and Rhosneigr. On the main road, so you would need to get there early in high season.

SIGHTSEEING

Plas Newydd: National Trust show place, brilliantly sited on the shore of the strait, with Snowdonia bristling on the far side of the water. View stretched by Rex Whistler's imagination into something even more exotic in huge mural in diningroom. Also Whistler exhibition. Belonged until 1976 to the Marquesses of Anglesey. Open Good Friday-end Oct (not Sat except Bank Hol) from 12-5. Admission charge.

Close by on other side of main road is Marquess of Anglesey's Column, commemorating first Marquess who was second-in-command at Waterloo where he was injured. 115 steps to the top, with dizzy view from the platform. Tickets from column keeper's cottage with plastic roses round the door. Admission charge. Off A4080, south coast.

Penmon Priory: cluster of treasures out on eastern headland. Ruined monastic buildings of the 13th c joined by Prior's House (still lived in) to St Seiriol's Church. Cool dark nave has wonderful treasures, two Celtic crosses and a font of 1000AD. Carved figure of dragon on tympanum above south doorway. Sunday services in Welsh and English. Signposted out of Beaumaris on B5109. Footpath leads past clogged-up priory fishponds to St Seiriol's cell, with spring where he baptised converts in the 6th c. Dovecot nearby built about 1600 has charming domed roof with small cupola. Room for 1,000 birds. Road leads on to Black Point, free if you're walking, charge for a car, with lighthouse, coastguard cottages, Pilot House café and a good view of Puffin Island.

Llaneilian: small beach with pebbles, sand at low tide. Good swimming, rock-pools, water skiing. Car park at top of the hill. Amazing church here with tiny medieval chapel joined on at an odd angle, both full of extraordinary delights. High up in nave and chancel are carved figures – musicians in the chancel, two trumpeters and two pipers. Intricately carved oak rood-screen with arresting skeleton painted in the centre, surmounting gloomy motto: 'Colyn angau yw pechod' ('Sin is the sting of death'). Church normally locked, but key available from splendid caretaker at Pedwar Gwynt. About 1 mile off A5025 between Cemaes and Amlwch.

Llanddeusant: tiny village off the beaten track in the pleasant northwestern corner of the island, 3 miles inland from A5025. Two good mills here, but you'll need an Ordnance Survey map to find them. Ancient windmill and outbuildings on west side of the village (ref 341853) and splendid restored watermill towards Llantrisant (ref 351845). It's called Howell's Mill, built of rugged blue stone with slate roof and overshot wheel taking water from the Afon Alaw. Very narrow track, best to walk there. Tregwehelydd standing stone south of the village.

Rhoscolyn: on southernmost tip of Holy Island down a very narrow winding lane that finishes in dunes and sea. Good beach, wide and sandy with safe bathing, quiet and uncommercial. Good walks over the headland past St Gwenfaen's Well and pretty cottages at water's edge. White Eagle Inn at the village and just up the road at Four Mile Bridge a huge bonus, Jill's Home Cooking, picnics packed, cakes, pies, pizzas etc. All take-away and cooked by the cheery owner (tel Trearddur Bay 741285). Open seven days a week, lots of space to park.

Brynsiencyn: on A4080, jumping-off spot for various lanes that lead down to unusual and rather lovely stretch of shore running parallel with the mainland at Caernarfon. Small jetty at western end of shore road, with pub, the Mermaid, handsome,

solid building, basket meals. At the other end of the road is McCreadie and Teck, an oyster hatchery. It's a small business but the owners happily show people around. Best to telephone first (Brynsiencyn 411). Oysters and lobster occasionally available to buy.

Further east, secretive lane leads to exceedingly spooky spot, Llanidan Church, empty, with ruined 15th c arches, stretching into the churchyard smothered by yew. Romano-Celtic earthwork at Caer Leb, a rough pentagon with two banks and ditches. Earlier neolithic camp at Castell Bryn-Gwyn nearby.

South Stack Lighthouse: thrift and bladder campion bloom brightly on this headland, bordering the dizzy zigzag of steps that leads down the

cliffside and over a small suspension bridge to the lighthouse. Spectacular cliff scenery, with sea-birds wheeling out from vertical rock faces. Royal Society for the Protection of Birds reserve here. Lighthouse open (if foghorn's not blowing) weekdays noon-1 hour before sunset.

Llanddwyn Island: subject of a seductive leaflet issued by Tourist Board, rendering its fragile beauty and status as a National Nature Reserve even more precarious. Access – admission charge – along Forestry Commission road, through the strange wastes of Newborough Warren. Good walk along Llanddwyn beach to island at west end with cross, church dedicated to Dwynwen, patron saint of lovers, beacon and

Sixth-century Penmon Priory, rebuilt after being sacked by Vikings.

small row of cottages, restored and furnished as folk museum. Magic place, tread carefully.

SPECIALITIES

Windmills: must once have been as thick here as on Crete. None now working, but distinctive stone towers still remain. Some heavily disguised as des. det. res.

Antiquities: island is thick with them: 23 in the care of the Welsh Office but many more besides. Best of the many burial chambers is Bryncelli-ddu, carefully restored to a mound, with sheep doing a cheap mowing job. Inside is dark and mysterious, with huge stone pillars (patterned one is replica). Most disappointing is Barclodiad-y-gawres. The Giantess's Apronful, also with unusual patterned stones, but reconstructed with a heavy hand and many prestressed concrete beams.

Churches: enchanting, tiny buildings, often far from any settlement. Many, against the most basic tenet of faith, are locked, so that one is reduced to prowling round the outside of these ancient places of refuge, peering through cupped hands into the still interiors. Unusual island church of St Cwyfan, nr Aberffraw, approachable only at low tide. Two totally isolated ones in Llaniestyn rural area, the first on the side of a hill fort (OS map ref 588815), the second to the

east of Llandonna (ref 585796) with a pattern of vine leaves and grapes carved on the eaves of the porch. Llaneugrad Church on Parciau estate, nr Llanallgo, is still used, the churchyard marvellously silent, full of wild garlic and campion, hemmed in with trees.

ACTIVITIES

Fishing: localities, tackle suppliers, boat owners are fully detailed in 'Angling Guide to Wales' published by Wales Tourist Board, Welcome House, Llandaff, Cardiff. Menai Strait is good for bass, cod, whiting and conger. Boat fishing along rocky north coast for shark, tope and ray. Angling trips in MV Starida from Beaumaris Pier (tel Beaumaris 810746) or in Mary of Garth from Menai (tel Menai Bridge 713258). Licences for fresh water angling issued by Welsh Water Authority, Penrhosgarnedd, Bangor, Gwynedd (tel Bangor 51144).

Sailing: Royal Anglesey Yacht Club (Hon Sec R. Jones, tel Beaumaris 810295) welcomes visitors with boats. Dinghy sailing off Treath Bychan with Red Wharf Bay Sailing Club (Hon Sec Dr L. Fairman, tel 061 485 1799). Yachts for charter from Mermaid Marine Enterprises, 3 Bay View Court, Benllech (tel Tynygongl 2545).

Walking: 'Wales Walking' (Wales Tourist Board) lists 23 walks on the

island including the nature trails organised at the Wylfa Nuclear Power Station and the South Stack Lighthouse. Hendai Forest trail (Forestry Commission) near Newborough passes over lost village of Rhosyr, now buried beneath shifting sand (leaflet available at trail start). National Trust owns several tracts of land on north coast, the long shingle bank and headland at Cemlyn Bay and the coastline to the east of Cemaes.

Amlwch old port, down Quay St, is a good place for budding industrial archaeologists. Harbour, once greatest copper port in world, made of slate slabs laid vertically. Old Custom House with tower of 1853.

At Dulas old harbour to the east, now almost landlocked, the sea takes a great bite into the land. Footpath leads along the shore of the estuary, dead calm, with the sound of the sea breaking outside the bar. Salty sea kale grows vividly green amongst the dry grass. Take the No Through Road immediately after the chapel on the right-hand side of road at Llaneuddog, between Llanallgo and Amlwch.

Weaving: Bodeilo Weaving Centre, Talwrn, Nr Llangefni (tel Llangefni 722465), hand-spinning, natural wool dyeing and weaving on old wooden looms. Tuition available. Museum showing history and techniques of handloom weaving, concentrating on Anglesey and North Wales – also looms from Africa and Asia. Admission charge. Museum and shop open 10-6 in summer, weekends only in winter. Café serving vegetarian food.

Bird-watching: excellent chapter on bird-watching by Dr Richard Arnold in the official guide. Best site for seabirds is South Stack RSPB reserve, especially busy early May-mid-July. Guillemots, razorbills, possibly ravens and choughs. Puffins nest among pink thrift on the lower slopes. Walk from Porth Wen to Porth Llanlleiana to see kittiwakes, ravens, and white-throats. The wardens on Llanddwyn Island are immensely kind and helpful.

Golf: courses at Beaumaris (tel Beaumaris 810231); Trearddur Bay (tel Trearddur Bay 2119); Rhosneigr (tel Rhosneigr 810219); Bull Bay (tel Amlwch 830213).

Briefing by Anna Pavord

South Stack, best-known of Anglesey's lighthouses, atop a 100 ft off-shore islet.

BARDSEY

BY CHRISTOPHER WORDSWORTH

It is sometimes easy to forget that Anglesey is an island at all, but there is never any doubt that Bardsey belongs to the sea. Standing on the headland north of the beach at Aberdaron, the upper jaw of Hell's Mouth where the Lleyn Peninsula cranes a long neck towards Ireland, you feel you can almost use the island like a footstool; and in fact a good outboard will get you across into the anchorage on the eastward side inside a quarter of an hour when the sea is calm. Five significant monosyllables – 'when the sea is calm'. It is not for nothing that Bardsey in Welsh is Ynys Enlli, 'the island in the tides'. There are times when the Sound is a maelstrom and for all practical purposes the island two miles off is as remote as Tristan da

Some of the Connemara ponies bred on Bardsey by Jane Strick.

Cunha. They will tell you that there are 27 several and highly idiosyncratic currents in the tide-race, something which the gulls tend to verify when they settle on an apparently sleeping patch of water and are whisked away at a mysterious rate of knots.

Temperamental waters indeed, and to the uninitiated the Welsh boatmen at Pwllheli (three hours for the crossing), Abersoch (two hours) and Aberdaron may seem equally temperamental, not to say devious, when you parley with them about a passage. Respect will come. So, apart from oilskins, wellingtons, sleeping bag, binoculars, torch, iron rations (not forgetting milk-substitute), the best equipment for Bardsey is a good supply of fatalism. Many of those who have skimmed across with a packet of sandwiches on a still morning have been older, wiser and considerably hungrier by the time they set foot on the mainland again.

Bardsey was inhabited in neolithic times; there are traces of hut-circles on its gorse and bracken-covered hump. Here were brought the Thirteen Rarities of King Arthur's regalia to the House of Glass, and here Merlin is buried. The first Abbey was built in the sixth century, and throughout the Dark Ages Bardsey was a holy and mystic place.

Its links with the old Celtic Church, before it was made to conform by the Princes of Gwynedd, are lost in the sea-mists of history but the pilgrims' way, via the ancient battened-down church on the Aberdaron strand, where picnickers sometimes crack their hard-boiled eggs on indecipherable headstones, was as famous once as Iona or Lindisfarne. In the Middle Ages three pilgrimages to Bardsey equalled one to Rome. Twenty thousand saints on this western threshold of Heaven are reputed to be buried here, and any spade in the shallow soil would grate on bone.

The tower of the 13th-century Augustinian Abbey is the only remaining relic, its ruin rubbing shoulders with the Victorian-ornate cemetery of a later community. Until the 17th century it was a nest of pirates (read 'local gentry'). A community, twice evacuated this century, hung on until after the last war, farming sheep on the 440 acres and making lobster pots from the withy beds, but dwindling inevitably as the school closed and the resident minister was withdrawn. There was a crisis when the second private purchaser in five years treated the place as a private bolthole and discouraged visitors.

Today it is secured by the Bardsey Island Trust to ensure that its tradition and archaeology, as well as wild life, are protected. There are no known rights of way, but the Trust ensures limited public access. There are sturdy boats from Pwllheli on Saturdays between April and November which cater for weekly visitors only. Day returns are available only by private charter. Some of the old buildings – impressively solid and laagered against wind and sheep by fortress-thick walls – are now hostels. In the ornithological lull before the autumn migrations, families with children can stay in a handsome double farmhouse (attendant warden, Tilly lamps, Calor gas, Elsans). There are two provisos: book in advance, bring your own requirements with a margin for safety. There are two goats, no cows, one tractor, no electricity apart from the farmer's private generator, no telephone (the lighthouse transmitter in emergency) and no guarantee that you and the tide-race will see eye to eye about your date of departure.

The 'mountain' where Bardsey turns its back on the mainland and looks out towards Ireland (Wexford is visible on a clear day) and the gleaming red-banded Trinity House lighthouse at the tip of the isthmus, linked by the solitary cart track, command the eye as you put in to the Lilliputian harbour. Between them, from the scatter of buildings under the lee of the ridge, the ground slopes gently down to a rim of rocks and coves – with one sandy beach for the summer children – where the grey seals breed and bask, a green counterpane of tiny, dampish fields divided by earth dykes, bobbing with post-myxomatosis rabbits and starred with yellow flags and marsh marigolds in the spring. The seaward aspect of the whaleback is spectacular where it plunges steeply into the Sound, with the rare chough and raven nesting in its crags and a thronging cacophony of gulls and cormorants.

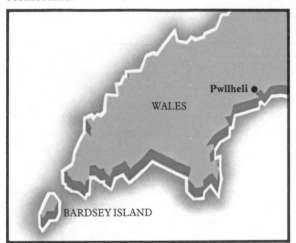

Bardsey seen from the mainland and (bottom right) *sheep being loaded on to the ferry.*

Trees on Bardsey are as infrequent as modesty in Parliament and for much the same reason, wind. So are vermin; there are no rats, the most unwelcome colonists being crows. A new species of pest, however, is beginning to infest the peace and threaten its tranquil future. The unpolluted waters have become a growing attraction to skin divers. Lobsters, which with sheep were once the mainstay of the economy, are increasingly hard to come by and the easier-caught crayfish have dwindled to vanishing point, according to Edward Strick, the island's fisherman-farmer. Since this is bound to have an unsettling effect on the seals also, there is a crying case for protective legislation.

This is truly an enchanted place, a place of ancient blessing – when words have blown away like spindrift you hear it in the deep heart's core. On a dark night when the Manx shearwaters come homing in to their burrows, with that weird sound like the cry of souls in torment, or with the rim of a moon on the mountain's shoulder and an opal-eyed white Connemara mare etched against a creaming sea, the present tense with all its imperatives seems curiously irrelevant.

CHRISTOPHER WORDSWORTH

APPENDIX: TRAVEL INFORMATION

——SHETLAND——

HOW TO GET THERE

By boat: P & O overnight car ferry departs Aberdeen 6pm three times a week all year arriving Lerwick approx 8am (connecting bus service for Yell, Unst and Fetlar). Sea-sickness sufferers beware – some very choppy waters south of Shetland where North Sea and Atlantic meet at Sumburgh Roost. P & O also run long weekend Mini-Cruises April, May, June, Sept and good value package holidays (eight days, nine nights) May to mid-Sept. Full details from P & O Ferries, PO Box 5, Jamiesons Quay, Aberdeen AB9 8DL, tel Aberdeen 572615: or Beaufort House, St Botolph St, London EC3A 7DX, tel 01-283 7272.
By air: frequent flights daily from Aberdeen to Sumburgh. By perverse rules of air travel it can be cheaper to fly to New York from London than to Shetland – no reduced fares are available. Apex fares can be booked from Scottish airports but not all the way from London. Flights most days from Wick, Inverness and Edinburgh.

GETTING AROUND

By road: drive-on drive-off ferries make it easy to get to major islands (see below). Muckle Roe, Burra and Trondra are linked by bridges. Plenty of self-drive car hire firms in Lerwick and Scalloway – Bolts, has airport desk, tel Sumburgh 60331 and A. J. Eunson, has office close by, tel Sumburgh 60209.

Sometimes better to park into wind because in gales doors can be damaged if opened carelessly, and salty mist is lethal to cars, so make sure windscreen-squirter is full and working. Bikes are ideal on calmer days – in Lerwick can be hired from Eric Brown, 7 Commercial Rd. John Leask & Sons, Esplanade, Lerwick, tel 3162, run coach tours all around Mainland and to Yell and Unst. Buses are not frequent, coming in from outlying districts to bring workers and shoppers to Lerwick early morning, and leaving Lerwick depot again 5pm, but you can use them to get to rural areas to spend a night or so.
By air: Loganair operate regular all-year service between Whalsay, Fetlar, Unst, Fair Isle and Mainland terminal at Tingwall 5 miles north of Lerwick. From mid-June to end Aug there's also a special service to Foula and Out Skerries. Details of fares, and times tel Gott 246. Loganair also operate a daily direct Tingwall-Edinburgh service.
By boat: Shetland Islands Council runs the excellent and very cheap passenger/car ferries. Timetable from Tourist Organisation. Vehicles best booked up to three days in advance by ringing: for Yell, Unst and Fetlar, Burravoe 259 or 268; for Whalsay, Symbister 376. Bookings not necessary for Bressay.

ACCOMMODATION

Best arranged through the Tourist Organisation which produces a comprehensive list ranging from plush and expensive hotels to hospitable farmhouses, youth hostels (one YHA, one private), self-catering cottages (which can be as primitive as a böd, traditional fishing station with hammocks etc), caravans and camping. If you decide on price range, and whether you want more central amenities of Lerwick and Mainland, or a remoter island, Tourist Organisation will do the rest. Always use first-class mail, and book at least 2 months in advance (oil men have caused a shortage), by March for self-catering.

INFORMATION

'Good Evening Shetland' – lively local radio programme on the air 92.7mHz 6.05-6.30pm with each day's news and forthcoming events. *The Shetland Times*, published Fri, is a good guide to entertainments, regattas etc. Travel books include: Eric Linklater's very readable 'Orkney & Shetland' (Hale); 'Traditional Life in Shetland' (Hale) by local author James Nicolson and 'The Windswept Isles' (Gifford) by Elizabeth Balneaves – both full of detail on history, crofting etc; 'The Natural History of Shetland' by R. J. Berry and J. L. Johnston (Collins) is comprehensive but specialised. Information-packed book on hundreds of types of rock found here from HMSO. Shetland Times Ltd and Hjaltland Bookshop, both in Commercial St, Lerwick will send publication lists and advance orders for those who want to read more before they go. 'Shetland Holiday Planner', from Tourist Organisation, is invaluable.

——ISLE OF WIGHT——

HOW TO GET THERE

Several routes to choose from. Hovercraft crossing Portsmouth and Southsea to Ryde is fastest at 7 mins, $1\frac{3}{4}$-hour journey approx from London.
Passengers: BR Sealink ferry Portsmouth/Ryde. Rail connection to Brading, Sandown and Shanklin. Hovercraft services – Hovertravel operate Southsea/Ryde, reservations tel Portsmouth 29988 or Ryde 65241; Hydrofoil – Red Funnel Services operate Southampton/Cowes, reservations tel Southampton 27599 or Cowes 292704. Coaches also run to Portsmouth and Southampton terminals and in summer sometimes cross on ferry as well. Details from local company or National Travel, Victoria Coach Station, London SW1W 9TP, tel 01-730 0202.
Cars: for peak summer holiday times it is essential to book as far in advance as possible. Some people book

as soon as they return from one year's holiday for the next. Sealink have two routes, Portsmouth/Fishbourne and Lymington/Yarmouth. BR computer slots in bookings in order of receipt Jan onwards, July-Aug Fri nights and Sats fully booked by April. For really early start, cars can go on 3am mail or 5am newspaper boats, daily except Sun. 24-hour Dial-a-Brochure service tel Portsmouth 751751, reservations tel Portsmouth 27744. Local Red Funnel line runs Southampton/Cowes. Bookings accepted Oct onwards for following year, July-Aug Sats fully booked by Jan, mid-week bookings can usually be managed 2 to 3 weeks beforehand. Reservations and timetables from 12 Bugle St, Southampton SO9 4LJ, tel Southampton 26211.

GETTING AROUND

By car: the most convenient way but roads can get congested in summer and parking places in towns difficult to find. Most towns have taxi service and self-drive car-hire firm.

By bus: service is good – open-top double-deckers blow the cobwebs away between Sandown and Ventnor in summer, and No 46 is useful route running hourly along coast between Yarmouth and Shanklin. Details of various Rover tickets giving unlimited bus/train travel, and timetables from Southern Vectis Omnibus Co Ltd, Nelson Rd, Newport PO30 1RD.

By coach: several companies run tours around the island. Details from Tourist Board or individual operators: Southern Vectis, depots in the principal towns; Moss Motor Tours, head offce 5 St John's Rd, Sandown, also booking offices in Ryde, Lake and Shanklin; West Wight Motor Bus Co, The Avenue, Totland or kiosk at Yarmouth Slipway, their starting point; Seaview Services Ltd, Seafield Garage, Seaview; Paul and Sons, 2a Union St, Ryde.

By bike: list of bike-hire companies available from Tourist Board.

By train: now only between Ryde, Brading, Sandown and Shanklin.

ACCOMMODATION

Half-inch thick brochure of places to stay: star-rated hotels, guest-houses, self-catering bungalows, flats, cottages, holiday camps and caravan and camping parks, from Tourist Board, Newport (address p. 29). Leaflet gives details of the island's camping sites. Red Funnel and Sealink organise package holidays combining ferry and hotel, details from Tourist Board.

INFORMATION

Best guide book is 'The Isle of Wight' by Pennethorne Hughes, one of Faber's Shell Guides, out of print but well worth getting from the library; 'Portrait of the Isle of Wight' by Lawrence Wilson gives historical background (Hale); for architecture read 'Hampshire and the Isle of Wight' by Nikolaus Pevsner and David Lloyd in The Buildings of England series (Penguin); 'First and Last Loves' by Sir John Betjeman has essays on the island (John Murray); six-page down-to-earth guide published in *Holiday Which*, December 1979, is stocked by most reference libraries; Tourist Board's 'Treasure Island' guide gives useful maps of towns, events – carnivals and so on – and entertainments list etc as well as accommodation; local CAMRA guide usually available from most of the real ale pubs, about half of all those on the island. The *Isle of Wight County Press*, good local paper, comes out every Sat.

ORKNEY

HOW TO GET THERE

By boat: from Scrabster nr Thurso to Stromness, P & O car ferry up to five times a day June-Sept, daily except Sun Oct-May. Takes 2 hours – fine views of cliffs of Hoy. P & O also offer 4-day package holiday on Orkney for motorists. Details and reservations from P & O Ferries Terminal, Pierhead, Stromness, tel Stromness 850655, or P & O Ferries, Beaufort House, St Botolph St, London EC3A 7DX, tel 01-283 7272. Also passenger ferries between John o' Groats and South Ronaldsay in summer, details from Thomas & Bews, Windiekap, Brough, Caithness, tel Barrock 619 or John o' Groats 353.

By air: two British Airways flights Mon-Fri from Aberdeen to Kirkwall connecting with planes from Heathrow. Fares expensive, but Apex fares available from Aberdeen and London. Flights from other Scottish airports by British Airways and Loganair (tel Kirkwall 3025).

GETTING AROUND

By boat: the Orkney Island Shipping Co operates regular services to both the northern and southern islands. They run round trips in large, comfortable passenger and cargo steamer Orcadia from Kirkwall to Eday, Papa Westray, Sanday, Stronsay and Westray twice a week. Leaves Kirkwall at 6.30am so good idea to spend night on board – cabins inexpensive. Short stays at each island while cargo unloaded – not much time for exploring. Weekly services to Egilsay, North Ronaldsay, Rousay and Wyre and daily services to Shapinsay. Also boats to southern islands, Flotta, Graemsay and Hoy from Stromness, and from Scapa (nr Kirkwall). Further details from Orkney Island Shipping Co, 4 Ayre Rd, Kirkwall, tel Kirkwall 2044 or 22 John St, Stromness, tel Stromness 850381. Also private boats to Hoy and Rousay (see *Where to Go, Islands*).

By air: Loganair operates invaluable scheduled service to all the most important islands. Tiny planes, only take eight passengers, local people use them a lot so always book in advance, especially in summer. Further details from Loganair, Kirkwall Airport, Kirkwall, tel Kirkwall 3025. Air charters and round trips also available, tel Kirkwall 2420.

By road: taxis are very expensive. Six self-drive car hire firms in Kirkwall, eg Scarth, Great Western Rd, Kirkwall, tel Kirkwall 2601 – they have desk at airport, tel Kirkwall 2125. Three self-drive car hire firms in Stromness eg E. M. H. Bain, 34 North End Rd, tel Stromness 850317. Cycles can be hired in Kirkwall, eg Rent-a-bike, Albert

St, tel Kirkwall 2995, and Stromness, eg Groat & Leask, 65 Victoria St, and on most of the islands – ask locals. The perfect transport, if it's not too windy.

Coach tours: operate in summer to visit major historic sites, details from James D. Peace, Junction Rd, Kirkwall, tel Kirkwall 2866. There are scheduled bus services, but buses few and far between.

ACCOMMODATION

Ranges from pleasant hotels, nothing exotic or very special, bed and breakfast or farmhouse accommodation – to self-catering houses and cottages all over Mainland and on most of the islands. The Tourist Office issues a booklet, 'Where to Stay in Orkney', that lists most of them. It is important to book early, especially for self-catering accommodation in the summer – January would be safe. If you write to the Tourist Office telling them the kind of place and setting you are looking for they will advise you. They also run an emergency booking service for people who arrive in Orkney with no reservations at their Kirkwall and Stromness offices.

There are seven hostels on Orkney for very cheap, basic accommodation. Two on Hoy and one on Mainland at Birsay are run by Orkney Island Education Dept, Council Offices, Kirkwall, tel Kirkwall 3535. Mainland hostel for parties, others open to anyone, phone or write to Education Dept to be sure of a bed. Scottish YHA hostels in Kirkwall and Stromness, both grade 2, open May-Sept. Also private hostels in Stromness – Mrs Brown, 47 Victoria St, tel Stromness 850661 – and Eday – W. Gray, School Place, Eday, tel Eday 263.

INFORMATION

The Orcadian, excellent local paper, comes out every Thurs. Radio Orkney's 'Morning Magazine', VHF 93.7 at 8.10-8.30am Mon-Fri has very good local weather forecast and travel information about the day's boats and planes plus local news.

Useful books include: 'The Ancient Monuments of Orkney' (HMSO); 'Orkney and Shetland' (Hale) by Eric Linklater – himself an Orcadian – vivid and readable about history and character of place. Almost all George Mackay Brown's writings, poems and prose, are marvellous evocations of atmosphere of Orkney, eg 'Greenvoe' (Penguin). Among many useful booklets obtainable at Tourist Office 'A Car Trail in Orkney's West Mainland' is especially good.

— THE CHANNEL ISLANDS —

HOW TO GET THERE

By air: Jersey and Guernsey: Flights to both islands from airports throughout the British Isles. Major companies like British Airways and British Caledonian fly to Jersey only; smaller airlines like British Midland and Air UK fly to both.

Alderney: Aurigny Air Services Ltd offers several flights daily from Southampton. Also flights several times a week from Shoreham. Restricted service in winter. Tel Eastleigh 612829 for more information on their services.

By sea: Sealink operate passenger/car ferries both from Weymouth and Portsmouth to Guernsey and Jersey. Daily crossings during summer months, less frequent winter service. From Portsmouth overnight journey, but from Weymouth choice of overnight or day journey; cabins can be booked. Fares slightly higher from Portsmouth. Sealink also do combination rail/steamer tickets, or special package holidays. Advisable to book early. Tel 01-834 2345 for details.

GETTING AROUND

By boat: Jersey to Guernsey/Sark/Alderney. Condor operate a hydrofoil service to each of these islands. During high season there is at least one a day, sometimes several, but only two weekly to Alderney. Address: Commodore Shipping Services Ltd, 28 Conway St, and Albert Quay, St Helier, tel Jersey 71263. Sealink operate a steamer to Guernsey from Jersey every day during the season, journey takes approx $1\frac{3}{4}$ hours. Address: 7 West's Centre, Bath St, St Helier. Tel Jersey 77122. Many travel agencies offer excursions to the other islands from Jersey. Two in St Helier are Summerday, 64 The Colomberie, tel Jersey 27841, and Bellingham, 6 Caledonian Pl, Weighbridge, tel Jersey 75019/71447. **Guernsey to Herm:** Herm Seaway, opposite Town Church in St Peter Port, runs daily boats throughout the season, tel Guernsey 24161, as does Trident, who have a kiosk by the Weighbridge Clock Tower (tel Guernsey 21379). Herm Seaway also does special afternoon and evening cruises; Trident does a disco cruise. **Guernsey to Sark:** Isle of Sark Shipping Company run several boats daily from St Peter Port – try to take the Ile de Serk cargo boat, all wood panelling and brass. Less frequent service in winter. Address: White Rock, St Peter Port, tel Guernsey 24059. **Guernsey to Alderney:** by Condor hydrofoil two days a week. Address: Passenger Dept, North Pier Steps, St Peter Port, tel Guernsey 26121.

By air: Jersey/Guernsey/Alderney: are linked by up to 18 flights daily operated by Aurigny Air Service. The planes are bright yellow 8- and 16-seater Trislanders, so small that passengers are sometimes seated according to weight. No telephone bookings, offices at airports and in St Helier (tel Jersey 35733), St Peter Port (tel Guernsey 23474) and St Anne (tel Alderney 2609). Essentially for commuters, best to avoid peak hours (8-10am and 4-6pm).

Within Jersey and Guernsey: speed limit on Jersey is 40mph, on Guernsey 35mph, and disc-zones are common – limited period parking for which you set a disc that comes with the hire car. If driving your own car, get discs at the Town Hall in St Helier, or from the Police Station in St Peter Port. Scores of car hire firms to choose from, but driving can be a problem for two reasons: Jersey has one of the highest ratios of cars to human beings in the world, so traffic is very heavy, while Guernsey has 300 miles of small non-signposted lanes – difficult for the solo driver to navigate. Ordnance Survey maps can be difficult to find, but most local bookstores stock the very useful Perry's Guide Maps. Even better is to use the efficient and comprehensive bus services, or go around the islands by bicycle.

ACCOMMODATION

The States Tourist Boards of both Jersey and Guernsey operate strict control over accommodation, using inspectors and grading systems, so standards are high and rooms often quite inexpensive. Self-catering is rarely available in Jersey because of the housing shortage, but there are lots of hotels, guest-houses and camping sites. Guernsey boasts a sea view from most accommodation in St Peter Port, self-catering and camping also available. For complete lists of accommodation on Guernsey, Sark and Herm write to: States of Guernsey Tourist Committee, PO Box 23, St Peter Port, Guernsey (tel Guernsey 23552). Mark envelope 'Accommodation'. For accommodation in Jersey write to: States of Jersey Tourism Office, Weighbridge, St Helier, Jersey (tel Jersey 78000). The Jersey Tourist Office also run a room-booking service (see *Jersey, Information*).

INFORMATION

'Guide to the Channel Islands' by Janice Anderson and Edmund Swinglehurst (Hamlyn Paperback) is an up-to-date, comprehensive guidebook. Useful for anyone planning a long stay. 'Portrait of the Channel Islands' by Raoul Lemprière (Hale). 'The Channel Islands' (part of the Island Guidebook series) by Peter Haining (New English Library). Volume on Channel Islands in the 'Islands' series (David & Charles).

——THE INNER HEBRIDES——

HOW TO GET THERE

Regular ferry service from Kennacraig terminal, Kintyre, 6 miles south of Tarbert on the road to Campbeltown. Through-route signposting invisible: look for indicator at the site – jetty, huts and (in high season) a small queue of cars. There is a choice of two lines: Caledonian MacBrayne go to Port Ellen twice daily May-Sept (similar winter timetable from end Sept). 2-hour journey. Ferry goes to Port Askaig once daily May-Sept (there you can get the 5-minute ferry to Jura). Western Ferries go to Port Askaig only, 3-hour journey, twice a day weekdays May-Sept, once Sun, less frequent winter service from end Sept. Caledonian MacBrayne officially demand reservations, plus cheque, not later than a week ahead of embarkation. Inquiries – see *Information*.

Loganair service between Glasgow and Islay, 2 to 3 flights a day in summer Mon-Sat. Less frequent winter timetable. Tel Glasgow 889 3181.

INFORMATION

If you want to read more than brief local brochures (not always reliably up-to-date and frequently unavailable), don't count on getting books on the spot. Here are several which we have found helpful. If you can, buy, borrow or consult them in a reference library: some are out of print. 'The Isle of Mull' by P. A. Macnab (David & Charles). The author has published an excellent pamphlet 'High-

ways and Byways in Mull', on sale at the Tourist Information Centre in Tobermory. 'Hebridean Islands: Colonsay, Gigha, Jura' by John Mercer (Blackie). 'Jura' by Donald Budge (John Smith). 'Colonsay and Oronsay' by J. V. Loder (1935). 'The Crofter and the Laird' by John McPhee (Angus & Robertson, 1972). 'Columba' by Ian Finlay (Gollancz). 'Skye and the Inner Hebrides' by Alasdair Alpin MacGregor (Hale, 1953). 'The Lands of the Lordship' by Domhnall MacEacharna (Argyll Reproductions, Port Charlotte, Islay). 'The Islands of Western Scotland' by W. H. Murray (Eyre Methuen). 'Six Inner Hebrides' by Noel Banks (David & Charles). For natural history 'The Highlands and Islands' by F. Fraser Darling and J. Morton Boyd (Collins).

Oban, Mull and District Tourist Organisation publish accommodation list (Mull, Coll, Tiree, Colonsay) and sell many of the local guides: Information Centre, Argyll Square, Oban, Argyll, tel Oban 3122/3551. Area accommodation list including Islay and Jura, from **Mid-Argyll, Kintyre and Islay Tourist Organisation,** The Pier, Campbeltown, tel Campbeltown 2056. Ferry timetables from Tourist Offices or Caledonian MacBrayne Ltd, Ferry Terminal, Gourock PA19 1QP, tel Gourock 33950. Western Ferries timetables and details of their cruises from 16 Woodside Crescent, Glasgow G3 7UT, tel Glasgow 332 9766. For those who want to visit several islands, 8 or 12-day Highlands and Islands 'Travelpass' gives unlimited travel on most buses, trains, ferries – June, July, Aug, Sept have slightly higher rates than other months. Details from Pickfords Travel, 25 Queensgate, Inverness, tel Inverness 32134.

Jura

HOW TO GET THERE

Western Ferries car ferry sails from Port Askaig, Islay (see ISLAY – *How to get there*) to Feolin about 12 times a day weekdays May-Sept, Sun 3 or 4 times. During winter, twice a day Tues-Fri, once a day Sat, Sun, Mon. No booking. Address for inquiries, see *Information*.

Colonsay

HOW TO GET THERE

Caledonian MacBrayne car ferry departs Oban May-Sept 3 times a week (winter timetable from end Sept). $2\frac{1}{2}$-hour journey. Address for details, see *Information*.

Mull

HOW TO GET THERE

Caledonian MacBrayne run regular 45-minute car ferry service Oban to Craignure roughly 6 times a day weekdays May-mid-Oct (reduced winter service from mid-Oct), 4 times Sun May-mid-Sept (no Sun service after mid-Sept).

A more frequent, but smaller (6 cars) 15-minute service runs from Lochaline in Morvern, 72 miles north of Oban (via the Corran ferry), to Fishnish, 5 miles north of Craignure, approximately 14 times a day weekdays June-mid-

Oct (10 times in winter), 18 times Sat (14 times), and 10 times Sun. No booking.

GETTING AROUND

Local buses between Craignure and Fionnphort (for Iona), Tobermory and Craignure; Tobermory and Calgary; Salen and Ulva. Consult the Tourist Information Centre, Tobermory for details. Limited services, especially Sun. Hire bikes from Brown's, Tobermory (tel Tobermory 2020); cars from Bruce Lindsay, The Depot, Craignure (tel Craignure 374) and Duncan MacGilp, Tobermory (tel Tobermory 2103). Bowmans run circular coach tours of island, including visit to Duart Castle, and trips to Iona, daily in summer. Advisable to book in height of season. Full details from their Booking Office, North Pier, Oban, tel Oban 3221, or tel Craignure 313.

Iona

HOW TO GET THERE

A bus from Craignure on Mull goes to the Iona ferry at Fionnphort three times daily, once on Sun: it takes 1 hour 35 minutes. The Iona ferry runs frequently every day of the week, all year, weather permitting, till early evening; Sept-May until later afternoon (not Sun). The trip takes 10 minutes. The current ferry-boat has been on duty for a few years only, but it has a pedigree of at least 14 centuries, which gives the service a claim to be Britain's oldest.

If you don't want to cross Mull, and are short of time, Caledonian MacBrayne runs the Sacred Isle Cruise from Oban twice a week early May-end-Sept leaving at about 9 o'clock, giving you a look at Staffa (no landing), usually allows an hour on Iona and gets back to Oban early evening.

Western Ferries offer a cruise on a high-speed catamaran from Oban three times a week until beg Oct. This leaves Oban at lunchtime, offers about 2 hours on Iona, weather permitting, and returns to Oban early evening. Sun till end Sept there is a cruise from Oban around Mull, including Iona, where you have about $1\frac{3}{4}$ hours: it leaves Oban at lunchtime, returning early evening. For addresses of both companies, see *Information*.

Coll

HOW TO GET THERE

May-Sept Caledonian MacBrayne car ferry departs Oban 4 times a week. Cars must be booked, passengers with sleeping berth reservations can stay aboard the night before sailing. Different winter timetable. Address for details, see *Information*.

Tiree

HOW TO GET THERE

Loganair's 16-seater flies to Tiree's Reef airfield once daily Mon-Sat in summer. Different winter timetable. Tel Glasgow 889 3181. May-Sept Caledonian MacBrayne car ferry departs Oban early morning, usually calling at Mull

and Coll on the way. Cars must be booked, passengers with sleeping berth reservations can stay aboard the night before sailing. Different winter timetable. Address for details, see *Information*.

ISLE OF SKYE

HOW TO GET THERE

By boat: at Kyleakin and Kylerhea, Skye is less than 5 mins by ferry from the mainland. The crossing from Mallaig to Armadale takes 30 mins, views of Skye are splendid. Big car ferries on this route five times a day (not Sun) mid-May-late Sept. In winter less frequent passenger service only. The most straightforward crossing is from Kyle of Lochalsh to Kyleakin. On weekdays two ferries operate in summer to minimise delays, fewer crossings Sun. Both ferry services run by Caledonian MacBrayne, information and booking tel Gourock 33755. Oldest and shortest crossing from Glenelg to Kylerhea, small car ferry, weekdays only, runs frequently 9-5. Details from M. A. Mackenzie, tel Glenelg 224.

By air: from June-end Sept, Loganair runs a midday flight from Glasgow to Broadford on weekdays, takes 1 hour. Out of season fewer flights. Details from Loganair, tel Glasgow 889 3181. Comprehensive and invaluable guide 'Getting Around the Highlands and Islands' is available, free, at most Scottish Tourist Board offices, or direct from Highlands and Islands Development Board, 27 Bank St, Inverness.

GETTING AROUND

By road: good main roads from Kyleakin to Portree, Uig and Dunvegan. Most others are single-track with passing places, so parking is sometimes difficult and caravans can be a menace. Self-drive car hire from Beaton's (tel Portree 2002), Ewen MacRae (tel Portree 2554) and Sutherland's Garage (tel Broadford 225/226). There are taxis in Portree and Armadale and a minibus for hire, tel Portree 2996. You hire bicycles from Kyleakin (tel Kyle 4532) and Portree (tel Portree 2521). There are daily bus tours and Highland Omnibuses run a long-distance service from Portree to Inverness and from Uig to Glasgow. You can use these to get from north to south of island, but they're not cheap. Local bus services from other parts of island to Portree tend to be geared to people coming into work or school, so you can use them if you want to spend the night in a rural B & B. Post-buses with a few seats do circuits in some outlying areas. Some buses from Portree to Uig to tie in with ferries to Outer Hebrides. Information from the Highland Omnibus Office, Park Rd, Portree (tel Portree 2647).

By boat: drive-on drive-off ferry to Raasay sails from Sconser weekdays, 3 trips a day in school holidays. You could spend day there, leaving Sconser at about 10 and returning from Raasay in the afternoon (there is an earlier and later boat in term-time). Isle of Soay (off west coast opposite Cuillins) is privately owned, but you can get permission to land – telephone Mallaig 2440 – and charter boat from Elgol, tel Loch Scavaig 225/213.

ACCOMMODATION

Skye has some splendid gentlemanly hotels. The most famous of these is the Sligachan Hotel (tel Sligachan 204), owned by Ian Campbell, convenor of the Highland Regional Council. From here pre-war climbers made pioneering ascents in the Cuillins – fascinatingly documented by them in Scottish Mountaineering Club's Climbers' Book, which you can see at hotel. Kinloch Lodge Hotel, Lord Macdonald's ex-shooting/fishing lodge in isolated position on edge of loch on Sleat, is very comfortable, with excellent varied food cooked by Lady Macdonald (tel Isle Ornsay 214). Isle Ornsay Hotel (Gaelic name is Tigh-Osda Eilean Iarmain) is another ex-shooting lodge beautifully situated on harbour promontory. Four-poster beds, Gaelic-speaking staff, owned by Iain Noble. (Tel Isle Ornsay 266.) Skeabost House Hotel (tel Skeabost Bridge 202) is in grand old manner, with billiard room, log fires, the day's catch of fish laid out on a marble slab at door. Good food. Flodigarry Hotel (tel Duntulm 203), close to Quiraing, with Flora Macdonald's cottage in grounds, is worth a visit for its British Raj-type interiors, like an Ealing comedy set. Food from hotel's own farm. Attractive old inns include the Ardvasar Hotel (tel Ardvasar 223) at Armadale, with good food, and Stein Inn (tel Waternish 208). All but the Ardvasar Hotel and Isle Ornsay Hotel shut in winter, some only open end May, so check.

There are many more good hotels on Skye, also comfortable guest-houses, and B & Bs all over the island. Plenty of self-catering croft cottages and caravans – some astonishingly cheap; caravan and/or camp-sites at Staffin, Portree, Edinbane, Dunvegan, Broadford, Glen Brittle. Youth hostels at Uig, Glen Brittle, Broadford.

The Isle of Skye Tourist Organisation produces a Holiday Accommodation Register, they will send you this booklet and for small fee will book you into the place of your choice. If you are touring, you can use Book-A-Bed-Ahead scheme at any Scottish Tourist Board Office.

INFORMATION

West Highland Free Press comes out Fri (see *Specialities*). Derek Cooper has written three books on Skye: 'Hebridean Connection'; 'Road to the Isles' and 'Skye', with gazetteer and anthology packed with fascinating information. (All Routledge & Kegan Paul.) Scottish Mountaineering Club's district guide, 'The Island of Skye' by Malcolm Slesser, has useful sections on geology, flora and fauna etc, and detailed descriptions of the peaks in the Cuillins. 'Skye Directory', profits from which go to the local hospital, is an excellent introduction to the island. Portree High School produced 'Skye Today', a serious attempt by the pupils to counteract the 'misty isle' romanticism of most tourist literature and talk about current issues, as well as drawing on their families' memories of the past. Now a bit out of date but still well worth reading. Tourist Organisation's guide 'Over the Sea to Skye'. Ordnance Survey cover Skye, sheets 23 and 32. OUP publish combined volume of 'Johnson's Journey to the Western Islands of Scotland and Boswell's Journal of a Tour of the Hebrides with Samuel Johnson', hardback and paperback. Dent also publish Boswell's 'Journal of a Tour of the Hebrides' in their Everyman library.

Muck

HOW TO GET THERE

Caledonian MacBrayne passenger ferry leaves Mallaig two or three times a week. Some sailings direct, but on others passengers take Isle of Muck launch from Eigg which connects with ferry. Details from Caledonian MacBrayne, The Pier, Mallaig (tel Mallaig 2403) or The Pier, Gourock (tel Gourock 33950).

Arisaig Marine run day trips from Arisaig 4 times a week. For details, tel Arisaig 224/678. Charter boats also available from Isle of Muck Farms (tel Mallaig 2362), Bruce Watt (tel Mallaig 2233/2320), Arisaig Marine (tel Arisaig 224/678), Eigg Estate (tel Mallaig 82413).

Eigg

HOW TO GET THERE

Caledonian MacBrayne passenger ferry calls at Eigg four times a week, with two departures Sat in summer, leaving from Mallaig on the mainland. Details from Caledonian MacBrayne, The Pier, Mallaig (tel Mallaig 2403) or The Pier, Gourock (tel Gourock 33950).

Day trips in summer normally available from Glenuig on the mainland. Fare and schedules from The Estate Office, Isle of Eigg, Inverness-shire (tel Mallaig 82413). Also from Arisaig Marine (tel Arisaig 224/678) and Bruce Watt, The Pier, Mallaig (tel Mallaig 2233/2320). Charters can be arranged through Eigg Estate, Bruce Watt, Arisaig Marine and Isle of Muck Farms (tel Mallaig 2362).

Rhum

HOW TO GET THERE

Caledonian MacBrayne passenger ferry calls at Rhum four times a week (two departures on Sat in summer), leaving from Mallaig. Details from Caledonian MacBrayne, The Pier, Mallaig (tel Mallaig 2403) or The Pier, Gourock (tel Gourock 33950).

Day trips June-Sept and charters usually available from Arisaig Marine Ltd, Arisaig, Highland Region (tel Arisaig 224/678) and Bruce Watt, The Pier, Mallaig (tel Mallaig 2233/2320). St Just Marine, Oban (tel Lochavich 212) take in Rhum on longer trips and may do charters. Strollamus Boats on Skye (tel Broadford 596/7) arrange charters.

Canna

HOW TO GET THERE

Caledonian MacBrayne passenger ferry calls at Canna four times a week, with two departures on Sat in summer, leaving from Mallaig. Details from Caledonian MacBrayne, The Pier, Mallaig (tel Mallaig 2403) or The Pier, Gourock (tel Gourock 33950). Day trips or charters may be available from Bruce Watt, The Pier, Mallaig (tel Mallaig 2233/2320). St Just Marine, Oban (tel Lochavich 212) take in Canna on longer trips.

THE OUTER HEBRIDES

HOW TO GET THERE

By sea: Caledonian MacBrayne offer a car ferry service to every island except Benbecula, which has no commercial port. Ferry to Lewis leaves from Ullapool, on the mainland, ferries to Harris and North Uist depart from Uig on Skye, ferries to South Uist and Barra leave from Oban, also on mainland. There is at least one boat daily to each island, except Barra, which has four weekly from June-end Sept but fewer in winter. Sleeping berths are available at an extra charge. Cheaper excursion tickets are available but valid for 4 days only and you must return by the same route. A scheme called 'Island Hopscotch' includes all the islands, leaving from Oban and returning to Ullapool, or vice versa. Reduced fares during winter months, but service is also less frequent during the off-season. For more information contact: Caledonian MacBrayne Ltd, Ferry Terminal, Gourock PA16 1QP, tel Gourock 33755.

By air: British Airways fly to Stornoway daily except Sun via Inverness or Glasgow. To combat expensive air fare from London, fly Apex via Inverness – for some inexplicable reason cost is much lower. British Airways also fly to Benbecula from Glasgow daily except Sun. The Scottish airline Loganair flies to Barra from Glasgow daily (no Sun service Sept-May). This is a most enchanting route, soaring over mountains and many of the Inner Hebridean islands to land on Barra's gleaming, sandy runway.

GETTING AROUND

The Highlands and Islands Development Board publish an invaluable book called 'Getting Around the Highlands and Islands', with details of ferries, planes, bus routes. Available from Stornoway Tourist Office.

By road: a car is essential for anyone with a family or staying outside major communities. Buses do run, but not very often, and they might not take you where you need to go. Car hire is fairly scarce – several firms in Stornoway but cars get booked up quickly; on smaller islands there may be one firm or none, with most cars off the road due to rust-inducing sea air and/or batterings from the small and congested lanes. Tourist offices can help, but visitors would be well advised to bring their own.

By air: Loganair operate at least one flight daily except Sun from Stornoway to Benbecula. On some days the plane continues to Barra but times vary according to tides and weather conditions. Tel Stornoway 3067 or Benbecula 2310.

by boat: Caledonian MacBrayne run car ferries from Tarbert in Harris to Lochmaddy in North Uist. Also a service from Lochboisdale in South Uist to Castlebay, Barra. Mr D. A. Macaskill operates a private ferry for passengers only between Leverburgh, Harris and Newton Ferry, North Uist, tel Berneray 230. Donald Campbell and his dog Splash will take carless passengers from Ludag, South Uist to Eoligarry in Barra, tel Lochboisdale 216. These boats and drivers can sometimes be chartered for trips around the numerous smaller islands.

ACCOMMODATION

The Western Isles Tourist Organisation produces a comprehensive accommodation list which ranges from luxury hotels in Stornoway to crofters' homes on the islands. Also included is self-catering – mainly caravans but one or two private concerns rent cottages; check with specific tourist office on each island. For copy of accommodation list write to Western Isles Tourist Organisation, 4 South Beach St, Stornoway, Isle of Lewis, Outer Hebrides; the Tourist Organisation also includes Caledonian MacBrayne ferry timetables and, if requested, will add a list of caravan and camping sites.

The Book-A-Bed-Ahead scheme allows you to reserve a room for the following night from the Scottish mainland or one of the other Hebridean islands. Specify type of accommodation required and number of beds to the nearest tourist office plus small fee and deposit, payable in advance, they will arrange it for you. There is also a local booking service for personal callers only. All tourist offices in the Western Isles are open May-Sept for late ferry arrivals, and the Stornoway office is open all year round.

INFORMATION

Mainland newspapers (Scottish and English) arrive in Stornoway on the plane from Glasgow and are in the shops by 11.30am, be prepared to queue. Sun papers arrive 1pm Mon and remain in shops all week. Hotels on other islands often have subscriptions to mainland papers, otherwise fairly hard to purchase one. Local papers are the *Stornoway Gazette*, published on Thurs, or the excellent *West Highland Free Press*, published on Fri.

Useful books include 'Lewis and Harris', 'The Uists and Barra', 'St Kilda and other Hebridean Outliers' (which includes many of the small offshore islands) by Francis Thompson, published by David & Charles. Unfortunately only the Uists book is still in print, the others, however, are commonly available in libraries. Acair Ltd is a small publishing company with offices at Cromwell Street Quay, Stornoway. They have recently published seven titles, all of local interest, including an English/Gaelic dictionary, 'A Hebridean Naturalist' by Peter Cunningham, and children's books. For brochures and prices write to above address. 'Folk Songs and Folklore of South Uist' by Margaret Fay Shaw is the definitive work. Published by OUP.

SCILLY ISLES

HOW TO GET THERE

By boat: classic and cheapest way, but people on dry land have been known to feel seasick just looking at the Scillonian ploughing her way across to Penzance harbour. Summer season (late March-mid-Oct) daily boat leaves Penzance Mon-Fri, two boats on Sat in high summer. Trip to St Mary's takes 2½ hours. Winter sailings depend on flower trade. Full details from Isles of Scilly Steamship Co Ltd, St Mary's, Isles of Scilly (tel Scillonia 22357).

By air: seven flights most days till end Oct (more Wed and

Sat) by helicopter from Penzance to St Mary's. Choppers are Sikorsky S61s and take about 20 minutes to do crossing. Comfortable and quick, but only carry 32, so essential to book. Information from British Airways Helicopters, Penzance Heliport, Penzance (tel Penzance 3871/2). Car park on the spot. Brymon Airways fly to St Mary's from Newquay, Plymouth and Exeter with connecting services from Heathrow, Gatwick and Manchester. Information from Brymon Airways, City Airport, Roborough, Plymouth (tel Plymouth 707023).

Bus shuttles from St Mary's airport into town and does regular service round island, no need for car. There's only 11 miles of road on St Mary's, perhaps a mile or so on each of the other islands.

GETTING AROUND

Very simple. You go when the boatman says he'll take you. When you're *there*, you walk. Cycling is ideal for St Mary's, though unnecessary on off-islands. Bikes can be hired from P. Guy at Atlantic View, High Lanes, St Mary's or from Buccabu, Littleporth, St Mary's. If you are booked for holiday on off-island, launch will have been arranged to collect you from St Mary's Quay. Charges depend on number sharing boat.

Network of inter-island trips posted up daily on all islands, at Timothy's Corner, Tresco, outside PO on St Agnes. Boats leave St Mary's Quay twice daily for off-islands.

ACCOMMODATION

The Council of the Isles of Scilly, Town Hall, St Mary's, produces an accommodation list each year for all the islands, ranging from poshest hotels to smallest campsites. Essential to book, or you may find yourself turned firmly back to the mainland. Use first-class mail and send sae. They also have simple guide and map of St Mary's.

Tresco, the most sophisticated of the off-islands, is also the most geared to visitors. The Estate Office, Tresco (tel Scillonia 22849) will send information about the Island Hotel, the New Inn (exceedingly good) or the 15 holiday cottages and flats in Tresco Abbey available to let. Time share scheme for some cottages offers an annual week for 40 years, prices vary considerably according to season. Bryher has brand-new Hells Bay Hotel (tel Scillonia 22947), St Agnes and St Martin's no hotels at all, but good small guest-houses.

INFORMATION

Scillonian magazine, published by Mumford's on St Mary's twice a year, is packed with island events and gossip. Useful books include: 'Portrait of the Isles of Scilly' (Hale), a local's view by Clive Mumford, editor of *Scillonian*; 'The Fortunate Isles' by R. L. Bowley (Bowley Publications), excellent on history, especially Civil War, and legends; good series of small guides by David Hunt and Frank Gibson, eg 'Wild Flowers of Scilly', 'Sea and Shore Birds of the Isles of Scilly'; all locally available. 'Islands' by John Fowles and photographer Fay Godwin (Cape), has vivid text and pictures; 'Island Camera' is fascinating collection by John Arlott and Frank Gibson of

old Scilly photographs (try to get it from library). 'Sunset over Samson' is record of music and songs from Scilly made by local people, from Bulb Shop and other St Mary's shops – also available cassette 'Talking About Scilly', all proceeds to Royal National Lifeboat Institution.

————ISLE OF MAN————

HOW TO GET THERE

By boat: Steam Packet Co ferries sail daily all year, except winter Sun, between Douglas-Liverpool, mainly drive-on/drive-off. Journey time $3\frac{3}{4}$ hours. Sealink Isle of Man vessel sails between Douglas-Heysham daily all year, all drive-on/drive-off. Journey time $3\frac{3}{4}$ hours.

In summer, Steam Packet Co sails between Douglas and Fleetwood, Ardrossan, Belfast, Dublin, Llandudno, mainly drive-on/drive-off except Llandudno, which is passenger only. Standard fare same as Douglas-Liverpool.

Full details: The Steam Packet Co, PO Box 5, Douglas, Isle of Man, tel Douglas 3824. Sealink Isle of Man, The Harbour, Heysham, Lancashire, tel Heysham 53802.

By air: flights daily to Ronaldsway, about 8 miles from Douglas, from main airports Belfast, Liverpool, London/ Heathrow, Manchester, plus less-frequent service from other airports, by three carriers – Air UK, British Midland Airways, Dan Air.

GETTING AROUND

Summer surfeit of trains, steam and electric, provides element of fun as well as transport. Narrow-gauge steam, running from May-Sept/Oct, chuffs from Douglas to Port Erin in an hour or so. Steam Railway Museum at Port Erin, open 10-5 while railway running. Electric railway, running April-Sept/Oct, with superb coastal views, takes $1\frac{1}{4}$ hours from Douglas to Ramsey. Also trips from Laxey to the top of Snaefell. Various runabout tickets for trains and buses. Full details: Railway Terminus Building, Strathallan Crescent, Douglas, tel Douglas 4549; Central Bus Station, Lord St, Douglas, tel Douglas 3464. Plenty of car-hire firms, rates are reasonable. Drive 'as in the United Kingdom'.

ACCOMMODATION

Several hundred establishments registered with Tourist Board, most aiming at the family market, ranging from good hotels to cheap B & Bs; also tourist flats, holiday hostels and camping sites. Free classified guide from Tourist Board Information Bureau, 13 Victoria St, Douglas, tel Douglas 4323. Free Findabed service, Central Promenade, Douglas, tel Douglas 24464, Mon-Fri 9-5.30, Sat 9-1.

INFORMATION

Manx Radio on 219 medium wave and 96.9 VHF put out 'Summertime Spotlight' about places tourists can visit, Mon-Fri mornings 9.15-9.45, with a repeat on Sat 1.10-1.40. 'Sunday Magazine' round-up goes out 9.30-11.30am; a guide to what's on during the week happens sometime between 5 and 6 on Sun evening. Newspapers, all weekly; *Courier, Examiner, Weekly Times, Manx Star, Peel City Guardian.*

Useful books include: 'Isle of Man' (Geographia Guide) for basic touring; 'Portrait of the Isle of Man' by E. H. Stenning (Hale) for a general picture; 'The Isle of Man' by R. H. Kinvig (Liverpool University Press) for history; 'The story of the Isle of Man' by C. W. Airne (Norris Modern Press, in two parts) for intriguing historical anecdotes. 'Isle of Man – A Book About the Manx' (Arts Council, hardback or paperback) has photographs of places and people plus preface by John Berger and a castigation of the State of Man by the emigré Manx photographer who took the pictures, Christopher Killip.

ST KILDA

HOW TO GET THERE

As the gannet flies, St Kilda is about 100 miles west of the mainland of Scotland and 40 west of the Outer Hebrides. Unless you hire your own boat, you can get there only with the assistance of the National Trust for Scotland which sends work parties out each summer to maintain the houses, the schoolhouse and the church, or by going on one of the cruises organised by Hebridean Holidays Ltd. There are usually about five work-parties a year, for 2 weeks at a time. Applicants are selected in Jan for the coming year. More important than special skills, says the NTS, are 'a sense of humour, an ability to work in a group in all weather conditions, and some zest for the project'. Details from St Kilda Secretary, National Trust for Scotland, 5 Charlotte Sq, Edinburgh EH2 4DU (tel Edinburgh 226 5922). Some of Hebridean Holidays' cruises visit St Kilda, mountainous seas permitting, for up to 10 days and passengers can explore. Full details from Hebridean Holidays Ltd, 91 Rose St, Edinburgh EH2 3DT (tel Edinburgh 225 9530/1).

LUNDY

HOW TO GET THERE

The island's 200-ton cargo boat *Polar Bear* takes 12 passengers and leaves three times a week from Ilfracombe. Bookings for *Polar Bear* through Lundy Administrator (see below).

Comfortable Millcombe House, open April-Oct, is the island's hotel, built in 1835 in classical style. It has a pleasant country-house atmosphere and excellent food. There are 10 self-catering cottages scattered about Lundy. Some are historic buildings – indeed two are inside the Marisco Castle keep; others are rather more recent, but all are comfortable. There is a self-catering hostel at The Barn, another in the former lighthouse keepers' quarters at the Old Light, handsome granite

buildings. It offers good, if basic, accommodation.

The island shop stocks most necessities, but fresh meat and some other fresh supplies have to be ordered in advance. Shop and Tavern prices are subsidised so that they are not much more than on the mainland, but accommodation is not cheap. Information and bookings from the Administrator, Lundy, via Ilfracombe, Devon, tel Barnstaple 73333.

ARRAN

HOW TO GET THERE

Caledonian MacBrayne run two car ferry routes: Ardrossan-Brodick, 1 hour, 5-6 sailings weekdays, less on Sun. Cheaper off-season fares, when there are slightly fewer sailings. Claonaig-Lochranza, 30 mins, about 8 sailings daily, April-Oct only. Island Hopscotch tickets allow you to use one ferry route to get there and leave by the other. Advisable to book cars for weekend Ardrossan-Brodick sailings. Claonaig-Lochranza not bookable. Full details from Caledonian MacBrayne Ltd, Ferry Terminal, Gourock PA19 1QP, tel Gourock 34568.

GETTING AROUND

Buses are rather infrequent, especially on western side of island. Self-drive cars need to be booked in advance from Arran Transport and Trading, Brodick, tel Brodick 2121 – they also run taxi service. Bikes – one of the best ways of seeing the island, but there are a few steep climbs – can be hired from several places. A list is available from the Tourist Information Centre.

ACCOMMODATION

Tourist Information Centre produces register of hotels, guest-houses, self-catering houses etc. Island gets fairly crowded July and Aug, so it's wise to book early. Two Scottish YHA youth hostels, one at Lochranza, one at Whiting Bay, and several approved camping sites – list from Tourist Information Centre. Farmers not listed may allow camping if you ask.

INFORMATION

Highly recommended book by local author Robert McLellan, 'The Isle of Arran' (David & Charles). Diminutive local paper, *The Arran Banner* – named after the celebrated local potato – comes out Sat, has news of discos, fêtes. And, of course, the Tourist Information Centre at Brodick.

BUTE

HOW TO GET THERE

Caledonian MacBrayne operate two car ferry routes: Wemyss Bay to Rothesay, 30 mins, about 10 sailings weekdays, fewer on Sun. Colintraive to Rhubodach, 5 mins across Kyles of Bute, shuttles back and forth daily. No need to book cars on either route. Timetables and inquiries – Caledonian MacBrayne Ltd, Ferry Terminal, Gourock PA19 1QP, tel Gourock 34567.

GETTING AROUND

Adequate local bus service to beaches etc. Cars can be hired from Bute Motor Co, Union St, Rothesay, tel Rothesay 2330, and bikes from Calder Bros, Bridge St, Rothesay. Coach tours of island start daily in summer from Albert Place, Rothesay. Some also cross on Rhubodach ferry for trips to Oban, Loch Lomond etc – these need to be booked in advance at Tourist Organisation, which also has leaflet giving details.

ACCOMMODATION

Tourist Organisation publishes register of hotels, guesthouses, self-catering flats etc. Most are in Rothesay but there are also a few at Kilchattan Bay, small village at south end of Bute with red sandy beach. Booking needs to be done well ahead for July and Aug, especially for the Glasgow Fair weeks, usually last two in July.

INFORMATION

The Buteman, published Fri, has details of local events. 'What's On' is main entertainments guide, delivered weekly to all the hotels. Useful guides include 'Walks and Drives in Bute', and 'Visitor's Guide to Rothesay and the Island of Bute', readily available locally. The best book is 'The Island of Bute' by Ian S. Munro (in David & Charles's Islands series). If you can get a copy, you'll find some entertaining stories in 'Bute and the Cumbraes' by R. Angus Downie (1934).

———— LINDISFARNE ————

HOW TO GET THERE

Lindisfarne is reached by causeway – note tide timetable displayed on approach road and on island. Buses every day from Berwick-upon-Tweed July and Aug, but only twice a week throughout rest of year. Here again times depend on tides, as does the length of the time one can spend there – 3 to 6 hours. On certain days, there are connections to and from Newcastle, Morpeth and Alnwick. For further information contact Northumbria Tourist Board, 9 Osborne Terrace, Jesmond, Newcastle, tel Newcastle 817744: National Trust Information Centre, Main St, Seahouses, tel Seahouses 720424: Berwick-upon-Tweed Tourist Information Centre, Castlegate Car Park, tel Berwick 7187: Alnwick Tourist Information Centre, The Shambles, Northumberland Hall, tel Alnwick 603120.

Priory ruins open April-Sept 9.30-6.30 daily, Oct-March 9-4 weekdays, Suns 2-4. Department of the Environment. Small admission charge. Castle open beginning April to mid-April Wed, Sat, Sun 2-5, mid-April-Sept daily except Fri (open Good Fri) 11-1, 2-5; Oct Sat and Sun 2-5, National Trust. Admission charge, special rates for parties.

Boats to the Farnes leave Seahouses harbour on average three times daily July-Aug, otherwise twice daily, provided weather is reasonable. Telephone first if travelling from any distance, W. Shiel, tel Seahouses 720308, H. J. Hanvey and Sons, tel Seahouses 720388, W. McKay, tel Seahouses 720155. 2-2½ hour trip. Warm waterproof clothing essential always, boats are open and it can be rough and damp. Small children and babes in arms cheerfully taken with their parents. Parties landed whenever possible – ie nearly always – on the Inner Farne for about 45 mins, which gives plenty of time to explore. Sheer cliffs on south, young children must be closely watched here. No dogs. NT. Landing fee charged. W. Shiel's morning trips usually land on Staple Island, excellent place to photograph birds, some others go to Longstone Island. Private charters may occasionally be booked in advance from W. Shiel for all-day trips.

There is plenty of good accommodation available in the area: contact Northumbria Tourist Board. Several local landowners have excellent cottages which have been converted for family holiday lets within easy driving distance of Lindisfarne and the Farne Islands.

———— ANGLESEY ————

HOW TO GET THERE

Rather a cheat as an island, because you can drive all the way. Telford's great bridge over the Menai Strait, opened in 1826, put an end to the ferryman's trade. The railway bridge to the west was built 24 years later by George Stephenson's son, Robert. Big fire in 1970 provided excuse for new road bridge on top of railway, officially opened by Prince Charles in 1980.

GETTING AROUND

Bikes are better than cars on the maze of tracks and lanes inland and the country is reasonably flat. Buses operated by Crosville Motor Services (tel Bangor 2445) run between Beaumaris and the main resorts of the north coast, Benllech, Amlwch (every hour) and Cemaes Bay (every 2 hours). Buses from Menai Bridge through Llangefni to Holyhead (every hour) and through Newborough (every 2 hours).

ACCOMMODATION

The island has a long history as a holiday base and is well covered with hotels of all sorts, bed and breakfast, campsites. Many advertise in the official guide, and the Tourist Office operates an accommodation register.

INFORMATION

Holyhead and Anglesey Mail, and *Holyhead and Anglesey Chronicle*, out Thurs, are both full of local news, entertainments etc. For details of all sorts of local events contact Recreation Dept, Isle of Anglesey Borough Council, Llangefni (tel Llangefni 722966). Useful books include: 'Companion Guide to North Wales' by Elisabeth Beazley and Peter Howell (Collins), good chapter on Anglesey; 'Portrait of North Wales' by Michael Senior (Hale), two chatty chapters on Anglesey; 'Hidden Haunts in Gwynedd' by David Price, useful little pamphlet available locally. Read 'Wild Wales', George Borrow's Victorian classic, for interest rather than information.

BARDSEY

HOW TO GET THERE

To stay, must book 14 days minimum in advance through Mrs Helen Bond, 21 Gestrige Rd, Kingsteignton, Newton Abbot, Devon (tel Newton Abbot 68580). Dogs and camping not permitted.

Official boat plies every Saturday in season, or first fine day following, from Pwllheli at Lifeboat House. Cars can be left safely in car park. Private charter available. Shorter, cheaper trips sometimes possible from Aberdaron, weather and boatmen willing. Protect belongings in large polythene sacks. Local contact for help and on-the-spot information: David Thomas, Tyddyn Du Farm, Criccieth, Gwynedd (tel Criccieth 2239).

INDEX

ACKNOWLEDGEMENTS

The Observer Magazine thanks the following, whose photography was commissioned for the original pull-out series: Christopher Cormack – on pages 137–9, 152–67, 210–14; John Earle – on pages 186, 189 (*top*); Alain le Garsmeur – on pages 60–76, 184–5; Peter Howe – on pages 200, 225, 228, 231; David Paterson – on pages 83–5, 90, 93–119, 136; Glyn Satterly – on pages 190–96, 204–9; Philip Sayer – on pages 26–38; Pamla Toler – on pages 82, 86–9, 91, 140–51, 180–83, 202; and Denis Waugh – on pages 6–21, 46–58, 120, 123–5, 129–32, 179, 222.

Credit for additional photographs is due to the following: Heather Angel – on pages 43, 168, 169, 171, 172; Bardsey Trust Collection – on pages 201 (photo by Barry Wilkinson), 233 (*top*), 233 (*bottom*, photo by Susan Cowdy); Alastair Black – on pages 3, 217; Bruce Coleman Ltd – on page 170 (photo by Gordon Langsbury); John Earle – on pages 187, 188, 189 (*bottom*), 203; Richard and Sally Greenhill – on page 121; Colin Molyneux – on pages 224, 226, 227, 229, 230; National Trust for Scotland – on pages 23, 24–5; David Paterson – on pages 81, 173, 174; John and Patricia Woolverton – on pages 44, 126, 127.

Other illustrations drawn by: Bob Bampton *Isolation of Species*, Rachel Birkett/Garden Studio *Life on the Beaches*, Brian and Constance Dear *Revelation in the Rocks*, Kai Choi *The Kindly Lights* (based on drawings from '*Lighthouses: their Architecture, History and Archaeology*' by Douglas B Hague and Rosemary Christie, Peter North/Garden Studio *From Gigs to Sixareens*, Liz Pepperil/Garden Studio *Salt on the Petals*, Gillian Platt/Garden Studio *A Seabird Spectacular*.

Maps drawn by Illustra Design Limited

Designed by Roger Walker

Research organised by Pamela Brown and Sarah Howell.